D0758066

BLUEJACKET ODYSSEY

GUADALDANAL TO BIKINI NAVAL ARMED GUARD IN THE PACIFIC

William L. McGee

Dedication

To the men of the U.S. Naval Armed Guard and U.S. Merchant Marine who delivered the goods during World War II, and to the atomic veterans and civilians who took part in America's tests at Bikini.

ACKNOWLEDGMENTS

This book could not have been done without considerable help from some very talented professionals.

Samuel Loring Morison, accomplished naval historian and nonpareil researcher, provided me with valuable documentation from our nation's archives.

Richard F. Cross III, Washington, D.C.-based historian and photo consultant supplied me with more than 1,000 negatives to choose from for this book and another "work in progress."

Contributing writers Jonathan Weisgall, author/attorney, and Oscar Rosen, Ph.D., former National Commander, National Association of Atomic Veterans, documented the dangers of radiation inherent in nuclear weapons research in Chapter 18.

I also want to thank Kay Strom and Dan Klein of Santa Barbara Literary Service, who critiqued and edited some of the early chapters. Their evaluations and suggestions were very helpful. Thanks also to Spencer Boise for his valuable suggestions and proofreading expertise.

A special thanks to Mr. Bernard Cavalcante, Mrs. Cathy Lloyd and the staff at the U.S. Navy Department's Naval Historical Center; Mr. Gary Morgan and his staff at the Military Reference Branch; as well as the staff of the Textural Reference

Division, Suitland Reference Branch (both part of the National Archives and Records Administration) for their collective research and encouragement.

I am indebted to the many Task Unit 32.4.4 survivors who shared their memories with me and to my *Fall River* shipmates and other atomic veterans who granted me interviews.

I would also like to thank the many individuals and organizations who filled my photo requests, especially the Still Photo Sections of the National Archives and the Naval Historical Center. Special thanks are due Chuck Harberlein, Ed Finney, Jack Green, and Pamela Overman at the latter facility for putting up with my requests during a week long search of their files.

Thanks are also extended to Jan Adelson for the long hours of manuscript typing and interview transcripts and to Jeremy Adelson for his microfiche/film research.

A very special thanks to my beautiful wife, Sandra, for her encouragement and support when I thought this project would never end. Thanks also for the hundreds of hours of proofreading and editing she endured on my behalf.

Finally, there would not be a book without the peerless efforts of the Glencannon Press staff who listened to my protestations against dividing the original manuscript into two books. Walter Jaffee, who edited this book, revealed a remarkable amount of patience along with his substantial editing skills during the entire process.

Contents

LIST OF MAPS

FOREWORD

I first met Bill McGee by telephone in 1992 when he called after visiting the historic Liberty ship, SS *Jeremiah O'Brien*, in San Francisco. Bill is an Armed Guard veteran and talented author. He immediately began gathering the research necessary for this ambitious book project — including all available back issues of our "Pointer" newsletter. It wasn't long before he realized he needed the help of a Washington, D.C.-based professional. Lady Luck must have smiled on him because the next thing I knew, Bill had retained the research services of Samuel Loring Morison, author and historian in his own right, and grandson of the famous naval historian, Rear Admiral Samuel Eliot Morison. Bill's been writing ever since.

The importance of logistics — the branch of military science having to do with procuring, maintaining, and transporting materiel and personnel — has remained unchanged throughout history. Yet it is usually down-played, if not ignored, by military leaders and historians.

The Allies nearly lost the war at sea in 1942 when our supply lines were stretched dangerously thin. In the end, the race between American ship construction and sinkings by the enemy was won by the Allied convoy system and naval superiority in combating the submarine menace, and an unprecedented mass production shipbuilding program.

The U.S. Merchant Marine and Naval Armed Guard took part in every major campaign in World War II. Consider this:

Up to V-J Day, 733 American merchant vessels of over 1,000 gross tons were sunk during the war; victims of torpedoes, bombs, mines, and marine disasters largely caused by war conditions.

There were only about 55,000 merchant seamen and officers sailing in December 1941. The War Shipping Administration established a recruitment/training program which turned out 262,474 graduates during the war. This program resulted in a peak seagoing force of 250,000 Merchant Mariners.[1]

A total of 6,700 merchant mariners were killed or missing in action and presumed dead; 670 were made prisoners of war.

A total of 144,970 Armed Guard enlisted men and officers served on 6,236 merchant ships (American- and foreign-flag) between 7 December 1941 and 30 September 1945. Armed Guard personnel peaked on 1 November 1944 with a total of 112,108 men.

A total of 1,810 Armed Guard officers and men were killed or missing in action and presumed dead; 14 were made prisoners of war.

The merchant mariners who operated the ships were civilians, but they were also under government control and subject

---

[1] The War Shipping Administration also controlled many foreign flag ships. Several hundred merchant mariners and Armed Guard personnel were lost serving on these ships.

to disciplinary actions by the U.S. Coast Guard and, when overseas, by local U.S. military authorities. The Merchant Marine served alongside the Armed Guard and together we delivered the goods. In times of trouble, they passed the ammunition and gave us a helping hand whenever needed. As Mike Molinari, an Armed Guardsman said: "When a ship is sunk, there is no difference between the Armed Guard sailor and the merchant mariner. They fought and died together as brothers and shipmates. Nobody can take that away from them."

Merchant seamen were finally recognized as veterans by an act of the U.S. Congress in 1988, forty-seven years after America's entry into World War II, and after many thousands of those who had served had passed away. I stand proud to have supported their efforts to obtain veteran status.

The mission of each Armed Guard crew was to protect the ship and its valuable cargo and crew from enemy attacks and sabotage from the day we boarded each vessel until we were properly relieved upon completion of the voyage.

The USN Armed Guard Veterans and the American Merchant Marine Veterans accept each other as members in our respective organizations. This book is a fitting tribute to the U.S. Merchant Marine and the defenders of their ships, the U.S. Naval Armed Guard.

The Naval Armed Guard's motto was "We aim to deliver" (and we did!) with the help of the merchant seamen, our escort vessels, and the grace of God.

Charles A. Lloyd, Chairman,
U.S.N. Armed Guard Veterans of WWII
Raleigh, North Carolina
Summer 1997

PREFACE

They say there's a story behind every story. Here's mine. My Navy hitch was supposed to be a single chapter in a planned "Family History." Then I noticed a picture of the now-famous Liberty ship, SS *Jeremiah O'Brien*, in a San Francisco newspaper in 1992 and decided to pay her a visit. There I met the *O'Brien*'s Shipkeeper, Bob Burnett. Before I knew it, Bob had convinced me I should write up my experiences on the four merchantmen I had served on during the war for the *O'Brien*'s library. He even told me how and where to write to request previously classified documents from our national archives. He also told me about C.A. Lloyd and the Armed Guard Veterans group and showed me a copy of a "Pointer" newsletter, their official publication. That did it.

After a year of research gathering, I "launched" this book on a freighter trip to South America — the wanderlust bug never leaves you. I've been accused of living in the past ever since by friends and family. But in preparing this book, I was constantly reminded of how little we servicemen knew about the war around us, let alone the big picture. One example: two out of three cargo ships in our little convoy of three Libertys and three escorts were torpedoed by Japanese subs in the dark of night on

June 23, 1943 after leaving Guadalcanal. I was on the lucky ship but, because we were ordered to hightail it out of there by the Escort Commander, I never knew until fifty years later both ships were sunk. Furthermore, I didn't even know the names of the ships or their hull numbers. But I've never forgotten the date or place. Declassified documents supplied the missing information. Fortunately, I was able to track down and interview forty some survivors. I don't call that living in the past. It's researching the past to update history. And it provides closure on an event that happened early in my life.

I hope, in some ways, this book will illuminate some of the events of World War II in the Pacific and the atomic bomb tests at Bikini. Perhaps through its pages the reader will achieve some small degree of closure of his or her own.

William L. McGee
Santa Barbara, California
May, 1997

INTRODUCTION

    This is a factual account of the first twenty-one years of my life with the emphasis on my four-year "Kid's Cruise" in the U.S. Navy during World War II. The Navy termed my "hitch" a Minority Enlistment because I had just turned seventeen and needed parental consent in order to enlist. I also had to agree to serve in the regular Navy — as opposed to the reserves — until I was twenty-one. Rumor has it, some salty old bosun tagged such enlistments a "Kid's Cruise."

    This book, three plus years in the making, is both a labor of love and a test of perseverance and commitment. It began as one thing, then seemed to take on a life of its own and became something else, then — thanks to a very talented and patient editor — was changed into two works in progress. What you are about to read is usually classified as a memoir. (The next book, *Pacific Express*, is a military history of the Solomon Islands campaign from a different perspective and will be published in early 1998.)

    This book can be divided into three parts: Chapters 1 and 2 provide an eyewitness account of growing up in Montana in the depths of the so-called Great Depression followed by two restless years on the road until I turned seventeen and joined the Navy in October 1942.

Chapters 3-15 depict the full range of maritime adventures and mishaps from boot camp through Naval Armed Guard duty on four merchantmen during the war, starting with my first trip to the Solomons in 1943 — and the ill-fated voyage of Task Unit 32.4.4. All are told from an enlisted man's perspective. In this part, the story of the forgotten men of the U.S. Naval Armed Guard and Merchant Marine who manned the freighters, tankers, and troopships to deliver everything from food, clothing, and medicine to combat troops, fuel, and ammunition to the Pacific battlefronts is chronicled.

I made every effort to convey the reality of shipboard life ranging from long, tedious weeks at sea to endless waiting while riding the "hook" off hot and steamy Pacific islands. From the heart-stopping encounters with the enemy, to storms at sea, to the battle of wills between a tyrannical old master and the gun crew over the use of the liberty boat, to the donnybrooks, tattoo parlors and brothels experienced by bluejackets who "wanted to do it all," the complete story is told.

In Chapters 16-19, I describe my peacetime Fleet duty on the heavy cruiser, *Fall River*, flagship for Commander Naval Task Group 1.2, for the first full-scale tests of the Atomic bomb at Bikini, Marshall Islands, in 1946. Following her maiden voyage through the Panama Canal to Hawaii, then on to the Marshalls, we undergo weeks of pretest preparation and training. Finally come the "Able" and "Baker" tests, with the assistance of Bikini participants I interviewed.

Contributing writers Jonathan Weisgall, adjunct professor of law, and Dr. Oscar Rosen, Ph.D., former National Commander of the National Association of Atomic Veterans, document the dangers of radiation inherent in nuclear weapons research in Chapter 18 and explain how macho military men and careless and/or subservient scientists ignored common-sense precautions in their headlong pursuit of nuclear superiority.

1

BIG SKY COUNTRY

My parents were married in Wilsall, Montana, in November 1920. Doris, my oldest sister, was born on the Lyon home ranch near Wilsall in 1922. Betty came along in 1923 while Dad was running the Catlin ranch in Meagher County for my Uncle Clyde. She was born in White Sulphur Springs, north of Wilsall. I was born in Livingston, Montana, about forty miles north of Yellowstone Park, in 1925.

The following year Dad accepted a job with the U.S. Border Patrol working out of Loring, Montana, a wide spot in the road just south of the Canadian border. I still can't believe he left one of the best parts of Montana for a place where it seems like snow and cold weather are produced and shipped to most other states each winter. What a shock the move north must have been to Mother. They rented a house in Malta, the Phillips County seat, about thirty miles south of Loring.

Vivian (Lyon) McGee with daughters Betty and Doris on Catlin Ranch, 1923. Author.

Malta got its start on August 13, 1887 when the St. Paul, Minneapolis and Manitoba Railway, which later became the Great Northern, reached siding 54 on the Hi-Line. (It was called the High-Line — later shortened to Hi-Line — to distinguish it from Northern Pacific's route through southern, or lower, Montana.) With a population of 2,500 plus or minus a cow or two, Malta, like most western towns, has a colorful history including a gold rush in the Little Rockies south of town and the 1901 Kid Curry train robbery just four miles west of town. The town sits on the banks of the Milk River. The river's headwaters are located in the eastern part of Glacier National Park where it runs northeast into Canada then drops down to Hi-Line country near Havre about 100 miles west of Malta. Eventually it dumps into the Missouri River near the Fort Peck Dam.

Once we made the move to Phillips County we saw less and less of Dad. He worked a big chunk of the border — mostly on the lookout for bootleggers. I remember him coming by the house on more than one occasion with handcuffed bootleggers in the back seat of his car. Dad also developed a profitable sideline, thanks to his reputation as a top hand with horses. He bought a small ranch not far from Loring and was soon buying and breaking saddle horses on a part-time basis. He sold most of them to the Border Patrol.

My little brother Bobby was born in the fall of 1927. It wasn't long after that, Dad began referring to us McGee kids as Shotgun (Doris), Buckshot (Betty), Billy and Bob. I was never quite sure why.

Mother spent more and more time with her church friends as she saw less and less of Dad. I've been told that Dad was

Malta, Montana in the 1930s. Author.

seen many a night in Malta in the saloons playing poker with his pals when we didn't even know he was in town. I guess their marriage went from bad to worse because they separated in 1930 and were divorced on October 11, 1932 shortly after my seventh birthday.

"Shotgun," "Buckshot", Billy and Bob, c. 1931. Author.

Times were tough. The Great Depression started in 1929 and Dad had contributed nothing since the divorce.

During Roosevelt's "New Deal," work was started on the Fort Peck Dam near Glasgow, Montana, some sixty-five miles east of Malta. Phillips County benefited from this "make work" project — at the time, the largest earth-filled dam in the world — in a number of ways. The minimum wage set by the government in 1933 was forty cents an hour. We had two "rock pickers" boarding with us for quite some time while they gathered prairie boulders in an old dump truck, then unloaded them along the railroad tracks for later shipment by rail to the dam.

In order to put food on the table, our family, like many others, operated like a cooperative. Every penny earned went into a household "kitty." Mother worked part-time for a paint and wallpaper store, learned to restore and bind books at the library and took any other work that came along. My two sisters got all the baby-sitting and housework they could handle while still attending school. As for me, by the time I was nine, I was shoveling snow, mowing lawns or bagging groceries when I wasn't out at the ranch. Brother Bobby did his share as he got older, too.

In spite of this all-out family effort, there were times we might have missed a meal had it not been for the generous farmers and ranchers who attended the Malta Community Church. We received many a gift of dairy products and farm produce from them.

Much of our life in Malta centered around the church. The congregation was a mix of town and country people. The church doctrine was similar to the Baptist faith. In addition to four or more hours of Sunday services, including Sunday School which we kids were expected to attend, Mother usually went to Prayer Meeting on Thursday evenings. We had old-fashioned revival meetings each summer and sometimes a visiting missionary, home on leave from Russia, China or the Philippines, would be a guest minister. I enjoyed their stories of far-off people and places. Most of our social life involved other members of the congregation; great food and fellowship at one home or another, usually following Sunday church services.

The Malta Community Church as it appears today. Author.

Four ministers served our church during the 1930s. The one I remember best was Reverend Leon Hawley. He had a great sense of humor — rare in ministers. He always addressed mother as Fibber (McGee) and liked to say to me, "You may be Wild Bill in Montana but where I come from, you'd be just Sweet William."

In the mid-1930s, we moved into a bigger house so we could take in boarders to generate additional income. Many ranchers had to keep a place in town so their high school-aged kids could go to school. Others, particularly if they only had one child in high school, found it less expensive to put them up in a boarding house.

From about 1934 on we always had boarders. Mostly they were country kids but I remember one older lady who worked in town. Three meals a day and a place to sleep was $7 a week. This included a hand-packed lunch of two sandwiches, a piece of fruit, and coffee if they provided a Thermos jug. My two sisters were both good cooks and knew how to clean house as well as any adult. My brother and I had chores, too. All in all, the boarding house concept was quite successful.

Most of us were dominated by what was called the Protestant Ethic. In its simplest form, it held that thrift, piety and hard work were the pathways to redemption and heavenly rewards. Even those Americans with little or no religious faith believed that thrift and hard work insured worldly success.

The Great Depression pushed prices to their lowest levels in decades. Ice cream cones were five cents and coffee was a nickel a cup. A shave and a haircut were, typically, two bits (a quarter). Movie tickets were usually ten cents, at least for Saturday matinees. A gallon of milk was only twelve cents; a dozen eggs, twenty-two cents; and two loaves of bread, just ten cents.

I felt we were fortunate to grow up in Montana during the depression. We could always put food on the table and clean clothes on our backs. Occasionally the diet wasn't balanced and the clothes may have been patched hand-me-downs but we did okay. And it wasn't all work and no play. We had free sports like swimming, ice skating, fishing and hunting — Canadian ducks and geese heading south for the winter, and grain fed pheasant along the river — or roller skating and bowling for a small fee.

In the spring of 1933 I was sitting on the front porch one Sunday when Carl and Louella Holm came by after church and asked me if I would like to spend the summer with them on their ranch. I said, "yes." I loved the country and everything it represented and I knew it meant one less mouth for mother to feed.

So about the middle of May 1933 at age seven, I said "So Long" to my family, climbed in the Holm's Model-T, and headed for their ranch in the Bennett Lake community some twenty miles south of Malta. The dirt road was very rough with deep ruts — the result of snow melt and spring rains — so it took the better part of an hour to reach the ranch. The grey, weather-beaten ranch house was built on a hill overlooking the barn and some other buildings. The nearest neighbor, the Christofferson family, was more than two miles away. Carl had added two rooms and a porch to the original homestead shack. On first sight the ranch house was downright depressing even to a seven-year-old. But that wasn't the half of it. There was no water, gas, electricity or telephone service. And, of course, there was no indoor plumbing. But I soon learned to manage.

Carl must have noticed the disappointment on my face. "Come on, Bill," he said, "I have something to show you down at the barn." Well, as soon as he introduced me to a little brown and white pinto named Paint and said, "He's yours for the sum-mer," I forgot all about the bleak-looking ranch house and its lack of conveniences.

The first two days were one new experience after an-other. Carl showed me how to bring in the work horses (with Paint, of course), feed and harness them, and hook them up to the farm machinery. He still farmed with horses even after many of his neighbors got tractors, preferring to think of himself

as a cow man who only farmed for diversification. He ran about
200 head of mother cows and an equal number of calves, mostly
on government Grazing Association land on Beaver Creek. He
was a top hand at "gentle breaking" both saddle horses and work
horses. He always seemed to have one green bronc in training,
so to speak, whenever he was plowing or doing other heavy
work that would sap some nervous energy out of a snaky three-
year old.

Louella counted on me to take chores off her hands, too.
I soon learned how to feed the cows, chickens and hogs in addition to the horses. Other jobs "inherited" from Louella that
first summer included separating milk, churning cream into butter, gathering eggs, gathering cow chips, and weeding her gar-
den. The list seemed endless. I didn't mind these chores that
much except for the way they kept me away from Carl and a
"man's work." But, by the end of my first summer, I knew what
it was like to round up and brand cattle, fix fence, put up hay and
harvest wheat.

We worked from dawn til dark almost every day. About
the only time we took a break was to go to town once or twice
a month on Saturdays to barter our farm products such as eggs,
butter and cream for staples like flour, sugar, coffee and beans.
In most cases cash never changed hands.

We also went to a little country church on Sunday morn-
ings when and if a visiting minister was scheduled to preach. As
the members were more likely than not to be Scandinavians,
some sermons were even "Paa Norsk" — in Norwegian. During
the warm summer months, a potluck social might follow the
service with great down-home food topped off with homemade
ice cream and cake. Those were always enjoyable gatherings. It
was about the only time we saw our neighbors so there was
always lots of catching up to do.

Louella was even more religious than my mother. She
read from the Bible every evening after dinner and would then
lead us in prayer. She even made me stop using "swear" words

Gathering Holm cattle, c. 1935. Author.

Branding spring calves, c. 1935. Left to right: Carl Holm, William McGee, Ralph Bergsagel. Author.

like gosh, darn and heck because, in her book, they meant God, damn and hell, respectively.

Louella was a hardy worker but she constantly complained about the tough times like many others throughout the community. You could see and hear despair everywhere during those drought and depression years. But I also remember those years as times of family solidarity and courage. A sense of unity developed between neighbors and friends.

Then there was the weather. If Montana is a land of extremes, the Hi-Line country goes to super extremes. Phillips County's range of record temperatures is from sixty degrees below to 115 above. Furthermore, thanks to Chinook winds, shifts of fifty degrees in one hour are not uncommon. Not exactly farmer-friendly country.

Carl was a good teacher. Each year he taught me to do more until by the end of my sixth summer on the ranch (the fall of 1938) I was capable of doing a man's job. I was a big, strong thirteen-year old by then. I knew how to break a colt, shoe horses and roundup, brand and ship cattle. I could also handle most farm jobs such as plowing with four or six head of horses or seeding and harvesting wheat, as well as various other chores like milking cows, which I hated, to haying, hauling water, and fixing fence.

That summer there was more and more news about the problems in Europe. I heard heated discussions among friends and neighbors as to whether we should be standing by doing nothing as we watched Hitler take over one country after another. The isolationists warned against U.S. involvement in other nations' differences whereas conservatives — which included my family and most of our friends — felt that Hitler had to be stopped.

That fall, Carl surprised me by loaning me a team and hayrack so I could make a few extra bucks during the "cooperative" wheat harvest in our community. (It was near the end of the binder and threshing machine era and just before combines took over.) Most dryland farmers and their hired hands joined forces as a community harvesting crew moving from place to place until all grain had been harvested. You got $5 a day, if you furnished your own team and rack, to gather and haul the bundles of wheat from the field to the threshing machine. As a field pitcher (loading the hayracks) or as a spike pitcher (unloading the racks into the threshing machine) you made $2 a day.

That first little taste of entrepreneurship made me realize it was time to renegotiate my "room and board deal" with Carl Holm or look for summer work with someone else who could afford to pay me wages. If I could do a man's work, why not try for a man's paycheck? Over the Christmas holidays, I posed the question of wages to Carl Holm. I was pretty sure I knew what his answer would be but had to ask. He simply couldn't afford to pay me the $30 a month plus the room and board I wanted and said so. But he quickly added, "I'm proud of the way you've learned here on the job. You're worth every penny you're asking. Let me know if I can help you find work next summer."

Many of the immigrants who settled in Phillips County were Scandinavians — hardy Norwegians and Swedes. The Kroon family was representative of these pioneers. We numbered them among our best friends. The Kroon boys, Melvin, Roy, Paul and Karl, were in many ways like substitute fathers to my brother and I. When school let out in May 1939, I went to work for Roy Kroon, the oldest of the Kroon boys, on the "ditch" — irrigatable farm and ranch land in the Milk River valley. While working for Roy, I learned what it was like to farm with a reliable source of water — just the opposite of dryland farming. I also learned how quick and easy it was to complete many jobs with a tractor. Roy raised alfalfa, sugar beets, corn, wheat, barley and oats, so I soon learned the differences between flood and row crop irrigation.

But, the plentiful supply of water had one big drawback — mosquitoes. And with respect to quantity and size of mosquito, the Milk River valley takes a back seat to no other place. At thirteen, I was driving a tractor and a truck and helping Roy with myriad tasks — some old, some new. I enjoyed using the tractor to cultivate the corn and sugar beets but you can have the ditch-digging and irrigation chores. They seemed to go hand-in-hand with the hoards of mosquitoes that hang out near water.

We put up two crops of alfalfa that summer and harvested the grain before I moved back to town for school. I couldn't believe the yields. Carl Holm got five to seven bushels of wheat per acre in a good year. At times he didn't even get his seed back. Roy got sixty-plus bushels per acre. Some difference, thanks to irrigation.

I missed not working with horses. In fact, I already had doubts about my long-term interest in farming. But ranching is another story. I dreamt about owning my own spread with lots of cattle, a few good horses, and enough water to raise alfalfa.

That was the first summer I got the itch to travel. One of Roy's alfalfa fields was between the Great Northern's tracks and U.S. Highway 2. I watched the trains and cars going by wondering where they had been and where they were going. Sometimes people waved and I waved back. The hoboes riding the freights were a friendly lot, too, shouting their greetings as they went by. I promised myself then and there that I would take a trip to some exciting place, and soon.

The war expanded in Europe. The German blitzkrieg struck Poland. Great Britain and France responded by declaring war on Germany after Hitler ignored their demands for German withdrawal.

That same fall, I saw Dad for a few emotion-packed minutes. He was called up by the Secret Service to help guard President Roosevelt during his trip to Montana to dedicate the Fort Peck Dam, the WPA project east of Malta that was nearing completion.

In late '39, Dad was transferred by the Border Patrol to Plentywood, Montana. Then in 1940 we heard he quit the Border Patrol and left for Alaska — "Montana was getting too crowded." Years later, I learned he joined the Secret Intelligence branch of the OSS (Office of Strategic Services) in 1942 for the duration of World War II. Afterwards, he became part-owner of a hunting and fishing lodge on the Kenai Peninsula southwest of Seward.

When I entered high school, I faced the same dilemma I had in 1937 when I started the seventh grade. How do I go out for football and basketball and still earn enough money to contribute my fair share towards household expenses? Mother and my sisters convinced me it could be done if I was very selective as to the kinds of work and the hours required to get the job done. They were partly right. I simply worked less after school hours the days we had practice sessions. I worked various part-time jobs that school year, ranging from clerking in the Malta Mercantile store to my on-going position as janitor of the Community Church.

We heard more and more talk about the war in Europe. Many people became fed up with the isolationists in Washington.

During the early months of 1940, Allied losses, in what became known as "The Battle of the Atlantic" between German U-boats and Allied merchant ships, mounted at an alarming rate — nearly 4.5 million tons of ships sunk during the first two months of the year alone.

I went back to work for Roy Kroon in May 1940. Not long after that Germany invaded France. By the end of June, Hitler controlled most of western Europe. The British and French armies were still reeling from the effects of the disaster at Dunkirk. Things looked very bad. In July, the German air force launched the first aerial attack on England in "The Battle of Britain." Most everyone was convinced that an invasion would follow soon.

2

WANDERLUST

It was mid-July 1940 when John Rood, Bob Kinney and I decided to work the wheat harvest in Pondera County about 200 miles west of Malta. John told us about a call from his uncle Hank who expected a better than average yield in August and needed two or three strong backs to haul grain.

We agreed to travel light, carry our belongings in duffel bags and try our hand at hitchhiking. My wardrobe consisted of two sets of work clothes, a Sunday-go-to-meetin' outfit, and a letter sweater with the big M for Malta Mustangs on the front. (The sweater would turn out to be one of this hitchhiker's best friends.)

Hank Rood was one of relatively few dryland farmers to have his own combine, a major investment in those days. The machine "combined" the functions of the binder that cut the grain with that of the threshing machine that separated the grain from the chaff. It shortened the entire harvesting process and made it much less labor intensive.

Over supper that night Hank explained his game plan. He had almost 400 acres of winter wheat and another 200 plus acres of spring wheat to harvest. The winter wheat was already ripe and waiting for us. Hank and/or his hired hand would operate the combine. The three of us plus one other guy would haul the grain using the two trucks parked outside.

For the better part of the next two weeks we worked our tails off. One crew followed alongside the combine in the truck taking on grain while the other crew hightailed it to the nearest granary and shoveled nonstop through a small window high in the wall with scoop shovels until the truck was empty. The last two truck loads of the day were taken to a grain elevator operator in Conrad so that Hank could "pay his bills."

During the last week of harvesting discussions about visiting the Northwest "as long as we've come this far" got serious. We heard about the shortage of workers on the West Coast as well as the big bucks being paid for construction work in Alaska.

After a brief discussion, we decided to head for Seattle. I was dying to see the other side of the mountains and had a good month to do it in before school started. We agreed to hitchhike south about 125 miles, then catch a free ride on a Northern Pacific freight train heading for the West Coast. As it turned out, that was a lot easier said than done.

We headed south the following morning. It didn't take long to catch our first ride but it only got us ten miles down the road. After two or three more short rides we turned down several others before "Mr. Right" came along and took us straight to the freight yards in Missoula, Montana.

The ever-changing countryside was impressive. I had never been so far from home nor had I ever seen real mountains. You can't compare the Little Rockies to the Rocky Mountains. When we crossed the Continental Divide, west of Helena, I realized I'd never seen real forests before, either. Then, as we dropped down into Missoula, we saw the Bitterroot Range off to the southwest. What a sight!

We picked up several valuable tips that evening from the old-timers we met in the hobo[1] jungle. We learned how to tell the difference between the through tracks and switching tracks used to make up trains in a big freight yard. Also, since there are no published schedules for freight trains, we tried to learn where to catch a freight headed in the right direction and, if possible, when it might leave. Once in a while a friendly brakeman or engineer might help, but they could just as easily report you to the railroad bulls (police). We learned how to spot the bulls, too.

Most of the hoboes we met were unemployed men with a sense of wanderlust. They claimed to be honest guys who worked when they could and that seemed to be true. Of course, there was always the chance they would "just as soon slit your throat as look at you," so we watched out for each other. We also hid our folding money in our boots.

The railroads had another name for hoboes — transients. And they had another word for their wanderlust — illegal. No one questioned the railroad's right to enforce the law against illegal rail travel. After all, the rolling stock was not designed to transport people. It was also dangerous, opening up the possibility of lawsuits. Even the old-timers agreed. They referred to train wheels as "salami slicers."

With the help of one very patient senior hobo, we caught our freight for Seattle, even though it was pitch dark. Throwing our duffel bags into the first open boxcar while slowly running alongside, we climbed aboard. Standing by the door we watched the Missoula lights fade as the train picked up speed. It turned chilly almost at once so we slid the door closed to keep out the wind only to discover none of us had a flashlight. We lit a few matches to make sure we were the only occupants of the car, then picked out some space at one end for a bed.

---

[1] Hobo lore has it the originals carried hoes with them for field work, hence the name "hoe boy," later shortened to "hobo."

It got colder and colder. The train labored up a steep grade and it wasn't long before we added another layer of clothing to offset the elevation gain. None of us got much sleep that night due to the cold and the hard floor of the boxcar.

We were spotted by a railroad bull that morning as we pulled into Spokane. As it happened there was a severe shortage of migrant workers in the Wenatchee Valley — home of the famous Wenatchee apples — about 100 miles west of Spokane. An unskilled labor shortage of this type was quickly solved; the Apple Growers Co-op called the sheriff who, in turn, called the railroads.

The bulls, with the help of the sheriff's deputies, gathered close to sixty apple pickers off our train alone. We were loaded into flatbed trucks for the ride to Wenatchee and our home for the night, a migrant workers camp outside of town. We weren't arrested, but it was implied we would be if we didn't agree to pick apples for a dollar a day. We picked apples from sunup till sundown the next day and after dark, took off.

Another freight that night on the outskirts of Wenatchee took us to Everett, Washington, about thirty miles north of Seattle. It was raining so we splurged and bought bus tickets to Seattle. In Seattle, we stayed in a rooming house, "a cut or two above a flop house" we were told, near the city's illustrious waterfront and skid row. The price and location were right for our purposes.

It took the better part of a day to track down the name and address of the general contractor for the Alaska construction work. Bob Kinney was hired, subject to reference checks, to drive a truck at an unbelievably high wage but the bad news was that John and I were underage.

The next morning we took an electric bus out to Boeing's big airplane manufacturing plant. It took almost an hour to fill out their job application form and then we waited to be interviewed. Bob was hired again. He now had a choice of jobs. John and I were told to come back when we turned eighteen. That was about a year's wait for John and over three years for me.

Luckily, we found a Seattle painting contractor who had temporary work painting a bunch of new two-story military-type barracks located between Seattle and Tacoma. He offered us $6 a day and a free new pair of coveralls if we started then and there. We did. The job only lasted two weeks but we made good money and became pretty good painters, too.

Bob sailed for Alaska and we had a bon voyage party for him on the waterfront. All I remember of that night was ending up at an old-fashioned vaudeville theater with striptease artist Sally Rand headlining the show.

John and I then went to Portland, Oregon, to visit some of his relatives. They liked Portland's small town friendliness, quality of life and year-round recreation opportunities. Their recommendations sold John. He wasn't sure whether to finish high school, find a job, or both. But he decided to stay.

Now it was decision time for me. It was near the end of August. School would start back home in about ten days. But the open road called — California and Arizona especially. I started school late more than once in order to help out on Carl Holm's ranch. Why not swing through California, Arizona, Utah and Wyoming on my way home and really see the West?

I hitchhiked all the way except for a few short bus rides to get in or out of a big city. My letter sweater worked like magic. To most drivers, it meant I was still in school and probably couldn't afford a train or bus ticket. Many of them stopped. Consequently, I became selective as to whom I rode with. They didn't seem to mind my qualifying questions, either, such as — how far are you going? Are you planning any stops en route? Or would you like some help with the driving? The net result: far fewer but much longer rides each day.

The scenery on the trip south through Oregon and Northern California was stunning. One mile after another of beautiful countryside with woods, lakes, rivers, farms and ranches. No wonder the Oregon Trail was so busy in the 1800s.

Next stop, Hollywood, home of the stars. I spent almost two days getting from Monterey to Santa Barbara on the Pacific

Coast Highway. The beauty of the mountains to the east and the Pacific Ocean to the west as you wind around one hairpin curve after another is an unforgettable experience. From Santa Barbara, I took a Greyhound bus the rest of the way into Hollywood. I wanted to see some movie stars but didn't have the time or money to hang around town hoping it would happen. I spent one night there sleeping in the back seat of an old junk heap on a used car lot.

The next day I caught a local bus for Pomona, California, east of Los Angeles and hitchhiked again. Destination: Arizona, home to some of the best known dude ranches in the west. Ever since I saw an article on the subject in one of the photo magazines, I wanted to see what they really looked like, and, if I liked what I found, to look into the chances for employment. I couldn't remember any of the names of the dude ranches covered in the article but I did remember at least two of them were near Tucson. That became my next destination.

My travels took me through California's Coachella and Imperial Valleys to Yuma, Arizona, and then east to Tucson. At this point, according to my map, I was about 1,100 miles south of my home town. My deadline for getting back for school, September 12th, rapidly approached. I left Tucson September 8, 1940 and hitchhiked back to Montana by way of Phoenix and Flagstaff, Arizona; Salt Lake City, Utah; Pocatello, Idaho; and Butte, Helena, Great Falls and Havre, Montana.

Arriving in Malta on September 12, I started my sophomore year of high school the following Monday. It was really hard to crack the books again. I thought football and basketball might get me back into the swing of things but it didn't happen. I guess you grow up faster when you experience life on the road. I always had a few older friends. Now, most of my classmates, especially the guys, seemed so young and naive. It took a lot of perseverance just to stay in school. I knew it would be my last year.

The war clouds grew darker.

September 1940:

The United States and England announced a Destroyers-For-Bases deal trading fifty old U.S. destroyers for the rights to several British bases in the Western Hemisphere.

The first call-up of National Guard units was announced and on the same date the Selective Service Act passed Congress requiring all males 21 to 36 to register for military service on October 16, 1940.

Japan joined the Axis powers by signing the Tripartite Pact calling for each of the three nations — Japan, Germany and Italy — to provide military assistance in case of attack by any nation not yet at war; e.g., the United States.

By the spring of '41 more and more Malta men were going into the service. National Guardsmen had already been called up by the Army. Others volunteered for the Navy or the Marines. I would have enlisted in the Marines myself had mother been willing to lie about my age but I couldn't talk her into it.

When school let out, I was ready to head for the coast again but, because I promised mother I would wait until fall, I went back to work for Roy Kroon on the mosquito-plagued "ditch." When the cars and trains went by heading west while I was working Roy's alfalfa fields, I pictured what they would see along the way.

The summer seemed to drag on forever. My job kept me busy physically but my head was elsewhere. Unbeknownst to me, mother was corresponding with Reverend Hawley — now Captain Hawley — at Fort Vancouver, Washington, across the Columbia River from Portland. He assured her that he could help me get a job. I wasn't too pleased with my "travel agent's" efforts but agreed to call the Hawleys upon arrival.

By mid-September I was on the road again. After taking U.S. 2 west through Glacier Park, south through the Flathead Lake valley, then west over the mountains across the Idaho panhandle to Spokane and into Portland, I called John Rood. He came out to pick me up in his new used car — a sharp-looking Model A Ford roadster. Over a couple of beers, I learned he was an auto mechanic. He was going to a mechanics' trade school part-time while holding down an apprentice position with the local Ford dealer. Pretty good for a guy still not eighteen.

Later, I took a bus to the Vancouver Barracks near the north bank of the Columbia River just east of the heart of town. The Army guard gave me a visitor's pass, and directed me to the Hawley's house on Officers' Row.

All the Hawleys were home for lunch that day and you'd have thought I was a long-lost son home from the wars by the greeting I received. After I gave them the latest news (gossip) of their former congregation, Reverend Hawley said he had lined me up for work at the post exchange — an army retail store on the post, simply called the PX — and in a nearby gas station, also on the post. Mrs. Hawley insisted I stay with them ". . . as one of the family. You'll have your own room, too." I was reluctant to accept as I liked my new-found independence. Finally, I agreed to stay for a trial period providing I could pay toward my room and board. Some nominal sum was agreed upon — too low, I'm sure — and I moved in.

I liked the Hawleys a lot, but living with them was restrictive. They treated me like I was still a kid. They were, of course, against dancing and movies. And now I had two more "sins" even Mother didn't know about yet. Once in a while I would smoke a cigarette and have a beer. So, after about three weeks I moved in with John's relatives as a boarder. The Hawleys were probably just as glad to be rid of the responsibility.

John was good friends with one of the guys he went to mechanics' school with by the name of Joe Rizzo. It wasn't long before we were like The Three Musketeers. Joe moved to Portland from back east — Brooklyn, New York, I think. He had a great sense of humor. He could break us up by telling jokes with his New York accent.

We had a lot of rain that Fall of 1941 — atypical, according to the natives. By Thanksgiving, we were sick of it. Joe proposed a long weekend trip to the snow country east of town in the Mt. Hood wilderness area. We stayed in a little motel and had a ball cross-country skiing in the daytime and partying at night.

Just before heading back to Portland, John said, "I've always wanted to see the 'biggest little city in the world' so why don't the three of us take a little trip to Reno over the Christmas holidays?" Joe and I quickly agreed. We made plans to leave the day before Christmas and return New Year's Day.

John was pretty sure he could wangle the time off. Joe had just quit his job and didn't seemed too worried about what he would do next. As for me, I was ready for a change. I was interested in getting in on the ground floor of the new Kaiser Shipyard under construction in Vancouver. I already had my name on a "to be called" waiting list for the boilermaker's union.

On Sunday morning, December 7th, John, Joe and I were walking down Broadway in Portland checking out the choice of movies, when someone opened a store door and shouted, "The radio says the Japs just bombed the hell out of us — somewhere called Pearl Harbor."

We were beyond incredulous. Like most Americans, we read and heard the so-called experts debate the ongoing threat of war with Japan. We held the average American's perception of the Japanese as small-bodied, smiling, bowing, inscrutable Orientals whose distant island nation produced unlimited numbers of cheap toys and trinkets for the rest of the world to buy.

Now, the facts of the matter were quite different. On that frightful morning — in a long-planned secret attack — some 400 Japanese warplanes took to the skies from the flight decks of six aircraft carriers that were supported by twenty-eight other warships and twenty-seven submarines. Precisely at 7:55 a.m., the warplanes appeared suddenly over the unsuspecting Pearl Harbor U.S. Naval Base. They proceeded, as if at a turkey shoot, to bomb or aerial torpedo what was then the mightiest U.S. naval force in history.

Sneak Attack, Sunday, December 7, 1941, Pearl Harbor. U.S. Navy

The Japanese sank or severely damaged eight U.S. battle-ships, three cruisers, three destroyers and five other special-mission vessels. The attack destroyed 177 Navy and Army aircraft. And, worst of all, more than 2400 Navy, Army, Marine Corps and civilian personnel were killed, 960 were missing and more than 1100 were wounded.

We were in a state of shock. The movies were forgotten and we headed home to listen to the radio. We were still stunned when we heard President Roosevelt's tensely-awaited broadcast the next day in which he unforgettably labeled December 7th "a day which will live in infamy" and declared war on the Japanese.

I was gung-ho to join the Marines or the Navy. I checked with both recruiting offices the next day to see if they were making any age exceptions now that there was a war on. Their answer: no way at age sixteen; okay at seventeen, providing one parent will sign a consent form; and okay at eighteen, period.

On December 11th, the U.S. also declared war on Germany; we would be fighting two wars simultaneously.

Hickam Field Disaster. U.S. Navy.

And suddenly the war was getting close to home. On December 20, 1941, a Japanese submarine sank the U.S. merchant ship SS *Medio* off Eureka, California. She was the first U.S. merchant ship sunk in the Pacific.

We weighed the pros and cons of sticking with our upcoming trip to Reno and decided it was still a "go." Early on December 24, 1941 we drove toward Reno, Nevada, some 600 miles to the south. Our route took us through Salem, Bend and Klamath Falls, Oregon, then across the northeast corner of California and on into Reno. As we pulled into town from the north, we saw the world-famous arch spanning Virginia Street lit up in neon lights claiming Reno as "The Biggest Little City In The World."

We were really excited. We heard all the stories about the wide-open casinos that never close — with their gambling, beautiful showgirls, bars and restaurants. We found a room at the Nevada Hotel on Second Street near the heart of the action. Because it was Christmas we splurged and had a great dinner at the Riverside Hotel's casino restaurant. Then for the next four days we saw and did just about everything Reno had to offer — and loved it.

Now it was decision time again. Joe wanted to head south for Las Vegas. As he put it, "We've come all this way . . . it's only another 400 miles and, besides, I hear you can have twice as much fun there."

John and I called our respective employers and were straightforward with them. No excuses. They, in turn, were frank and honest with us. "Sorry to lose you . . . have a great trip."

We also had a serious discussion about money that day. Most cities had a vagrancy law calling for the arrest of anyone caught wandering around without a permanent home or employment. The cops, in many cases, used money as a means test for vagrants. We finally agreed to not let our collective financial resources go below $100 without replenishing the supply.

Las Vegas had the same attractions as Reno only more so. It was also warmer. We worked as shills[2] on New Year's Eve and most of New Year's Day. I made over $100 in tips from one high roller who bet with me at the crap table every time I had the dice. Each time we won he tossed me one or two $5 chips. I made my point seven times in a row one time before I crapped out. He made several thousand that time alone.

We learned how to make two surefire bets (well, almost) one night from a beer distributor who was in Vegas for a convention. The first one sounds unbelievable. You bet someone they can't taste the difference between coke, ginger ale, and 7-Up while blindfolded. We watched him win this bet three times in a row. The second bet surprises most everyone, even West Coast natives. Bet someone that Reno is west of Los Angeles. They will usually think you are crazy until they look at a map.

On January 2, 1942 we left for Southern California with Joe at the helm. Someone recommended Westwood as an

---

[2] A shill gets paid to gamble with house money to give the appearance the tables are busy. Many high rollers won't play at slow tables.

inexpensive place to stay, saying, "You can rent a small apartment there for peanuts." Availability was another thing. But, we finally spotted a "for rent" sign and managed to convince the landlady we were UCLA undergrads.

Even though I disliked Los Angeles, I liked California a lot. Its climate, diversity and wide range in scenic beauty made a lasting impression on me as did the endless days of bright sunshine, the Pacific Ocean, High Sierras, expansive deserts, green, fertile valleys, the Southwest/Spanish architecture, the citrus groves, avocado trees and vineyards. Compared to the subzero winter months in Montana, it was no contest.

After a few days of playing tourist — we took in everything from the beaches to Hollywood studio tours — Joe and John decided it was time to get a job and settle down "for the winter." I wasn't so sure.

The next day I headed for Arizona to see if there were any openings on the dude ranches. I also decided to take a bus to Pasadena with the idea of catching a Santa Fe freight heading for Barstow, then east to Flagstaff, Arizona.

I won't forget that freight ride if I live to be one hundred. As the evening wore on, it got colder and colder. It was a clear night and close to a full moon. How in the world can a desert get this cold, I wondered. When the train pulled into the little town of Needles, California, I hopped off and shouldered my duffel bag. All I could think about was a hot cup of coffee and a good sandwich, then a warm place to sleep.

Unfortunately, the Needles police chief saw me jump from the boxcar. As I crossed the street, he pulled up, threw his spotlight on me and said, "Hold on there. Let's see your I.D.!" My heart pounded and the light blinded me. My first instinct was to run. But, knowing I hadn't done anything worse than ride the freight, I pulled out my billfold, offered my driver's license, and waited.

After a long minute he said, "You're a long way from home, aren't you, son? You look cold, too. Come on, I'll buy you a cup of coffee."

We went into a little cafe on the main drag and I had my coffee and a sandwich — both on the Chief. Furthermore, he offered me one of the jail bunks for the night. I gladly accepted.

The next morning I hitchhiked south toward Yuma, Arizona, on U.S. 395. My second ride was with a "good old boy" from Oklahoma. He was heading for San Diego in his dump truck and talked me into going with him as far as Indio, "just ninety miles to the west, right on the SP line." I hesitated, but when he asked me to drive so he could get some shut eye, that did it. I had driven trucks before but never a big rig like this one. By the time I pulled into Indio it was getting dark. I woke my new Okie friend with a few gentle shakes, said thank you and good-bye, then headed for the nearest gas station to wash up.

It was too early to go to sleep so I explored the town and wandered into Indio's brightly lit post office. I was looking at various notices on the walls including several FBI "Wanted" posters when in walked a man, fifty something, all duded up in a western-cut suit, alligator cowboy boots and a ten gallon Stetson.

As he walked by I said with a smile, "That's a good lookin' pair of boots you're wearing . . . and the hat's not bad either."

He stopped, turned, and said, "Thanks very much. Where are you from? You don't look like you're from around here." When I replied, "Montana," his face lit up and he said something like, "Do you know anything about horses?"

When I said yes he smiled and said, "If you're looking for work, I would like to hire you. Where are you staying?" I told him I had just arrived in town. He said, "Fine, come with me. You can stay at the ranch tonight and start work tomorrow."

I picked up my duffel bag and followed him out the door to his big black Cadillac. As we got in the car he said, "Oh, by the way, my name is Walter Kirshner. What's yours?" I told him and we shook hands.

Mr. Kirshner drove west toward Palm Springs for about five miles, then turned south and followed a country road another

mile. He pulled into a tree-lined driveway and stopped in front
of a big white Spanish-style house.

Two beautiful women, in their late twenties or early thirties, came out to greet us. After the introductions, Mr. Kirshner
said, "Come on Bill, let's get you something to eat," and led me
through the living room and out to the kitchen. He introduced
me to Maria, his Latina cook, with instructions to "take good
care of Bill."

We all sat around the big kitchen table and got better
acquainted while I tried to eat my sandwich. I learned that one
of the gals was a nurse, the other a secretary. They worked for
and traveled with Mr. Kirshner.

After eating, Mr. Kirshner showed me to my room at the
far end of the house. I was stunned. The bedroom was the size
of many a living room and came with its own bathroom.

When Mr. Kirshner asked if there was anything else I
needed, I said, "That should do it . . . at least for now," with a
big grin. He knew I wasn't used to that kind of luxury.

Early the next morning, I surveyed my new home while
everyone else slept. The ranch was really an estate on a quarter
section of land. The buildings were tucked behind several rows
of tall stately date trees and groves of grapefruit and oranges.
The white stucco house with its red tile roof was shaped like a
giant "L" with a swimming pool in the center. The stables, one
hundred yards or more behind the house, were also white. Several palomino mares and their colts and a young pinto gelding
were in one of the paddocks and a big beautiful palomino stud
pawed for attention in one of the stalls.

As I leaned against the corral admiring the horses, the
ranch manager introduced himself as Ed Martin. He and his
wife, Agnes, lived in a house trailer on cement blocks behind the
stables. Ed and several Mexican farm hands took care of the
farm and gardening work. He was glad I would be taking over
the horses.

Ed invited me to have breakfast with him so he could fill
me in on some of my duties and responsibilities. I had lots of
questions for him, too. Like, who is Walter Kirshner and how

did he make his fortune? Ed told me that Kirshner was a self-made man. He was a major stockholder in Robinson's Department Stores, a regional chain in Southern California, and Grayson's, a national chain of women's clothing stores. Beverly Hills was his primary residence but he spent several weeks each winter in Indio. He was divorced and enjoyed keeping beautiful young ladies around. The horses were a hobby and, maybe, a tax write-off and he didn't ride.

My primary duties, according to Ed, were to feed, exercise, and groom the horses, and to "gentle break" the two- and three-year olds. One of the Mexican hands would keep the stalls cleaned out and put down fresh bedding. Mr. "K," as Ed called him, liked to enter the palominos in horse shows and parades of all kinds, from rodeos to the Rose Bowl. "In fact," as Ed put it, "the stud just returned from 'starring' in the Rose Bowl parade a little over a week ago.

"Then, there's the stud service," Ed said. "You'll get calls every so often from a "horsey type" with a mare in heat. You'll want to schedule these on the calendar in the tackroom to avoid conflicts."

After breakfast I went out to get better acquainted with the horses. The tack room with its pungent smell of leather and horses at one end of the stables was well stocked with western gear. It was also clean and neat. I saddled up the stud, Champion, and took him for a ride. He had a comfortable single foot gait — perfect for a parade horse.

Walter Kirshner and Ed Martin were waiting at the stables when I got back. I could tell they were checking me out. After all, Mr. Kirshner had hired me based on my say so. He needed to know if I was qualified for the job. They seemed satisfied with what they saw and, from that day on, never questioned my qualifications for handling horses. That made me very proud.

In no time at all, I settled into an enjoyable routine. The weeks seemed to fly by.

The war news went from bad to worse.

January 1942:

Japan takes control of the Philippines as General MacArthur with-
draws to Corregidor.

German bomber and torpedo planes increase their attacks on
Russian-bound convoys.

Roosevelt and Churchill agreed after a Washington Conference
that Allied strategy will be to defeat Germany first, then Japan.

The first American troops arrived in Europe since the end of
World War I.

Later that month, I got the thrill of a lifetime. General
George Patton showed up at the ranch. Mr. "K" had met him
somewhere and told him all about, "his prize-winning palominos" and to "come out for a ride anytime." I took him out to
the stable and you could tell in a flash he knew and appreciated
good horseflesh. Saddling up Champion for him and a gelding
for myself, we rode together for more than an hour. He was a
sight to behold, with his old-fashioned cavalry-style boots and
britches and his famous pearl-handled pistols. He was a top-
notch rider, too.

General Patton was training his tank crews about fifty
miles east of Indio at the Desert Training Center. The training
ground sprawled over 18,000 square miles in California, Nevada
and Arizona. (It was chosen to train soldiers for desert conditions they would soon face battling German forces in North
Africa. More than one million soldiers trained there before it
was closed in 1944.)

Mr. "K" hosted a different company of Patton's soldiers
every Sunday to a poolside barbecue from that day forward as
long as the troops were stationed there. They arrived with large
appetites and even bigger thirsts. But they were also badly in
need of showers. Part of their training was to get by on one
helmet of water a day — for drinking, shaving and washing.

Young Montana Cowboy William L. McGee at the Kirshner ranch. Author.

Consequently, they arrived with sand in their hair, shoes, and just about every where else. By the time they all took a swim, the bottom of the pool was covered with sand.

February 1942:

A U.S. carrier task force under Vice Admiral William L. Halsey conducts the first U.S. carrier offensive of the war — a strike against the Japanese-held Marshall and Gilbert Island groups.

Japanese carrier- and land-based bombers attack Darwin in northern Australia.

Roosevelt approves controversial plan to remove Japanese-Americans from the West Coast and intern them in camps in Colorado, Utah, Arkansas and other interior states.

A Jap submarine shells an oil refinery at Ellwood near Santa Barbara, CA — the first attack of the war on the U.S. mainland.

The destroyer USS *Jacob Jones* (DD-130) is hit by torpedoes from a German submarine off the Delaware Capes blowing off the ship's bow and stern. Only eleven men of a crew of 125 survive.

I ate with the Martins when Mr. "K's" cook was away. Agnes Martin introduced me to chili beans with hot out-of-the-oven cornbread. And Ed made his contribution, too — cornbread in a bowl of milk lightly sprinkled with salt and pepper. Every time I eat cornbread, I think of my old friends, the Martins.

Patton's troops enjoy a poolside party. Author.

March 1942:

A second Japanese air attack was launched against Pearl Harbor by two Jap flying boats.

General MacArthur left the Philippines for Australia vowing to return.

The first orders were issued under Executive Order 9066 — a decree signed by President Roosevelt on February 19, 1942 — calling for the evacuation of more than 110,000 Japanese-Americans living on the West Coast to relocation camps in Utah, Wyoming and Arkansas and other interior states.

The war news bothered me. I liked my job but it was hardly supportive of the war effort. I voiced my feelings to Mr. "K" in early April and he couldn't have been more understanding. We agreed I would stay until the end of the month. He also assured me I could have my job back at anytime. Having given notice, I made plans to return to Portland to work in the shipyards at least until I was old enough to enlist in the Marines or Navy.

The April war news was mixed.

April 1942:

Seventy-five thousand American and Philippine troops surrender to the Japanese after stoic resistance to overwhelming odds.

The U.S. Navy begins partial convoying of merchant ships along the Atlantic seaboard after German U-boats sink forty-eight merchant vessels during March.

East Coast "dim outs" — the extinguishing of bright lights — is also ordered to prevent the silhouetting of ships and to cut down on U-boat night attacks.

Selective Service registration begins for all American men between ages forty-five and sixty-four.

Sixteen B-25 bombers, led by Lt. Col. James Doolittle, are launched by the USS *Hornet* (CV-8) from a position 800 miles east of Tokyo in a daring raid on Tokyo and other Japanese cities.

On May 1, 1942 I packed up my duffel bag, said my last good-byes and, in a final gesture of hospitality, was driven to the bus depot in Indio by Mr. "K." He thought he had talked me out of hitchhiking north, but my ticket only went to Beaumont, about fifty miles west. I wasn't about to spend my hard-earned money on Greyhound when I had my trusty letter sweater with me.

My last ride dropped me off in Oregon City, south of Portland, about five o'clock. John Rood was home and picked me up within an hour. During the drive into town he explained he was working the graveyard shift (midnight to 8 a.m.) for Kaiser Shipyards in Vancouver, across the river, where he was an apprentice machinist. He was positive they would hire me even though I was still sixteen. John still lived with his relatives in Portland; "You can't beat the rent, but I don't want to commute to Portland anymore." He wanted me to share "the perfect Vancouver studio apartment right on the bus line to the yards" with him.

By the end of my second week back in the Northwest, I was working for Kaiser Shipyards as an apprentice welder on the day shift (8 a.m. to 4 p.m.) and John and I had moved into that "perfect studio" in Vancouver.

The coming of the war forced the Maritime Commission to develop the Liberty ship as an "emergency standard" cargo carrier which could be built in new shipyards. This resulted in the construction of Libertys while the yards themselves were still under construction. In all, eighteen yards containing 210 slipways with a work force that swelled to more than 650,000 people by mid-1943 built more than 2,710 Liberty ships between 1941 and 1944.

Before World War II, Vancouver was a quiet town of about 18,000 people. Work on the new Vancouver shipyard started in early 1942 while I was still in Southern California. In less than a year, a huge shipyard emerged on what was once a dairy farm.[3] By the end of 1942 its population soared to some 100,000 mostly because of the Kaiser shipyard which alone employed 38,000 workers.

The Vancouver yard, like all merchant shipyards, became a gigantic factory designed to mass-produce ships with assembly-line methods. On any day, ships in varying stages of completion — from keel block to finished hull at the moment of launching, to the outfitting docks — could be seen.

Before I joined Kaiser, the U.S. Maritime Commission had already awarded the Vancouver yard a contract to build several hundred Liberty ships. But almost immediately the contract was reduced in order to start work on higher priority Navy shipbuilding orders. We stopped Liberty construction after only two ships. (The surplus Liberty material on hand was transferred across the river to Oregonship. Early in 1943, about the time I sailed out of San Francisco on my first Kaiser-built

---

[3] Construction on Oregonship, the first Kaiser shipyard in the nearby Portland area, began in February 1941.

Liberty, the Vancouver yard reverted to Liberty construction long enough to build eight more ships before it resumed production of military vessels — this time transports.)

The first of the Navy's orders came through right after I started welding school. It was for an undisclosed number of LSTs (Landing Ship Tank.) Later, fifty escort aircraft carriers (baby flatops) were ordered.

My first day on the job was mind-boggling, to say the least. The size of the yard far surpassed my expectations. There were assembly buildings, storage sheds, piers and offices in various stages of completion along with the skeleton-like frames of two ships on the ways. Cranes, forklifts and trucks seemed to be moving every which way. The workers — from skilled pipefitters, machinists and shipfitters to welders, burners and warehousemen — seemed to be moving to the clang of metal, the crackle of a welding rod or the sparks from a burner's torch. I was proud to be joining them.

My two weeks of on-the-job welding school went quickly enough. As our instructor put it, "You will be trained to specialize in one or two tasks initially using sub-assembly methods to the maximum. By applying mass production technology to shipbuilding we can reduce slipway times substantially." I soon learned the difference between flat, vertical and overhead welding and how each method got progressively harder to do right. I also began to understand why and how welding was so important to merchant shipbuilding speed. To build a ship similar to the Liberty in the first World War required some 650,000 rivets; new welding techniques in the Kaiser yards cut this to 25,000 rivets.

My first day in a pre-assembly building after completing welding school was an eye-opener. As welders put parts together, cranes turned them over so that nearly all welding was done in the "down hand" or welding below the waist position so that the molten metal flowed into the joints by gravity. To weld overhead took arm strength and skill, but almost anyone, including some very petite women, learned to weld at low-level quickly.

USS Casablanca *(CVE-55), right, about to be launched at Henry J. Kaiser's Shipyard, Vancouver, Washington, on April 5, 1943. Two of her forty-nine sister ships are under construction at left. Naval Historical Center.*

(Welding was also much less demanding than working with heavy rivet guns.) From that day forward I found myself going to work early and/or staying late just so I could walk around the yard on my own time to learn the what, why, where, when and how of shipbuilding.

May 1942:

In the "Battle of the Coral Sea," U.S. Navy planes severely damage a Japanese fleet and turn back an invasion force en route to capture Port Moresby, New Guinea. For the first time in Naval history, the battle is fought entirely by carrier-launched aircraft — the opposing ships never see each other.

General Rommel begins a major offensive in Libya with his Afrika Korps against the British Eighth Army.

Kaiser Co. Shipyards, Vancouver, Washington. Naval Historical Center.

The first thousand-plane raid of the war is carried out by the RAF Bomber Command on the German city of Cologne.

The U.S. Women's Army Auxiliary Corps (WAAC) is created. Later it is shortened to the Women's Army Corps (WAC).
Gasoline rationing goes into effect and price ceilings are implemented on many retail products.

John and I lived and worked in Vancouver but played in Portland. It had the friendliness of a small town with the advantages of big city cultural events and entertainment. We managed to negotiate swing shift (4:00 p.m. - midnight) assignments after I finished welding school to avoid conflicts over sleep and leisure time activities. That gave us a lot of daytime hours for sight-seeing so we got to know Portland in a short period of time.

June came and went before I knew it. The big news for the month was the decisive defeat of the Japanese at Midway.

June 1942:

American Lend-Lease to the Soviet Union begins with war materiél initially shipped through Iran and Alaska.

The Japanese are decisively defeated by the U.S. Navy in "The Battle of Midway" — the second crucial carrier battle in the Pacific war.

The Japanese invade Attu and Kiska in the Aleutian Islands after their carrier-based aircraft strafe and bomb Dutch Harbor.

Eight German saboteurs land at various points on the East Coast from submarines. They are quickly captured and tried as spies. (Six are executed.)

A Jap submarine shells Fort Steven at the mouth of the Columbia River near Portland, Oregon, and makes all of us at the yard work just a little bit harder!

View of Mount Hood from Portland, Oregon in the 1940s. Oregon Historical Society.

As my welding abilities improved through on-the-job training and experience, my assignments became more interesting and challenging. By the end of July, I had progressed from the assembly buildings to working on the ways. This included joining the steel plates over a newly laid keel, as well as vertical and overhead welding, as we secured the giant sections hoisted aboard by the cranes. At this stage, you understood how your work contributed to the team effort.

July 1942:

U.S. Army Air Force pilots make their first bombing run in Europe as part of an RAF raid against German airfields in Holland.

Japanese troops launch their Papua, New Guinea campaign with a landing near Gona.

The U.S. Women's Naval Reserve is established as the WAVES (Women Accepted for Volunteer Emergency Service).

The aircraft carrier USS *Essex* (CV-9) is launched at Newport News Shipbuilding and Drydock Company in Virginia. (She is the first of seventeen fast carriers that will enter service during the war, forming the backbone of the U.S. Navy's fast carrier strike force.)

John and I discussed the pros and cons of enlisting in the marines or Navy versus staying with the shipyard. John's mind was set. He would stay with the yard providing he got a promotion from apprentice to journeyman machinist soon. I planned to enlist on September 30th.

The first major offensive against the Japanese in the South Pacific was big news in August.

August 1942:

In the first U.S. Amphibious landing of the war, the U.S. 1st Marine Division under Lt. General A. A. Vandegrift lands on

Guadalcanal and Tulagi in the Solomon Islands northeast of Australia. (It is the beginning of a two-pronged offensive aimed at dislodging the Japanese from islands that will provide stepping stones to the eventual invasion of Japan.)

U.S. and Australian warships are surprised in a night attack by Japanese cruisers and destroyers while standing guard for the Guadalcanal landing in the "Battle of Savo Island." Three U.S. heavy cruisers and one Australian cruiser are sunk, and three U.S. destroyers are damaged.

The Germans begin an offensive against Stalingrad that is expected to complete their conquest of the Soviet Union.

Six hundred mounted Italian troops rout 2,000 Soviet soldiers at Izbushensky in "history's last cavalry charge!"

In the third carrier battle of the Pacific war, the "Battle of the Eastern Solomons," U.S. Naval forces defeat the Japanese Navy as they attempt to screen reinforcements for Guadalcanal.

U.S. troops land on Adak Island in the Aleutians group.

In mid-September John and I took what would be our last day trip together — this time to the Pacific coast, an hour's drive west of town. Even though we had made this trip before, the coast always seemed like a make-believe realm of mystical fogs, driftwood-strewn beaches, tide pools, forests of cedar and spruce, rugged headlands, and wind-raked dunes — a great change of pace. We strolled the beach and checked out two or three small coastal towns — always on the lookout for single young ladies, of course.

During the trip, John tried to talk me into waiting to go into the military, at least until I was old enough to be drafted, but my mind was made up. Like a whole lot of teenagers at the time, I wanted a piece of the action. It never once occurred to me I might not come back. At sixteen, I was invincible . . . or so I thought.

3
BOOT CAMP

I had wanted to be a Marine since Pearl Harbor. But when I tried to enlist on my seventeenth birthday in downtown Vancouver, Washington, the Marine doctor discovered I had a minor hernia and rejected me. He said, "It seems to me you have two choices. You can get the hernia operated on, then come back and see us or you can go next door and join the Navy. They will probably take you with the hernia and if it starts to bother you, they'll operate." (In retrospect, that minor hernia might have saved my life. The odds of a Marine living to a ripe old age weren't all that good in 1942.)

I walked out of the Marine recruiting office in a state of shock. How could the Marines *not* want me, I wondered. I had done a man's work for several years on Montana ranches. And what about my current job with the Kaiser shipyards? The more

I thought about it, the more I was convinced that the Marine Corps' loss would soon be the Navy's gain.

I explained my experience with the Marine doctor for the Navy recruiting officer. A Navy doctor quickly confirmed the slight hernia. He assured me the Navy would take me "as is" and perform surgery to fix the hernia should the need arise. I was told to come back the next day for a more complete physical but first I had to complete and mail a consent form to my mother in Montana.

The next morning at the recruiting office, several dozen men waited in line for their examinations. Once the physicals were completed the recruiting officer told us we would not be sworn into the Navy for approximately three weeks, for a special reason. All October recruits in the greater Northwest were to be sworn in by America's first lady, Eleanor Roosevelt, at one giant ceremony on Navy Day, 26 October 1942 in downtown Seattle. I suppose it was special to a lot of people, but many of us questioned why our training was delayed three weeks when the country was at war.

The three weeks passed slowly. My head was in the Navy but my hands still built ships.

September 1942:

A Japanese submarine launched a floatplane off the coast of Oregon. Its mission: drop incendiary bombs on the forests near Brookings, Oregon. Two fire-bombing missions were flown, each carrying two 154-pound bombs. (News of the attack was voluntarily withheld by the U.S. media. It was the only bombing of the continental United States during the war.)

Three RAF squadrons comprised of American pilots who volunteered prior to the U.S. entry into the war are transferred into the U.S. Army Air Force. The Americans shot down seventy-three enemy aircraft while serving in the RAF.

The morning of October 25 about fifty of us boarded a special bus for the U.S. Navy Recruiting Station in Seattle where we joined several hundred other recruits from all over the Northwest. We were assigned army cots in a large Navy barracks, then given the rest of the day off.

About 1100 the next morning we were loaded on buses and taken to the Bon Marche, one of Seattle's leading downtown department stores. I thought, what a strange setting for a Navy function. Recruits were standing anywhere there was space — in the aisles, between clothes racks. Fortunately, the ceremony was brief. A Navy band played some Sousa marches. Several Seattle dignitaries and some Navy brass said a few words. Then, with a drum roll, Eleanor Roosevelt was introduced. After a few kind words about the Navy — it was Navy Day, after all — she conducted the swearing-in ceremony and we all took the oath.

We spent the rest of the 26th and most of the 27th learning what it means to "hurry-up and wait." During that time it didn't help to read in the *Seattle Post-Intelligencer* that the Japs flew over Pearl Harbor again.

October 1942:

A Japanese submarine launches a floatplane for a reconnaissance flight over Pearl Harbor. After the pilot radios his report, the aircraft is apparently lost at sea.

A Japanese submarine sinks a Soviet sub some 500 miles west of Seattle, WA.

The Japanese submarine *I-25* fires two torpedoes at the tanker *Camden* off Coos Bay, Oregon while the vessel was stopped, making engine repairs. Six days later, while under tow, the ship bursts into flames and sinks.

In the "Battle of Cape Esperance" in the Solomons-New Guinea campaign, American cruisers and destroyers decisively defeat a Japanese task force in a night surface encounter.

The U.S.-flag Camden *sinking under tow, October 10, 1942. Naval Historical Center.*

Lt. Gen. Bernard Montgomery and his British Eighth Army open an offensive against Rommel's Afrika Korps. (It was the start of a 1,750-mile drive to join the Allied troops that will land in French North Africa in November.)

The afternoon of October 28 we were loaded into buses for the ride to the train depot. Destination: sunny San Diego — or so we thought! It didn't take long for the real destination to get out. We were heading East, not South, to a new Naval Training Station called Farragut, located in the upper panhandle of Idaho.

My reactions were mixed. I left Montana to see the world. Why was I heading back to where I came from? The Navy and Idaho — where was the fit? As it turned out, the "fit" was a body of water called Lake Pend Oreille in a serene mountain setting. The only real negative was that winter was right around the corner.

Our Northern Pacific train picked up milk cans, mail and other light shipping as well as passengers. But this "milk train" had the only service into Athol, Idaho, so it got most of the eastbound Farragut business.

During the ride we got better acquainted. Most of us were volunteers in our late teens — still single and gung-ho to take on the enemy. (The Army got most of the draftees.)

That night as I listened to the clickety-clack of the train rolling down the track from my berth, I remembered my first freight train ride over these same rails in 1940.

We were met at the Athol train station and loaded into a "cattle wagon" for the five mile ride to our new home — the United States Naval Training Station (USNTS) in Farragut, Idaho.

I don't know what I was expecting but it certainly wasn't unfinished new construction in a sea of mud. We soon learned we had the dubious honor of being among the first recruits to call Farragut "home."

The cover to the indoctrination pamphlet. Roger E. Glans.[1]

The cattle wagon dropped us off near a chow hall for our first official Navy meal. As we milled around wondering what to do a Chief Petty Officer grabbed a mike near the mess hall door and barked, "Now hear this. You're in the Navy now so pipe down, put out your cigarettes, and line up. We're going in and get some chow. The rest of the day will be fun and games."

It was only fitting that our first breakfast at Farragut was chipped beef on toast. (The messmen called it "shit on a shingle.") After chow we were marched — herded is a better word for it — to a large building that was part of the Receiving Unit. Each man was given a cardboard box and told to remove all his clothes, put them in the box, and write his home address on the label so they could be shipped home.

---

[1] All Farragut photographs in this chapter, unless otherwise noted, are courtesy of Roger E. Glans.

The "cattle wagon" brought new recruits into the camp.

Next we were issued soap and a towel and told to hit the showers at the far end of the building. At this point the only thing we had in our possession was the soap and towel. After the shower we didn't have that. The next two hours were spent standing in line, buck-naked, waiting to receive the first in a series of vaccinations and get another physical examination.

We were then asked to sign a Navy form confirming we understood that our salary as apprentice seamen would be $52.50 a month; our clothing allowance was a one-time $133.81.

Everyone was measured for clothing and shoe size. Talk about feeling lonely in a crowd. Still naked as jaybirds, we were shepherded along counters, staffed with nearly-bald recruits, each, of course, an expert at issuing proper-fitting clothing.

"Put on a pair of drawers, pull a skivvy shirt over your head and put the extras in your sea bag. Put on one pair of dungarees and a blue denim workshirt. Keep moving."

"Excuse me, what are dungarees?"

"Well, they're not your dress blues, stupid. Keep moving!"

And so it went. Shoes, socks, leggings, neckerchiefs, hammock, dress blues, ditty bag, toothbrush, towels, bedding, white uniforms, and always with the admonition, "Keep moving!"

By the time we were dressed, we realized privacy was not in the Navy's lexicon. It's a good thing that kind of experience comes to a person when he is young, resilient and adaptable. The change from civilian life to that of a boot is traumatic, to say the least.

Next we got our haircuts — the same skinhead cuts sported by those who yelled at us when we arrived. At least now we had earned the right to yell at the next arrivals.

We also learned why it's called Boot Camp. The leggings looked a little like the upper part of a pair of boots on your leg. And since they were part of the uniform of the day for all apprentice seamen, we were called boots.

When we reached our assigned barracks — our home for the next several weeks — the head facilities were another shock. There were no stalls; just a line of about eight porcelain thrones along one wall, the sight of which constipated some of the shyer guys. The showers were wide open, too, but somehow that didn't bother anyone. The shower felt so good we didn't mind the lack of privacy.

One of our first duties was to stencil our names on each piece of clothing.

We were also officially assigned to a company and met our Company Commander, J. J. Murphy, Chief Petty Officer, USNR. He talked tough, chewed you out for no reason, but in the end turned out to be a pretty decent guy. Murphy quickly introduced us to the basics of marching, then gave us an orientation "tour."

The Farragut camps used exclusively for training incoming recruits were laid out the same. Each camp had twenty-two, two-story barracks housing forty-four recruit companies surrounding a fourteen acre drill field called the "grinder." A typical company was composed of 120 recruits. Twenty companies formed a regiment. All

This cartoon postcard captures one of the paradoxes of recruit life. Naval Historical Center.

camps were laid out in an oval configuration that included a mess hall that fed 5,000 bluejackets in two shifts of 2,500 men in an hour-and-a-half.

At the opposite end of the grinder was the recreation building (ship's service). Alongside the grinder, midway between the mess hall and the recreation building, stood a huge drill hall containing six basketball courts, a boxing ring, and a 50' x 75' swimming pool. (Approximately thirty percent of the recruits could not swim when they joined the Navy. The goal was to teach them to swim within three weeks.) Interspersed among the barracks were laundry buildings with "scrub decks" where we boots washed our clothes.

There were two medical dispensaries (sick bays) in each camp staffed by Doctors, Dentists, Pharmacist Mates and Hospital Corpsmen. Personnel with more serious illnesses were transferred to the Farragut Naval Hospital.

Each camp had its own indoor rifle range with eighty firing positions in addition to the large outdoor range shared by all camps.

In every recruit's life, there is one man he remembers as long as he lives — his company commander. The C.O. (Commanding Officer) takes raw recruits and turns them into "fightin' bluejackets" in six to eight weeks. He does this through threats, physical exercise, psychological terror and hazing. The entire process was built on fear. The brainwashing never stopped, morning, noon and night. No matter what you did, you were told it was wrong. Murphy never ran out of tortures, from cleaning the barrack's head with a toothbrush to an extra turn around the obstacle course. He intimidated us at every opportunity, ordered us to address him as "Sir" and controlled our every move. Replies to questions were never satisfactory. The purpose of all this was to break us down and then rebuild us into the sailor the Navy wanted — one who would never question an order, who would always worry about his shipmate and who, someday, would walk as tall as Admiral Farragut.

At seventeen, I was young, very independent and, to some extent, undisciplined. J. J. Murphy soon took care of that. In fact, it wasn't long before it dawned on me that the Navy was the first father figure I had ever really known. It took care of all my needs. Like most father-son relationships, at first it was a love-hate relationship.

Each day's routine became like the next except that the weather changed. We saw our first real snowfall the second week of November. It added to the sloppy conditions on the obstacle (commando) course. Some of our Southern mates griped about the cold temperatures but it did them little good. The news that Congress had approved the drafting of eighteen and nineteen year olds was a slight consolation.

November 1942:

British and American troops under the command of Lt. General Dwight D. Eisenhower land at three points along the coast of North Africa.

A Japanese Naval force is defeated off Guadalcanal rendering the Japs unable to reinforce their troops on that island. The first Jap battleship to be lost in the war, the *Hiei*, is heavily damaged and scuttled. U.S. losses include the cruiser *Juneau* (CLAA52), whose sinking takes the lives of the five Sullivan brothers.

Many of the local families in Coeur d'Alene invited us to their homes for meals, skating, sledding and ice fishing. I remember spending a delightful Thanksgiving with one couple who had two boys in the service. We were all cheered by the occasion.

They say time flies when you're having fun. Boot Camp was hardly fun but Chief Murphy kept us so busy the weeks went by quickly. Our company was scheduled to graduate between Christmas and New Year's. There was lots of talk about what duty we would apply for and what schools we wanted to

The main entrance to Farragut.

*Indoctrination included innoc-
ulations, ten of them. Note the
iodine number on the "boot's" chest.*

*Inspection in formation soon became
part of the routine.*

*Training in Idaho included
marching in the snow.*

attend. Of course, at this point, we expected the Navy to grant our every wish.

We were promised Christmas day off but there was no change in our routine Christmas Eve. The plan of the day included calisthenics, jogging and marching in the morning and the obstacle course after lunch. About mid-morning I noticed a sharp pain in my right side. I tried toughing it out because Chief Murphy let us know early on that anyone who complained of feeling sick for whatever reason was goldbricking — that's Navy jargon for faking illness to get out of work. The second wall I had to scale did it. I went back and told Chief Murphy I couldn't continue and told him I was pretty sure I had appendicitis because the pain was so localized in my lower right side. They took out my appendix later that day.

In those days, you stayed in bed two full weeks after an appendectomy. Then it took another two weeks just to get your strength back. I have two pleasant memories of my first hospital stay — nurses and Waves. I think I fell in love several times that month.

January 1943:

Emperor Hirohito gives Japanese commanders permission to evacuate Guadalcanal and accept the American victory.

Allies capture Buna in New Guinea.

Soviet forces raise the siege of Leningrad.

President Roosevelt and Prime Minister Churchill begin Casablanca Conference.

Unfortunately, all that time in the hospital took me out of the training cycle. I had to join a different company when I got out. Joining my new company the third week in January 1943, I graduated on February 10 with new rating of seaman second-class (S2/c). On graduation day, we marched together for the last time on the parade grounds of Camp Ward. We may not have been seasoned Bluejackets, but we looked the part. For the first time our C.O. smiled — before he said good-bye. At last, no more apprentice seaman leggings. We also received a hefty $4.20 a month pay raise.

Now it was career decision time. What did I *really* want to do in the Navy? When I enlisted I told the recruiting officer I wanted to make the Navy my career. My "Kid's Cruise" made me a member of the regular Navy — not a reservist. We could sign up for schooling in different ratings (occupational fields) or simply specify sea duty and take our chances that we would learn the rating of our choice. Scuttlebutt had it that if there was a wait for the service school of your choice, you spent months peeling potatoes or serving chow or at some other equally unrewarding job. I had a preliminary meeting with a Navy career counselor. After a brief review of my Navy Classification Test scores — which were pretty good — he suggested I review three chapters in *The Bluejacket's Manual*: "Educational and Commission Opportunities," "Duty Assignments and Advancements" and "Classifications, Rates and Ratings." My service school preferences were Submarines, Guns, and Quartermaster school. My preferred duty assignment could be summed up in two words: sea duty.

The following day, my counselor explained there was a nine month wait for submarine school providing I met all requirements. Quartermaster school had at least a four month wait. However, if I "volunteered" for the Naval Armed Guard, I could go to gunnery school immediately and be at sea within six to eight weeks.

Since I had never heard of the Armed Guard, I asked the counselor to explain. "The Armed Guard," he said, "is a special arm of the U.S. Navy that defends cargo ships, troop transports, tankers and other support-type vessels from enemy air attacks and submarines. On average, there are between fourteen and twenty gunners, one signalman and maybe a radio operator in each Armed Guard crew. The rest of the ship's company is made up of civilian Merchant Marine personnel."

"It's volunteer duty at this time," he added, "due to the extremely hazardous Murmansk run to Russia. Allied convoys run the gauntlet of German U-boats, aircraft, and surface raiders and about twenty percent of the ships never make it back. But if you like guns, are eager to see action, and want to go to sea almost immediately, it should be just the ticket."

I signed up for the Armed Guard then and there.

On 15 February 1943, I was officially transferred to the Destroyer Base in San Diego, California, for Armed Guard gunnery school.

As new trainees, we came from all walks of life. Rich and poor became as one. We were shoved together to eat, sleep, work, play and train with our company mates. The officers and our company commander terrified us at first. And the rules and regs took getting used to, but we survived.

As the years passed most of us remembered the humorous side of Boot Camp. Here are some of my most (un)forgettable memories:

1. The day of arrival before assignment hearing the skin heads hollering, "Fresh meat! Wait 'til you get that square needle! You'll be sorry!"
2. The way the mess cooks slopped chow on your tray.
3. The psycho doctor who asks, "Do you like girls?"
4. The Ensign MD and the final physical. A buck-naked male factory with iodine numbers on our chests and backs.
   "Bend over and spread your cheeks" — a Navy finger wave.
   "Short-arm inspection — Skin it back and milk it down. Next!"
5. The injections (all ten of them — ouch!).
6. Reveille: "Drop your cocks and grab your socks. Hit the deck sailors, it's 0430! Rise and shine with the maritime."
7. The skinhead haircut.
8. The first visit to the canteen — get me five Hershey bars.
9. The sea bag — better learn how to pack it.

10. Punishment: Sea bag on your back, six times round the track.
11. Marching — two left feet; hup, two, three, four.
12. Morning calisthenics — stand in back so you don't have to jump as high.
13. Your first experience in the head with 24 other guys.
14. The gas chamber drill — brought tears to your eyes.
15. Guard Duty with a wooden rifle. How ridiculous!
16. Rifle Range — marksmanship scores.
17. Swimming test.
18. Obstacle course.
19. Barracks inspection — the white glove routine.
20. Square that hat, sailor!
21. Mail call! No letter today.
22. Graduation — at last!

Physicals . . .

. . . barracks inspection, above, boathandling, right, . . .

. . . swimming (including making a life vest of your pants) . . .

. . . and the obstacle course led to . . .

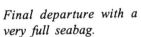

Final departure with a very full seabag.

4

GUNNERY SCHOOL

t was a cold winter day, the temperature near zero, as I
waited for my train in Coeur d'Alene. Pulling my peacoat
collar up around my neck, I walked back and forth along the
station platform. After the camaraderie of the last three months,
it seemed strange to be heading for San Diego alone. Didn't any
of the other guys want the Armed Guard? Was I nuts or what?

The train pulled in and I climbed aboard.

As the train slowed to a stop in Spokane, I saw civilians
and servicemen waiting to board. A cute little gal, probably
nineteen or twenty, said, "Is this seat taken?"

"No, ma'am," I replied. "Here, let me help you with that
bag."

Her name was Donna and she was a new war bride. Her
husband had just left for England with the Army Air Force. She
had coal black hair, was about 5' 2", weighed maybe 110 pounds
and was very pretty. She was from South Dakota and was going

to Portland, Oregon to get a job in defense work. Because I was from Montana and had worked in the Portland area, we had a lot in common and in no time we were gabbing like old friends.

When it turned dark outside, the conductor came by passing out blankets. We took a blanket to share and were soon cuddled up next to each other like two high school kids on a date. It seemed the attraction was mutual.

The train ride between Spokane and Portland proved to me that "time definitely flies when you're having fun."

The next morning when we pulled into Portland, she got off. We must have behaved like a married couple because several of the through-passengers in our coach later asked, "Where is your wife?" I simply replied, "She's visiting relatives."

As the train headed south out of Portland I thought, it's a good thing I have to report to the Destroyer Base in two days or Donna and I might get into trouble.

January/February 1943:

The U.S. Eighth Air Force based in England fly the first American bomber raid against Germany, striking the port of Wilhelmshaven.

The last German forces encircled at Stalingrad are destroyed or surrender to Soviet troops.

Marines unloading supplies on a Guadalcanal beach, December 1942. National Archives.

U.S. Marines take control of Guadalcanal after four months of savage combat in which they were cut off from supplies and were reduced to eating roots. FALSE

Officially, I was "Received Aboard" the Destroyer Base in San Diego, California, at 1600 on February 18, 1943 to attend gunnery school. A Bosun's mate at the receiving desk assigned someone to show me to my barracks. They looked like those at Farragut only older and maybe cleaner. The bunks were stacked two-high. The head was at one end. It, too, looked familiar: open thrones, latrines and showers.

The next morning after chow I was assigned to a gun crew consisting of twenty-one new arrivals. Our crew plus four others made up a company of 105 men. The company commander (C.O.) was a typical "old salt." A weather-beaten chief gunner's mate (CGM),

ARMED GUARD TRAINING SCHOOLS. There were three schools: Little Creek, Virginia (later moved to Camp Shelton), Gulfport, Mississippi (after the Great Lakes Training Station was closed) and San Diego, California. The San Diego gunnery school was established in the fall of 1941 as part of the Destroyer Base even before the repeal of the Neutrality Act. According to the Navy's Bureau of Personnel, 16,931 enlisted men and 1,273 officers received their training there before the school was disestablished on January 27, 1945. Most of the San Diego-trained men shipped out of the Armed Guard Center at Treasure Island.

he had hash marks from the bottom of his sleeve to his elbow, representing over thirty years of service. He was also a Pearl Harbor survivor and not too happy with his Stateside training duty.

He explained an Armed Guard crew can vary from ten to eighteen men depending on the ship's armament. We could expect to have a 30-to-90-day wonder as our Commanding Officer plus one gunner's mate petty officer. We might also have a Navy signalman and/or a radioman, depending on where our ships were headed and whether traveling independently or in convoy. As for gunnery training, "We've developed a four week

U.S. Destroyer Base, San Diego, California. Naval Historical Center.

crash training schedule that should really take three months. In week one you'll get the basics on small arms and some old relics from World War I like the .30- and .50-caliber[1] machine guns and the outdated 4" and 5" broadsides that the Fleet has been casting off as they've re-gunned.

"The remaining three weeks will be devoted to the 20-mm Oerlikon antiaircraft cannon and the 3"/50 and 5"/38 dual purpose guns. Some combination of these guns is now being installed on most new merchant ships.

"As for liberty, it will be kept to a minimum due to the crash nature of the course. You'll have reading assignments most nights. But you can count on Sundays off and maybe one weeknight liberty. It depends on your progress.

"And finally," the C.O. said, "I want all of you to remember this as long as you are 'cannon cockers.' A gun out of action from neglect is little different from a gun that has been put out of commission by direct enemy action."

---

[1] Caliber, applied to naval guns, has two meanings: first, it refers to bore diameter, expressed in inches or millimeters (mm); second, it expresses the ratio of the gun's length in inches divided by the bore diameter; e.g., you can find the barrel length of a gun by multiplying the bore diameter by the caliber of the gun.

Our instructors were regular Navy gunner's mates with sea-duty experience. They ranged from good to indifferent — depending on their interest in teaching. We learned a lot in four weeks. For example:

It would be our job to defend our ship, merchant crew and valuable military cargo from enemy aircraft, submarines and surface raiders as long as our guns would fire.

The Navy provided merchant ships with ammunition, magazine storage space, splinter protection for the bridge and radio shack, and berthing and messing space for the gun crew.

During the early days of the war, some innovative merchant marine skippers had their carpenters build gun tubs fore and aft containing creosote-soaked poles that looked like broadside guns to discourage enemy submarine commanders from surfacing to use their deck guns, a common practice then, to save torpedoes. Merchant ships were highly vulnerable to attack owing to their low speed, lack of armor and few watertight bulkheads. Hence the all-out effort to increase their surface and antiaircraft armament.

Armament priority was still given to vessels sailing to the most dangerous areas such as North Russia, the Mediterranean, the Indian Ocean and the Persian Gulf. Because President Roosevelt and Prime Minister Churchill at the January 14, 1942 Washington Conference agreed that the Allied strategy would be to defeat Germany first, then Japan, Pacific Ocean runs carried a relatively low priority. For this reason, we probably wouldn't see many 5"-38 guns for at least another year.

In early 1942, the Secretary of the Navy authorized the arming of not over forty foreign flag ships a month. Norwegian, Danish, Dutch, Polish, Greek and other ships flying the flags of Germany's victims were demanding American guns because they were bravely and effectively serving the common cause, too.[2]

---

[2] At first only Panamanian ships were provided with U.S. Naval Armed Guards. Then in April 1942 the Navy began furnishing them to large French and British passenger ships carrying U.S. troops. They also supplied Armed Guard communications personnel such as signalmen and radiomen.

Armament would differ from one ship to another depending on age, type and speed of ship, as well as when and where it was armed. The supply of guns and ammunition available for merchant ships was still inadequate. If we were assigned to an old rust bucket that was armed on the East Coast in '42, we would almost certainly need to know the basics of some of the World War I relics. But if we caught a new Liberty ship our chances were pretty good we'd have more modern weapons.

Our first training was in a small arms classroom. There we learned to break down, clean and reassemble pistols, rifles and Thompson submachine guns. In time, we were expected to do the entire "drill" blindfolded. We then moved up to .30- and .50-caliber machine guns. These were World War I vintage but still in use on some ships. We studied both air- and water-cooled Lewis and Browning machine guns, some on old Army tripod field mounts. We were relieved to learn the 20-mm Oerlikons with tracer bullets were fast taking their place. Finally, still in week one, we studied the old 4"/50, 5"/50 and 5"/51 broadsides with the help of Bureau of Ordinance training manuals. Part of this training included working the bigger surface and dual-purpose guns mounted in back of the classroom building. We practiced simulated loading and firing with dummy ammunition. We also learned how to take the breechblocks and firing mechanisms apart, and how to clean and reassemble them.

The 20-mm antiaircraft gun — more correctly called a Oerlikon 20-mm — was a Swiss-designed, rapid-fire, antiaircraft gun used by Allied and Axis navies during World War II. (The original guns were of Swiss manufacture, but soon they were being produced in the U.S.) We learned the 20-mm Oerlikon operated on the blow-back principle, with the explosive force of the propellant moving the breech to accept the next round. The gun's high rate of fire (450-480 rounds per minute), range of about 4,000 yards, its light weight, and the fact that it could be bolted to the deck without electrical connections made it suitable for ships and small craft of virtually any size.

The dual-purpose 3"/50-caliber and 5"/38-caliber guns were used against both surface and air targets and operated differently:

Table 1. Differences in Guns		
	3"/50	5"/38
Range in yards	14,000	17,300
Rounds per minute	20	15-22
Projectile weight in lbs.	13	55

The 3"/50 is a case gun, meaning the propelling charge of powder is contained in a metal cartridge or case. Ammunition for case guns is either fixed or semi-fixed. The 3"/50 takes fixed ammunition, that is the propellant powder case and projectile are

Above, left, "Guns" explains the breech mechanism of a 3"/50; above, pointer and talker; left, gunnery practice with dummy shells. U.S. Navy.

attached as one unit. Semi-fixed ammunition has two parts: powder case and projectile. The 5"/38 uses semi-fixed ammunition.

Both guns have these components in common: stand, carriage, slide, housing, barrel, and breech assembly. We soon learned that while all are important, it's the breech assembly which houses the firing mechanism that ignites the powder primer in the propellant case, and the extractors that remove the fired (empty) cases from the gun chamber, that require constant cleaning and oiling by a gun crew.

We learned how to pass the ammunition, load the gun, set sights, point (elevate), train (rotate), and fire each gun. And, of course, we had to strip (take them apart), clean, oil and reassemble them.

My first Sunday afternoon liberty in San Diego was spent getting a long-promised picture taken for my mother in my dress blues.

In our fourth week of gunnery training, we were retrained on firefighting methods, first aid and the use of gas masks. Then came our first real gunnery practice aboard ship. Early one morning, we were ordered to pack our sea bags, lash them up in our hammocks and stand by to leave. At 0800 we were bussed to a nearby pier along with several other gun crews. Shouldering our sea bags we clamored up the gangplank of the USS *Sacramento* (PG-19), an old World War I gunboat and Pearl Harbor survivor.

Sailing out the channel to the open sea, I think we all felt a little more like sailors. The first day we concentrated on surface targets with an old 4"/50. The gun crews took turns and while a crew was at "bat" the positions on the gun such as pointer, trainer and loader were rotated.

That night some of us were in for a shock. We had to sleep in our hammocks — but you first had to be assigned a spot. Eight of us drew the ship's galley. That evening, when the galley was as closed as it ever gets, we were "granted

permission" to string our
hammocks between jackstays.
We were warned that if we
tossed and turned, we could
easily end up on the deck. Two
of our group found out the hard
way. That wasn't the only
disturbance. One "cookie" or
another clanged pots and pans
all night. At 0400 we were
rousted out of our hammocks
so they could prepare breakfast.
Talk about a long first night at
sea.

The second day we prac-
ticed shooting at a target sleeve
pulled by an airplane. This time
we took turns firing two 20-mm
Oerlikons and a 3"/50.

*Seaman 2/c William L. McGee, age
seventeen, Armed Guard Gunnery
School, San Diego, March 1943.
Author.*

USS Sacramento *(PG-19). Naval Historical Center.*

When that old gunship reached port that evening we looked forward to sleeping in our bunks again. Our crew was offered liberty but we were too tired to go out. But staying on the base had its attractions. We attended a concert starring Marlene "See what the boys in the backroom will have" Dietrich. What a show! She had everyone in that hall eating out of her hand.

Our gunnery training continued with dummy ammunition for another week but it was never quite the same after experiencing the real thing.

> **USS *SACRAMENTO***
>
> The *Sacramento* was commissioned in 1914. She and other PG Gunboats were classified as Patrol Craft during World War II along with eighteen corvettes and eleven converted yachts. On December 7, 1941, she was part of a concentration of cruisers, destroyers and various auxiliaries at the Pearl Harbor docks and piers of the Navy Yard east of Pier 1010 that received very little attention from attacking Japanese planes. Some of these "Kates" (Japanese torpedo bombers) chose points close astern of the *Argonne* (AG-31), *Ramapo* (AO-12) and *Sacramento* (PG-19) from which to launch torpedoes at the battleships.

There is an old sailor expression: "Getting stewed, screwed, and tattooed." The night before we completed training, eight members of our gun crew decided to do just that in Tijuana. The stewed and screwed part was easy, but when the chips were down, only six of us actually got tattooed.

I didn't remember what happened until I woke up the next morning to a throbbing left arm. It gradually dawned on me what I had done. That's when I discovered a blood-soaked paper towel wrapped around my arm. Of course, both the blood and the towel were dry by then. Heading for the shower to soak the towel I hoped my choice in artwork was acceptable. Fortunately, it was, thank the good Lord. It simply said "USN" below a picture of an American flag with a ship's anchor.

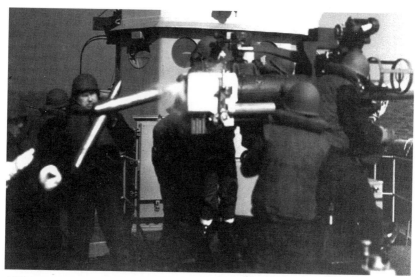

3"/50 in action during gunnery practice. Hot Shell man at left, with white asbestos gloves, catches case while Ammunition Handler, with shell in hands, stands by to load a fresh round. Naval Historical Center.

5

TREASURE ISLAND

On March 18, 1943, the Armed Guard gun crews in San Diego that completed training were transferred to the Armed Guard Center (Pacific), Treasure Island, San Francisco, California. We were a happy bunch as we boarded our train. Sea duty was right around the corner. We pulled into the Oakland train station early the next morning and transferred to grey Navy buses for the short trip to Treasure Island (TI).

As our bus headed up the eastern section of the San Francisco-Oakland Bay Bridge, the driver became tour guide. "You're looking at TI down there on the right. It's a man-made island, you know, and was the home of the recent World's Fair. Straight ahead, we're coming to Yerba Buena Island. Some old timers still call it Goat Island. It anchors the suspension bridge going on into San Francisco."

Without warning, he made a sharp right exit that had us grabbing for armrests and wound down the eucalyptus-covered

Reporting aboard Armed Guard Center (Pacific), Treasure Island, for the first time. U.S. Navy

western slope of Yerba Buena over a causeway connecting the two islands and on to the main gate at TI. We were all eyes, ears and mouth. Before the driver could answer one question, he was interrupted with another. Most of our questions went unanswered because the bus pulled over just inside the gate and let us out in front of a large former World's Fair building — TI's administration headquarters.

We were greeted at the front door by a young ensign who took our orders and other paperwork. Lining us up, he said, "Welcome aboard," took muster and gave us directions to the Armed Guard Center. "It's about three-quarters of a mile down the street. Two tractor-trailer rigs from the transportation pool will come by for you in about ten minutes, so pick out your sea bags and be ready to board."

Author's collection.

The cattle cars arrived on schedule. The lady driver, an attractive forty-something civilian, climbed down from the tractor and showed us how to stow our sea bags so there would be room for all sixty-five of us bluejackets on board. The road from the administration building to the Armed Guard Center hugged the tree-lined western side of the island. Shortly after passing a water taxi pier on the left we arrived at the Center, consisting of several buildings off by themselves and, we later learned, directly alongside the ammunition storage area. As one gunner put it, "We're going to be riding ships loaded with ammo. It figures."

A lieutenant greeted us as we fell in for muster. Welcoming us aboard, he turned to a second-class gunner's mate and said, "After muster, give them your ever-popular orientation tour of the Center and be back here in thirty minutes."

"Gun's" tour was quick, all right. He pointed out where we would eat, sleep, and get our mail. He also told us about Saturday inspections, linen exchanges, early morning calisthenics, port and starboard liberty sections, and more — all in less than twenty minutes. "How in hell can we remember all of that?" said a gunner behind me.

"You've got to work at it, Sailor," Guns fired back. "From now on, when someone says 'Now hear this' or 'Listen up' within earshot, you better do just that . . . case closed."

We then lined up in front of the main Center building to hear Lt. Cmdr. E. D. Flaherty, USNR, the assistant C.O. His speech, obviously given many times, went like this: "Armed Guard personnel are assigned 'permanent duty station' at one of three Armed Guard Centers located in Brooklyn, New Orleans, or here in San Francisco.

"In spite of the military's reputation to the contrary, Armed Guard assignments usually make geographical and economic sense. In other words, if you received your gunnery training in San Diego, you were probably assigned to us here at Treasure Island.

"All Armed Guard Centers provide many important services. For example, each Center will:

"Serve as a home base for gun crews awaiting their next ship assignments with ample opportunities for liberty, recreation, and entertainment.

"Provide ongoing refresher training in gunnery and communication skills as well as firefighting, abandoning ship, chemical warfare, lookout, recognition and reporting.

"Be there for each man's family when/if needed while he is away.

"Provide medical, dental, and religious services.

"Process mail, pay records, leave and shipping orders, and much, much more.

"Finally, it is the mission of this Armed Guard Center to assemble, equip, train, retrain, and furnish the finest Naval gun crews anywhere to all merchant ships originating trips from any/ all West Coast ports."

We were then addressed by a personnel officer who gave us two well-received points of information: first, we were all being promoted to seaman first-class (S1/c), and, second, we were granted liberty for the rest of the day. Most of us doubled back to the barracks, staked out bunks, stashed our sea bags, washed up, and headed for the mess hall. Why pay for chow in the City (there are many cities in the greater Bay Area but there is only one the local residents refer to as "the City," with a capital C, which is, of course, San Francisco) when we could get good meatloaf, mashed potatoes and gravy plus a piece of apple pie and coffee for free?

A dozen of us decided to hit the City right after chow, so we got liberty cards and caught a cattle car to the main gate, then transferred to a bus headed for the East Bay Terminal in San Francisco. Just about everyone wanted to explore San Francisco's fabled Market Street, find the beer joints and, of course, locate the girls.

I had a different objective in mind: locate a good, inexpensive tailor to make up a set of sharp dress blues, fast. They were called "tailor-mades" because they were cut from a quality gabardine fabric and custom-fitted to your body. They also stayed pressed much better than the Navy issue. When I first saw them in San Diego I asked a couple of "old salts" if they were legal, and their approximate cost. They told me the blues were legal and cost about a month's pay.

I soon found out that selling uniforms was a big, highly competitive business. Some tailors on Market Street had sales-people standing outside their stores trying to lure passing sailors into buying. Now that I was getting a $12.60 raise (to $69.30 per month) and would soon be at sea, I owed myself a pair of tailor-mades, right? I quickly found a tailor and ordered them for delivery in three days. As an added inducement, they prom-ised to throw in a gold dragon stitched into the lining of the thirteen-button panel above the crotch.

February/March 1943:

The Afrika Korps of Field Marshall Erwin Rommel defeats U.S. forces. But American troops regroup under the new com-mand of George Patton and stop Rommel's drive.

The U.S. Navy scores another major victory over a Japanese convoy in the "Battle of the Bismarck Sea" off New Guinea.

The largest convoy battles of the "Battle of the Atlantic" are fought, marking what would later be called the turning point in the U-boat war.

Meanwhile on the home front, U.S. rationing regulations were announced for meat, butter, and cheese. (Gasoline, coffee, and shoe rationing were implemented earlier.) Attempting to stem inflation, President Roosevelt announced he would also freeze wages, salaries and prices effective April 1, 1943.

The next afternoon, we began enhancing our skills. One group listened to a boatswain's mate explain how to abandon ship, while in a pitch-black room another petty officer offered techniques for developing "night" vision. Meanwhile, still others honed their plane-recognition-and-reporting skills with the help of models and flash cards.

Most classwork instruction was mandatory. If you spent any amount of time at the Center you received training or refresher training in all of the above skills plus first aid, chemical warfare, ammunition handling, firefighting, sound-powered phone techniques and, of course, gunnery exercises. Even communications personnel honed their skills in separate classes.

The daily routine at TI was easy compared to Boot Camp and Gunnery School. Calisthenics were at 0700 followed by morning chow, then classes before lunch. Afternoons were free and usually spent playing ping-pong or visiting the canteen — if we didn't have liberty.

March 27, 1943, was the day I looked forward to for months. During morning muster, fifteen names (including mine) were called out for sea duty. We were to be, in Navy jargon, "detached this date to the SS *Nathaniel Currier*," a brand new Liberty ship. Those curious about the destination were told to wait, with the reminder, "loose lips sink ships."

As the crew gathered we introduced ourselves and soon discovered there were thirteen gunners and two signalmen in our crew. Petty Officer Leo Russell, gunner's mate third-class, ("Guns" for short), and Eluterio Barela, signalman third-class, ("Flags" for short), were the only men with sea time. The rest of us had the same rating, seaman first-class.

The photographer arrived, lined us up two deep and took our picture — a routine that was repeated each time we were "detached" from TI.

Our commanding officer (C.O.) was Robert L. Miller, Lt.(j.g.) — a recent "90-day wonder" graduate — who arrived as the bus pulled up. "Guns" had mustered the group. After a quick handshake with the C.O. we climbed aboard and headed for our ship. You could sense our excitement by our chatter as we crossed the Bay Bridge. Everyone was eager to do battle

The first Armed Guard Gun Crew of the SS Nathaniel Currier. *Top Row, left to right: Grady Murphy, Bill McGee, Duane Curtis, Lee Gibe, Bill Sutton. Middle row: Leo Russell, GM 3/c, Joe Bergin, Eluterio Barda, SM 3/c, Gerald Olsen, Joe Jurgens. Bottom row: Art Lindstrom, Joe Skalenda, Frank Gassen, Rex Meadows, Russell Haynes. All S 1/c unless otherwise indicated. Author.*

with the Japs, including Lieutenant Miller. Like most of us, this was his first trip to sea.

As the bus took the off-ramp leading to the waterfront, we watched for Pier 3 and our ship. The San Francisco waterfront on the Embarcadero was a bustling, noisy, but exciting place. Trucks, railroad engines and freight cars, cranes, forklifts, and longshoremen were everywhere. The Navy bus driver skirted in, out, and around dozens of trucks like he was cutting cattle out of the herd. When he finally stopped we were on Pier 3, about twenty yards from the bow of the *Currier*. President Roosevelt might have called the Liberty ship an "ugly duckling," but to me she was a beauty. She was my passage to adventure!

Naval Armed Guard crew load their gear en route to duty aboard ship. Note method of tying hammock with seabag. National Archives.

6

DESTINATION:
SOUTH PACIFIC

We were a sight that afternoon as we marched single file up the gangplank with our sea bags over our shoulders. Our excitement was so high we looked and acted like a bunch of city kids arriving at our first day of camp. Our average age couldn't have been over nineteen or twenty. Lt. Miller (C.O. hereafter) had toured the ship earlier with the master, David Hassell (also called the Captain, Skipper or The Old Man) and knew his way around. The C.O. said, "Pick up your sea bags and follow me," then led us to the fantail (stern) to discuss gun and quarters assignments. With steam-powered winches hoisting cargo from the dock and lowering it into the holds, we had to pay attention or pay the price.

"First," the C.O. said, "let's decide on gun assignments since your gun station dictates where you will bunk. Do any of you have a preference?" I put up my hand immediately and asked for one of the bow 20-mms. "You've got it," he said. Others requested the 3"/50 caliber stern gun just above us and in

San Francisco waterfront. Naval Historical Center.

less than five minutes, all gun stations and quarters were assigned.

Three gunners along with "Guns" Russell, gun captain, manned the 3"/50 and two other men would handle the two 20s on the stern. The six of them were assigned accommodations in the afterhouse. The rest of us bunked in the gunners' accommodations in the midships house. "Flags" Barela and Joe Bergin, a signalman striker (studying to earn a signalman's rating), were also quartered midships since their duties were largely on the bridge deck.

After showing us where to bunk, the C.O. gave us the rest of the morning to unpack with orders to meet in the gunners' mess for chow at 1200.

We were pleasantly surprised by our relatively spacious quarters. There were sixteen bunks in four midships compartments. (The extra bunks would be needed on later trips.) The double-decker bunks or "racks" were comfortable and we each had a locker. Furthermore, we had our own head just down the passageway.

All U.S. merchant ships were manned by two distinctly separate crews. The merchant marine or civilian crew operated

Kaiser Permanente No. 1 where the Nathaniel Currier *was built. Naval Historical Center.*

the ship and the Navy Armed Guard crew manned the guns. The *Currier* was a new ship so the civilian crew was still assembling. The merchant marine steward, cooks and messmen weren't due until the next day. Chow was takeout food from a nearby deli, courtesy of the C.O.

While eating lunch, the C.O. laid out the rest of the day for us. First, there would be a tour of the ship led by Chief Mate Robert Yates. Then "Guns" and the C.O. would hold an indoctrination meeting on the fantail where, among other things, liberty sections and port security watches would be discussed.

Yates' tour was interesting — particularly to someone such as I, who helped build ships. However, what I saw as a welder during the early stages of shipbuilding was far different from a completely outfitted ship like the *Currier*. Chief Yates explained that the SS *Nathaniel Currier*, classified as an EC-2 Liberty dry cargo carrier, was built by Kaiser's Permanente Metals Corp. Yard No. 1 (Hull No. 529) in Richmond, Calif., and completed in March 1943. Her overall length was 441 feet, 7 inches with a beam of 56 feet, 10 inches. Her draft when loaded was 27 feet, 7 inches. For propulsion she had a single screw driven by a 2,500 horsepower steam reciprocating engine. Her cruising radius was 17,000 miles at a speed of ten to eleven knots. The ship's net tonnage was 4,380, deadweight tonnage 10,800, and displacement tonnage 14,100.[1] The ship flew the U.S. Flag and was registered in San Francisco, California.

The armament of the *Currier* consisted of one 3"/50 dual-purpose gun on the stern and nine 20-mm antiaircraft cannons — three forward, four on the bridge, and two aft. Our Armed Guard crew included our C.O., Robert L. Miller, Lt. (j.g.), thirteen gunners and two communication liaison personnel for a total of sixteen. The merchant marine crew consisted of the master, David W. Hassell, plus a deck department of eighteen, engineering department of thirteen and a steward's department of nine for a total of forty-one.

The master or captain had three assistants under him in the deck department; the chief (or first) mate, second and third mates. The deck crew included a Bosun with six able-bodied seamen (AB), and three ordinary seamen (OS) under him. In addition, there was a radio operator, a deck cadet (in training), a carpenter and a clerk-typist. The chief engineer also reported to the captain. He was in charge of the engineering department and had three assistants that reported to him: the first-, second- and third-assistant engineers. Additional members of the "black gang" — as the engineering crew was called — included a deck engineer, engineer cadet (trainee), three oilers, three firemen/water tenders, and two wipers. The steward's department included a steward, a chief cook, second cook/baker, assistant cook,

---

[1] Gross tonnage is the entire internal cubic capacity of the ship expressed in tons of 100 cubic feet each. Net tonnage is derived by subtracting from the gross tonnage the cubic capacity of certain internal spaces not available for carrying cargo such as machinery compartments and crew's quarters. Deadweight tonnage is the carrying capacity of a ship in long tons of 2,240 pounds each.

A sister ship to the Nathaniel Currier *in 1943. Note the lifeboats rigged out for immediate launching. George H. Dern courtesy William F. Hultgren.*

three messmen and two utility men. Some ships also carried a purser who ran the slop chest (store) and the ship's business accounts.

The *Currier* was built for the U.S. government's War Shipping Administration (WSA). In addition to purchasing or requisitioning vessels for its own use or for use of the Army, Navy, or other government agencies, the WSA also repaired, armed, and installed defense equipment on WSA-controlled vessels and Allied vessels under lend-lease provision. Because all ships were requisitioned by the WSA, qualified ship operators became operating agents for the government. In our case, WSA chartered the *Currier* to R. A. Nicol and Co.

Our indoctrination meeting later that afternoon was short and sweet. The crew was divided into two liberty sections: port and starboard. Under normal circumstances, one half the crew would have liberty while the other half shared the duty. The duty section handled gangway watch and any other posts our C.O. deemed necessary.

With the ship and her equipment being new, only routine maintenance would be required on our first trip. But Guns always found a job to keep us busy anyway. For starters, we had to strip the cosmolene — a glue-like grease applied by the manufacturer to prevent rust — from all the 20-mm guns.

It was difficult to concentrate on work that afternoon. I was fascinated with the cargo handling. The steam winches chattered loudly. Longshoremen shouted and cursed as they went about their jobs. The scent of the dock — from coffee beans to hemp to copra meal — evoked "far away places with strange-sounding names."

The next day, Lee Gibe, a lanky six-foot-four Oklahoma transplant, and I decided to go on liberty together with a grand total of $7.25 between us. We didn't get past a little bar on the next pier. Thanks to some generous longshoremen we played country tunes on the Nickelodeon and consumed enough beer to float a tugboat. Every time "Remember Pearl Harbor" came up on the jukebox, the entire bar crowd "remembered" and sang along. Gibe and I were reminded we might soon "meet the foe." Not exactly Hollywood's idea of a sailor's night on the town, but I think we had a good time.

The days flew by. Installation of armament and loading of ammunition was completed on April 2. Then, on April 3 came: one fire control phone system with seven bridge phones, three forward sets and one aft; sixteen life jackets; forty-one helmets (twenty-five for the merchant crew ammo handlers); sixteen sets of foul weather clothing; seven sets of special winter clothing (for lookouts); twelve sets of lookout goggles (six light- & six dark-density); sixty-one gas masks (forty-five for the merchant crew); three binoculars; and sixteen Army cots. We also received: one set of boxing gloves, one Chinese checker board, one sack of marbles, one chess set, two sets of checkers, two cribbage boards, one Acey-Deucy game, two sets of dominoes, six decks of playing cards, two decks of pinochle

[2] "Armed Guard Center Report of Materials Furnished To Armed Guard Units."

cards, one set of books for men at sea, one phonograph with records, one medicine ball, and one fishing kit.[2]

The five holds swallowed an unlimited amount of general/military cargo consisting of drummed aviation gasoline and diesel oil, ammunition, small stores, beer, soft drinks, and miscellaneous items. We watched as the stevedore crews topped off each hold, hoisted the strongbacks (beams) and hatch boards into place and covered the hatches with canvas and cross battens. Departure was close at hand. The C.O. confirmed this by canceling all liberty.

World War II poster by Anton Otto Fischer. Naval Historical Center.

Then the stevedores loaded a "deck load" of construction equipment and landing barges on top of the hatches and on the main deck of the ship. Everything was secured with heavy cable and turnbuckles to avoid shifting at sea. Finally, a catwalk, a wooden walkway with railings, was built over the top of the barges and/or construction equipment fore and aft so we could get to our guns. Of course, the merchant mariners used these catwalks, too.

Later that afternoon, the master and our C.O. left the ship to get our sailing orders.

On April 4, 1943, at 1620 with pilot aboard, the *Nathaniel Currier* slowly inched away from the pier with the aid of two tugboats. Destination unknown. The C.O. promised to tell us where our first stop would be after we cleared the harbor. All Armed Guard were at their assigned gun stations for this momentous occasion.

As the pilot navigated the *Currier* between the other ships dotting the Bay and the submarine nets protecting the harbor near the Golden Gate Bridge, we saw fog rolling in. It turned chilly as we gained speed and the sun disappeared.

I felt a strange combination of apprehension and excitement. I was proud to be serving my country. We had our headsets on so there was some chatter, but I think most of us were deep in thought. What lies ahead? Will we see action? Will we make it back? Why are we sailing alone instead of as part of an escorted convoy?

Leaving the Golden Gate, the ship began pitching and rolling, just enough to remind us — as if we needed a reminder — that we'd better develop our sea legs, and fast. The pilot boat pulled alongside bobbing like a cork and the pilot climbed over the gunwale and descended the Jacobs ladder. In some ways, it was like cutting the umbilical cord to the U.S.A.

As it grew dark, the C.O. set Condition 3 — meaning only one of three sections, the 1600-2000 watch, had to be at their assigned lookout stations. Since I was part of the first day's 1600 watch, I moved forward to the lookout's position in the bow guntub as we passed the Farallon Islands. It was 1700. The seas got rougher. The ship slowly pitched up and down as we headed into the big Pacific swells. I was glad I had on my Navy peacoat and watch cap. If it was chilly now, what would it be like by 2000? Then, because of the heavy blanket of fog, it quickly turned dark.

I was thankful for our sound-powered phone system. (No electrical power was necessary: the user's voice acted on a carbon-filled cell and diaphragm to generate current to power the circuit.) The phone system was like a party line — everyone could talk and/or try to listen at the same time. Hearing other voices relieved the feeling of loneliness one gets on a dark night at sea. We weren't supposed to chitchat while on watch, but we

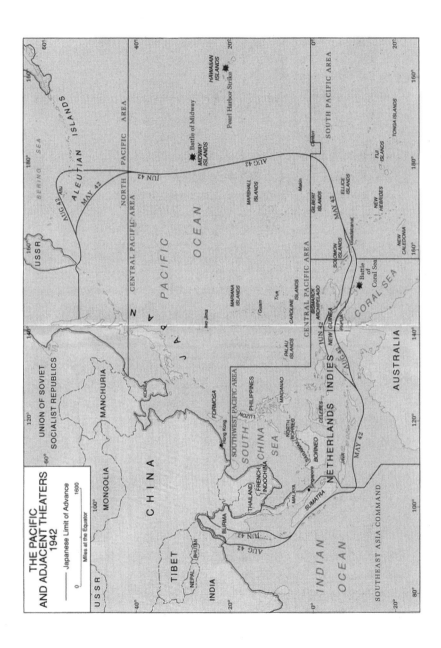

THE PACIFIC
AND ADJACENT THEATERS
1942

Japanese Limit of Advance

Miles at the Equator
0 — 1600

Gunnery practice on the 20mm. Mounted on Mk. 2 mount with adjustable trunnion, height is controlled by a large handwheel on opposite side of the mount. Naval Historical Center.

20mm antiaircraft gun in action aboard a Liberty ship. Note the simple ring sight. Naval Historical Center.

had to check in with the other lookouts from time to time. My thoughts drifted from one subject to another. I always valued alone time. It looked like I'd be getting plenty while on watch.

At 1945, Russell Haynes, my relief, arrived. He warned me about a couple of tight turns to watch out for on the catwalk leading back to the midships house. He also informed me the gunner's messroom was almost empty. I guess I wasn't the only one feeling queasy. Working my way along the catwalk, I slowly made it to the midships house.

I headed straight for the messroom. I was hungry in spite of being a little nauseated. There wasn't a soul in sight. It seems that when we changed from a westerly to a south/southwest heading about 1900 the ship went from pitching stem to stern to rolling side to side. And this rolling motion created seasickness — sometimes even among old salts.

The night cook had put out cold cuts, bread, and condiments, so I made myself a sandwich, poured a cup of coffee and sat down to eat. After a few bites I, too, lost my appetite and headed for my bunk.

The next morning the General Quarters (GQ) alarm sounded at 0345. All Armed Guard members not already on watch were called to their battle stations on the double. It was only a drill, but it was also the start of our morning GQ training sessions. This was a rude awakening for most of us — not only the early hour but the difficulty of getting to our stations when it's still pitch-black outside. From that day forward we were at General Quarters (Condition #1) before sunrise every morning we were at sea — starting about 0500 and ending one and one-half to two hours later. The same routine applied prior to sunset, around 1800, and lasted about an hour. Of course, the GQ alarm sounded only when it was a special drill or the real thing. On all other occasions we were awakened by someone or told when GQ started so as not to alarm the Merchant Marine crew unnecessarily.

During most GQs we held gun drills. For example, the twice-daily 3"/50 drill always included a recoil cylinder check, firing circuit test, and elevating and training the gun through maximum arc.

The start of GQ each morning was the equivalent of reveille for the first two weeks we were at sea; then, for some reason, the C.O. called for reveille ten minutes prior to GQ. It went a lot smoother after the change.

We had a number of other routines — some daily, others less often:

Daily: Ammunition magazines inspected/temperatures taken.
          All guns cleaned and oiled.

Weekly: Aircraft identification drills.
~~All gun tubs, mounts and decks cleaned/inspected.~~
Monthly: Living quarters and heads cleaned/inspected.
20-mm sights drill.
Sight setter drill for 3"/50.
Gunnery training for merchant crew and passengers, if any.
Personal gear inspected.
Instructions on
  a) behavior on shipboard,
  b) relative bearings and keeping lookout,
  c) aircraft lookout and reporting,
  d) tracer control and lead firing,
  e) military courtesy.
Calisthenic drill—while in port, only.

On April 7, the 3"/50 caliber gun crew got to test fire four rounds off the stern: one round at zero degrees elevation; three rounds at five degrees less than maximum elevation. The test results: The foundations holding down bolts, the gun platform and other installations were examined and found to be in good condition. The 3"/50 gun was ready for immediate use.

On April 12 at 1330, target practice was held. Sixty rounds were fired from each 20-mm gun at a target balloon. Six shells were also fired from the 3"/50. The results were not bad although the balloon was still in one piece when last seen.

It felt good to get a few bursts in with my "own" gun. It also gave us the opportunity to get acquainted with our Merchant Marine ammunition loaders. These men were strictly volunteers. My loader, David Powers, was an AB (able-bodied) seaman and part of the deck crew.

On April 11 three old salts from the Merchant Marine, backed up by our very own Guns Russell and Flags Barela, let it be known that we would be passing a "mail buoy" on the 12th and if we wanted to write letters home, they could be placed on the buoy for pickup by the next ship heading for the States. I didn't fall for their little joke mainly because I had written home just before leaving TI, but about a dozen green guys from both crews were the butt of the "mail buoy spoof" for the rest of the trip.

On April 18, we crossed the equator at 1330. King Neptune Rex (Guns Russell), Queen Aphrodite (Flags Barela) and Davy Jones (Bosun' Bill Olsen) duly initiated all Pollywogs into the Royal Order of the Deep. Thirteen out of fifteen of the Armed Guard unit (counting the C.O.) were landlubber Pollywogs — having never crossed the equator before. (We were never sure, but about half of the merchant mariners were supposedly Pollywogs, too.) However, with the exception of Bill Olsen, most of the merchant crew stayed on the sidelines.

All of the royalty were bearded and wore grass rope skirts and sandals. In addition, the queen wore a brassiere stuffed with a couple of grapefruit. King Neptune had a trident spear, the queen a scepter with a star of gold on the tip, and Davy Jones was blackfaced and wore an eyepatch. The Jolly Roger flag was hoisted right on cue as King Rex said, "Let the ceremony begin."

The king, queen and Davy Jones all sat on their thrones high above the poor Pollywogs come to pay them homage. Pollywogs had to stay behind the Lubbers' Line until they were summoned. For starters, grease was applied to their shaved heads as anointing oil. Our C.O., was handcuffed and had a large anchor ball tied around his neck as penance for not having crossed the equator before. He was then asked to kneel before the queen, where he was touched on his backside by the electrified scepter and jumped a foot.

Frank Gassen, a little on the chubby side, had to remove all of his clothing and wear a diaper fastened with a large spike. The 3"/50 gun crew (minus Guns Neptune, of course) were blindfolded, armed with boxing gloves — and told to let swing. Davy Jones would tap one of them on the head and stand back as the Pollywog swung like a gate.

Joe Bergin was drenched with sea water from a fire main, then, on hands and knees, forced to push a piece of clothesline

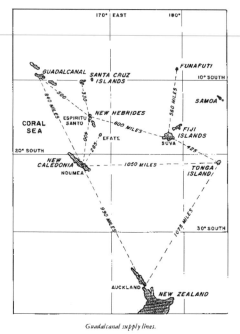

Guadalcanal supply lines.

with his nose across the equator. To encourage him, Davy Jones used his trusty paddle. Try pushing a limp line with your nose with someone wielding a paddle on your behind.

I was part of the last group of guys initiated. We had to disrobe and take turns wielding the paddle on each other as we moved around the steel deck in a circle on our hands and knees. It was midday. The deck was hot.

The ceremony was fun for everyone. Once initiated as full-fledged Shellbacks, we could look forward to our next crossing without trepidation. (Some might even look forward to "getting even" by taking it out on new Pollywogs.)

On April 21, we crossed the International Dateline north of the Fiji Islands and lost a day in the process.

With no doctor or corpsman on board, we all hoped and prayed we wouldn't get sick but on April 23, Donald Phelps, ordinary seaman (OS), was put to bed with an ice pack and placed on a liquid diet. Diagnosis by the master: appendicitis. Fortunately for Phelps, we were nearing our first foreign port.

On April 25, our bow lookout spotted the New Hebrides Islands at 0920 off the starboard bow. The first leg of the *Currier* maiden voyage had passed.

At 1140 we dropped anchor in destination port No. 1 — Espiritu Santo in the New Hebrides. The C.O. secured sea watches and set gun watches on Condition 2 — meaning we were in an area where submarine, surface, and/or air attack could occur at any moment. In this case, the entire gun crew was at

Aerial view of Espiritu Santo in the New Hebrides. Seabees.

The Waterfront with a Liberty ship unloading, ca 1943-44. Seabees.

ESPIRITU SANTO

The New Hebrides, in the western South Pacific, consists of some eighty tropical islands with a land area of about 5,700 square miles. Of the thirteen main islands, the most important are Espiritu Santo, Efate, and Malekula.

Espiritu Santo is about 100 miles north of Efate. Santo is the main town. In mid-May 1942, Admiral Ghormley and Generals Patch and Chamberlain, headquartered in New Caledonia, decided that, in order to counter the new Japanese base at Tulagi, another advanced air and naval base must be set up at Segond Channel, Espiritu Santo.

Soldiers, Seabees and Marines started a road from the harbor to the airfield site and had the first runway open for the Guadalcanal campaign on D-day, August 7.

On July 10 ComSoPAC (Ghormley) received the operation order of CinCPAC (Nimitz) for the seizure of Tulagi and Guadalcanal. Within a few months Espiritu Santo became the principal advance base for the support of Operation "Watchtower," the occupation of Guadalcanal and Tulagi.

GQ, but divided into two lookout sections of two hours on and two off. Thirty minutes later the C.O. changed back to Condition 3 — our regular lookout watches at the guns of 4 hours on and 8 off. (Condition 3, we learned later, is sometimes called for in unguarded anchorages or roadsteads like Espiritu Santo.)

This was our first foreign port. There were ships of every kind in the roadstead. Small craft darted between them and the island like toy boats in a bathtub.

Base Button, at Segond Channel, was rapidly becoming an advance naval and air base. Espiritu Santo, 560 miles SE of Henderson Field and 409 miles north by east of Noumea, New Caledonia, was considered a far healthier place than Guadalcanal. By the time we arrived, the anchorage was ample and well protected and the first of several wharves under construction was completed by the Seabees. The shore installations, mostly on a slope facing the fresh trades, and the Pallikulo airfield, a few minutes' drive over coral-surfaced roads, was second in importance only to Henderson.

The next morning at 0645, shortly after our usual GQ drills, we weighed anchor and got underway. The C.O. set sea watches on Condition 2, then informed us we were heading for our next port, an island not too far to the southwest, and that we could expect more information soon. It made us wonder: Why all the secrecy?

The evening of April 27 while at GQ, I reported a large island off the port bow. The C.O. told us over our sound-powered phones we were looking at New Caledonia. He also explained it was a French colony, which triggered chatter about Frenchwomen, and more, until the he finally said, "Knock it off, you guys. Don't set your hopes too high."

We dropped anchor at 1825 about a mile from Grand Terre, the main island. We could see the lights of the capital city of Noumea being turned on along the coast. Hopefully, the next day we could meet the natives.

The C.O. secured GQ and set the gun watch on Condition 3. It looked like half of Admiral William F. Halsey's South

Pacific Force was anchored around us. That gave us a good feeling. The storied carriers like the *Saratoga* (CV-3) and the *Enterprise* (CV-6) looked big and formidable. And the sleek cruisers and destroyers made me feel, for the first time, like I might have made a mistake in my choice of sea duty. After all, the Armed Guard is a <u>defensive</u> unit. Maybe I should be on a combat ship that goes <u>looking</u> for a fight with the Japs!

We mustered at 0800 for morning orders, a calisthenics drill, and liberty information. (The calisthenics was a first on this trip and set a precedent for things to come when in port.)

The starboard section would get the first look at Noumea with an abbreviated liberty from 1300 to 1800. Liberty section muster was set for 1245: uniform; dress whites. Hot damn.

We soon learned Noumea was the nerve center for the South Pacific campaign where Admiral Halsey, with a seasoned staff of officers and bluejackets, ran the entire South Pacific Force of Navy, Army, Marine Corps, Seabees; ships, boats, freighters, net tenders; search radars, antiaircraft batteries; service of supply

NOUMEA

New Caledonia stretches about 250 miles and has a maximum width of about thirty miles. It is mountainous and surrounded by coral reefs. Its highest peak is Mt. Panie at 5,413 feet. The interior contains plateaus and deep valleys. The island also has extensive forests.

By the time Vice Admiral Ghormley, Commander South Pacific Forces and Area, arrived at Noumea May 17, 1942, New Caledonia and all the French Islands in the Pacific except Wallis had declared for General de Gaulle. Many of the local French were pro-Axis and ship and troop movements were constantly reported to the Japanese.

At Admiral Ghormley's request, RAdm John S. McCain was appointed Commander Aircraft South Pacific Area. McCain set up headquarters on board U.S.S. *Tangier* in Noumea Harbor and exercised operational control of all Allied planes in the South Pacific. Sixteen Catalinas were based on the tender *Tangier*; four Flying Fortresses and thirty-four Army fighter planes were on the Gaiacs field at the center of the island, and the advanced base at Efate was operating under difficulties imposed by malaria, terrain, and lack of bare necessities.

and repair stations; camps, hospitals, officers' and enlisted men's clubs; and a hundred other groups and forces, not to mention the thousands of men who were just passing through. But Noumea was not a place to relax. Lights burned late on the docks where soldiers and sailors tried to relieve supply-line congestion, and in naval headquarters where staff officers worked over reports, orders and dispatches.

The skipper and our C.O. were going ashore for a port director's meeting, so they took our entire Armed Guard liberty party and several merchant mariners with them in one of the ship's lifeboats — a fat whaleboat that carried about twenty-five people comfortably.

If you looked past the throngs of servicemen, Noumea was an unpainted, ramshackle town, but the climate and the surrounding scenery were superb: a picturesque-ly-indented coast, dazzling coral sand, wood-ed vales and well-cultivated fields, the right amount of rainfall, temperatures seldom above eighty-six degrees, cool nights with trade winds and no malaria-carrying mosquitoes!

The native kanakas seemed friendly enough although we heard they fought regularly with the French gendarmes. I purchased a French phrase book at the first opportunity but soon found that most shopkeepers understood English. A few of the guys went looking for the local house of ill-repute. The rest of us had a pretty good meal in a French restaurant topped off with a couple of beers. Not an exciting first liberty on foreign soil, but a nice change of pace from shipboard life.

Everyone was at the boat dock by 1700 waiting for the skipper and C.O. They had little news when they finally showed up. It seemed we were witnesses to another example of "hurry up and wait." There had been a change in Admiral Halsey's plans but that was all they could or would tell us.

The ship remained off Noumea for six more weeks. During this time, we had more liberty than we could afford and got to know the merchant crew a lot better. Made up of civilians from ages sixteen to sixty, their job was to operate and maintain the ship. Thousands got their training in Maritime schools. The physical training and discipline was akin to the U.S. Navy's Boot Camp, and the six months of technical training and testing was condensed and vigorous.

We had lively debates with the merchant crew about who had the best deal. The disparity in pay between us was the biggest bone of contention, and here there was really no contest. The mariners won this one hands down. They earned separate voyage, area, and explosive bonuses in addition to their base salaries, overtime and security watch pay. All told, their monthly income averaged about ten times that of the Armed Guard crew.

The six weeks in Noumea taught us the meaning of "channel fever" and boredom with a capital "B." I purposely cultivated my friendship with Stuart Churchon, the Merchant Marine radio operator ("Sparks," for short). As a news junkie who always wanted to know what was happening in the war as well as on the home front, Sparks was my primary source for news. From him I learned there were three significant war developments in April and May.

In a pincer action, Patton and Montgomery linked their armies in Tunis, forcing the surrender of all German and Italian troops in North Africa.

U.S. troops invaded Attu in the Aleutian Islands.

A Jap submarine torpedoed the Australian hospital ship *Centaur* and 299 persons died when she sunk.

Learning about Adm. William Halsey's naval headquarters in Noumea where he and his staff planned and coordinated the South Pacific campaign with Gen. MacArthur's staff reminded me once again just how little the average enlisted man, or officer for that matter, knew about the big picture. Hell, we didn't even know where our ship was headed next, let alone the plans of

Halsey's task force or MacArthur's army. The sailors in the fleet at least had the news piped over their ship's sound systems periodically. It was usually after the fact, but at least they had a pretty good idea what was happening. I had to count on my radio pal Sparks to keep me informed.

7
TASK UNIT 32.4.4
PART I

We had been anchored off New Caledonia since April 27, 1943. It was now June 9. Everyone was broke and most had a bad case of "channel fever." So we were eager for a change when we weighed anchor and joined six other ships in a U.S. Navy Task Unit designated 32.4.4.[1]

In addition to the *Nathaniel Currier*, there were three U.S. Navy cargo ships: *Aludra* (AK-72), *Celeno* (AK-76), and *Deimos* (AK-78), all Libertys (each AK's armament consisted of 5"/38 and 3"/50 guns on the stern and bow respectively, plus eight 20-mm antiaircraft cannons), plus our escorts: the destroyer *O'Bannon* (DD-450), fast transport *Ward* (APD-16), and mine-sweeper *Skylark* (AM-63). Additional protection was scheduled

---

[1] Task forces are divided into task groups, with numbers following a decimal point, and the groups into task units, with numbers following a second decimal point. TU 32.4.4 means the fourth Task Unit of the fourth Task Group of Task Force 32 of Admiral Halsey's Third Fleet.

Convoys allowed escort vessels to concentrate their defensive weapons on several ships at once. Naval Historical Center.

during the last two days of the trip north as we sailed through "Torpedo Junction" — that part of the Coral Sea between the Solomon and the New Hebrides Islands regularly patrolled by enemy submarines.

Convoy speed was set at ten knots. Ships were grouped in convoys to maximize the defense capabilities of the escorts — radar, sonar, depth charges and guns. For security reasons, we bluejackets — and most officers for that matter — never knew where we were headed until we were well underway, and sometimes, not until our destination was in sight. In fact, most Pacific islands had code names. Furthermore, we seldom knew the names of the other vessels in a convoy. The Coast Guard ordered the nameboards on the midships house reversed on all merchant ships, and the U.S. Navy displayed hull numbers only on the bow.

The promised additional protection in the form of land- and carrier-based air cover was provided on June 12-13 as we sailed through "Torpedo Junction." At least half the gun crew

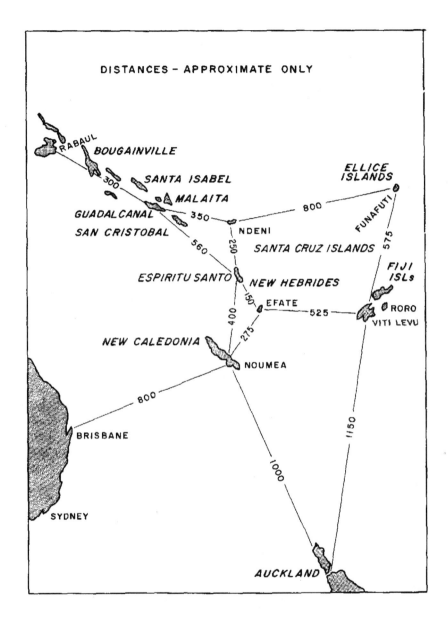

DISTANCES – APPROXIMATE ONLY

was constantly at battle stations with lifejackets nearby. Some men slept by their guns all night.

On June 14, we dropped anchor off Guadalcanal, ten months after the U.S. Marines first landed on this mountainous island of the Solomons group. Enemy troops — stragglers who missed the evacuation boats — were still being pursued in the distant hills by our soldiers. We soon realized our days of practice were behind us and that the next GQ bell could be the real thing. In fact, we were introduced to the Japanese our first night off the "Canal."

To pester Marines, bluejackets and aviators alike, the enemy had one or two aircraft — usually single-engine float planes that circled for an hour or more over Henderson Field and Ironbottom Sound, released an occasional flare for visibility, then dropped small bombs at irregular intervals to make sure we didn't sleep too soundly. The exasperated Americans listening to the peculiar chug-chug of their engines named these nocturnal pests "Washing-Machine Charlie," "Louie the Louse" or "Piss-call Charlie."

At 2305 on June 14, we experienced our first real General Quarters alarm. We scrambled to our gun stations only to hear "Washing-Machine Charlie" off in the distance somewhere over Henderson Field. He putt-putted around for over thirty minutes, then dropped what sounded like a small bomb and took off in a northerly direction. That was it. No big deal, but he managed to cut into our sleep.

Bright and early the morning of June 15, a Seabee crew (1st Special Naval Construction Battalion) came aboard to begin off-loading. They rigged the booms with the help of the *Currier* deck department and lowered the deckload of landing barges into the water, then filled them with construction equipment, all before lunch. By afternoon they were off-loading drummed aviation gas from the holds into two Navy LSTs (Landing Ship, Tank) — one on each side of us. They finally knocked off about 1900.

Later, the Seabees worked far into the night. This meant sacrificing the safety of blackouts to expedite off-loading. However, with radar and coastwatchers providing early warning signals there was ample time to darken the ship. With every alert, landing craft and barges were under orders to cast off immediately. If it was daylight they headed for the safety of the beach, but at night they simply scurried out into the dark and waited for the all-clear signal.

SS *Nathaniel Currier*

The Seabees were back on the job the next morning by 0700. Right after noon chow "Sparks" Churchon received a Radio Guadalcanal Yellow alert signifying that Jap planes were headed our way from the northern Solomons. They were first spotted by a Coast Guard patrol plane. Sparks sounded the GQ alarm and all hands were soon at their battle stations.

Upper left, Seebees working in cargo hold of Liberty ship. View of the deck, above, as they take a break. Lower left, cargo of lumber is loaded onto barge tied alongside. Claude Gulbranson.

At 1350, we received a Condition "Very" Red signal with orders to get underway immediately. We watched impatiently as the *Celeno* immediately stood out towards Koli Point in a northeasterly direction, followed closely by the *Deimos*. The *Skylark* was already some 500 yards to the north in a screening position and the *Aludra* was getting underway off Koli Point.

The two LSTs tied up alongside the *Currier*, the "353" and "398," seemed to take forever getting underway. In the meantime, Airsols' fighter pilots went into action. It was a confidence-builder for us newcomers, watching them take off, one after another, to intercept the incoming force of Japanese bombers and fighters. There were Navy Wildcats and Hellcats, Army P-40 Warhawks and P-38 Lightnings and, last but not least, Marine gull-winged Corsairs.

While we waited at battle stations our imaginations ran wild. The chatter over the battle phones picked up in volume and intensity. You could hear excitement and apprehension in every voice. To the few sailors in TU 32.4.4 who had already seen action, the wait was probably tolerable since they only concerned themselves with what the enemy would do, but those of us without experience were anxious about our own reactions as well as the enemy's actions.

Duane Curtis, Gunner: "I felt that I didn't know what I was gittin' into and when the air raid hit, I wondered if I was gonna get out of it. It's surprising what will go through a man's mind. I also remember seeing the ship's carpenter on the stern. He broke down and cried like a baby during the attack."

The C.O. told everyone to pipe down, but it did little good. He even tried group therapy on us — like how to get a laugh out of stressful situations. I'm the first to admit that laughter relieves stress. We proved it with some very corny jokes that day as we watched and waited.

The weather was typical of the South Seas — hot sun, mild trades, with only a few scattered cumulus clouds. We were on the lookout for high-altitude dive bombers as well as low-flying torpedo planes. Hundreds of *(text continues on p. 108)*

AIRSOLS

The Solomon Islands Air Force (Airsols) was a heterogeneous mix of U.S. Army, Navy, and Marine Corps airmen as well as the New Zealand Air Force. Marine, Navy, and Army fliers flew on missions together, lived through bombing raids together, and many died together aloft or in foxholes.

Airsols' fighter planes kept guard over ships off Guadalcanal and over convoys running north of Espiritu Santo; its deep-chested Fortresses (B-29s) and Liberators (B-24s) pulverized enemy airfields; its PBY-5A "Black Cats," equipped with radar and landing wheels as well as pontoon hulls, conducted night-time scouting and anti-submarine patrols, rescue missions and bombing and gunfire spotting; its PBY "Dumbo" rescue planes picked up shipwrecked mariners and bailed-out aviators, delivered rations to beleaguered coastwatchers, and rushed spare parts to the fighting front. And, to reduce the enemy's fondness for night air attacks, night fighter squadrons of Corsairs (F4U-2) and Vega Venturas (PV-1) were added to the mix of Airsols' firepower.

The F6F Hellcat, left, a faster, more heavily armored plane, replaced the Navy's Grumman F4F-3A Wildcat, bottom. Left, Naval Historical Center, bottom, National Archives.

AIRSOLS (continued)

Commander Aircraft Solomon Islands (ComAirSols) in June 1943 was RAdm Marc A. Mitscher,(command of Airsols rotated between the U.S. Army, Navy, and Marine Corps.) By the spring of 1943, Airsols had gained the advantage in quality aloft and sometimes in numbers, too. Many changes based on combat experience were made in older models of American planes — more power, more heavily armed and armored with longer ranges. New types were the F6F-Hellcat and the F4U Corsair fighters, and the B-24 Liberator, which was capable of carrying more bombs longer distances than the older B-17.

Airsols bombers included the B-17, above, on a bombing mission over Gizo Island, and the PB4Y (the Army Air Corps version was the B-24), below, taking off from Carney Field, Guadalcanal. Above, Naval Historical Center; below, National Archives.

AIRSOLS (continued)
Just two of many Airsol pilots to distinguish themselves were Marine Medal of Honor winners Capt. Joe Foss and Major "Pappy" Boyington. Both would become top Aces during the August 1942-April 1944 period — Foss with 26 victories and Boyington with 28.

The P-38 Lightning was new to the area and with its twin engines was more than a match for the enemy Zero. Above, on the ground, below, over New Georgia. Top photo National Archives, bottom author's collection.

(continued from p. 104) watchers strained their eyes to the horizon and directly above but saw nothing. It was maddening. Where the hell were they? Our 3"/50 gun crew on the stern was ready to reach out seven or eight miles to greet the raiders if they could only see a target.

We later learned that many of the enemy planes were directly overhead at 18,000 feet, their well-camouflaged undersides invisible from the surface.

It wasn't until 1410, a full twenty minutes after receiving the "Red," that our ship was able to move out and start zigzagging. The C.O. had just finished reminding us to keep a close watch for enemy planes that might sneak over the 'Canal's mountains when, at 1413, as the ship was making its first hard turn to starboard, all hell broke loose. Japanese "Val" dive-bombers and Zero fighters appeared from nowhere, coming in at all directions and angles.

Lt. Miller, Flags Barela, and Joe Bergin tried to spot enemy planes and report them to us over the battle phones, but Dave Powers and I had all we could do just to cover our own "zone of influence." Dave, my loader, tapped me on the shoulder and pointed out approaching bogeys (unidentified aircraft). I swung around ready to fire if they were Japs. It happened that fast.

From the Armed Guard Officer's Action Report:

> The *Currier* had just turned in a northeasterly direction when a Val dive bomber appeared out of a low-hanging cloud over Guadalcanal headed for the stern of the ship at an angle of about thirty degrees. (Vals were easily identified by their non-retractable "pants down" landing gear.)
>
> Duane Curtis, manning the after starboard 20-mm gun, immediately started shooting and his line of fire was observed directly in front of the attacking plane. The pilot banked sharply to port to avoid Curtis' 20-mm fire and dropped three bombs prematurely. One bomb missed abaft starboard, another directly astern missed by 40 or 50 yards, and the third missed by about 75 yards off the port

quarter. Keith Sutton, the after port 20-mm gunner, and Gerry Olson, the after port bridge gunner, also opened fire as the plane drew away, but no hits were observed.

In the words of our C.O.: "There can be little doubt that the combination of the hard right turn

A Japanese "Val" divebomber in action during the raid of June 16. Naval Historical Center.

made by the Captain and the prompt and accurate fire laid down by Curtis, Sutton and Olson saved the ship from a bomb hit."

As more enemy planes came, Duane Curtis was credited with splashing one Nip and a flagpole. "I was following this Jap over the top of the ship and when I got to the smokestack stickin' up there I stopped. They say I was shootin' between a boom and Bill Sulton on the opposite side of the ship and the flagpole got in my way and before I could get my finger off, I shot it. I don't even remember having a stop on the gun, but of course all the guns had stops to prevent us from hitting the ship, and each other. When I hit the pole, I just spun around and took after another plane. The first one I was shootin' at was smokin' and that's the one the guys saw go in [the water].

"I remember, when the flag fell, a Merchant Marine — I think he was a cadet — grabbed the flag and tied it up on the stump of the pole."

Almost immediately afterwards three Japanese planes were seen diving on *LST-340* about 300 yards west of the port bow of the *Currier*. The leading plane commenced his long, whistling dive on the target and dropped three bombs from a very low

Duane Curtis downed the first plane of the battle for the Currier *Armed Guard crew. Duane Curtis.*

altitude and appeared to get one or two direct hits before banking away sharply abreast of our portside. Joe Jurgens and Gerry Olson, manning the forward and aft port bridge guns respectively, hit the plane with several long bursts that raked the entire length of the fuselage. Joe Skalenda, our bow gunner, also put several tracers through it. The plane began smoking heavily and crashed on the beach about 200 yards inshore. The loud, tension-relieving cheers of our forward gun crews when that Jap plane hit the beach were like the '49ers had scored a touchdown in the last five seconds to win the Superbowl.

A second Val attacked the same LST from the port bow with bombs and machine gun fire, but narrowly missed the target. The plane was hit many times by both the *340* and *Currier* forward gunners as it passed overhead. We saw the plane crash some 500 yards off our starboard bow. (Our C.O. didn't see this one splash and refused to credit us with even a half-plane kill.)

A Japanese "Val" dives toward the ship through a sky peppered with anti-aircraft fire. Naval Historical Center.

We starboard gunners got in some valuable practice on another Val (Aichi) bomber while *LST-340* was under attack off our port side. Flags Barela reported this one from his spotter station on the flying bridge. I opened fire as the Nip was making his run on our starboard bow with his machine guns blinking. I remember thinking for the first time that, hell, I might die at seventeen and never get to own my own ranch or raise a family. About the time my tracers began disappearing into the nose of his plane, he gunned his engine and banked sharply to port and ran smack into a lead curtain put up by Gibe and Gassen on the starboard side of our bridge. The Jap pilot never released any bombs but was soon greeted by a very daring U.S. Army P-38 flyboy who zoomed out of nowhere for this easy kill of the cripple. As we watched him splash the Val some 1,000 yards off our starboard quarter, I wondered if we could have claimed the plane had it not been for the P-38 pilot's interception.

P-38s were new to the area. Leonard Honeycutt, radarman on the *Skylark*, recalled: "A couple of us were standing on the fantail. We were off Guadalcanal, watching the 'air show' when we saw this Jap plane fly over a hill on the 'Canal, and right behind him was a P-38.

"Now this was when P-38s first came into being and I'd never even seen one before. I remember it like it was five minutes ago, my shipmate saying, 'My God, that guy must be going 300 miles per hour!' Remember, that speed was unheard of in those days. Anyway, both planes disappeared over the hill and three or four minutes later here comes the P-38 so we assumed he splashed that Jap."

When the *LST-340* attack ended, enemy bombers and fighters made the first of several passes at the *Celeno* (AK-76) — about 1,000 yards southwest of our port quarter. Each of the planes peeled off in succession with the sun behind them from a height of several thousand feet, dove on the ship and dropped bombs and/or strafed her in a stern-to-stem direction, then leveled off near the *Currier*. As each plane passed by, it was fired on by every gun we could bring to bear.

Left, a Japanese "Val" eludes antiaircraft fire during the battle of June 16, 1943. National Archives.

The first Val to attack the *Celeno* scored a direct bomb hit near the stern. All four of our port side 20s shot at this one. The second or third attacking plane also hit the unfortunate AK somewhere aft of midships. It passed almost directly over the *Currier* at a height of about 500 feet. Our crew put several bursts into the plane as it came over, before it went into a glide, smoking heavily, and crashed into the sea about a mile off the starboard bow.

Another plane was hit by us as it traveled abreast of the *Currier's* port side, then made off trailing smoke and was promptly pounced on and splashed by a Marine Corsair pilot.

While the foregoing action was taking place, a single enemy fighter — a Mitsubishi type "O" Zero — was spotted by Dave Powers coming in on the starboard side about 150 feet above the water. I hesitated, at first, thinking it must be one of our fighters. By the time I opened fire and Gibe and Gassen joined in, it wasn't more than 150 yards out. He bracketed the *Currier* with two light bombs, probably 100 pounders. One exploded about 100 feet to starboard and the other some fifty feet to port. It happened so fast, we only winged him.

Another plane, out of nowhere it seemed, was hit several times as it went by the starboard side. It, too, became a "smoker" before it passed out of range, but no one saw it crash. However, a member of the Seabee battalion who observed the action from shore told our C.O. several days later that the plane crashed about one mile inshore.

About ten minutes later, two Zeros passed by the *Currier*'s stern and were fired on and probably hit by the after guns, but no material damage was seen.

At the same time two Val dive bombers approached the bow in a low-level run. They were spotted by Skalenda, Haynes, and my loader, Dave Powers, about 1,000 yards away. We opened fire immediately and the planes banked off sharply at about 100 yards without

A Japanese Aichi B3A "Val" dive bomber goes down smoking during the attack of June 16, 1943. Author's collection.

dropping their bombs. All three forward 20s appeared to score hits as we bracketed the Vals but they didn't seem to be seriously damaged.

At about 1430, three Mitsubishi "Betty" twin-engine bombers — the only Bettys I remember seeing on the 16th — made a bomb run over the Guadalcanal base — now referred to as "Mainyard" — escorted by two Zeros. I was amazed to see several American fighters wade into them ignoring A/A flak from both ship and shore batteries. (They were well out of range of the *Currier*.)

We fired on several other planes that attacked shore installations or other ships from time to time as they passed

Left, a Mitsubishi G4M1 "Betty." Below, a low-level attack through antiaircraft fire by "Betty" bombers off Guadalcanal. Naval Historical Center.

overhead — most of them beyond the range of our 20-mm guns. Several shells fired by our 3"/50 gun crew, captained by Leo Russell, GM 3/c, burst fairly close but no damage was observed.

USS *Deimos*

The *Deimos* crew had a different view of the battle. The ship got underway at 1352 after receiving air raid warnings by both radio and visual signals. She stood out towards Koli Point at a speed of ten knots. Eight or nine Japanese planes attacked her directly. Of the eight, three were sure kills, two were possibles, and three were damaged.[2]

---

[2] USS *Celeno* Action Report, 22 June 1943.

THE ENEMY IN THE AIR

Allied pilots found the Japanese airmen far superior to the stereotypes depicted by WWII U.S. journalists and cartoonists. In fact, the first American air crews to return from combat knew they had faced some of the world's most experienced combat pilots equipped with formidable airplanes. Early in the war, Japanese training of airmen was tough — reportedly far beyond the limits of U.S. Marine Corps boot training. But by the spring of 1943, their edge wore thin as they lost many of their most experienced pilots and flight commanders along with their aircraft. Even the most experienced pilots eventually came up against a losing roll of the dice. To make matters worse, every Japanese plane was highly inflammable for lack of self-sealing gas tanks. As RAdm. Morison put it: "'Val' was a slow and easy target for an American fighter plane or anti-aircraft bullet. 'Kate,' the torpedo-bomber, lacked speed and endurance compared with the American TBF (Avenger). 'Betty,' the twin-engined torpedo-bomber, was fast and long-winded but horribly quick to catch fire. Japanese Army planes, seldom seen in the Solomons, were subject to the same defects. And the enemy made no provision for pilot survival. Many an aviator prematurely joined his ancestors because he was unprotected by cockpit armor. There was no rescue organization similar to our 'Dumbo,' and aviators, like other Japanese fighting men, were indoctrinated to die rather than surrender. An air squadron was often kept flying until completely wiped out, instead of some of the veterans being saved to instruct young aviators.

Lester Ray Weathers, Boatswain's mate 2/c: ". . . We were unloading on some barges and one of the barges, when they sounded GQ, pulled away and he was only fifty yards beyond us, maybe not that much, when they got one straight in the middle. There was nothing left of it.

"I seen the bombs coming in and I thought we had them because they always look like they're coming straight at you. They went on over and they caught the barge on the other side."

Robert E. Vorhies, Seaman 2/c: "We had just started unloading, the Seabees were unloading us, when the red alert came on, some of those Seabee boys didn't even wait for the landing craft or anything to take them to the beach. They just started swimmin'."

Richard Thomas Rogers, Gunner's mate 3/c: "I was on the bow underneath the 3-inch gun when GQ sounded. I was up

USS Deimos *AK-78. ELSILRAC Enterprises.*

there taking a sunbath. I ran towards my 20-mm on the bridge right away. What we did — you know we shot by tracer control — I used to put two or three tracers into the magazine first on my gun and then about the fourth round I was right on the plane."

Kenneth F. Keller, Ensign: "We were fascinated by the call we got from the Coast Guard up in New Georgia that said 130 planes had just taken off and were headed our way. When we got that message someone moved the lunch hour up a half-hour or so — so we could get our lunch before they got there. We were underway full steam when the planes arrived. There were black clouds all around, you wouldn't believe what a noisy place it was. We saw very few enemy planes because they came over the hill and by that time they were pretty close. That's when we'd start shooting at them."

Stanley Reid Voorhees, Radioman 1/c: "We received information to button up the hatches, 'cause we were unloading. It was calculated there was somewhere around seventy bombers and some Zeros coming into Guadalcanal. So we had a little time to get out and maneuver in the bay. And that's what saved our neck."

J. B. Morrison, Seaman 1/c: "I kinda wondered why those 'ole boys wanted to get off that ship. They was scratchin' metal goin' over the side to them barges, yellow alert or red, they got outta there in a hurry."

Richard Rogers: "They were coming out of the sun. The *Celeno* was on the starboard side of us and there were Zeros right over the top of her, and they were strafing. I was screaming, because our rigging was in the way, too. Our old man was screaming and I was screaming to get the rigging out of the way."

Bob Voorhies: "I was forward on the 3"/50 passing ammo out of that little elevator. The crates were upside down — gray-painted boxes. There was two 3" shells in each container and they had six screws in them. I was so scared I couldn't get the screwdriver in the holes. And finally a Spanish boy, can't remember his name, came down to relieve me. I couldn't hit those screwholes. I got about three of them."

Edval Helle, Sr., Shipfitter 1/c: "I was pullin' anchor. I seen some of the planes that was shot. We got credit for three planes, I think. I seen some of those Japs . . . our pilot would get a Jap on his tail and he'd hit the dive and the Jap would go in the water. I seen that happen two or three times."

Richard Rogers: "I had one Zero come in and I could see the pilot. I was shooting right into him 'cause I was on him so fast. Then some rat went and took that plane from me. Shot him down. So I claimed him. But they claimed him too. We put seven [Japanese flags to indicate "kills"] on the bridge. We just took what the guys said altogether 'cause Jap planes were comin' from all directions."

Bob Vorhies: "Our gun crew painted five Jap flags on the bridge. I know there were planes falling but who was knocking them down, I couldn't tell you. I know the shore batteries were opening up, too, with 105s."

Bob Phillips: "I was loader on a 20-mm on the port side, right on the fantail. One of them hit real close to us. That sucker splashed water on us. We got the dive bomber but he released his bombs first. We was shooting at him all the way down. He was comin' in on the starboard side of the stern."

Stanley Voorhees: "I was on the deck near the aft radio room. All of a sudden, straight over us — possibly a couple thousand feet — was this group of planes and they immediately peeled off and started to dive-bomb us. One released this bomb and the gunners got him before he got maybe 500 or 600 feet from the ship. They hit him broadside. I think it was one of them 5" shells that got that plane. I think he was only 100 feet away when he tried to pull up because you could just see a big grin on his face."

Bernard Barker, Radioman 2/c: "I watched them [bombs] fall just like feathers, just so slow — pretty in a way. They just whirled down there, then they bounced off the gunwale. I turned around to sit down because we were getting so much machine gun fire."

Pat Paones, Shipfitter 1/c: "I remember them dive-bombing at us, and they were comin' in so close I could see their big buck teeth."

Bob Vorhies: "I remember two, possibly three, across the bow. They said we had nine near-misses. I know when they turned those bombs loose, you could see the plane jump back like that and as the bombs were coming down they start spinning. When they're cutting that wind and you hear 'tswshshsh,' they're close. You could see the paint on 'em."

Ken Keller: "I got a Purple Heart out of that because one of the bombs just barely missed the gunwale where I was standing. Matheson, our Exec on the con, and a helluva good Navy man, had made a hard right turn and that Jap pilot who had aimed right for us, by the time his bombs got there we were just out of the way by inches. As soon as they hit, the shrapnel came up and it ripped the whole rib cage off this guy that was standing right next to me. Someone hustled him to the doctor's right in the middle of the battle.

"I got a piece of something — I always thought it was a monkey wrench that we sent over to them before the war. It hit me right in the back, knocked me down, but didn't really hurt me much. Cut into the skin pretty deep but the doc was able to fish it right out."

Jay Rider: "We were sitting in the radio shack, and I had a typewriter on the desk in front of me and was copying messages. We heard the bomb coming and they told me later that that bomb was about three feet off the bridge. It went over the railing and exploded on the port side. After it was all over with they put a boat in the water and went to look for damage to the hull."

Mike Hosier, Gunner's mate 2/c: "We got off maybe a dozen three-inch shells, something like that. There was this guy, from Oklahoma or Tennessee or somewhere — I don't think he knew how to spell his own name. He was one of these kind of cruddy guys. Nobody liked him so they put him on a forward 20-mm.

"I remember very clearly a plane come down and swooped right there. I don't think he missed hitting the ship with his plane more than ten feet, and I could have swore he would have hit that gunner. I just happened to look over and here was this guy, he was strapped in shooting like a son-of-a-gun. He wasn't ducking, he wasn't getting down. He was shooting. I'll always remember that. I never even knew the guy's name."

Bob Parker: "They were using what we called at the time, grasscutters — Anti-personnel bombs that scattered 'cause we caught a lot of light shrapnel. I got a piece in the shoulder. In fact, a corpsman hit our gun tub and told me I was bleeding. I told him to get the hell outta there. I was so goddamned scared I wanted to stay with the gun.

"Our own planes were supposed to be giving us lights. I know there were a few friendlies got shot at because they came in too close. I said later, I'd of shot a seagull if he came in low enough, lights or no lights."

Erwin Holan, Boatswain's Mate 2/c: "The Japs had so much shrapnel flying against the ship, they punched holes in all our lifeboats."

Ray Weathers: "Some of those fighters, they strafed everything. They shot the booms and a couple of them guys even turned in close enough — in front of the foremast up there — and just looked down and smiled at you like it was a nice day."

J. B. Morrison: "Them bombs blowed mud out of that water. Shrapnel everywhere. That shrapnel done lots of damage to everything. One hit me right on the head. If I hadn't had my helmet on I'd of been killed deader than a doornail."

Bernard Barker: "I was Commodore Hayes' talker on the flying bridge. We took a lot of machine gun fire. I remember sitting there behind the gun tub by the 20-mm ready box. I was looking at the stack and you could just see the paint spatter where the slugs were hitting it."

Richard Rogers: "They dropped two bombs off the bow. They were really close — about five feet. They hit the water. When those bombs went off, we shipped water — I don't know how many feet — over the bow. We went right under. We thought we were going to sink. Then, off the fantail, a Betty bomber was coming in low there. She was going to try and land, or something, on the fantail and they put a shell right through her nose. Pieces of her were going all over the ship."

Ken Keller: "Everything was chaos and we saw the *Celeno* heading for the beach — it looked like she needed to hurry."

Bob Vorhies: "I remember looking over to the beach and seeing the *Celeno* on fire. The smoke coming out. How long the raid lasted I don't know. It seemed like eternity to me. After it was over, I couldn't sit down, I couldn't lay down, I couldn't get still in any way. I know I was scared to death."

Bob Parker: "The thing I remember about the *Celeno* was that she was loaded with bombs in 1, 2, 3, and 4 holds and number 5 was hospital supplies. That's where she took the hit — luckily. Somebody told me that right after this thing happened. They said the *Celeno* was hit and I said, 'Yah, the number 5 hold. They had hospital supplies in there. If they'd taken it in any other one they'd still be on the way up!'"

USS Aludra

The *Aludra* was also discharging cargo when she received the yellow alert at 1320. She got underway off Koli Point about

1350, after receiving an air raid warning (Condition Red) over the radio and visual signals from the Navy Signal Station at Lunga Point.[3] She was attacked by enemy dive bombers and fighters. Crew members remember bombs falling "too close" for comfort.

Roy Lucy, Radioman 3/c: "In addition to the thousands of barrels of high test gasoline down in those holds, we had fifty

USS Aludra *AK-72.* *National Archives.*

tons of dynamite and fourteen tons of nitroglycerin caps. I've always remembered that because the chief said if we ever get hit, we can walk to Tokyo!"

Eugene Hopper, Boatswain's mate 2/c: "We were un-loading onto barges and they had tugboats alongside. We had Army or maybe Seabees. The day of the big air strike, all them guys wanted to do was get off that ship."

William Earl Hartman, Chief Boatswain's Mate: "I was on watch and Hopper was up there with me. All of a sudden, we saw our planes taking off from Henderson Field *en masse* and we got to talking about how the Japs were going to catch hell today, boy, because those bombers and fighters were just zooming out of there. Then the Japs hit all over."

Ross C. Osborn, Seaman 1/c: "I was part of an amphibi-ous group that was supposed to get off somewhere — not sure where. Anyway, they kept us on as *Aludra* ship's company.

---

[3] USS *Celeno* Action Report, 22 June 1943.

That air raid come over and we was runnin' around with the boats. We were told to get out of there so we headed for the beach — and a foxhole."

Eugene Hopper: "The sky was just full of black spots and airplanes."

Bill Hartman: "I almost got me a Wildcat (Grumman F4F-3 fighter) that day, too. It was coming down and, boy, they were screaming at me from the bridge, 'Cease fire! Cease fire!' I almost got him."

Roy Lucy: "The first-class radioman, the Chief and I were out on the port side of the bridge and somebody had hung his helmet on one of those ribs sticking out and the Jap planes were shooting, we were underway by then. Anyhow, the ship hit a swell and rolled. That helmet came down and hit the deck and it sounded exactly like the rat-a-tat-tat of a machine gun and all three of us went through that hatch at the same time. Don't ask me how we did it. Man, we were moving!"

Marvin W. Acree, Boatswain's Mate 1/c: "I remember seeing *LST-340* get hit on our starboard bow.

"The USS *O'Bannon* was doing figure eights at full speed and you could see the lead filling the sky. She was firing all her AA guns and what a wonderful sight to see in action. It was then I decided I wanted my next ship to be a destroyer."

USS *O'Bannon*

The USS *O'Bannon* (DD-450) (LCmdr. Donald J. MacDonald, USN, Commanding) started the day patrolling as a unit in the outer antisubmarine screen 6,000-8,000 yards off Lunga Point, screening Task Unit 32.4.4. The Task Unit commander was in *Aludra*, the screen commander in *O'Bannon*. Highlights from the *O'Bannon*'s Action Report follow:

> The *Aludra* and *Schley* were off Togoma Point, while the other three AKs were unloading between Lunga Point and the Tenaru river. Also in this area were several LSTs and many smaller craft. No other escorts were available at this time.

USS O'Bannon *DD-450.   ENSILRAC Enterprises.*

Air Attack and Narrative: At 1337 L (0237Z), 16 June 1943 considerable information commenced coming in over fighter control circuit stationing fighter groups. Bogies were reported at this time.

1346 condition red over Cactus was reported on Harbor circuit. All hands were called to General Quarters, speed increased to 25 knots, and course set to close cargo ships. Speed was shortly thereafter increased to 30 knots.

1346 the escorts were ordered by me to close cargo vessels and screen in accordance with our prearranged plan. This plan provided for one escort vessel in each quadrant distance 1,500-2,000 yards.

1347 condition red over Cactus received over fighter control circuit.

1349 the Waters was again ordered to close, which she did.

1355 Bogies were reported southwest of Cape Esperance-distance 25 miles. SUGAR CHARLIE radar picked up unidentified planes bearing 275 degrees T-distance 28 miles. Tracking was started.

1358 condition red reported existing over Tulagi.

1403 SUGAR CHARLIE radar reported unidentified planes bearing 353 degrees T-distance 7.5 miles.

1405 Bogies reported as closing on Henderson Field from southeast 15 miles. At this time our radar could not pick up enemy aircraft, having lost them in land mass. Several friendly planes over Henderson Field were giving us friendly indications.

The Cargo Ships were beginning to clear beach area and head in a northerly direction. Practically all small craft began to move away from beach area. A sort of formation was being taken by Cargo vessels but the Celeno was lagging well behind. The Aludra and Schley were well to the east.

1409 Bogies were reported over Henderson Field, Angels 15. This altitude was above the cloud banks which were directly overhead. We also had friendly fighters overhead. In fact, there were a number of friendly planes all around the area. The sun was bearing in direction of Savo Island at a position angle of about 50 degrees. Great stress was laid to watching up in the sun. The *O'Bannon*'s position was on the port quarter of the formation, toward the sun.

1410 Bogies were reported over fighter number two. My radars were unable to pick them up. All guns that could bear were trained in this direction.

1410 The Commanding Officer saw a group of planes, possibly 12 in a Vee formation appear in a hole in the clouds at an altitude that must have been about 15,000 feet. He could not identify them, but ordered Control to commence fire on them, giving bearing and approximate position angle. At practically the same moment, they began to peel off coming down in dives that were nearly vertical. Most of the group pulled out at about 500 feet and then attempted to strafe ships. Several never pulled out. I believe the LST that was damaged was hit by a crashed plane.

At about 1411, fire was actually commenced by this vessel by all guns including the machine guns and 1.1" on the starboard side at planes just pulling out of dives. Control was unable to get on planes until they were half way down in their dives. After following a few in, our 5" fire was finally raised to planes still overhead just about to dive. Another group estimated at about 12-15 in number were frustrated by our 5" fire so that they never did make a bull's eye attack.

The *Celeno* and the damaged LST were hit by what I believe were the first bombs dropped.

The Jap bombers were Aichi 99s with wheels down. They were carrying at least two bombs and possibly three apiece; one large bomb under the fuselage and 1-2 wing bombs. My Air Defense Officer reports seeing several Type Zero's with square wings in the melee strafing our shipping. This I believe is true because I saw several Jap single engine planes with wheels retracted strafing us.

Some of our fighters came in with the second attacking group. A P-40 and a P-38 were definitely identified and, unfortunately, they were shot at, but I do know the P-40 got through without crashing.

Bombs were dropped all around our formation by the first Jap group. There were 3 dropped in this vessel's vicinity, the nearest exploding about 100 yards on the starboard beam, two others fell about 200-300 yards on port bow.

All planes coming within range were taken under fire as fast as targets could be shifted. This vessel shot at approximately seven planes with its machine guns, and besides breaking up second attack by 5" fire, fired at several at low level. One plane being fired at by our machine guns was definitely seen to crash while at least two, and possibly four others, were seen to catch fire and start smoking while clearing the immediate vicinity. My repair personnel claim that one of our 5" projectiles burst inside one plane. I can not confirm this as I did not see it.

The main action was taking place on our starboard hand but I did notice about four splashes on our port bow which possibly could have been planes crashing. By the gunfire of all vessels, it is believed that at least five planes were shot down, many of the planes being shot at by different vessels at the same time and possibly claimed by each.

1415 Firing ceased. The ship was still being maneuvered around as a unit of the screen for the cargo ships. One LST was on fire forward and burning fiercely. The Celeno had a fire aft, emitting great volumes of black smoke.

1420 Bogies were reported over Tulagi. Skylark was ordered from screen by me to protect the cripples, who were about 2,500 yards from beach never having really gotten very far before being hit.

1430 Several small craft from landing area came out to assist cripples.

1504 Message was received by me from the Shore Station that two submarine periscopes were sighted from Tulagi toward Lunga. This was passed by me to the *Strong* who was in that area and later at 1522 the *Waters* was ordered to proceed to that area and investigate.

1517 condition green over Cactus was announced on all circuits.

Damage And Casualties: The only apparent damage inflicted in this vessel was a 20-mm hit fired by a friend which penetrated the 1/8 inch side shield of 5" gun #1 exploding inside, severing the hydraulic lines in two places and starting a small fire in the warm oil. The fire was quickly put out by gun crew.

Ammunition Expended and Remarks: The following amounts were expended: 30 rounds of 5"/38 AA common, 1,500 rounds of 20-mm, and 344 rounds of 1.1". We have two Mark 14 sights on 20-mm's and one in our Mk. 51 Director for the 1.1". All personnel on these sights claim they could not pick up and follow the targets fast enough. In all cases they had to shift to open sights to pick up planes and use tracer fire for spotting.

Comments and Remarks: It is believed that the big Jap air offensive of the 16th had as its objective, Blue Shipping in Guadalcanal area. If, in fact, submarines were present as reported on the 16th, and later on morning of 17th by an LCT and a plane, then no doubt the offensive was to have been a well coordinated attack, with the air flushing the shipping out for the Subs. The raid on Tulagi on the night of the 17th would bear this out. Or the Subs were being used solely for intelligence. So far there have been no attacks made by subs. Searches made by escort ships have all been negative.

The AKs and Merchant Ship did very well considering the short notice that was given. They should definitely be instructed to make maximum speed and radical changes of course if not closed up in formation where Unit Commander can exercise control. Both the LST and the *Celeno* were lagging well behind, only being clear of beach area by about 2,500 yards.

Shore batteries did not fire. Cloud cover was such that planes flying at 15,000 feet could not be seen.

The USS Ward *(DD-139) as a flush-decker, and a four-piper prior to conversion to APD-16. First Shot Naval Vets.*

The shipping off Lunga Point was attacked by 18-24 Jap dive bombers with several Zero's coming in to strafe. Some of our own fighters were staying outside of range to get them as they cleared, so that very few finally got away. A number of friendly planes as mentioned before closed our formation and unfortunately were fired at by some ships. Information regarding friendly aircraft was passed over TBS by this vessel to stop other ships from shooting at friends coming in to land.[4]

USS *Ward*

According to her historical sketch, the USS *Ward* (APD-16), our high-speed transport escort, ". . . helped to beat off the Japanese air attack in the Guadalcanal area on 16 June, her gunners claiming four attacking aircraft."

USS *Skylark*

The USS *Skylark* (AM-63), our minesweep escort, (Lt. Roy H. Jones, USNR, Commanding) was steaming as antisubmarine screen for the *Nathaniel Currier* on a course parallel with

---

[4] USS *O'Bannon* Action Report for 16 June 1943.

USS Skylark *AM-63. ELSILRAC Enterprises.*

beach east of Lunga Point the night of 15-16 June 1943. Highlights from her diary on June 16:

1349 Sounded General Quarters upon receipt of condition red from radio, enemy bombers sighted north of here.

1359 Bomb hits in water off Savo Island.

1401 Changed speed to standard ahead, USS *Celeno* and USS *Deimos* underway.

1406 Upon signal from Senior Officer Present Afloat (SOPA) maneuvering to take station on port quarter off *Celeno* and *Deimos.*

1412 Changed speed to full ahead. Commenced firing at enemy dive bombers.

1413 USS *Celeno* hit on stern and burning.

1414 One enemy aircraft knocked down on starboard side.

1417 One enemy aircraft knocked down on port side.

1418 Enemy plane hit and downed forward of port bow.

1419 4 enemy planes observed down and burning in water. LST 340 on fire.

1424 Ceased firing. Still maneuvering at flank speed.

1500 Secured from General Quarters. Preparing to standby to assist USS *Celeno.*

1508 Sounded General Quarters.

1519 Secured from General Quarters.

1530 Screening USS *Celeno* on various courses and speeds.

USS Celeno *AK-76. Naval Historical Center.*

1605 Received orders from task unit commander in *Deimos* to screen SS *Nathaniel Currier.*
1620 Commenced screening *Nathaniel Currier* according to instructions.
1830 Commenced patrolling sector . . .
2015 Sounded General Quarters upon sighting 3 red flares from beach.
2022 Changed speed to standard 15 knots.
2045 Secured from General Quarters.[5]

USS *Celeno*

The *Celeno* was about midway between Lunga and Koli Points and one-and-one-half miles offshore when eight enemy bombers and Zeros made the first of several dive bombing and strafing runs on her at 1410.[6] Anthony "Tony" Gray, quartermaster third-class had a 360-degree view of the action from his battle station on the flying bridge as the C.O.'s messenger: "When we got the red alert, you're kind of wondering, 'where the heck are they?' As I remember it, they came in real high in line with the sun. There were a few scattered clouds. All at once the devils were comin' right at us."

At approximately 1416, the first bomb made a direct hit forward of the #7 20-mm platform, continuing on through the

---

[5] USS *Skylark* (AM-63) War Diary Wednesday 16 June 1943.
[6] USS *Celeno* (AK-76) Action Report, 22 June 1943.

main deck and exploding below. (It also jammed the rudder full right, rendering it inoperative and, at the same time, flooded the shaft alley.) The second direct hit was in No. 5 hold. Exposed parts of the ship were raked from stem to stern by enemy strafing.

Tony Gray: "The ship bounced like a rubber ball, up and down. We knew we'd been hit because we could hear and see the flying debris but I couldn't imagine that big ship going up and down like it was on one end of a teeter-totter."

There were four near-misses: one on the starboard side abreast of No. 4 hatch; two by the port side of the forecastle abreast the 3"/50 bow gun; and another very near-miss on the port side abreast the No. 3 hatch — all causing severe hull damage.

Fire broke out almost immediately in a deck load of gasoline and oil drums abreast of No. 5 hatch, and in No. 5 hold, which was nearly full of cargo. Before the fire could be brought under control it had spread to No. 4 hold, also nearly full of cargo.

Fire and damage control parties worked with *Celeno's* guns booming and chattering around them, seemingly oblivious to flying shrapnel and strafing bullets. In Tony Gray's words: "It was shrapnel and strafing bullets that got our people on deck. Shrapnel did a bad number. There was a Chief Fry, a piece of shrapnel ripped his stomach open and his intestines were just hanging there. It was really a shock. Then there was the dead lying around on the deck. I mean, guys that fifteen minutes before were racing up and down doing something. There they were, stretched out."

The gun crew manned all guns except No. 7 20-mm, which was put out of action, and the 5"/38 that received damage to its elevating and depressing gear. No shots were fired by the latter gun crew even though the Gunnery Officer, at main control, gave the order to "Commence Firing." The pointer on the 5"/38 and the gun captain left their posts before the first hit and went over the side into the water. They were picked up later by rescue boats. (Both men received general courts martial later on.)

There were two cases of misfire on the 3"/50 bow gun and it was finally placed out of service after a projectile became separated from its case when an attempt was made to remove the charge that had misfired.

Conning throughout the entire action was done by the C.O. from the flying bridge rather than from the safety of the enclosed wheelhouse where vision would have been greatly handicapped. With the ship's rudder jammed to the right, it was only by skillful handling and the prompt assistance rendered by the USS *Rail* (AT-139), USS *Vireo* (AT-144), and the USS *LCT-322* that the *Celeno* was able to beach herself off Lunga River, Guadalcanal.

The shaft alley, steering engine room, and No. 4 and No. 5 holds were completely flooded and the ship's counter at the main deck was under water. A limited amount of power was provided by the main engines up to the time of beaching at 1645.

From *Celeno* Action Report of Division Officer Lt. (jg) Edward O'Rourke:

> The explosions shook everyone off their feet. Generators continually kicked out and pumps stopped . . . but very little confusion existed throughout the entire bombing . . ."
>
> At 1425, the *Rail*, and later the *Vireo*, provided power and steerage from alongside the port and starboard quarters respectively to assist in fighting the fires.
>
> At 1535, the *Celeno* dropped anchor in 20 fathoms of water 800 yards off Lunga Point. At 1550 the all-clear signal was finally received from shore.
>
> At 1600, *Celeno* lifted anchor and made a run for the beach full speed with the *Rail* pushing on the port quarter until the *Celeno* was in 2 fathoms of water. At that point, the *Rail* ceased rescue operations.
>
> *LCT-322* furnished personnel to fight the *Celeno*'s fires and to evacuate her dead and wounded. Later she stood by to take the crew ashore. Boatswain Edward Mican also called on the *322* to

"come up under the *Celeno*'s starboard bow to take the starboard anchor as close to shore as possible . . ."

At 1706, by order of the C.O., the crew began disembarking the vessel with the exception of the ship's security watch.

On the lighter side, Tony Gray remembers: "There was this rope hanging over the side, and this sailor ran and grabbed that line — he wasn't going to take time to go down the cargo net — and the damn rope wasn't secured. It was kinda funny 'cause I saw him go over the rail with that rope and here comes the other end following behind him, don't even know if he got hurt. The silly things you remember."

Due to flooding and settling — and with No. 4 and No. 5 holds partially filled with cargo — shoring and plugging of holds from inside the ship was impossible. (Action, however, was started the next morning by salvage tug *Menominee* (AT-73) after receiving and rigging pumps.)[7]

The *Rail* was called upon once more that night to assist the *Celeno* under red alert conditions. At 2310 she arrived back at the *Celeno* to discover the ship had reversed headings. The salvage tug *Menominee* had arrived to assist and was standing by off the port side. By 2340 the *Celeno* received a work party of eight men and one officer off the *Menominee*, so the *Rail* headed for Florida Island to get some well-earned rest.

Tony Gray hasn't forgotten his time on the beach: "We had those damn air raids at night and we'd have to get to the foxholes. And it was rainy. It could rain for no reason at all. I remember another thing. They had those lister bags hanging from trees for drinking water. I took a big drink and happened to look down into the damn thing and it was just full of mosquito wigglers."

The *Celeno* was credited with shooting down three enemy planes and three possibles. Ammunition expended: 1,837

---

[7] War Damage Report, USS *Celeno*, 27 June 1943.

USS Rail *AM-26. Naval Historical Center.*

rounds, seven 3"/50, 860 20-mm, and 970 .30-caliber. She had fifteen men killed and nineteen wounded in battle.

With the exception of the two 5"/38 gun crew members who deserted their battle stations, ". . . the entire crew performed their duties in a most satisfactory manner," according to Lt. Cmdr. N. E. Lanphere, USNR, Commanding Officer. The C.O. went on to report, "Many of our men fought fire in the cargo, partly made up of ammunition and gasoline, after having received wounds from machine gun strafing, shrapnel, and from burning."[8]

The Commander Service Squadron, South Pacific Force, issued commendations to the *Celeno, LCT-322, Vireo* and *Rail* ". . . for saving USS *Celeno*, which received extensive damage as a result of 2 direct hits and 4 near-misses from enemy bombers."

USS *Rail*

The USS *Rail* (AT-139), a World War I minesweeper reclassified as tug (AT-139) on June 1, 1942, arrived in the

---

[8] USS *Celeno* Action Report, 22 June 1943.

Solomons in May 1943. The morning of 16 June, she picked up barge *PAB #6* at 1025 and towed it into position alongside the USS *Celeno*.

At 1212, *Rail* positioned another flattop barge alongside the *Celeno*. At 1350, she received a Condition Red signal from Radio Guadalcanal and went to General Quarters. From her June 16 log:

> 1352 - Underway from alongside of USS *Celeno* with flat top alongside to port.
>
> 1405 - Moored flattop alongside of *PAB #6*.
>
> 1409 - Underway various courses and speeds.
>
> 1415 - Observed about 30 dive bombers attacking U.S. ships in channel. US ships firing antiaircraft. *LST-340* hit by bomb, heading for beach burning. USS *Celeno* hit by bombs, burning and disabled. Proceeding to assist *Celeno*.
>
> 1430 - Moored starboard side of Celeno attempting to beach her and assisting to put out fire.
>
> 1530 - Fire under control.
>
> 1535 - *Celeno* dropped anchor off Lunga Point — apparently not aground.[9]

The *Rail*'s efforts to help salvage the USS *Celeno* took up the rest of the day and earned her a Commendation from the Commander Service Squadron, South Pacific Force.

USS *Vireo*

The USS *Vireo* (AT-144), another World War I minesweeper reclassified as tug (AT-144), first arrived at Guadalcanal on October 12, 1942 to take part in resupply operations for the Marines at Henderson Field. It looked like another routine day to the *Vireo* crew. At 1050, fires were lighted under #2 boiler, and at 1143 she got underway. The captain was at the conn, the navigator was on the bridge. Her speed was ten knots (105

---

[9] USS *Rail* Ship's Log, Wednesday, 16 June 1943.

RPM) as she steered various courses and speeds. At 1131, *Vireo* anchored in 7.5 fathoms of water off Togoma Point. At 1245, she commenced pulling *LST-340* off the beach. After completing this task, she got underway at various courses and speeds, having received the yellow alert.

The entries in the ship's log after 1400 tell the rest of the story:

1413 - General Quarters; about 40 enemy bombers over Lunga Point broke off in dives on shipping.

1415 - LST-*340*, off Lunga Point, hit by bomb and burning furiously.

1416 - USS *Celeno*, off Lunga Point, hit by bomb; down by stern and burning. Numerous enemy planes shot down by gunfire and fighters in vicinity of Lunga Point.

1445 - Proceeding to assistance of USS *Celeno*.

1512 - Moored to starboard bow of *Celeno* off Lunga Point.

1514 - Secured from General Quarters.

1515 - Commenced towing *Celeno* toward beach at Lunga Point at maximum speed with assistance of USS *Rail* on her port quarter.

1536 - Anchored *Celeno* in 20 fathoms of water 800 yards off Lunga Point.

1545 - Cast off from USS *Celeno*.[10]

The *Vireo* also earned a Commendation from the Commander Service Squadron, South Pacific Force.

USS *LST-340*

The *LST-340*, crammed with soldiers and loaded with vehicles, was a major casualty of the June 16 raid. Ironically, she was only about thirty yards off the beach waiting for the Army Engineers to complete construction of an unloading ramp when the GQ bell shattered everyone's nerves.

---

[10] USS *Vireo* Ship's Log, Wednesday, 16 June 1943.

At 1350 on June 16, 1943, a group of nine enemy planes was observed overhead at about 20,000 feet. Suddenly all nine planes went into a diving attack and peeled off in groups of three. The first three dive bombers headed straight for the *340*, dropping nine bombs of about 300 pounds each in sticks of three.

One of the planes that attacked from the port side registered a direct hit on the *340*'s main deck near the after cargo hatch on the port side. Two near misses from this same plane landed about fifty feet off the starboard side. Their explosions caused personnel at the waist guns and on the conning station to be drenched with water. This plane was hit by nearly a full drum [sixty] of 20-mm bullets and splashed on the starboard side. Another plane attacking from the port bow scored two near-misses on the port side, strafing the bow guns as it passed

After being hit by an enemy bomb, the LST-340 *was run aground at Lunga point. This photo was taken fifteen minutes after the bomb hit. U.S. Marine Corps.*

The LST-340 *aground at Lunga Point after the bomb hit. She is aided in her fire-fighting efforts by the* LST-353, *alongside. National Archives.*

over the ship. The shrapnel from these near misses and the strafing put more than 100 holes in the port side of the hull.

The plane was hit many times by the forward guns and crashed in the water on the starboard side after passing over the ship.

The direct bomb hit created a dreadful fire among the trucks — all with full fuel tanks and highly-flammable loads, such as cans of oil and gasoline, wooden crates, trunks, bedding, and barracks bags. The explosion and fire cut the water main and interior communications. Gun crews and all other personnel at battle stations continued the fight against the attacking planes in spite of the immense heat and frightful explosions.

James Stalp, Seaman 1/c, aboard the *340* proved himself that day. Stalp was at his gun post in the bow of the ship when the bombs hit, knocking out the gunner's mate, wounding the ship's communications officer and setting aflame the deck cargo of vehicles and gas. Stalp slung the officer over his shoulder and made his way through 100 feet of flaming deck cargo to the stern. Then he returned through the flames to his post where he found the gunner's mate had lost an arm. Stalp slowed the flow of blood with a tourniquet and lowered the man over the side. Next he threw overboard four 55-gallon drums of gas which were in the path of the oncoming flames. After that he climbed down a hatch and came up with a wounded New Zealand soldier who was pleading for help. Stalp lowered him over the side, too. Then he returned to his 40-mm gun post to shoot down a Jap bomber. Stalp received the Silver Star for "diving into the roaring flames to rescue three of his shipmates."

With no water to fight fires and the imminent danger of ammunition magazines exploding, the Army troops were ordered to abandon ship. Life rafts were cast loose and two ship's boats, which were trailing astern, picked up the troops.

The auxiliary engine room had to be abandoned because a bomb fragment that penetrated started a gasoline fire. Shortly after the direct hit, the port engine went out of commission. About five minutes later the main engine room reported it was impossible to remain any longer due to unbearable heat. But the skipper, Lt. William Villella, refused to give up. He ordered his engineers, at the point of suffocation, to set the starboard engine at flank speed ahead and then abandon the engine room.

All personnel, other than the gun crews and repair party, were then ordered to abandon ship. Some swam ashore. The others were picked up by nearby boats.

Villella headed the ship toward the beach at Tenaru, maneuvering to take advantage of the wind to prevent the flames from spreading. About 500 yards offshore, the clutch on the starboard engine kicked out, but the *340* beached herself on her own momentum with a little help from the wind.

Army passengers and crew casualties of LST-340 *being carried ashore at Lunga Point. Seabees.*

Flotilla 5 Commander Capt. G. B. Carter directed two sister LSTs to give the *340* assistance. The few personnel still on board then went by boat to the *LST-353* and directed her to the port side of the *340* where water was immediately played on the fire. Skipper Villella, spotting *LST-398* nearby, boarded that ship and asked her C.O. to maneuver alongside the *340*'s starboard side where hoses could get at the flames.

Anthony "Tony" Tesori, Lieutenant and first gunnery officer of *LST-340*: "All of our crew except those assigned to man guns had been ordered ashore the night of 15 June 1943. The ship was on the beach, bow doors open and ramp down, and very vulnerable.

"The next morning with the entire crew back aboard we made plans to unload the troops and cargo, but did not get the chance. We received another air raid warning. This time we raised the ramp and closed the bow doors and backed away from the beach. We managed to get away some distance and began to take some evasive action (which, because of their lack of maneuverability, is something of a joke among those who have served on LSTs).

"At 1 p.m. all ships in the flotilla came under attack from a large number of Jap planes. In less time than it takes to tell, we were badly hit and burning. The bomb had hit just forward of the conning tower, destroying the main and auxiliary engines as well as all communications."

Fortunately, the ship was underway at the time and headed toward the beach. When it became obvious nothing could be done to save her, the skipper ordered the ship abandoned. The fire had spread to all areas of the ship and was moving close to the stern.

Anthony Tesori continues: "The heat was threatening to explode the ammunition magazine located below the stern deck. The commodore, skipper, and I tried to start two handy-billy pumps in a last desperate attempt to flood the ammunition magazine, but failed.

"As far as we could tell, the three of us were the last to leave the ship. We left by way of a Jacob's ladder off the stern. By this time the steel deck was so hot our shoes seemed to be on fire. We also had a real fear that the magazine would explode. Apparently, the magazine locker was sufficiently below the water line to maintain a cooler temperature. Anyway it did not explode.

"Jap planes did try to strafe those of us in the water, but were driven off. Very shortly thereafter, an LST from our flotilla came along and picked us up. It also used its own fire fighting equipment to help fight the *340* fires."

USS *LST-353*

The *LST-353* was taking on a cargo of drummed gasoline and diesel oil from the SS *Nathaniel Currier* when Condition Red was received at about 1340. Lines were cast off and she got underway, zig-zagging in a big circle about a mile offshore. According to the *353* War Diary:

> Enemy planes overhead. All guns in action. Two planes shot down. At 1420, when the action subsided, *LST-353* proceeded to the aid of *LST-340* which had been hit and was beached in flames near Tenaru. Fire under control at 1900.

The *LST-340* fire remained under the control of the *353* throughout the night. But fires continued to smolder in isolated areas throughout the ship for two days and nights and it became necessary to employ cutting torches and rescue breathing apparatus to completely extinguish all fires.[11]

---

[11] War Diary of *LST-353* for Wednesday, 16 June 1943.

USS *LST-398*

The *LST-398* was secured to the port side of the SS *Nathaniel Currier* taking on cargo when General Quarters was sounded at 1340. After considerable delay she finally cast off from the *Currier* at 1405 with all engines ahead flank speed on a zig-zag course.

At 1415, the *398* was attacked by Japanese dive bombers. From her War Diary:

All possible guns firing. Plane dropped 3 bombs which struck water 50 feet off port side. No damage or casualties to this unit.

At 1402, *LST-398* secured from GQ and stowed her ammo in her bow. She then approached and tied to the starboard quarter of *LST-340* to assist in fighting fire. At 1540 she began playing water on the *340* with all available hoses.

At 2235, *LST-398* secured from fire fighting with fire under control of *LST-353*. The *398* then retracted from the beach and anchored nearby at 2355.[12]

USS *LST-340*

On the *340*, the cargo was completely ruined. An early summary of ship's damage included:

Main deck between frames 10 and 35 completely wrecked.

Officers' quarters gutted by fire, damaged by heat, smoke and water.

Galley and all equipment damaged beyond repair.

Numerous holes of various sizes throughout the ship made by bomb fragments, explosions and strafing, plus openings burned out to gain access for fire fighting purposes.

Port side of ship between frames 9 and 27 was punctured by seven 37-mm, fourteen .30 caliber and 43 bomb fragments — all above water line.

All electrical wiring (and many electrical fixtures) ruined by fire and water.[13]

---

[12] War Diary of *LST-398* for 16 June 1943.

[13] *LST-340* Ship's Damage Report, 22 June 1942.

The burned-out vehicles and debris were removed at Tenaru Beach by the *340* crew with the assistance of the 46th Seabee Battalion. According to *LST-340* survivor Ensign Don Sterling: "The *340* crew was billeted at the Australian Ration Dump near the Tenaru River for about four days before being transferred to Tulagi Island where a group of Quonset huts soon became known as 'Carter City' — headquarters for Capt. Grayson B. Carter, USN, the Commodore of LST Flotilla 5."

LST-340 claimed two planes shot down, four "possibles," and four "damaged." Ammunition expended: 910 rounds.

Casualties: One enlisted man killed and two seriously wounded, plus one officer and one enlisted man lightly wounded. Nine U.S. Army passengers were also killed in the action.[14]

USS *LCT-322*

The *LCT-322* also earned a Commendation from Commander Service Squadron, South Pacific Force for helping to save USS *Celeno*. From the commendation:

> On June 16, 1943, the USS *Celeno* was attacked by enemy bombers and suffered considerable damage from two direct bomb hits and four near misses. Notwithstanding this considerable damage and with fire raging on the ship and with no steering mechanism, the USS *Celeno* was successfully beached.
>
> No small amount of the credit due for the successful beaching of the *Celeno* goes to the USS *LCT-322*, who furnished personnel in fighting fires aboard the *Celeno* and evacuated their dead and wounded.
>
> The Commander Service Squadron, South Pacific Force hereby commends the Commanding Officer, officers and men of the USS *LCT-322* for their prompt and diligent efforts and courageous devotion to duty which contributed directly to the saving of the USS *Celeno* and the reduction of casualties to the minimum. Your action exemplifies the highest traditions of the Naval Service.[15]

---

[14] Action Report of USS *LST-340*, 26 June 1943.

[15] Commendation from Commander Service Squadron, South Pacific Area, 19 July 1943.

USS *CELENO* (AK-76)

The *Celeno* survivors spent two or three days on Guadalcanal living in tents and foxholes while a salvage crew made temporary repairs and pumped out the holds. As Tony Gray, captain's messenger recalled:

> We were then towed over to Tulagi — the rudder and shaft were badly bent, so we couldn't move under our own power — where further repairs were made.
> After about a month, we were towed down to Espiritu Santo where the *Celeno* went into a floating drydock to check the repairs. The shipfitters replaced some of the temporary patches and about 1 September we left for the States on a towline from two seagoing tugs. We reached San Francisco thirty days later and went into a Mare Island drydock for a stem-to-stern overhaul.

Most of the *Celeno* crew received survivors' leave while the ship was under repair and being outfitted for troop handling. In December 1943, the ship loaded at Oxnard, Calif., with a Navy ACORN Construction Group and headed back to the Russell Islands in the Solomons.

Celeno brought troops and cargo to Manus through the spring of 1944. She continued to operate throughout the Pacific until the war ended and was decommissioned at San Francisco March 1, 1946 and transferred to the Maritime Commission. She received three battle stars for World War II service.

SS *Nathaniel Currier*

By 1530 the sky appeared drained of enemy planes and our fighters began returning to Henderson Field.

Armed Guard gunners and Merchant Marine helpers swapped impressions. Cuts and bruises acquired in action were noted for the first time. We slapped each other on the back, telling and retelling what we had seen, as we celebrated shooting down our first enemy planes. We kidded around while waiting to secure from GQ, but relief was written on everyone's face. We had met the long-awaited "gut check" while under fire and passed the test. June 16 would never be forgotten. From that day forward, life would always be a bit more precious, to be enjoyed one day at a time. You could sense that some felt we were now invincible. It was a good feeling.

At 1559, we received the all-clear signal from shore and returned to the anchorage. From the time the ship got underway until the all-clear message was received, the skipper kept the ship zigzagging in a radical pattern at flank speed with a skill that reflected a lifetime of experience.

A total of 2103 rounds were fired from the 20s. Ten shells were fired from the 3"/50; one of which misfired. (One 3" shell was fired with an 800-yard fuse, four with 1500 yard fuses, and five with seven second fuses.) No damage was inflicted on the *Currier* by the enemy and there were no casualties, except for burns Grady Murphy received during the attack. To paraphrase our C.O.'s July 17 report: The after port 20-mm jammed because of an improperly loaded magazine. The jam was promptly reduced and the cocking lanyard placed over the cotter, but the gun was rolled too high on the mount to cock the gun from the shoulder bars. Enemy planes were coming in, and to save the time it takes to roll down the mount, Murphy seized the hot barrel of the gun with his bare hands and cocked the gun by pulling down on the barrel. His burns were immediately treated with tannic acid from the gun bag, and he continued to serve at his battle station on the 3"/50 gun for the balance of the action. After the ship returned to anchor, Murphy was treated by a naval medical officer ashore and returned to the ship.

Our C.O.'s report summarized the Armed Guard's defense of the *Currier* with these words:

> Two enemy planes were definitely destroyed by the fire from the guns of this ship, and two more were damaged — one was subsequently destroyed by a P-38 fighter plane, and the other possibly destroyed. Several other planes were hit, but no material damage can claim to have been done to them. At least three other bombers attacking this ship during the course of such raid were driven off.

Our gun crews were so busy shooting we had no time to count, but most of us felt the C.O. was low on all his tallies.

Also according to him, "The merchant seamen at the guns carried out their battle assignments quickly and efficiently and without any confusion or signs of panic."

The casualty count and damage to U.S. ships would have been far worse had we not had the protection of the Solomon Island Air Force ("Airsols"). Their fighter pilots were absolutely fearless — and a bit too trusting of A/A gunners.

The 1st Special Naval Construction Battalion (NCB) stevedore gangs discharged almost 6,700 tons of *Currier* cargo into or onto anything that would float ranging from 45-foot Landing Craft, Mechanized (LCMs), 117-foot Landing Craft, Tank (LCTs), 328-foot Landing Ship, Tank (LSTs), to 70-ton barges made up of pontoon cells — in only seven days — about 24-hours of which were lost due to air raids. (During the approximately eight days we were standing off Guadalcanal, there were thirteen air raids and/or red alerts. But the only instance in which a serious attempt was made to directly attack the *Currier* was on June 16.)

As efficient as they were, there were a few difficulties. Most of the newly-arrived LST "drivers" experienced maneuvering problems when attempting to come alongside and/or back away from the *Currier*. According to the *Currier*'s log:

> On 16 June 1943 while backing away, an LST fouled one of our life rafts which was subsequently lost overboard.
>
> On 18 June at 1710, while coming alongside to take on cargo, another LST fouled the bulwark abreast number 4 hatch on the starboard side and fractured the rail.
>
> On 20 June at 1920, yet another LST, '. . . fouled vessel at anchor while coming alongside and holed vessel on starboard side amidship in the 'B' strake. It also fractured the plate in same strake.'

The first U.S. Navy Stevedore Battalion in the South Pacific, the 1st Special NCB, earned high praise on Guadalcanal for its professional cargo handling talents while off-loading long-haul freighters and/or battle-loading the new landing craft. The Merchant Marine and Naval Armed Guard crews that manned the 6,000-plus long-haul carriers like the *Currier* were quick to recognize and appreciate the increased efficiency and shorter turnaround times. They were a pioneer outfit with an important mission: To increase logistical support for RAdm Richmond Kelly Turner's Amphibious Force South Pacific (PHIBFORSOPAC).

These revolutionary new landing ships and craft would soon prove invaluable as medium-to short-haul carriers of troops, war matériel and supplies between advance bases like Noumea, Espiritu Santo, and Guadalcanal and new amphibious operations such as the upcoming New Georgia campaign.

8

TASK UNIT 32.4.4
PART II

O n 22 June 22, 1943 at 0945, Task Unit 32.4.4, composed of *Aludra, Deimos, Nathaniel Currier*, USS *O'Bannon*, USS *Ward*, and USS *Skylark*, got underway proceeding through Lengo channel. From the *O'Bannon*'s Action Report:

> Preliminary Information — Task Unit 32.4.4 . . . departed Guadalcanal via Lengo channel . . . for points south via route Careen.

> Commander Task Unit 32.4.4 was LCmdr. Collins, USNR, the Commanding Officer of the USS *Aludra*. The Commanding Officer of the *O'Bannon* [LCmdr. Donald J. MacDonald] was the senior officer of the escort ships.

> After clearing the channel the *Aludra* was the guide followed by the *Nathaniel Currier* at a distance of about 700 yards; the *Deimos* was 1,000 yards on the *Aludra*'s starboard beam. The formation of the AKs and the merchant ship remained as mentioned above throughout the day and night.

Narrative — Speed of auxiliary ships was approximately 10 knots, we were zigzagging in accordance with plan #38 so the speed made good over the ground was approximately 9 knots. All screening vessels were patrolling station radically at speeds up to 14 knots. Prior to sunset of the evening of 22 June, 1943, the following night orders were received from Commander Task Unit 32.4.4:

1. At about 2022 zig zag will be ceased and mean course resumed together.
2. 2045-course to be altered by wheeling to true course 141.
3. 0100-course is to be altered by wheeling to true course 124.
4. 0130-commence zig zag in accordance with plan #38.

At 0445 L (1745Z) the formation was steaming on course 124 degrees at a base speed of 10 knots, zigzagging in accordance with plan #38. The moon was full and directly overhead, the sky was completely overcast, the sea was choppy, the wind was force about 3 from southeast. The indirect illumination caused by the overcast sky with a full moon above, caused our ships to stand out very clearly at a range of 4,000 yards.

It was at this time [0443] that two explosions, which seemed almost simultaneous, were felt by this vessel. The Officer of the Deck reported that the *Skylark* had changed course to Port and had just dropped depth charges. The Commanding Officer upon looking over the situation immediately realized that the auxiliary ships had been torpedoed. Radar screen showed nothing, nor had they shown anything during the night other than our own ships.

SS *Nathaniel Currier*

The *Currier* gun crew was at battle stations all night because we were headed south back through Torpedo Junction. At 0443, Joe Skalenda, our bow-lookout, sighted a torpedo wake and shouted, "Torpedo off port bow!" Our bridge lookouts also spotted the torpedo streaking toward us. Of course, there wasn't time to change course or maneuver. I no sooner picked up the fast-moving line of phosphorescent bubbles than it disappeared under our bow, only to emerge to starboard racing off through the early morning darkness.

We had barely absorbed the shock of this close call when the *Aludra* and *Deimos*, steaming abreast of each other just ahead, were each hit by torpedoes on the port side less than thirty seconds apart.

Duane Curtis was napping in his guntub on the fantail when Skalenda's shouts into the phones jarred him awake. As Duane remembers it: "I was still groggy when the first torpedo hit a few seconds later, but I was plenty awake and saw the second one hit."

According to our C.O.'s Action Report:

> The ships had been zigzagging all night and, at the time of the attack, had gone on the left leg of the convoy. This brought the three cargo vessels in a V-shape or triangular formation about eight hundred yards apart with the *Currier* the last ship in the convoy.
>
> Within a few seconds after the attack, Captain Hassell took charge of the bridge and the ship continued for several miles at flank speed in company with one of the escorting destroyers [*Ward*], using a radical zigzag pattern. A sharp lookout was kept in all sections, but the submarine was never sighted and no further attacks were made.
>
> Captain Hassell requested permission to return to render assistance to the damaged ships, but he was ordered to continue away from the point of the attack, which order he carried out. No shots were fired, and when last sighted, both ships which had been hit were afloat.[1]

The Action Report of *O'Bannon* continues:

> [The *O'Bannon*'s course] . . . was changed to starboard and a circle commenced to try and locate submarine on starboard side. Communications could not be established over TBS [Talk between

---

[1]   SS *Nathaniel Currier* Action Report 17 July 1943.

ships] with other friends, so the Commanding Officer was not aware at this time from which side the torpedoes had hit. A search to starboard was immediately made for the submarine although survivors in boats began flashing SOS over blinker lights. No attempt was made at this time to pick up survivors.

At 0529 L [local time] (1829 Z [Greenwich Mean Time]) a surface radar contact was made on bearing 033 degrees T[rue], distance 13,800 yards; speed was immediately increased to ultimate 30 knots and course changed to run down contact. It was at first thought that this might be the submarine, upon drawing closer, two contacts were definitely established and at 0600 communications were established with YPs *514* and *518*.[2] They were requested to come back and pick up survivors while this ship continued submarine hunt.

After the YPs were in the area, the Commanding Officer of the *O'Bannon* directed the *Skylark* and YPs to pick up survivors while the *O'Bannon* continued circling and to hunt for the submarine. Sunrise was at 0629. It was not until 0645 that communications were established with any of our ships over the TBS.

The *Currier* and the *Ward* stood on ahead on base course swinging clear of the crippled ships and, after getting about 10,000 yards away, were directed by me to proceed at best speed toward BUTTON [Espiritu Santo]. We were not able to establish definitely from which side the ships had been hit until 0720 and this was over the TBS at which time Commander Task Unit 32.4.4 said that they had been hit on the Port side of base course . . .

Rescue Operations — The *O'Bannon* continued to search for the submarine except as indicated below; to put a boat in the water and send a doctor to the *Skylark* at 0728. At 0743 *YP 514* reported sound contact off port bow and this vessel proceeded in that vicinity to search. Contact was false and nothing further was developed.

---

[2] These distinct patrol craft (a.k.a. YPs, "Yippies," "Yard Patrol Craft," "Cactus Navy," "Yard Birds," "Tuna Boats," or "Pineapple Navy") were small and slow, displacing between 50 and 150 tons. Mostly fishing boats from Hawaii or patrol craft from Hawaiian Sea Frontier Forces, they were converted for military use. Wooden-hulled and lightly armed, they were used as tugs, dispatch boats, rescue craft, troop and supply ferried and transports for minor amphibeous assaults.

At approximately 0900 a PBY approached and circled the formation. He was directed to go out to circle 25 miles and work in. Shortly thereafter, another PBY closed the formation and he circled the area, assisting in the hunt. A Flying Fortress closed the Unit and looked over the situation and then departed.

At 0933 the *Aludra* sank. At 1024, *YP 518* came alongside and transferred the Commanding Officer of the *Deimos* with 7 other *Deimos* officers and 41 enlisted men to this vessel.

At 1028, *YP 518* and *514* were directed to make final sweep for survivors. At 1055 this vessel went alongside the *Skylark* and transferred two containers of blood plasma.

At 1105 all ships made a complete sweep of the entire area and after ascertaining that there were no more survivors in the water, the Commanding Officer of the *O'Bannon* directed *Skylark* and the two YPs to proceed to Button at best speed.

Sinking of the *Deimos* — At 1200, after circling the *Deimos*, verifying that no contact was in the area prior to sending salvage party aboard, it was noticed that the *Deimos* was settling by the stern fairly rapidly so that her after gun was just going underwater.

After talking over the situation with the Commanding Officer of the *Deimos* and ascertaining the damage which had been done and her chances for salvage, it was decided that salvage would be impossible, so the *Deimos* was sunk by gunfire at 1233 . . .

TU 32.4.4 Search Continues — After the *Deimos* was sunk, a thorough [*O'Bannon*] search was started for any remaining survivors and also for the submarine. At 1400 radar contacts on unidentified aircraft bearing 060 degrees T, distance 10 miles began to come in. From 1400 until 1518 radar contacts were maintained on four different unidentified aircraft. One closed the range to 8 miles but was not identified visually. The others circled at ranges of 12 and 15 miles . . .

At 1830, just at dusk, this vessel was again back in the area of the empty life rafts and life boats that were still floating. At 2027 L (0927 Z) a black cat [Allied aircraft] circled overhead and gave us the proper reply. At 2046 a flare was dropped to the North of us; course was changed to north and speed increased to 30 knots to run down the vicinity of the flare. It was thought at first that the black cat had a contact and was illuminating it. After steaming on this course for 40 minutes with no radar contact and not being able to establish communications with the black cat plane over the common frequency, course was changed to rendezvous with the *Currier* and *Ward* which was accomplished the next morning at dawn.[3]

The "Casualty Report" from the *Aludra*'s medical officer reported that two crew members died of injuries on June 23 and were buried at sea the following day. Twelve crew members were wounded; four were transferred to Base Hospital #3. The casualty report didn't mention the military passengers who were killed.

The *Skylark*, (Lt. Roy H. Jones, Commanding) and two YPs, the *514* and *518*, rescued the *Aludra* and *Deimos* survivors.

USS *Skylark*

The *Skylark*'s War Diary describes the recovery action:

Wednesday 23 June 1943

00-04: In compliance with orders from COMTASK Unit 32.4.4 . . . patrolling station 45 degrees off port bow of guide ship of convoy, USS *Aludra*.

04-08: Steaming as before. 0443 Observed a high column of water with smoke coming from the *Aludra*; no flame or fire observed. 0443 Observed a large column of smoke and flames from *Deimos*. 0444 Sounded General Quarters and reversed course.

0448 Observed both ships to be dead in the water and appeared to be settling by the head; later known that *Aludra* was hit on the bow and the *Deimos* near the stern (#4 hold).

Continued on reverse course searching with echo ranging; began to search in all directions on the port side of base course and continued search tactics until 0615.

0630 Received orders to pick up survivors, DD 450 screening. 0635 Alongside first raft with nine men, none injured. 0652 All men aboard from second and third life rafts (17 men). 0710

---

[3] USS *O'Bannon* Action Report covering sub attack 23 June 1943.

Recovered two men clinging to wreckage, one injured. 0715 Four more men singly, two injured. 0730 One man recovered injured.

0735 *Aludra* sank, bow down. Recovered eighteen men, none injured. 0742 Twenty-nine men picked up from life boat, one seriously injured. 0754 Recovered Twenty-one men aboard, two badly injured.

0755 Received the doctor from *O'Bannon*. *YP 514* and *YP 518* joined the search for survivors.[4]

Leonard Honeycutt joined the *Skylark* in Noumea on his eighteenth birthday, June 6. Here's how he remembers the rescue operation: "I'd never even seen anyone seriously ill in my life when I joined the Navy, much less dead, and here we were bringing all these men aboard, some alive, some wounded, and some dead. It was still dark and we were pulling them aboard covered with oil, black from head to foot.

"We had the mess tables and decks filled with people. It was total chaos. We had our doctor there as well as one from the *O'Bannon*. I guess I was pretty much in shock because we had to stack the dead on the fantail for some time.

"We used our berthing compartments for the survivors and we stayed topside. Of course we were sleepin' topside anyway because of the heat."

08-12: 0803 Recovered seventeen men from life raft, two injured. 0813 Recovered eleven men from life raft, one injured. 0826 Recovered Three men from life raft, none injured. 0843 Recovered nine men from life boat, none injured. 0847 Recovered five men from life boat, none injured.

0847-1049 Continued to search the area for survivors. 1049 Doctor reported need of plasma and proceeded on a course in order that DD 450 could pass supplies by line. 1107 Medical supplies aboard by line from DD 450 and searching the area was complete.

---

[4]   USS *Skylark* (AM-63) War Diary for 23-24 June 1943.

USS *Aludra* Survivors

To those on the *Aludra* (AK-72) it was a morning they would long remember.

Bill Hartman: "It was my turn to go down and get the coffee and when I got back up in that [gun]tub, that's when it happened. It hit right beneath me and blew us right out of the tub. I was really buggered up from the waist down for about two weeks. We stayed right where we were until we heard the words, 'Abandon ship!'"

Eugene Hopper: "I was in the 5-inch gun crew sittin' up on deck. We'd been at General Quarters since 2230 that night. When that thing hit, it was still dark, it was like going full speed and hitting a brick wall. I just bounced across the deck."

Merle E. Luther, Shipfitter 2/c: "We slept at our battle stations that night with our life jackets on. At daybreak we were awakened by a loud bang.

"The aft mast came flying down but, thank God, it missed everybody. I was stationed on an aft 20-mm and my locker was just below on the main deck. Within minutes, the Captain ordered 'abandon ship' over the loudspeaker."

Roy Lucy: "I had just gotten off the midwatch and gone down to sack out on a cot by the No. 4 whaleboat aft of the bridge. I was awakened by this explosion . . .

"As I got up, I was looking at the *Deimos* and I saw her take a fish. Then I became conscious that the GQ bell was going off so I climbed up to the radio shack. Nobody was there — because I had missed 'Abandon ship!'"

Primo Saraiba: "I was sleeping topside behind the midships house. When that torpedo hit, the water came up over the gunwale and knocked me down on the deck."

Clinton Slater: "I was at GQ on the 5-inch gun on the stern. There was this sudden big boom, then the ship started shaking violently. As the bow went down, the stern went up and the ship kept turning and kicking up."

Eugene Hopper: "My abandon ship station was right there alongside the gun. It was my job to cut the rafts loose. But after the torpedo hit, we were taking water in the bow, the fantail was up in the air. We were empty anyway, so you're talking about thirty feet. The screw was goin' round as we circled. The screw wouldn't stop.

"I understand the chief machinist mate went back down and shut the engines off 'cause I wouldn't cut the rafts loose until the screw stopped because it was cutting the guys in half. They would scrape alongside the ship and that screw, about half out of the water, you could hear it, 'ba-bump, ba-bump, ba-bump.'

"When the engine stopped, I got a 4-inch mooring line and put a figure-eight in it and dropped it over the side. That's the way about eighteen of us went down to the raft so we wouldn't have to jump."

Clinton Slater: "My abandon ship station was the aft falls on a whaleboat. We were in the boat for eight to ten hours, a long time."

Primo Saraiba: "We went over the port side with a net and I got into a lifeboat. We wandered around for a little bit and the ship wasn't sinking so we went back aboard. We went to the armory on the stern where we had all the small arms. We busted the lock on it and got some guns, then we went back down into the boat."

Merle Luther: "I ran to my locker, grabbed a package of orange slices and pushed them into the front of my shirt. Then I abandoned ship twice. The first time, I slid down a line to my life raft but the fellows were yelling there's no more room. So, I went back up the rope hand over hand to the deck and ran up to the bow where there were still several men and the Captain. But there were no more life rafts available so the skipper said, 'Throw the hatch covers over the side and get on them.'

"So I abandoned ship again, only the hatch covers didn't float so well and they got all tangled up. So all we could do was stay in the water and hang on to them. The fellows in the boats and rafts kept telling us to 'watch out for sharks' which didn't make us feel very secure."

Bill Hartman: "My abandon ship station was a whaleboat and I'd done my job real well. It was actually overloaded, the boat, but I kept picking them up anyway 'cause you ain't gonna sink them whaleboats. Then for some ungodly reason, I'll never know, I went back aboard that stinking ship.

"I turned the tiller over to another guy and went back aboard to see what I could do. But there was nothing anyone could do, it was just a total mess up there. So I left with four other guys. The five of us shared a life raft and for the next seventeen hours it was touch and go."

Eugene Hopper: "We had eighteen guys on our raft. It was about three feet underwater. We had to ride it like a horse around the edges and there were guys inside, too.

"We stayed in the water until dark. I imagine they picked up the lone survivors first, before they hit the big groups. I don't really know how many hours I was on it."

Bill Hartman: "The four of us were on the life raft about seventeen hours. It was after dark when I heard this diesel engine running and thought we'd had it 'cause we figured it was an enemy sub that had surfaced in the darkness and was running on the surface looking for survivors. It circled, then approached. All of a sudden, out of the night, we hear, 'Ahoy there!'

"You talk about relief. We couldn't answer, you know and pretty soon here comes this little 'ole blockade runner, a little 'ole white yippie boat, converted San Diego tuna boat, and they took us aboard.

"They had a bunch of those boats down there — called 'em Yard Patrol or something like that. They'd been searching all day for survivors and the way I heard it, we were the last ones to get picked up.

"There were sharks. You damn betcha there were sharks there. The able-bodied tried to protect the wounded as best they could."

Eugene Hopper: "There were a lot of sharks. The *Skylark* crew, they used their machine guns on them."

Typical of the YP-type patrol boat that rescued the survivors was YP-552, *formerly the yacht* Kyma. *Credit: Naval Historical Center.*

Roy Lucy: "They were shooting at them [the sharks] from the *O'Bannon*, using rifles, .45s, and Tommy guns."

Merle Luther: "After about four hours, a converted tuna boat came along and picked us up. My orange slices were a gummy mess!"

Roy Lucy: "We lost some of our crew. I know we lost the chief warrant bo'sun' — his name was Brown — and we lost a third-class signalman named Franklin. He was a great guy, terrific fella, regular Navy. And Brown, he was up there with those passengers because that was his duty.

"And then we lost a machinist mate. Second-class, and a striker. They were both down in the engine room.

"We had about thirty-five passengers of Army, Navy and Marines, all headed Stateside on emergency leave or for some other reason. And they were asleep on top the number one and two holds. So we lost almost all of those guys, I understand it was at least seventy-five percent, poor guys. We picked some of them up but they died. They were wounded going into the water. We took them to the *O'Bannon* and a lot of them died."

Primo Saraiba: "All but one of the passengers were killed. He was sleeping on one of the hatch covers just right, I guess. When the torpedo exploded, it blew him over the side. When he landed in the water, he was still on that hatch cover."

Eugene Hopper: "As far as I know, we only lost three crew members. I think the *Deimos* lost more. And we had thirty military passengers. Half of them were malaria cases. I think it killed twenty-six of them. They were sleeping topside. We buried six guys at sea on the *Skylark* the next day. We slung guys over the side. What an awful feeling."

Roy Lucy: "We were picked up by the USS *John Penn* (APA-23) and taken down to Noumea, New Caledonia. Most of the guys went up to the 'Casual' camp — a receiving station of sorts, I guess, but we radio guys got assigned to ComSoPac.

USS *Deimos*

Events on the USS *Deimos* (AK-78) were equally memorable.

Bernard Barker: "I was on the flying bridge behind the stack — why, I don't know — lookin' off to port when I saw the phosphorescent wake. They make a helluva wake especially when it's that dark. I saw that and I knew immediately it was a torpedo so I let out a yell, 'Torpedo!' and just flopped down. As I flopped down, I could see the *Aludra* going up. Then we got a dull thud and then, wham! I asked later why there was two explosions. I didn't know it, but they tell me those torpedoes carried a penetrating cap, so the first thud was the cap knockin' a hole in the hull."

Charles Maiers: "I had just gotten off the midwatch and showered up and then apparently I dozed off on No. 5 hatch. The next thing I knew I was caught in the rigging — you know, steel cable and stuff — and that's the only thing that saved me from going overboard. I had been using my lifejacket for a pillow, but I guess it went one way and I went another. When I came to, the water was on deck from the explosion. So it was almost a miracle when I looked down and there was a lifejacket. Never mind who the hell it belonged to, it was a lifejacket and that was all that mattered to me at the time. Then it was only a few minutes before we abandoned ship."

J. B. Morrison: "I was in my gun tub on the bridge when the thing went off. I remember hatch covers flying up and away. We had a bunch of old trucks in the hold — taking them back for repairs or something. Blowed them out of the hold, too."

Edval Helle: "I was up at the anchor winch on the bow. There was a big flash [*Aludra*] and about that time somebody screamed and hollered, 'We're gonna get it next!' He didn't more than get it out of his mouth and we got it. One guy saw one of the hatch covers off No. 4 hold come over the bridge and land up on the bow near me."

Richard Rogers: "I left a lot of the guys around 2400 — they were playin' cards — and, 'stead of going to my bridge gun tub, I went up to the No. 2 hatch and stretched out. I was layin' there wondering what the devil I was going to do if we got hit, 'cause I couldn't swim.

"All of a sudden, I see a flash. It was the *Aludra* that got hit. Within about thirty seconds we got hit on the port side aft. I grabbed my lifejacket and then I see this big thing, like a horseshoe, comin' over the bridge and go right past me. I don't know where it landed but I thought of all our guys up there. Then I said, 'To hell with this!' and ran to the side and saw a lifeboat down there with about thirty men in it."

Ken Keller: "I was on the port side wing of the flying bridge looking through the damn telescope when I saw the explosion on the *Aludra*. So as soon as I saw that, I yelled at this guy, 'Take over, I'm going back to my station!' I ran down the ladder and across the boat deck. As I started down the ladder to the main deck, all these guys were asleep on that damn deck. I yelled at them, they better do something. The *Aludra* had just been torpedoed. I saw them raise up and start pulling on some clothes. Just as I got to the bottom, to the main deck, it was a matter of my life being saved by a second or two because had I been up on that ladder, that shower of debris would have cut me to pieces. As it was, the explosion underneath caused me to fall forward on my face.

"The damn, heavy oil line broke and I got sprayed with that. It was an awful mess. But the big mess was all those guys got blown right over the side. I finally got back on my feet. My station in a case like this — the captain had already yelled 'Abandon ship!' — was a raft by the after gun platform.

"I didn't get back there in time to see this but I was told later, two mess boys went right down the ladder and climbed into that raft. The screw was still turning, so they cut the damn line with a pocket knife — so there went a twenty-man raft with only two people in it all morning.

"Anyway, I saw a guy — I thought he was seasick. I cussed him out and said, 'Get up!' Then I realized he was unconscious. Another guy came along and we picked him up. It was hell because he had no clothes on. It had blown all his clothes off. How that happened, I don't know. He was covered with grease and we had a helluva time carrying him across the deck to the doctor's boat. We put a line under his arms and lowered him down. Suddenly we realized the doctor was sitting in water up to his waist. So, with our guy, he was still unconscious, we got the line back under his arms and dragged him back up on the boat deck.

"About this time, I spotted Carl Heiner's whaleboat — that old Navy man could really handle a damn boat — so I ran over and said, 'Carl, can we give you another passenger?' He said, 'Hell, yah, we can always take one more.' So this other guy and I lowered him back down and put him on the boat which was picked up pretty early in the game.

"Later, the doctor informed us that he was a member of the black gang. He also said he had a broken back! With all the things that we did to him — up, down, and around — it's a wonder he survived. I've never gotten over that."

Stan Voorhees: "I was on duty in the radio room when I heard the first blast — apparently the *Aludra*. A few seconds later we got hit. The ship lights and radio signals went out briefly, then came back on. Less than a minute later the captain was yelling, 'Abandon ship!' As I left the radio room, it was still not very light but I could see that the fantail was soon going to be under water."

David Haugh: "I was back on my gun station, sleeping at the time. The *Aludra* explosion jarred everyone awake. About the time I jumped up, the damn ship did a one-eighty. There was shit and corruption coming down all around us. We stood there at General Quarters and finally — it wasn't very long — the word was passed to abandon ship.

"There was a group of radiomen who were attached to the commodore of that little Task Unit in the aft radio shack and I thought, oh shit, those guys are probably locked in there and didn't get the word. So I went down and broke my way through to the radio shack only to find they were long gone.

"Right across the passageway was a storage locker for small arms and I said, oh, I'll get me a submachine gun or something and go out and fight. I got in there, but all I could find was an old rifle and a bandoleer. Then I tried to get out of there and couldn't find the hatch. It was pitch-black. I was in there screamin' and hollerin' and pounding. Some guy right outside the hatch opened it and said, 'Did you want to get out?' I said, 'You bet your life I do!'"

Pat Paones: "I was standing out on deck. I saw the ship *Aludra* alongside of us get hit. All I heard was a big boom.

"The next thing I remember, seconds later, we must have been hit because I found myself scrambling over twisted steel beams — I suppose hatch beams — and where I ran to, I don't even know."

Bob Parker: "We were sitting around our gun station. All of a sudden, we hear the *Aludra* catch the first torpedo port side forward. Our skipper, whoever was on the bridge, must have given a hard right turn order to the helmsman to get the hell out of the way. Luckily for the forward crew, anyway, he started to turn right. We took our torpedo that followed within a period of maybe thirty seconds or forty seconds, in No. 4 on the port side. The same side. So those two torpedoes were probably fired simultaneously, and the time it took for the first one to hit the *Aludra* and the second one to hit us was just the difference in distance of maybe 1,000 yards. I honestly believe that right turn saved my life because I'm sure we would have taken it port side forward and I wouldn't be here."

Mike Hosier: "I was sittin' in the little cantina having a cup of coffee and all of a sudden GQ sounded and I got up to start for my battle station when, whambo, right next to me that torpedo hit and just blasted the hell out of things. Damn near blew me overboard. I went right through them black-out curtains and hit the chain rail, and all I got out of the whole mess was a broken thumb."

Bob Vorhies: "We were goin' to have beans and cornbread for breakfast. Those beans had been simmering all night long. I had a gas mask, lifejacket, and helmet under my arm when they woke me and said, 'Cookie, it's time to start breakfast.'

"I remember walkin' into the galley and layin' my lifejacket on the peelin' table we used to prepare vegetables. Then I got a big 'ole pan and headed for the forward storeroom right beneath the 3"/50 — we stored cornbread and other dry produce there.

"There were two watertight doors and, if I'm not mistaken, six dogs on each hatch, and as you go through, you dog them behind you. Well, I went through the two, got my cornmeal, came back out and dogged the doors behind me.

"There was a meat block just outside the ice box. I set that cornmeal on the meat block and I pulled the plunger on that big 'ole ice box door, opened it, pulled off my old cook's hat that I had on, and just as I bent over, I hear the explosion. But, at first, I thought, my God, what's happened? I thought maybe we collided 'cause we were runnin' pretty close together. I ran for that plunger and when it didn't open I said, oh, my god! I picked up a couple of boxes or crates or something and I ran at that door and when I hit it with my shoulder, it swung open.

"I looked down the ladder and saw that stream of water comin'. I ran up that ladder and I'm goin' to get my lifejacket. But somebody had taken it. I remember runnin' forward. My division officer said, 'Vorhies, get to your abandon ship station.' I don't know what I said to him but I kept runnin'!

"That's when I jumped off the bow of that ship and it seemed to me like it was thirty days before I hit water. I remember reaching for my legs and I can't feel a thing. My God, what's happened, what's happened, I wondered.

"I remember goin' by that hull and seein' the oil splattered around where the torpedo had entered. I could hear that water making kind of a sucking sound. Then I finally got hold of a boat skid and hung on to that for I don't know how long. Withers, he was a first-class cook, got a hold of me and got me to a donut raft. It was for sixteen people and there were twenty-seven of us hanging on it.

"Bowie, he was a mess cook for the officer's wardroom. The back of his head was blown out and you could just see the inside of his head."

Don Waterhouse: "Rider and I had just gotten off duty in the main radio shack. It was too hot to go inside but since we couldn't find any space on deck, we ended up in the aft radio shack. That's where we were when the torpedo hit."

Jay Rider: "I had just gotten up on the bench to stretch out when it hit. I went up in the air and I'm sure Don did, too. Those metal lockers came down with a bang and blocked the door, but we were able to shove them out of the way. We started to open the portside hatch to get out of there, but water was flowing down the deck lickity-split. About that time somebody came by and said, 'There's nothing but a big hole that way. Go out to the starboard side.'

"There was so much oil on the main deck I went up to the boat deck. A pharmacist mate had somebody in his arms, rocking him, trying to get him to come to or whatever. I asked him if he needed any help and he said, 'No, go ahead.' So I went up this twisted old ladder to the captain's promenade. I was going back into the main radio shack when the communications officer came out and said, 'I've taken care of all the secret stuff. I deep-sixed all the coded stuff. So go abandon ship.'"

Erwin Holan: "The fellas that manned the boat made one mistake. The bowman unhooked the forward falls before the rear and it capsized the boat."

Bernard Barker: "I went topside and helped load a couple whaleboats, and then I jumped over the side when the skipper — he gave three calls to abandon ship, two calls and then every man for himself! I went over the side and hung on to the side of a whaleboat and somebody puked in my face.

"I let go and got on this boat skid with Morris D. Martin — he was yelling at me. I remember another guy, a teeny black guy named Ferguson. He was rattling around on something and offered free rides to San Francisco for ten bucks or something. Everybody got a big bang out of it. Real nice guy."

Stanley Voorhees: "My raft had been blown off the deck by the concussion of the explosion, so I assisted some shipmates in lowering a whaleboat. Six or seven of us went down the rope ladder into the boat. All of a sudden a big wave capsized the boat dumping us all out. We finally noticed an upside-down whaleboat and swam to it, got on the back of it until we were picked up."

Charles Maiers: "When I jumped over the side everything was thick with oil, but there was this capsized lifeboat that was not very far out with a bunch of guys hanging on it, and that's what I got hold of."

Mike Hosier: "Our guy knocks the pin out so the raft can drop into the water, but somebody forgot to secure the painter [line] to the ship, so I look out and there's the goddamn raft back there about a quarter mile. So I went over the side on a cargo net, got into the water, and someone picked me up. I think it was Lt. Bailey."

Walter Ballow: "The life rafts had been secured with lines when the ship was down in the water, when the draft was deep. When they cast them loose the damn rafts came to the end of the line before they hit the water and they broke lose. So I was assigned to a whaleboat and the sea was kind of rough. I was on the net going down and the damn whaleboat already had too many people in it. Then a wave came and before they got it unhooked, it capsized.

"There were more on that net than me — we just jumped off and I got tangled up in that damn net and I thought I was never going to get back up to the surface. But I did. Then we just swam in the water. It seemed like there was quite a current in there.

"Finally, it started to break day. Four or five of us were bobbing around in the water and we saw one another. I suppose we just happened to be floating close. So we kind of got together in a bunch and later on in the morning the destroyer picked us up."

Bob Parker: "I got in the number 2 lifeboat, portside forward. While we were in the water the *O'Bannon* was running around dropping depth charges trying to get that sub."

David Haugh: "Mr. Heiner, an ensign, and a Mustang, was the boat officer. He was in the boat and they began to lower it away and I jumped in real fast. Heiner wanted to pull away from the ship but the captain said, 'Stay there, we got wounded we can put in there.' Finally, the captain said in disgust, 'Okay, shove off.' So we did.

"Those whaleboats were a pretty good size. We had maybe fifteen guys, so we were in luxury. Then we started picking up the guys that were floating in the water around us."

Richard Rogers: "I didn't hear any 'Abandon ship.' I didn't hear anything. I saw them all in the lifeboat, everybody was yelling, and somebody let go of the forward fall to that boat and it went down just as I was gonna jump on it. So I went right by the engine room in the water and all that hot oil. I was an oil-baby there. I couldn't see anything.

"All of a sudden I was splashing around there. I was on my back and I lost my spare lifejacket. I had one on. I was floating around there and I couldn't see anything. I was taking in an awful lot of water. I could feel myself — it was the only time I got just a little religion — I could feel myself lifting right out of the water. I felt like I was two feet above the water. I think I was drowning. Then something hit me in the face. It was the keel of an overturned lifeboat. I didn't care what the hell it was, I climbed on it.

Ken Keller: "We were hanging on to the boat cradle or skid, probably eight of us on it. The water was something like eighty degrees, but by the time we got picked up some six hours later you couldn't stop your teeth from chattering. God, it was cold!"

Erwin Holan: "The skipper said, 'Well, now or never,' so we all jumped into the water with our lifejackets on and that was it. He said to swim out as far as we can from the ship in case it starts sinking.

Pat Paones: "I was vomiting and coughing when I was in the lifeboat and the ensign, with a revolver, threatened to make me jump overboard if I didn't stop but a little seaman and some other guys reminded the ensign he would go overboard first. I don't remember how I got into the lifeboat and many other things. We were picked up by a tuna boat and later by a destroyer."

Bernard Barker: "I think we were all pretty much in shock. We saw this YP off in the distance and it was coming toward us at, I suppose, twenty knots, and we thought it was a Japanese destroyer. We were trying to decide whether we'd just drown ourselves when we saw the American flag. Martin and I just about cried."

David Haugh: "There were personal tragedies in that boat, too. There was this little machinist mate, an Italian kid, and he was scared and seasick. When he'd throw up he'd make the most god-awful noise you ever heard. And old Heiner, who had been sunk off of North Africa, you'd think he'd know better but he was really upset. He had his .45 automatic out and he told this kid, 'I'm gonna shoot you if you throw up again.' It's funny now, but it was just scary then. I was sure glad I had that rifle.

The yacht Elgra *was pressed into service as the* YP-546, *typical of patrol boats used in rescue operations in the South Pacific. Naval Historical Center.*

"We all had bunker fuel in our hair, in our mouth. We were covered in it. There was a young fellow, a cook, and his side was laid open. You could see his ribs. One of those big ole' hatch covers had hit him. He was pretty good. He didn't make much noise.

"We rode around and picked up a few more people. Then those destroyers, like the *O'Bannon* would come up and slow down and we'd row like hell to get over to them and they'd take off. I can't blame them because that Jap was still out there."

"We swam over to this overturned whaleboat — six of us — and grabbed the bars along the bottom and rode it out. If it hadn't been for those bars we couldn't have hung on, those waves would have just kept slopping us off. That little design feature probably saved our lives.

Stan Voorhees: "We were in the water about two to three hours until the *O'Bannon* picked us up and, by the way, we were completely covered with bunker oil — this dark, greasy, black oil."

Pat Paones: "There was an electrician we had aboard, and a shark come up and tore his whole arm off."

Walter Ballow: "Oh, God, there were lots of them [sharks] but we never had any of them attack. We were sure we'd get eaten up by the sharks if the damn Japs didn't get us. Our rescue ship, the *Skylark*, shot at quite a lot of them with their 30-caliber machine guns."

Edval Helle: "When they pulled me up out of the water, a shark made a pass at me and the chief fired his .45. I don't know if he hit him, but the shark didn't get me."

Ken Keller: "We pulled up to that little reefer boat — I think it was Zane Grey's yacht they'd converted to carry food from the south up to Guadalcanal — anyway, as we were inching our way over to go up the ladder, I thought I kicked the navigator, Bill, and I apologized to him. I said, 'Sorry, Bill, for kicking you.' He said, 'Hell, you didn't kick me.' Sure enough, when we got aboard, the guys up on deck didn't say a word, but that goddamn fish had been going back and forth, I guess, figuring out which one of us was the most tender. We all got aboard and not one of us had any problem."

Bob Vorhies: "Those bodies that were floating out there, every once in awhile you'd see the fins come through the water, then you'd see the bodies bob. They'd pick up some of the dead bodies and the sides of their faces might be torn off and you'd just see their teeth. It was just awful."

Ray Weathers: "I seen plenty of sharks. In fact, after I was picked up, there was this guy out there hanging onto a gas drum. When the *Skylark* backed down to get him, the sharks ate him before you could blink. There were lots in that area."

David Haugh: "Some of those YPs were tuna boats from San Pedro with big reefers on them so they could carry fresh food up to the 'Canal. Finally one of them pulled up and we got aboard. We kind of overwhelmed them because they had a small crew and small ship. But they were wonderful.

"They helped pick up quite a few survivors. I didn't see it 'cause I was too sick and I wanted my mother. I was seasick. The water was pretty rough but it was that damn fuel oil. I still can't stand the smell of it. They turned over their bunks to us.

I climbed in there all oily. Those poor guys probably ended up throwing all their bedding away. I didn't even go out on deck to watch the *O'Bannon* sink the *Deimos*. I wasn't about to lose my bunk."

Walter Ballow: "They would cast a line to us but that damn captain didn't want to slow that destroyer down enough so we could grab on. Hell, if you caught the line you couldn't hold on 'cause you were going through the water just flip-flopping.

"Eventually, he slowed it down so we could grab on, then they pulled us in with the line."

Mike Hosier: "A little banana boat, a YP, picked up four or five of us guys with a lot of oil and stuff on us and the crew tried to clean us up. Their skipper told them to give us some clothes, so they took us below and gave us socks, dungarees, skivvies, stuff like that. Then afterwards they were gonna serve us breakfast. Who the hell could eat!"

Bob Parker: "While we were in the water, the *O'Bannon* — they used to call her the 'Little Helena' — was running around dropping depth charges. We were picked up by a YP and transferred to the *O'Bannon* later. When we boarded her, each crew member grabbed a survivor and they gave us clothes and stuff.

"We stayed there all day long trying to find that sub. The Skipper was really hot."

Richard Rogers: "The *O'Bannon* came over and picked us up. It was real light by then. We climbed up a net, just the two of us. They took us to the mess hall and we got under a table. I remember the doc reaching down, putting cotton to my face and wiping it off. I don't even remember getting clean clothes. They were operating on guys on the table.

Stan Voorhees: "The escort ship *O'Bannon* pulled alongside and six of us climbed up the rope ladder to safety. We were a beat-up bunch, all covered with black bunker oil. Her crew offered their spare clothes to us. We looked like we'd been in a wreck.

The USS Ward *APD-16. Her war record began at Pearl Harbor when she sank a Japanese midget submarine on December 7, 1941. Naval Historical Center.*

"The next morning, we held memorial services — we had some burials at sea. I believe it was somewhere around a dozen."

Bob Vorhies: "They put me in a bunk on that Yard Patrol. Oh, Lord, I couldn't move. My legs were paralyzed. It happened when I jumped. I either hit something, debris in the water, maybe it was the way I hit. I don't even know how many feet I fell. I don't. I just know I jumped."

Jay Rider: "I got picked up by a YP. The guys that were injured in any way were put in the bunks of the crew. One of the other fellas and I were out on the deck heaving our guts out. We were as green as could be from vomiting. Even though I didn't taste any oil, I could smell it, a real strong smell, and it made us sick."

"We were at General Quarters, or we could have lost more of the crew. The torpedo narrowly missed the engine room or all men on watch down there might have been killed. Black gang crew members were marked men in a sub attack."

Bob Vorhies: "I remember them burying six of the boys that they picked up. Some of them had their lifejackets on and

The crew of the Ward *pose with their "scoreboard" in June of 1944. Naval Historical Center.*

their heads were down, just their bottoms bobbing up. They just reached down and bow-hooked them.

"There was a chaplain aboard, gave the burial services. I remember they were wrapping them in canvas and shoving them overboard. I think they took some ballast out of the ship and tied it to those bags. Now who they were, I don't know. I didn't know who the boys were they picked out of the water."

Most T.U.32.4.4 survivors were back in action within two weeks. Some examples:

> Eugene Hopper and Ray Weathers returned to Guadalcanal to catch the *Rail* (AT-139) and *Menominee* (AT-73) respectively — tugs that had helped save the *Celeno* on 16 June.
>
> Charles Maiers and Walter Ballow served together on amphibious transport *George Clymer* (APA-27) for the Bougainville invasion.
>
> Bob Phillips and Erwin Holan ended up together on the *Crescent City* (AP-40). They also made the Bougainville invasion.

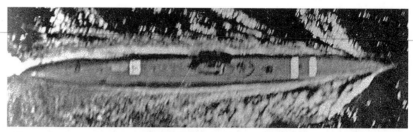

This aerial view of a Japanese RO-100 Class submarine was taken in 1943 near Rabaul, New Britain by Allied aircraft. Naval Historical Center.

Richard Rogers and his Deimos buddy, Snorgraff, served together on minelayer *Breese* (DM-18) during the Philippine campaign.
Bill Hartmann and Jay Rider returned to the Solomons on subchasers *644* and *531*, respectively.
Ken Keller was shipped back to Guadalcanal so fast he made the New Georgia campaign as skipper of an LCT.

The *O'Bannon* picked up the *Ward* and the *Currier* on her radar at 0635 on June 24 and joined formation taking station in screen at 0714. These remnants of Task Unit 32.4.4 sighted Espiritu Santo Island at 1705 bearing 115 degrees T., distance about 25 miles. The *Skylark* and YPs *514* and *518* joined formation at 2048 and took position astern.

There is some question as to how many enemy subs were lying in wait for us that night. RAdm Samuel Elliot Morison documents four subs: "Japanese submariners accomplished even less than their flying countrymen in hampering preparations for the New Georgia invasion. Captain Theiss's convoy was not even sighted by four submarines lying in wait off San Cristobal. One of the group, *RO-103*, did, however, sink Liberty ships *Aludra* and *Deimos* returning empty from Guadalcanal on 23 June."[5]

---

[5] Morison, RAdm. Samuel Eliot. *Breaking the Bismarcks Barrier*, Vol. VI, p. 141.

Taken at Yokosuka Naval Base in September, 1945, this photo shows the RO-58 in the foreground, several "Kairyu" midget submarines to the right and the transport submarine, I-369 in the background. National Archives.

The *Ward* (APD-16) historical sketch described a single submarine attack: ". . . Japanese submarine *RO-103*, commanded by Lt. Rikinosuke Ichimura, slipped past the [T.U.32.4.4] screen and torpedoed and sank two cargo ships — *Aludra* (AK-72) and *Deimos* (AK-78), which proved to be Ichimura's only 'kills' of the war."

There was no sign of the *RO-103* after her last report on July 28, 1943 north of New Georgia.

From *O'Bannon* Comments and Remarks:

It is not known how the submarine made his attack but it is the belief of the Commanding Officer that the Submarine ran up the port side on the surface avoiding detection by the screening vessels on the port hand and made his final approach submerged. The visibility would have greatly aided him in such an attack. There is no doubt that the task unit from the very beginning was shadowed and there is a possibility that aircraft may have assisted in the attack as noticed by the *Ward*. If there was an aircraft in the vicinity at the time of the torpedoing, my radar screen did not indicate this. As our unit passed the western end of San Cristobal at a distance of approximately 10 miles lights were observed on the beach. A submarine was reported as being in the vicinity of the eastern tip of San Cristobal at 1930 the night before. There is no doubt that this submarine was probably the one which made the successful attack.

It is definitely felt that for three large vessels steaming at such slow speed the screen was inadequate; this coupled with the fact that the screening units had never worked together before. Although all escorts had radar equipment, some of their personnel were still inexperienced in its capabilities. I understand that the *Skylark* had a surface radar contact about 1 hour prior to the torpedoing, but due to inexperience of personnel this contact was never developed. I now understand this contact was on the screen at range of about 10,000 yards on her port quarter. The *Ward* did not have it, nor did the *O'Bannon*.

Our ill-fated convoy, composed of four Liberty ships and three escorts, left Noumea June 6, 1943 for Guadalcanal. Two weeks later we were down to just one freighter, the *Nathaniel Currier*.

An estimated total of 1,250 crew members manned the seven ships. The *Celeno* suffered the heaviest casualties: 15 KIA [Killed In Action]; 19 WIA [Wounded In Action]; and 2 MIA [Missing In Action]. The *Deimos* lost 6 to 8 KIA. The *Aludra* had 2 KIA and 12 WIA, with MIA still a mystery. She also lost an estimated twenty-five military passengers.

The U.S. Navy only had 160 AKs and 108 AKAs in its Auxiliary Fleet during WWII. All but three survived the war. The *Aludra* and *Deimos* were two of those three. The USS *Aludra* (AK-72) and the USS *Deimos* (AK-78) each earned one battle star for their brief but courageous World War II service.[6]

The rest of our return trip to San Francisco was uneventful. About two days out, Flags Barela introduced us to a novel lottery — the anchor pool. The C.O. had already told us we should arrive in San Francisco on July 17. The big question: What time would we drop the hook or tie up to a pier? Flags

---

[6] *Dictionary of American Naval Fighting Ships.*

sold twenty-four chances — each with a different hour between 0000-2400 — at $5 per chance, so the winner could net a potential $115. We all bought at least one chance and the Merchant crew took what was left.

It's almost impossible to describe my inner feelings and emotions when we sighted the Golden Gate Bridge. All of us choked up and our hearts beat just a bit faster. After less than four months, here we were, back in the good old U.S. of A. And grateful to be in one piece! Our emotions ranged from elation to sadness.

As we steamed under the bridge we could see the stream of cars overhead carrying people home from work. Back to reality or was it another world? The sky was relatively free of clouds and even the fog cooperated by staying out to sea. It was going to be a beautiful evening for liberty in the City by the Bay.

We had the answer to the anchor pool at 1900 when we dropped the hook off Alcatraz Island on July 17, 1943. Sea watches were secured and port security watch was set. Lee Gibe won the pool and we all lost out on liberty that night because we remained at anchor until the next day.

Talk about channel fever. To travel thousands of miles and get to within a half-mile of a great city like San Francisco only to have to wait to experience her charms, was pure torture. But we survived. On July 18, at 1330 a pilot came aboard, we upped anchor, and moved slowly into Pier 17 on San Francisco's waterfront, not far from where we started our voyage.

The C.O. awarded the port section first liberty from 1600 to 0700 the next morning. Those of us in the starboard liberty section consoled ourselves with the abundance of fresh milk, fruit and vegetables that came aboard almost immediately. It's funny how fresh produce tastes so much better when you've been denied it for months. And fresh milk. Some of the guys consumed a gallon or more within an hour.

On July 19, at 0800 muster, the C.O. announced that six of our gun crew would be transferred to the Armed Guard Center on TI for reassignment and that they would be replaced by fifteen new men. Of course, all six shipmates felt that fifteen new men to replace six old salts who had seen action in the Solomons was only proper.

The change in crew, scheduled for July 20 at 0800, meant that our Liberty section would have to say our good-byes before going ashore. There was the usual exchange of home addresses, handshakes, and "See you around TI" good-byes before we went on liberty that afternoon. It was a strange feeling — like losing part of your family. We were together less than four months, but our shared experiences would last a lifetime.

Curtis, Gibe, Russell, and I were the only crew members staying with the *Currier* in the Starboard liberty section. So we took departing crew members Jurgens, Murphy and Sutton down to Pier 31 for a few rounds of farewell drinks.

We played the hits of the day on the juke box and talked to any single ladies who came in, while waiting for a live combo to start playing at 2100. By the time the combo showed up, we were too high to fully appreciate them, thanks, in part, to some very generous "Pier 31" regulars. But we had a really good time hosting our departing shipmates and no one threw a punch or otherwise embarrassed us.

We later learned our Merchant Marine skipper, D. W. Hassell, sent a very complimentary letter to the commanding officer of the Armed Guard Center on Treasure Island when we got back. His final paragraph quoting the Seabees makes me particularly proud:

. . . It is my belief that the reason we sustained no casualties or damage was the volume and accuracy of the barrage put up. Officers and enlisted personnel of the Seabee battalions in the Cactus-Ringbolt area [Guadalcanal] repeatedly asserted that they had never seen a merchant ship put up such a volume of fire as this ship did.

Our gun crew received a commendation from the Chief of Naval Personnel for the June 16 enemy action, which reads, in part, as follows:

A report of the experience reveals that this ship and the areas about her were subjected to a vicious attack by a formation of enemy dive bombers. Disregarding the danger from falling bombs and flying shrapnel, the Navy gun crew fought back gallantly, setting up an accurate and sustained barrage of shellfire which shot down two planes, inflicting severe damage on two others, and aided in driving off the rest . . .

9

NEW GUINEA

O n July 20 at 0815, a gray Navy truck pulled up to the foot of the *Currier* gangway with a load of sea bags. Behind it was a small gray bus with fifteen new crew members. The C.O. held muster for both new and old hands on the aft gun deck. He asked for gun preferences, did some juggling in order to have two men for each 20-mm, one new and one experienced, then assigned sleeping quarters.

I was moved to the forward starboard 20-mm on the bridge with Lloyd Caldwell, one of the new men, as my loader. Of the fifteen new crew members, three had seagoing experience: Marvin Waterhouse, GM3/c; Bill Cairns, S1/c; and Felix Perez, S1/c. The replacement personnel changed the makeup of our gun crew substantially:

We went from fifteen to twenty-five men — twelve with previous sea duty.

A second Gunners Mate third-class was added so we could have a petty officer on each watch.

We would now have two Armed Guard gunners on each 20mm plus three for the 3" gun, excluding the petty officers. (On our first voyage we had one Armed Guard gunner and one merchant seaman as loader on each 20mm.)

Our crew was now closer to minimum requirements established for Armed Guard crews by the Navy's Bureau of Personnel than on our previous voyage. Consequently, we would not have to rely as heavily on volunteer merchant mariners to pass or load ammunition.

The merchant crew was practically all new, too. Only the master, the third mate, the deck cadet and my friend, Stuart

SS Nathaniel Currier *new Armed Guard crew members for Voyage No. 2. Top Row, L to R: Hubert Cooper, Bill Cairns, Tom Roberts, Harold Murray, Larry Burke. Front Row L to R: Raymond Ferris, Thomas Graham, Lloyd Caldwell, Unknown. U.S. Navy.*

Churchon, radio operator, now wearing a second hat as the ship's purser, shipped over from the first trip. We had a total of forty new mariners and a net increase of three men in the total crew.

One night, several of us, including my good buddy, Lee Gibe, decided to pay another visit to the Fife and Drum, the friendly little tavern on lower Market Street we discovered before our first trip. In no time at all we were "drunker than skunks" thanks to the regulars who continually set us up with drinks.

The next thing I remember, I was awakened by a very nice lady who said, "Wake up Bill, my name is Mary. You have to get back to your ship," as she handed me a cup of coffee.

As I raised up on my elbow to thank her and take my first sip, I realized we weren't alone. Another gal was fixing breakfast. She pointed to the bathroom and said, "Good morning, Bill. Why don't you go ahead and take a shower. Breakfast will be ready in ten minutes. By the way, I'm Lisa."

My head was pounding, the room was spinning and food was the last thing on my mind. "What happened and why am I here?" I asked.

Mary's answer surprised me. "You were drinking with us and didn't want to leave when your shipmates did, so we promised them we'd get you back to your ship safe and sound. Later on, we brought you home with us and you promptly passed out on the bed. That wasn't exactly what we had in mind, but drink your coffee. Maybe next time."

I was embarrassed. I explained that I wasn't a drinker, had never really been drunk before, and had never known what a hangover felt like until then. They both laughed and may have even believed me. Lisa called a cab and I took my leave while they got ready for work. But not before I got their address and phone numbers and promised to call them the next time my ship was in San Francisco. They were both nice looking gals with a sense of humor. They were also a good ten years my senior, but I was big and tall and looked older than my seventeen years. They took care of me and probably saved me from the Shore Patrol. I wanted to return the favor some day.

The next few days flew by. On July 24 workers from Permanente shipyard showed up to fix an ongoing problem with one of our ammunition lockers. Because the C.O. knew about my Kaiser shipyard experience, he decided I should be the one to show them the problem locker.

I gave them a copy of the C.O.'s Report of July 17 to the Vice Chief of Naval Operations.

> The after starboard ammunition locker is virtually useless in a tropical climate. On 15 April, the daily inspection disclosed that the temperature of this locker was 101 degrees at 1500 which was approximately 5 degrees higher than the ready boxes which were exposed to the sun . . . While the ship remained in tropical waters, the temperature registered over 100 degrees nearly every day. Mr. Noble, the chief engineer, found that a steam pipe without insulation . . . was so hot that it was uncomfortable to touch . . . Mr. Noble advised me that the blower in the magazine is wholly insufficient . . . It is recommended that (1) the live steam pipe be insulated, and (2) that the ventilation be improved and, if possible, a stronger blower be used.

Then, I showed them the locker, which we had just emptied, and watched as they insulated the steam pipe and installed a new blower. In three hours they were finished.

At the same time the stevedores were busy loading a partial cargo of drummed gasoline. During the loading approximately forty-five drums in leaking containers were taken aboard the *Currier*. These drums were set aside and plainly marked as leaking. The Coast Guard firewatchman brought this to the attention of the loading officer but they were nevertheless loaded in No. 5 hold. The next morning this was reported to the Port Director who inspected the hold but failed to find leakage, and so refused to order the defective drums unloaded. Consequently, the mariners were forced to adopt special fire precautions until the drums were discharged from the ship.

At 1830 on August 3 the *Currier* left the dock and moved out into the Bay to adjust compasses. We departed San Francisco on my mother's birthday, August 4, 1943, at 1340 hours

— a good omen, I thought. The C.O. set sea watches on Condition 3 as the ship got under way. I had many of the same feelings I'd experienced on the first trip as we slipped under the Golden Gate. Where to this time? Will we be as fortunate as on the last trip?

The weather was partly cloudy and cool with the usual fog bank lying offshore. The ground swells were still there and promised to spoil a few dinners before the night was over. The new men asked many of the same questions we asked just four short months earlier. Only now there were more "old salts" to provide the answers.

I'm told the Navy fleet got their news over each ship's PA system. As a news junkie, I envied them. The only time I really felt informed was when we were in the States. As far as the war was concerned, it was all happening in Europe according to the major newspapers and radio networks.

June/July 1943

* The Combined Chiefs of Staff officially inaugurate an around-the-clock bomber offensive against Germany on June 10.

* U.S. forces make six separate amphibious landings in the New Georgia Group in the Central Solomons between June 21 and August 15, 1943. As the first large scale land, sea, and air offensive in the Pacific, the campaign represents the turning point in the Pacific war.

* Allied forces under General Eisenhower's command began the invasion of Sicily on July 9.

* The first air raid on Rome is made by 158 B-17 Flying Fortresses and 112 B-24 Liberator bombers. (The bombing was preceded by the dropping of warning leaflets.)

Raiders cross one of the many rivers encountered during the New Georgia campaign. (Note that two of the men are armed with .55-caliber antiank rifles.) U.S. Marine Corps.

New Georgia Campaign, 1943. This Marine F4U "Corsair" fighter was the first U.S. plane to land at Munda Airfield after its capture and reconstruction by U.S. forces, August 1943. Pilot was Maj. R.G. Owens,USMC. National Archives.

* Italian dictator Mussolini is overthrown by a coup on July 25. Field Marshall Badoglio takes command of both the Army and government.

We pulled into Port Hueneme harbor, about 100 miles northwest of Los Angeles, California, on August 6 and dropped anchor at 1700. Sea watches were secured and port security watch was set. The next morning a pilot came aboard and we moved alongside one of the Seabee's docks. After Guadalcanal, it was like seeing old friends.

The Seabee stevedore gangs started loading our deck with landing barges in the afternoon. Of course, this started lots of

Aerial view of Port Hueneme, circa 1960s. Seabees.

speculation as to where we were going. Could it be the Solomons again? New Guinea? Where else?

The starboard liberty section, now twelve deep, had liberty that night so we headed for Ventura. The town of Port Hueneme was mostly military, not the best of prospects according to our stevedores. We were all completely broke by this time but we went anyway.

You can never be sure when you just might get lucky and meet a girl who can show you the town. The important thing was to always have bus fare back to the ship.

Ventura, about ten miles above Port Hueneme, is much like other California beach towns with palm tree-lined streets leading down to the beaches. We toured the beach, admired the boats in the Marina and enjoyed the sunshine and warm weather. But it seemed like all the girls were in school or at work. Our fate was to have a hamburger and coke, then return to the ship. Maybe we'd meet the girl of our dreams in the next liberty port.

On August 10, 1943 Jerome Anderson, Signalman 3/c, reported aboard for duty as replacement for Joseph Bergin, Seaman 1/c (SM striker), who was detached for duty elsewhere. Most of us old hands knew this was a sign of convoy activity ahead because signalmen are important for proper communication between ships. Armed Guard crews usually included one or two people with the communications skills of signalman and/or radioman. When ships are grouped together into convoys, the need for communication between ships becomes obvious. A Signalman deals in Morse code, semaphore, and international code flags; a radioman with radio. Unlike gunners, communications personnel take orders concerning most of their work directly from the civilian captain. For responsibilities relating to the Navy, they take orders from the Armed Guard officer. Communications personnel are also taught to operate the guns in case a gunner is injured. In addition, they serve as phone "talkers" for the gunnery officer during enemy action.[1]

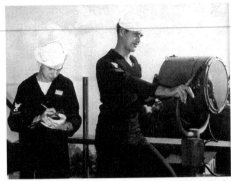

A signalman, right, mans the signal light while his assistant stands ready to write down the incoming message. U.S. Navy.

With the deck load of LCM's in place and the catwalk completed, sea watches were set and the *Currier* slowly moved out to sea at 2100 on August 10.

It was pitch black outside. We were sailing the first leg of this trip independent — meaning without escorts. As usual, we were at our General Quarters stations as we left port. There was the now-familiar nervous chatter on the phones between the new men.

The pilot's boat pulled alongside about 2130 but it was too dark to see his departure. Shortly thereafter the C.O. set Condition 3 and leg number two of trip number two began.

Our GQ gun drills each morning and evening were identical to Trip No. 1. The same can be said for the other daily and weekly routines at sea such as aircraft identification drills,

---

[1] Signalmen and radiomen also served in a little-known special Armed Guard service called Convoy Control meaning they were assigned to foreign flag merchant ships. In most cases, they sailed with ships' crews who often spoke no English, with the exception of the captain and senior officers, ate bad food, and suffered abominable living conditions. Sometimes, Armed Guard gunners were included in these special teams, sometimes not, depending on the ship's armament.

gunnery training, and, of course, cleaning and inspections of all kinds.

Some of the crew devised ways to vary the routine. Duane Curtis: "Lee Gibe, you know, he was from Tulare, California, he used to drive me crazy. He would get the victrola and go out on the deck, near my porthole, and play the record, 'No Letter Today,' over and over again. He was a good ole boy, an Okie, you know. Kinda like a gentle giant. You didn't ever want to get on his wrong side."

After two weeks at sea we introduced the new men to King Neptune and his court. We had just crossed the equator at 1106 on August 24 when the ceremony began. As usual, it involved heavy grease, rotten eggs, garbage, 80-pound fire hoses, naked Pollywogs, King Neptune, Queen Aphrodite, Davey Jones and some very enthusiastic "shellbacks" with paddles who initiated all "Pollywogs" into the King's "Royal Order of the Deep." Then the C.O. passed out Armed Guard Shellback cards to all hands, duly signed by King Neptune and witnessed by Lt. (jg) Robert L. Miller, USNR.

On August 26 at 1430, we held target practice. Sixty rounds were fired from each 20-mm at a target balloon released from the bridge of the ship. I was positive I hit the balloon but one of the aft gunners made the same claim. The C.O. called it a tie.

We released another balloon so the 3-inch gun crew could also get some practice. They fired five shells. The spotting results were:

* Shell #1: range 1600, scale 500, 25 yards short, deflection on.
* Shell #2: range 1700, scale 500, 25 yards over, deflection on.
* Shell #3: range 1750, scale 500, 10 yards short, deflection on.
* Shell #4: range 1800, scale 500, 50 yards short, ten yards right.
* Shell #5: range 1950, scale 496, 100 yards short, deflection on.

According to our C.O. we rated about a 3.6 on a Navy scale of 1 to 4 with 4.0 a perfect score. This was especially good considering the 3"/50 gun had no range finder or other modern

AUSTRALIA AND NEW GUINEA

Townsville, Australia. U.S. Navy LCVP lands on local beach during practice loading operations with the Army, 1943. Note Army 155-mm gun and prime mover in center. Naval Historical Center.

equipment found on fleet combatant ships. Everything, including the power, was manual.

We had aircraft identification every morning. Most of us had the enemy and our own planes down pat, but a few of the new men needed more work with the flash cards.

On August 29 we crossed the International Dateline and lost the 30th of August in the process.

The bow gun lookout spotted a coral atoll off the starboard bow on September 6 at 0600. The Skipper and our C.O. announced our first port of call would be Townsville, Australia. That coral atoll was the southern tip of the Great Barrier Reef. The whales and dolphins put on quite a show as we headed north in the calm protected waters inside the reef.

Most, if not all of us, had never heard of Townsville or the Great Barrier Reef but we had certainly heard great things about Australia and its beautiful women.

Townsville, is a relatively small city of about 75,000 in northern Queensland, a huge territory. General MacArthur's headquarters were in the territorial capital, Brisbane, some 600 miles to the south.

Sea watches were secured and port security watches set when we anchored. Everyone wanted to know the who and when regarding liberty but the C.O. said we'd have to wait for the Port Director's okay. Well, September 8th and 9th came and went and still no liberty. Both crews (Armed Guard and merchant marine) studied the shoreline carefully with binoculars hoping to spot a pretty figure but we were too far offshore for even the most far-sighted voyeur. We did identify some Army troops practicing beachings but nothing else.

WWII Convoy. U.S. Navy.

Lt. Miller mustered us each morning at 0700 for "morning orders and physical training," another term for calisthenics. Finally, liberty was scheduled on September 10 between 1200 and 2000 for the port section. I was still in the starboard section, of course. Later that night we got an earful of raves about the hospitable Aussies and their great beer. The next day, the starboard section got the bad news that there would be no more liberty in Townsville.

On September 12, 1943, sea watches were set on Condition 3 at 2140 as the ship weighed anchor and joined a convoy of eighteen ships with six escort vessels: average speed, eight knots. The convoy was made up of both old and new freighters ranging from new Liberty ships to an old Dutch-flagged Hog Islander.[2]

By now most of us were pretty sure we were heading for New Guinea. But still no word from the skipper or our C.O. We moved up the coast, protected by the Great Barrier Reef, amazed at the beautiful colors in the shallow water below. When we emerged from the safety of the reef *(continued on page 194)*

---

[2] So named because they were constructed at the Hog Island Emergency Shipyard in Philadelphia during World War I.

NEW GUINEA

New Guinea, the world's second largest island (after Greenland), lies immediately south of the equator. Its topography ranges from mangrove swamps in coastal zones to razorback ridges and towering mountains in the central regions.

When World War II began, the western half was a Dutch colony and largely unexplored; the eastern half was under British and Australian administration.

New Guinea and the Solomons marked the southernmost conquest of Japan's Pacific offensive in late 1941 and early 1942. Port Moresby, the colonial capital of Papua, and Milne Bay, about 200 miles southeast, were strategically important as advance bases for the Allies. The Japanese had to take them in order to cut the American-Australian lifeline.

When the Japanese began their Pacific offensive, most of Australia's troops were in North Africa fighting alongside the British Eighth Army. By March 1942, the north coast of Papua was dominated by the newly established Japanese stronghold at Rabaul on the eastern tip of New Britain and the Japanese moved into Lae and Salamaua unopposed, closing the Vitiaz Strait. The small Australian garrison withdrew to hold Port Moresby, preventing the Japanese from bombing Australia.

BATTLE OF MILNE BAY, 25 AUGUST-5 SEPTEMBER 1942

Located at the extreme southeastern tip of New Guinea, Milne Bay runs about twenty-five miles up into the land, is over seven miles wide at the entrance, and five miles wide at the head. It is flanked by dense jungle on both sides leading to mountains ranging to 4,000 feet in elevation. The bay's natural features and its position relative to New Britain and the Solomons made it an ideal airfield site and advance naval operating base for either side. It was a good staging point for offensive action.

Samuel Elliot Morison recorded the action in Milne Bay the summer of 1942:

> Because of the short and protected sea route, MacArthur beat the Japanese to Milne Bay. In early June 1942, a company of the 46th United States Army Engineers, a company of Australian infantry and an anti-aircraft unit, under the overall command of Colonel Frank L. Burns, USA, were sent up in the Australian SS *Islander*. Promptly they started work on an airfield for fighter and bomber planes on the Gili Gili plantation. A United States anti-aircraft battery was flown in on 19 August. Two or three days later, two KPM (the Dutch Koninklijke Paketvaart Maatschappij Company) boats and one British ship landed the 18th Australian Infantry Brigade, a veteran outfit from the Middle East, with the Australian overall commander, Major General Cyril

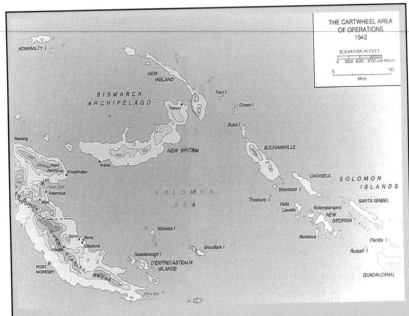

A. Clowes. This brought ground strength up to 8,500 Australians and some 1,300 Americans. Air forces at this time comprised thirty-four Australian P-40s (Kittyhawks) on the one completed airstrip two miles west of Gili Gili, but two other airstrips were under construction nearby (Gurney Field and Turnbull Field). Naval forces consisted of a few armed launches and auxiliary ketches.

On 24 August Japanes cruisers *Tenryu* and *Tatsuta*, destroyers *Tanikaze*, *Urakaze* and *Hamakaze*, and *SC-22* and *SC-24*, escorted transports *Kinai Maru* and *Nankai Maru* carrying over 1,900 tough Special Naval Landing Force troops against Milne Bay. A coastwatcher in the Trobriand Islands reported the convoy next day. By midnight 25 August, the Japanese convoy was well inside the Bay, anchored off Wanadala about nine miles east of the Australian headquarters at Gili Gili. About 1,200 men of the landing force poured ashore to fulfill their commander's orders to "kill without remorse." On Gili Gili airstrip the P-40s snarled aloft to cover several Flying Forts which arrived in the nick of time from their base on Cape York. The B-17s badly damaged transport *Nankai Maru*, then drove the other transport and her escorts out to sea, only partially unloaded. The Kittyhawks next turned their guns on the Japanese troops and supply dumps, giving the Australians opportunity to consolidate a line just east of the Kristan Brüder Mission.

Thenceforth the Battle of Milne Bay became an infantry struggle in the sopping jungle carried on mostly at night under pouring rain. After their first attack on the airstrip was thrown back with heavy losses, the Japanese attempted bringing in reinforcements by sea, but Allied planes caught and destroyed seven large barges at Goodenough Island where their crews were resting. Japanese air power, depleted by the Guadalcanal fighting and baffled by foul weather, could not help the stranded troops. Admiral Mikawa pushed through a relief convoy on 29 August, bringing 775 men under naval Captain

Minora Yano, who joined the troops already there in a furious night attack on Turnbull Field. At dawn on the 31st they withdrew, leaving 160 dead.

The Allies then took the offensive and pushed the dispirited Japanese back to KB Mission. Australians and natives mopped up the stragglers leisurely, snaring the last one in November.

Except for the initial assault on Wake Island, the Battle of Milne Bay was the first time that a Japanese amphibious operation had been thrown for a loss.[3]

BUNA-GONA CAMPAIGN, SEPTEMBER 1942-JANUARY 1943

When Gen. MacArthur finally took the offensive in the Solomons-New Guinea campaign, dubbed Operation Cartwheel, in late 1942, he began on the Kokoda Trail and at the Buna stand-off between the Japanese and a combined US-Australian force. As the Australians pushed the Japanese down the northern slopes, MacArthur ordered the U.S. troops on the beach at Pongani in Dyke Ackland Bay, twenty-five miles south of Buna, to move inland and join up with the Australians. Although bombed and strafed the entire way, the Americans finally met up with the Aussies on November 20 in the level fields between Dobodura and Soputa. There they built the airstrip that developed into the great Dobodura airfield.

Buna had no harbor and the sea approaches were difficult due to reefs that extended twenty-five miles out. Any reinforcements coming by sea had to be transported by small Dutch and Australian vessels manned by Papuans and Javanese. There were no LSTs, LCTs or LCIs in the South Pacific and merchantmen could not be expected to dodge enemy bombs by day only to be impaled on uncharted coral pinnacles at night.

The retaking of Buna, Gona, and Sanananda took six long months (much like Guadalcanal), three Allied divisions, and some of the most challenging ground fighting of the war.

The principal contribution of the U.S. Navy to the Buna-Gona campaign was a squadron of motor torpedo boats based on Milne Bay and later on Cape Nelson at Tufi, an ANGAU (Australia-New Guinea Administration Unit) station some 125 miles closer to the action. Every night PT boats went out searching for supply submarines and troops barges. They quickly became the nemesis of the enemy's wooden diesel-powered barges that traveled by night and hid out by day in sheltered coves or wooded creeks.

RAdm Morison closed out his coverage of the campaign with these thoughtful observations:

> With the collapse of Buna and Gona, as with the evacuation of Guadalcanal, the Allies in the Southwest Pacific suddenly found themselves recovering from a

---

[3] Morison, Samuel Elliott. *Breaking the Bismarck Barrier*, pp. 36-38.

Depth charge explodes astern of a speeding Higgins-type PT boat. Naval Historical Center.

year of defeat and retreat, from one illness and relapse after another. Now, they could hardly believe they had the enemy on the defensive--wondered if it were not an hallucination which Tojo would promptly dispel...

The loss of Buna-Gona and of Guadalcanal, occurring almost simultaneously, warned Japanese Imperial Headquarters that the war had entered a new and unsatisfactory phase. They decided to reinforce and strengthen the line Munda-Rabaul-Lae, to step up air bombing of recently won Allied positions, and to wait for the Allies to take the initiative.[4]

4 Morison. pp. 50-53.

(continued from page 190) into the Coral Sea and proceeded in a northeasterly direction, we were sure of our destination.

On September 16 at 1300, the C.O. secured sea watches and set the gun watch on Condition 3. We had arrived and anchored in Milne Bay, New Guinea.

While in Milne Bay, there were several air raid alerts. The general alarm for the first one came at 2235 on September 19. "Flags" Barela sprained his ankle in a collision with a mariner while hurrying to his battle station in the blacked-out ship. Barela was treated for three days with hot applications. There was a lesson learned from his mishap. On a blacked-out ship the watchwords are "Hurry Carefully" when responding to the annoying clanging of a general alarm.

While in port, alerts for air attacks usually came via radio from shore-based intelligence facilities based on radar findings, reconnaissance flights and/or coastwatcher reports. Usually we never knew what triggered an alert unless an air raid materialized. In this case, it turned out to be another "Washing Machine Charlie." He put-putted around for almost an hour then headed for home. To the new men on board it was "close but no cigar." They wanted a shot at the Japs but were also relieved when it didn't happen.

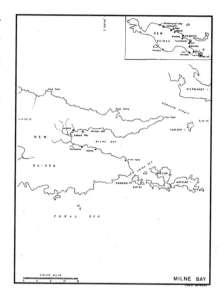

The naval base at Milne Bay was scheduled for development to provide facilities nearer the enemy and to relieve overcrowded Australian ports. Early Seabee construction included a major overhaul facility for

PBY Patrol Bomber, of a "Black Cat" Squadron takes off from its base at Samarai Island Milne Bay, New Guinea. Naval Historical Center.

Consolidated PBY-5 "Catalina" Flying Boat of a "Black Cat" night patrol squadron. National Archives.

PT boats, and a small seaplane base — the latter on the island of Samarai, southeast of Milne Bay. PBY "Black Cat" patrol bombers had just started using the new seaplane base when we arrived. They became one of our answers to "Charlie."

The entire ship's company — merchant marine and Armed Guard — were soon involved with stevedore work. Lt. Robert Holmes, acting Port Director, was understaffed both in his office and with stevedore gangs to work the cargo. He "requested" the merchant marine begin discharging the deck cargo into lighters on September 17. Little progress was made by September 20 and, because the equipment was badly needed ashore, our C.O. was directed to use any of the Armed Guard Crew not needed to discharge their military duties — e.g., to stand gun watches — to help unload the ship.

Our C.O. registered a detailed complaint with the Vice Chief of Naval Operations in his Voyage Report at the end of this trip:

> The unloading operations were inefficiently handled, the principal reasons for the undue amount of time consumed being as follows:
>
> (a) Insufficient barges in which to discharge the cargo.
>
> (b) Inefficient handling of the equipment and barges available.
>
> (c) Inefficient facilities ashore for discharging the barges, including insufficient equipment which was poorly handled.
>
> (d) Inefficient handling of the crews unloading the barges ashore.
>
> (e) Failure to assemble and make use of the barges taken off the *Currier*.
>
> (f) The fact that the cargo was consigned to two points in Milne Bay several miles apart, and the cargo was intermingled at Point Hueneme to such extent that the cargo consigned to one point could not be unloaded without also unloading the cargo consigned to the other point.

(g) Diversification of authority over equipment used to discharge the barges and the failure of those handling and
having authority over such equipment to cooperate and
coordinate their efforts.

The slow and inefficient handling of such cargo contrasted
sharply with the handling of this ship's cargo on the last trip when
a heavier cargo (almost 6700 tons) was discharged into lighters at
Guadalcanal Island in seven days, almost twenty-four hours of which
were lost during air raids.

I enjoyed the physical exercise although it was well over
100 degrees in the holds. I was one of a handful of men who
knew how to start up the D-8 Catapillars (CATs) — thanks to
my country boy roots. So one of my jobs was to start up and
maneuver the CATs to the center of the holds so they could be
raised with heavy cable slings and set down in the landing barges
alongside the ship.

There was no liberty in this port, nothing to see or do,
plus we had to remain on board in case of an air raid. Lt. Miller
devised a way to help break the monotony. He got Skipper
Hassell's okay to rig a mast and sail for one of our lifeboats so
he could go sailing. I never did figure out what would have
happened to our C.O. if there had been an attack while he was
out sailing. In any case, I was invited to join the C.O. with a
couple of other guys for an afternoon of sailing on my eighteenth birthday. It was really slow going but fun. We sailed part
way across the harbor at about one mile an hour. Then we
started up the outboard motor and went about a quarter of a mile
up a river. The Lieutenant then surprised us by breaking out a
few bottles of beer for my birthday.

On October 3, 1943 at 2110, the general alarm sounded
for another air attack. By the time we all groped our way to our
gun stations, donned our helmets and life jackets and reported in
to the C.O. on the bridge, we received word to secure.

Some of our crew had difficulty dealing with the demands of Navy life. Lt. Miller conducted mast (court) on October 8 with the following results:

Graham, T.W. found guilty of drunkenness and disorderly conduct on 11 September and assigned as punishment 30 hours of extra duty.

Cooper, H.L. found guilty of inattention to duty on 7 September (the day we arrived in Townsville) and assigned as punishment 30 hours of extra duty.

Caldwell, L.R. (my loader) was found guilty of inattention to duty on 7 September and assigned as punishment deprivation of all liberty ashore for a period of 30 days.

So our C.O. proved he was all business when need be. I was never able to get the full story out of Caldwell. He admitted he was in the wrong but thought our fearless leader — "Ahab," as he called him — went overboard with the punishment.

The last two days in Milne Bay, Army stevedores loaded 800 tons of crated engines needing repairs. Then on October 11, some twenty-five days after our arrival, we weighed anchor at 0900 and the ship pulled out of Milne Bay traveling independently: average speed 10.3 knots. Next stop: Townsville, Australia. We were there from 0700 October 14 to 2000 October 17. No liberty, no drunkenness, no problems.

After discharging the crated engines we sailed independently on October 17 for Sydney, Australia at a speed of 10.3 knots. In this case we were told the destination because we were traveling empty and there was no stop before Sydney.

Sydney was founded as a penal colony in 1788. It is Australia's oldest settlement. Its population surged during the Australian gold rushes of the 1850s and continued to grow until it had a population of some three million.

We took on a pilot and moved into the inner harbor with the able assistance of an Aussie tug. Approaching the Sydney Bridge, we were surprised to see it lined with people waving and shouting friendly greetings at us. As we passed under it, a few

Aerial view of Sydney Harbor from bridge to the Heads. Image Library, State Library of New South Wales.

even dropped flowers and/or notes inviting us to meet them on the wharf. What a welcome! We'd heard lots about our friendly allies down under, but never expected such a reception.

The starboard section had first liberty. We mustered at 1800 and were granted liberty until 0700 the next morning. Lee Gibe, Russ Haynes, and I headed for the gangway with but one thing in mind: to be the first bluejackets at the entrance to the wharf. Australians of all ages were lined up to meet us. It was unbelievable. Some offered ice cream and berries, others, various delicacies and still others offered home-cooked meals. We didn't want to appear ungrateful, but we had other priorities.

It was a good thing we started early because there was plenty of competition from both crews. Lee and I considered Russ our "bird-dog." He had the charm and sweet talk many women love, whereas Lee and I were more the quiet, country boy type. We had no sooner passed through the gate when Russ spotted three gals who seemed to be together and made his move. Soon, he waved us over to meet them. After introductions, we piled into a cab and headed for our new friends' favorite pub. Then we moved on to the Roosevelt night club. We received a

Dancing to Monte Richardson's Band at the Roosevelt night club. Image Library, State Library of New South Wales.

warm welcome but soon realized most patrons were officers. After a few dances and another beer we moved on. We learned later that the American's popularity with Australian women and our pay advantage of about fifty percent sparked several riots between Allied servicemen.

An Australian wit spoke for many diggers [Australian soldiers] when he penned these lines:

> To the yanks
> They saved us from the Japs
> Perhaps
> But at the moment the place is
> too yankful
> for us to be sufficiently
> thankful.

We got a little high on the Australian beer, about twice the alcoholic content of U.S. beer, then left and flagged down

Kings Cross section of Sydney, Australia.   Image Library, State Library of New South Wales.

another cab. The driver agreed to sell us a bottle of Gilbeys gin he just "happened" to have in the trunk, as we made our way to our new girlfriends' flat located in the infamous Kings Cross section of town. After chipping in to pay for the gin, we followed the gals up the stairs to their place.

Russ' gal, Liz, put on records while my new friend, Jane, got out glasses and Lee's date put out cheese and crackers. We drank, talked, and danced, well, sort of danced, until the gin was gone. Then Jane and I went for a walk. We were only gone ten or fifteen minutes but when we returned, the others were already in the bedroom.

Jane and I started making out on the sofa. She was about twenty-five and obviously more experienced than I. She knew what she wanted and wasn't afraid to ask for it. Just as we began making love, one of the roommates tapped me on the shoulder and said, "I say, ole boy, can you spare a rubber? I don't want no Yankee baby!"

Talk about *coitus interruptus*. After a few sidesplitting laughs that had us rolling on the floor, I dug the last Trojan out of my billfold and handed it to Jane's roommate. It was some night and our dates couldn't have been nicer. The next morning we made it back to the *Currier* with thirty minutes to spare.

Three or four days after we arrived in Sydney, I was watching the Australian stevedores, a.k.a., wharfies, load a bulk cargo of zinc ore for our return trip to San Francisco. Frank Gassen, one of our original gunners, sidled up to me and asked for a loan of $20. There was nothing unusual about that but when I asked him what he needed the money for, he wouldn't tell me. So I said, "Frank, if you can't tell me why you need it, then I'm not going to loan you the money."

Reluctantly he said, "I've fallen in love with this beautiful Australian redhead, Bill. It was love at first sight, just like in the movies, I swear. I want to marry her but there's a slight problem."

"What's the problem?" I asked.

Frank's answer really took me by surprise. "She needs some dental work and a complete set of false teeth, and I don't have the $150 to pay for them. She says if I really love her, I'll borrow the money. What do you think, Bill?" He added. "I know it sounds crazy but I've never felt like this about a girl before. Should I give her the money? If you loan me $20, I think I can raise the rest from the other guys. What do you say, friend?"

"Frank," I said, "she either really loves you or she plans to take you for a ride. Make the rounds of the other guys. You can count me in for twenty, if you can come up with the other $130."

He was serious about the redhead, no doubt about that. But when he had to tell her he couldn't raise the money, she dropped him like a hot potato. Frank took a lot of razzing before the trip was over but in the end decided we probably did him a favor.

Gibe, Haynes and I went on another liberty together before leaving Australia, only this time we did a day trip of the New

South Wales countryside west of Sydney by bus and on foot. The weather was great, the country beautiful, and the people most hospitable. Our country roots — Montana, Colorado, and Oklahoma/California — made us curious about Australian ranching and farming methods compared with our own.

One spread stands out in my memory. We stood by the road admiring the ranch when the owners pulled up and asked if they could help. I explained our country tour objectives and they insisted we come in for a visit. Before we knew it, dinner was on the table. Our conversation ranged from ranching to the status of the war up north in New Guinea and the Solomons. I will always remember their down-under hospitality.

My last liberty in Sydney was the best of all. Early in the evening, I met Gina, who was the Australian equivalent of a U.S. Navy WAVE, in a small, friendly pub. We hit it off at once and, after discussing our options for the evening, decided to see a movie. Before we parted that night we had enjoyed a simple but good pub meal and walked for miles. It was a particularly warm and beautiful night. We ended up on a Hyde Park bench looking up at the stars and talking for hours. Two lonely people, relaxed and comfortable with each other, and no one else to break the spell. We made love on the grass that night

Hyde Park, Sydney, New South Wales, Australia. Author.

as if we were made for each other. It was passionate and tender love, the kind one never really forgets. Then it was time to part. We retraced our steps until we found a taxi stand, embraced one last time and went our separate ways. As my cab pulled up to the wharf, dawn was breaking in the east.

The *Currier* was finally loaded with approximately 6,700 tons of zinc ore concentrate plus some tallow and eight liberty days later, on October 30, port watches were secured and sea watches set and we were underway for San Francisco, sailing independently at an average speed 10.2 knots.

One of the merchant marine officers was relieved of his duties shortly after we left Sydney. He made homosexual advances at just about everyone on the ship. He was even accused of forcing one of the youngest merchant crew members (age sixteen) to have sex with him. There was a "Kangaroo Court" held on the fantail of the ship one evening and a vote was taken as to whether or not he should be thrown overboard. Had the skipper not relieved him of his duties when he did, I think some of the old (and not so old) salts would have gladly tossed him in the ocean.

On November 5 we crossed the International Date Line. On November 7 we saw the first signs of a weather disturbance off our starboard bow. All guns were kept covered that night during General Quarters because of the inclement weather.

By November 9 the seas were shipping over the bow with such force, the C.O. moved the forward lookout to the flying bridge. The Pacific wasn't living up to its name and it seemed the farther north and east we steamed, the more violent the wind and seas.

Most discussions in the messroom centered around the question, are we in a gale or a storm, and more importantly, are we headed into a typhoon?[5]

The propeller was out of the water as often as it was in, causing constant "throttle watches" to keep the engine under

---

[5] According to the Naval Terms Dictionary, a typhoon or hurricane is defined as a destructive cyclonic storm with winds more than 65 knots.

control. Estimating the effectiveness of the propeller, the strength and direction of the current, wind and seas became a constant struggle. One twenty-four-hour run resulted in a net loss of ten to twenty miles according to the Chief Mate. Another estimate had us traveling seven miles forward and seven miles sideways that day. The seas ran extremely high and it seemed as if the miles traveled were mostly up, down and backwards.

On November 9 the weather got worse. The skipper ordered all lifeboats swung inboard and secured. We were now in fifty-knot whole gale winds making very slow headway through the heavy seas.

The next day I began to wonder if the ship might break in two. We all heard horror stories. While standing watch on the bridge, I was mesmerized by a small wire strung between the masts. One moment it was taut as a guitar string, the next, slack as a rope clothesline, as the ship pitched fore and aft in the heavy seas. The force and the size of the waves seemed to grow causing the ship to roll and pitch so violently that half the time the screw and rudder were out of the water and the bow was buried into a wall of green water. When the screw was out of the water, the ship shook like a Hawaiian hula dancer. Huge waves lifted the bow, ran along the hull, dropped the bow fifteen to twenty feet, lifted the stern until the screw and rudder were out of the water, then dropped the stern fifteen to twenty feet with a force that threatened to break the ship in half. Everyone was ordered to keep off the main deck because of the breaking seas.

During the five days it took to ride out the storm, we fought huge long-running seas with waves forty feet high and

---

A storm or meteorological disturbance, literally, has winds of 55-65 knots. A gale, or strong wind, is usually described as moderate (28-33 knots), fresh (34-40 knots), strong (41-47 knots), or whole gale (48-55 knots). Breeze, the general term for winds, runs anywhere from: 22-27 knots (strong), 17-21 knots (fresh), 11-16 knots (moderate), 7-10 knots (gentle), to 4-6 knots (light).

winds of whole gale force — at times estimated over sixty-five knots. On November 14 the weather finally moderated and at 1430 the Captain ordered the lifeboats swung outboard and secured — a good sign.

On November 23 we held target practice again.

On November 27 we could see the beautiful Golden Gate Bridge ahead as we passed by the Farallon Islands. The twenty-nine day nonstop trip from Sydney without seeing as much as an atoll was a record for me. Some ocean!

At 1630, the anchor was dropped in our home port, sea watches secured and port security watch set.

The next day the C.O. issued seventy-two-hour liberties to all gun crew members who would not be eligible for leave in December. That left seven of us on board to stand the port security watches. No problem. Besides, we had lots of fresh meat, produce, and dairy products to ease our pangs of envy.

On December 2, 1943, seven of us old-timers — part of the original gun crew — were detached from the *Currier* to the Armed Guard Center on Treasure Island for twelve-day leaves. (None of us had received any leave when we completed Boot Camp.) Lt. (jg.) R.L. Miller also "logged out" for leave to December 17. Marvin "Guns" Waterhouse was left in charge of the Armed Guard crew.

The news on the war was mostly positive.

August
The Allied forces complete the conquest of Sicily.

The Allies complete the occupation of New Georgia Island. (This was particularly gratifying since most of our Trip No. 1 *Currier* cargo was used in this invasion.)

September
Allied troops in New Guinea recapture Lae-Salamaua-Finschhafen. (Much of our Milne Bay cargo was used in this campaign.)

The Italian government surrenders unconditionally to the Allies. More than 700 ships deliver an Anglo-American invasion force to Salerno. British troops land at Taranto.

October

Approximately 100 U.S. prisoners of war on Wake are executed by Japanese Island Commander, Rear Admiral Sakaibara. (A reminder, if anyone needed it, of how ruthless the Japs could be!)

November

Allied forces invade Bougainville in the Northern Solomons on 1 November 1943, the final phase of the Solomons campaign.

The methodical destruction of Rabaul as an effective Japanese base begins in early November 1943 with attacks from the west (Gen. Kenney's land-based Bomb Group) and from the east (Adm. Halsey's new Essex and Independence class carriers).

U.S. Amphibious landings against Tarawa and Makin atolls in the Gilbert Islands begin on 20 November 1943.

Marine patrol crossing a river on a log "bridge," to get at Japanese snipers, soon after the Cape Torokina landings on Bougainville. Photo taken circa 1-7 November 1943. Naval Historical Center.

Bougainville Operation. A casualty is brought to the beach under fire, circa 1-9 Nov. 1943, during the early stages of the invasion of Cape Torokina.   National Archives.

President Roosevelt and Prime Minister Churchill meet in Tehran with Joseph Stalin — the first meeting of the Big Three. (It was revealed later that they conferred about the coming invasion of Europe.)

10

FROM HAWAII TO CALIFORNIA

O n December 2, 1943, the seven "old salts" in the *Currier* gun crew who had not received leave since joining the Navy were detached to Armed Guard Center, Pacific AGC(PAC) on Treasure Island. We secured our travel arrangements and leave papers before noon the following day and were on our way.

Two long days sitting up in a packed coach on a "milk train" carried me to Seattle, my mother and older sister's new city of residence. On my arrival Puget Sound was blanketed with a fog so cold that it penetrated my peacoat.

Mother and Doris made me one of my favorite home-cooked dinners the first night, meat loaf and mashed potatoes. They asked questions and listened to my stories with interest. A nice welcome home. But it didn't take me long to realize my life and interests were elsewhere and I felt guilty when the urge to return to TI and my shipmates set in after only three days.

SS Nathaniel Currier *"old salts" returning from shore leave. Top L-R: Kirby Girod, S 1/c; Russell Haynes, S 1/c; Bill McGee, S 1/c; Gerold Olsen, S 1/c; John McKay, S 1/c. Bottom L-R: Howard Bragy, GM 3/c; Frank Ewing, S 1/c; Lee Gibe S 1/c. U.S. Navy.*

On December 16 I reported back to TI. Two days later our leave contingent reported back aboard the *Currier.*

There was no liberty on the 19th, and on the 20th the Skipper and our C.O. received our routing instructions and sailing orders.

The *Currier*'s Official Log-Book carried an interesting last minute crew change on December 20.

—— left vessel on Dec. 15 at about 6:00 p.m. and up to Dec. 20th at 2:00 p.m. had not returned. Robert Riboli, Oiler was signed on as a replacement. —— declared to be a deserter.

[signed]   D.W. Hassell, Master

Scuttlebutt had it the deserter voiced his preference for a ship without munitions cargo. Had he been a member of the

U.S. Navy, the Code of Military Justice calls for a Court Martial and, if found guilty, a long-term prison sentence or even execution.

The merchant marine added two men to the Steward's Department for this trip giving a total of forty-six in the crew. The U.S. Navy Armed Guard Unit now numbered twenty-seven. Our outbound cargo, loaded at the Naval Supply Depot in Oakland, was munitions, beer, whiskey and miscellaneous military cargo.

On December 21 the ship got underway with sea watches set on Condition 3. We were part of a small two-ship convoy plus one escort vessel. We probably earned the escort because we were very heavily loaded with ammunition.

Shipboard life during our off time had its limitations. We didn't have movies or radio entertainment like the Navy fleet but that didn't bother us. There were always card games, checkers, dominoes, reading, bull sessions, and practical jokes.

It is said, "Games without gambling are like food without salt," and gambling was a way of life for some of the men. Any card games — bridge, pinochle, casino, hearts, gin rummy —

Naval Supply Center, Oakland, Calif. Naval Historical Center.

had bets on the outcome. Then there was the occasional anchor pool bet. Poker was very big, but blackjack or dice games were popular, too. Some poker games kept going with the same players for days, even weeks, at a time. You simply excused yourself to go stand watch and rejoined the game later.

Prior to this trip, I limited my game playing to checkers and dominoes because, I knew nothing about cards or gambling. Like smoking, drinking and "wild, wild women," they were off-limits, according to the doctrine of my church. However, since I was already violating some of these rules, I figured I might just as well learn how to play poker. "Sparks" Churchon, loaned me his book of "Hoyle" (*Foster's Complete Hoyle, The Encyclopedia of All Indoor Games*) and said "Here, read up on the game, then we'll play some practice hands."

Hoyle was just what I needed. In addition to forty-some pages on poker, it had "how to " information on practically all the other card games, too.

December 25th was my second Christmas in the Navy. The cooks prepared a delicious roast turkey dinner with all the trimmings, topped off with a choice of pumpkin or mincemeat pies. We listened to Christmas carols on our windup phonograph but that seemed to make everyone homesick.

We arrived in Pearl Harbor on December 29, 1943 and docked at 1815 — too late for liberty. The following morning was a shock for most of us. Oil still floated across the harbor and under the docks. The USS *Oklahoma* lay bottom up with some four hundred bodies still trapped inside. She had capsized on December 7, 1941 and we learned that trapped sailors were still heard tapping on bulkheads as late as December 24th, seventeen days later. What a ghastly price to pay for our national freedom!

The port section mustered the morning of December 30 and was granted liberty to 1730.

On December 31, New Year's Eve, the starboard section had its first Hawaiian liberty. Before going ashore, Lt. Miller warned us it would take a good hour to reach downtown

HAWAII

Following the Japanese attack on December 7, 1941, Hawaii was considered to be a war zone, an imminent target of invasion, and a potential refuge for enemies. The Act of Congress that had made Hawaii a territory allowed declaration of martial law in case of imminent threat of invasion. The Army took over the islands. Military officials appropriated more than 300,000 acres of land, from pineapple plantations to school buildings and campuses. The military ordered a strictly enforced nightly blackout and the arrest of anyone carrying lighted cigarettes, cigars, or pipes during the blackouts. They also set a 6 P.M. to 6 A.M. curfew for anyone not on official business and drew up intelligence reports on most Hawaiians. Everyone over the age of six was required to carry an identification card. Anyone caught without a card was subject to arrest.

One of the first notable U.S. war songs was "Remember Pearl Harbor" (words by Don Reid, music by Sammy Kaye and Don Reid). It was copyrighted a few days after the attack.

Let's Remember Pearl Harbor as
    we go to meet the foe.
Let's Remember Pearl Harbor as
    we did the Alamo. . .

The song title became a Pacific battle slogan, a rallying cry in politicians' speeches and in exhortations to war workers.

Aerial view of Pearl Harbor, Territory of Hawaii, October 1941, five weeks before sneak Japanese attack. Naval Historical Center.

Honolulu by bus and even longer for the return trip. It wasn't far but you couldn't be sure when a bus had room for you. Of course, taxis were available, but they were too expensive.

Lee Gibe, Russ Haynes, Gerry Olsen, and I clambered down the gangplank at 0900 and headed for the nearest bus stop just as the stevedore gangs started unloading our ammunition cargo.

Just about all sailors want the same thing on liberty: wine, women, and song, or the equivalent thereof. While on the way into Honolulu, several old timers suggested we head for Canal Street, "the best bet for bars and whorehouses." Alvin Kernan described Honolulu liberty in *Crossing the Line-A Bluejacket's World War II Odyssey*:

> A few minutes were spent in the New Congress Hotel, where the "French line" went up the long wooden stairs on the right, and the "old-fashioned line" ascended the left staircase. (Such sophistication? What could the Old Congress have been like?) Going once through each line — take your choice of the order — was considered a sign of true manhood, and the really virile went right back into the line rather than getting a few drinks before returning to the service of Venus.

This was followed by the unpleasant but necessary memory of the "Pro Station" where you squirted some stinging liquid up your uretha, washed up, and then topped it off with antiseptic cream. VD (venereal disease, today known as STD or Sexually Transmitted Disease) was no laughing matter and most sailors gladly took preventive measures to avoid it in those pre-penicillin days. Between honky-tonk stops, we all had our picture taken with the same beautiful Hawaiian girl.

Afterward, we enjoyed a cold Primo beer while listening to Glenn Miller on the jukebox. A brawl broke out between some sailors and

This same wahine posed with thousands of sailors. Author.

marines. Gibe wanted to join in, he loved a good fight, but cooler heads prevailed.

Meanwhile, I had other plans. I saw a tattoo parlor a block or so up the street and decided to go back for another piece of "body art" for my right arm. As foolish as this sounds today, tattoos were an accepted sign of a macho, regular navy man back then. There were no takers when I invited the others to join me, so I doubled back to the parlor, made my selection, a dagger and shield decorated with "Old Glory," and watched as the cute little tattoo artist needled me with red and blue ink. This time it was covered with gauze and a legitimate bandage, unlike the parlor in Tijuana, Mexico.

I was back at Pearl by 1700 having shared a bus with a bunch of bedraggled, drunk and noisy sailors from the fleet. It's a good thing I arrived when I did because my shipmates were in a shouting match with the marine guards over Gerry Olsen's lost liberty card. Since I was cold sober and vouched for him, they made an exception, and let him in.

Alvin Kernan summed up wartime Honolulu liberty with these words: "Weighed soberly, Honolulu liberty was not much, but it had the effect of making us glad to be, as sailors always are, aboard ship again."

"Sparks" Churchon brought me up to date on recent news:.

December

U.S. troops make a preliminary landing on the Arawe Peninsula of New Britain and on December 26 the main Allied assault of New Britain begins with the First Marine Division of Guadalcanal veterans, going ashore at Cape Gloucester.

On the home front, the Selective Service announces a policy of not drafting men who were fathers before December 7,1941.

The U.S. Army is ordered to take over the operation of American railroads to forestall a strike.

We were all relieved when we saw the last pallet of ammunition lowered to the dock. On January 5 the ship got underway sailing independently; average speed, 10.74 knots.

I spent a few hours on the return voyage on homework. First, I reviewed my Gunner's Mate training manuals, then I studied Spark's book of "Hoyle" on poker. I also watched a few more poker games in both the mariners' and gunners' messes and finally sat in on my first poker game with some of the gun crew. It was a penny-ante game with a five-cent limit. Believe it or not, I actually won a few bucks. The others called it beginner's luck. But, from that point on, I knew I was hooked.

According to all of the experienced players, the best poker player on the *Currier* was the bosun, Bernie Agostini. He ended up with most of the money on the ship and lent it back to the poker players or any one else who needed extra cash. Later, when the crew was paid off, "Boats" stood at the end of the mess table with his list of IOUs, collecting from every shipmate who owed him money.

On January 12 we ran into rain which continued the rest of the way into San Francisco. All the guns were kept covered. On January 13 at 0920 the ship was heavily shaken by either an underwater explosion or by striking a submerged object, we never learned which. Immediately afterwards a destroyer and a submarine (both friendly) were sighted by our bridge lookout at about 1,200 yards, relative bearing 315 degrees. Visibility at the time was about 1,500 yards. Except for the above incident, the voyage was entirely routine. (We never did find out what that "Tin Can" and Sub were up to.)

On January 14 at 0830 we had a special work detail prepare for an inspection of all guns, quarters, heads and material by the San Francisco Port Director. At 1230 the starboard section mustered and liberty was granted until January 15 at 1100.

Then, on January 15, a special four-day liberty expiring on January 19 was granted to twelve men. That meant the rest of us would go without liberty until they got back. On January

19 eight more men received four-day liberty passes good until 1100 on January 23.

Now it was time for me to say good-bye to my shipmates and the *Currier*. The hernia that kept me out of the Marines on my seventeenth birthday was bothering me, particularly when I lifted something heavy such as a can of ammunition. I decided to follow doctor's orders and let the Navy fix it. On January 19, 1944 I was detached from the *Currier* and assigned to AGC(PAC). My orders called for me to report to the U.S. Naval Hospital on Treasure Island, practically next door to the Armed Guard Center, the following day.

After the war, the *Currier* was eventually transferred to the Reserve Fleet, Site 4, in Mobile, Alabama and scrapped in December 1971 at Panama City, Florida.[1]

After reporting in to the Armed Guard Center I found an empty sack and locker, stowed my gear, and headed for the Treasure Island library. Lt. Miller arranged for me to take the Gunner's Mate third test on the 20th before checking into the hospital.

The next morning I was the first in line for the test. Then, after lunch, I checked out of the Center and into the hospital. The preparation, anesthesia, and surgery procedures were similar to my appendectomy in Boot Camp. The main difference from a patient's perspective was that they kept you in bed for three weeks instead of two. The only consolation was the nurses and WAVES seemed to be prettier than ever . . . or was it the year at sea?

As more and more of the Women's Auxiliary Reserve (WAVES) were added to the hospital complement, a separate building was constructed to house them and designated WAVE Hospital Corps Quarters. The original assumption was that WAVES would primarily perform clerical and administrative tasks, but due to manpower shortages, more than 200 shore jobs opened up to women, and they soon made their presence felt in

---

[1] Sawyer, L.A. and W.H. Mitchell, *The Liberty Ships*.

U.S. Naval Hospital, Treasure Island, San Francisco, Calif. U.S. Navy

Men and women in White. U.S. Navy

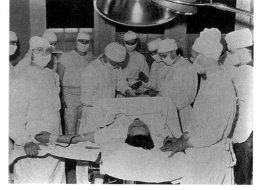

positions ranging from gunnery instructors and aviation machinists mates, to photographers and meteorologists, and, of course, hospital corps personnel.

The TI hospital had its lighter side, too, providing comfort and entertainment for both bedridden and ambulatory patients. Frequent visits from stars of stage and screen helped many a sailor get back on his feet.

I was as weak and unstable as a newborn colt after three weeks on my back, but a combination of youth and physiotherapy took care of that. Anytime I felt sorry for myself, all I had to do was look around at the men shot up in the war to realize I was the lucky one.

On February 19 I was transferred to the Navy's convalescent hospital in Santa Cruz about seventy miles south of San

Sonja Henie visits the wards. U.S. Navy.

Francisco. What a pleasant surprise. It looked more like a luxury resort hotel — which I learned it was before the Navy took it over. Furthermore, it was only a short walk to the beach and, instead of the usual hospital ward, I was assigned a semi-private room.

One of the few good things I remember about being hospitalized was the easy access to the news:

January/February 1944

Soviet forces open an offensive to relieve the German siege of Leningrad.

U.S. troops make an amphibious landing behind German lines at Anzio, just south of Rome, in an attempt to encircle German forces in Central Italy. Fierce fighting takes a heavy toll on both sides.

Eight hundred U.S. heavy bombers strike Frankfurt in the largest American raid yet made against Germany.

The U.S. Amphibious forces continue a step-by-step sweep into the Central Pacific with the 31 January invasion of Kwajalein atoll and the 17 February landings on Eniwetok atoll in the Marshall Islands.

Kwajalein Operation, January-February 1944. LST-476 and LST-479 land vehicles and supplies amid the Roi Island beach clutter and wreckage, circa early February 1944. National Archives.

Eniwetok Operation. Marines of the 22nd Regiment prepare to advance on Japanese 400 yards up the beach, on 19-22 February 1944. National Archives.

The destruction of Rabaul on New Britain is completed by U.S. Carrier-and land-based aircraft. The Nips abandon this valuable air base in February.

U.S. Army Air Corps and RAF commence massive heavy bomber attacks on German aircraft production facilities.

The Japanese seem more and more willing to sacrifice their pilots on suicide missions known as kamikaze attacks.

The Selective Service begins review of the occupational draft deferments of 5 million men in response to a shortfall of recruits.

Kamikaze pilot of Jap Zeke unsuccessfully tries to maneuver his plane onto deck of USS Missouri (BB-63) on 25 April 1944. He ends attack splashing into sea. Naval Historical Center.

There was no longer any doubt we would win the war, it was simply a matter of when. From a personal point of view, I wanted to ship out as soon as possible. I didn't enlist to spend time on the beach.

I spent a little more than four weeks in Santa Cruz, then was transferred to yet another naval hospital, this time in Shoemaker, California east of Oakland, "for further treatment and hospitalization." Finally, on May 3,1944, I was transferred back to AGC(PAC) by USNH Shoemaker. My service record simply states, "To duty. Treatment completed." What a relief.

As I was leaving Shoemaker, I was told why the "Docs" were so reluctant to release me. They were told that the Armed Guard didn't even have a pharmacist mate on board ship, let alone doctors, so they wanted to be doubly sure I was OK before clearing me for sea duty.

While reporting to the Center, I was officially informed I had passed my Gunner's Mate third-class test with a 3.7 grade, promotion effective July 1, 1944.

Meanwhile, the war continued:

March/April 1944

Gen. Orde Wingate's long-range penetration groups begin landing behind Japanese lines in Central Burma.

The Joint Chiefs issue orders for Gen. MacArthur and Adm. Nimitz to begin a dual advance to the Luzon-Formosa area by February 1945.

German troops occupy Hungary.

Soviet troops open an offensive in the Crimea and recapture Odessa.

A new Twentieth Air Force is activated under the command of Gen. Henry "Hap" Arnold, head of the Army Air Force, to direct strategic bombing operations against Japan.

The following morning, I met with the Center's Chief Gunner's Mate. He suggested I take a two day refresher course on the 5"/38 gun as most new Victory class ships had them on the fantail. Maybe he knew something at the time but wasn't telling, because, sure enough, my next ship turned out to be a Victory.

11

AMMO DISASTERS

O n the morning of May 6, 1944 our newly assembled gun
crew milled around outside the entrance to the Armed
Guard Center on Treasure Island, sea bags in hand. It
was early and there was a damp chill in the air. None of us
wanted to be kept waiting by our new leader, Lester Hayes Null,
GM 2/c, but wait we did, for almost thirty minutes. When he
finally showed up, his Southern drawl was even slower than his
punctuality. As the leading petty officer for our group, his orders
were to lead us to a new Victory ship in Portland, Oregon, providing, of course, we could catch our train which was due to
leave Oakland in forty minutes. Thanks to a patient Navy bus
driver who waited with us, we arrived at the train station with
three minutes to spare.

Our railroad car, called a "cattle car" by most servicemen, looked like a boxcar with stacked bunk beds. The oblong
side windows appeared to be the only feature different from a

boxcar. It made us feel like we were back in Boot Camp. We shared the car with about twenty-five other Navy men heading for the Northwest.

The trip itself was uneventful. Some guys played cards, others read and still others snoozed the miles away. I caught up on the news in the San Francisco papers.

April 1944

Allied troops land at Aitape and Hollandia in New Guinea.

Hollandia, New Guinea Operation. Troops of the 7th Amphibious Force land on a beach at Tanamerah Bay, 22 April 1944. This LCM carries a tank, armed with a short gun, in addition to the infantry. Man in right center has a Thomson sub-machine gun. Naval Historical Center.

Frank Knox, Secretary of the Navy, dies of a heart attack. He is succeeded by Under Secretary James V. Forrestal.

The U.S. Office of Price Administration ends most meat rationing.

We pulled into Portland the next morning, piled into a U.S. Navy canopied bobtail truck, and were driven to the ship where we reported aboard. I soon learned several interesting facts about our new home.

Built by the Oregon Shipbuilding Company, of Portland, Oregon, the *Yugoslavia Victory* was powered by an Allis-Chalmers engine. Classified as a VC2-AP3 Freighter, she measured 7,608 gross tons, 4,555 net tons and displaced 15,200 tons when loaded. Owned by the War Shipping Administration, she was chartered

SS Yugoslavia Victory *Armed Guard Crew, May 1944. Chambers, John Robin, GM 3/c; Dylina, Joseph John Jr., SM 3/c; Knecht, Martin Jerome, GM 3/c; McGee, William Lionel; Medearis, Freemen; Mendoza, Eugene Mike; Miller, Donald Jean; Milligan, Frank Milford; Montoya, Bennie; Mozzine, William Joseph; Muller, Theodore; Munguia, Ernesto; Neal, Hayden Gorham; Nelson, George Milton; Nogales, Alvaro Castillo; Norton, Ross; Nowak, Phillip James; Null, Lester Hayes, GM 2/c; Olinger, William Arthur; Olson, Clarence Dobble; Orloski, James Ralph; O'Rourke, Lawrence Thomas; Ortiz, Enrique Rodrigues; Owens, David Leroy; and Pederson, Richard Niels. All men are Seaman first-class unless otherwise noted. U.S. Navy*

to the Coastwise Steamship Company (PFE Line). Her armament consisted of eight 20-mm guns, one 3"-50 on the bow, and a 5"-38 on the stern. Commanded by Clyde F. Bryant, her merchant marine crew numbered fifty-six: twenty-one in the deck department, nineteen in the engineering department and fifteen in the steward's department. Our U.S. Navy Armed Guard Unit was twenty-six strong, commanded by Gilbert J. Rottman, Lt. (jg.), USNR, with twenty-four gunners and one communications seaman.[1]

I ended up with the Pointer's job on the 5" gun on the fantail — exactly what I wanted. Because of my gun's location,

---

1 Sources: Naval Armed Guard Voyage Report and Smooth Log; Port Directors' Supplementary Report of Supplies and Personnel; Arming Merchant Vessels Report; and Official Log-Book, Merchant Marine of the United States, SS *Yugoslavia Victory.*

SS Yugoslavia Victory *in wartime gray.* *Credit: Puget Sound Maritime Historical Society.*

I was assigned a bunk right below it in the poop deckhouse, no stumbling along a catwalk in the dark during GQ for me this trip.

By the time everyone learned where their battle stations and quarters were located and unpacked their sea bags into metal lockers, the day was almost gone. Nonetheless, the C.O. met with the Petty Officers and conducted a "Title B" inventory of all guns, telescopes, ring sights, magazines, binoculars, foul weather gear, gas masks, recreational gear, and so forth, with our help. This was particularly important with a new ship because key items were often missing.

On May 8 we received our ammunition for the voyage and stowed it in the magazines below deck. The next day we loaded the 20-mm magazine drums, then loaded and secured the ready boxes alongside each guntub. Following that we stowed twenty-four AA (Anti-Aircraft) projectiles and cartridges at the 5"/38 readybox on the stern and twenty-four AA shells at the 3"-50 readybox on the bow.

We were tied up to a pier in downtown Portland — one of the great liberty towns on the west coast — without liberty. Preparations continued as we connected and tested all the sound-powered battle phones. Then on May 10 the gun crew assisted in preparing the ship for degaussing.

Eventually Lt. Rottman heard from the petty officers that the sailors were unhappy, because at 1600 we were mustered on the fantail, liberty sections "A" and "B" were established, and section A was granted liberty from 1700 to 2400. Unfortunately, I was in Section B.

The next day port security watch was secured and Condition 3 sea watch was set as we sailed down the Columbia River. There would be no liberty for the B section that night.

We took on a pilot for the trip into Puget Sound and by 1300 were tied up at the ammunition dock in Muckilteo, Washington, thirty-some miles northwest of Seattle. There we watched for the next seven days as the stevedores filled our holds with ammo. We were occupied with gun drills, quarters and gun inspection by a Lieutenant from the Port Director's office and general quarters drills. But we had no liberty in Muckilteo.

Our primary cargo consisted of aircraft bombs. According to one of the Coast Guard officers supervising the loading, "The Navy and Army Air Force use a variety of bombs with high explosive, fragmentation, chemical, and incendiary warheads." High explosive bombs ranged in size from 100 pounds to 2,000 pounds; fragmentation or antipersonnel bombs came in twenty-, twenty-three-, and thirty-pound sizes. We also carried chemical bombs filled with phosphorus and titanium for producing dense white smoke and incendiary bombs weighing up to fifty pounds, usually packaged in clusters, to break apart over the target, each to ignite a fire.

We shifted to Seattle, Washington, where we docked at Pier 37. The C.O. took half the gun crew with him to the Exchange Building for all-day instruction on 20-mm gun and magazine assembly. School never seemed to end in the military. We still had no liberty.

Finally, on May 21 at 1200, Section B was granted liberty until May 22 at 0700.

It was only a few months since I was home on leave, so mother was both surprised and pleased to hear my voice when I called from the pier.

After dinner the conversation dragged so I excused myself and returned to the ship. I loved my family, but we seemed to have less and less in common. Besides, knowing how much it hurt mother, I still couldn't bring myself to smoke or drink in front of her.

Meanwhile, the mail brought me some good news: 1) My Gunner's Mate third rating would be effective July 1 with a big $12 raise to $78 a month, and 2) I was awarded a Commendation "for outstanding service as a member of the Armed Guard Unit aboard the SS *Nathaniel Currier* during action against Japanese aircraft off Guadalcanal on 16 June 1943."

On May 23 and 24 the stevedores finished topping off the holds with beer and general military cargo — filler on top of the ammo. Then they closed the hatches and added a deckload of Army trucks and jeeps. Finally they installed a catwalk.

On May 24 we tried leaving the dock but discovered the ship was grounded, so we had to wait until high tide. At 1815 we got away and calibrated the radio direction finder and compensated the ship's compasses. Finally at 2130 we set sail independently pursuant to Port Director routing instructions at an average speed of 15.7 knots.

The following morning while at battle stations, the C.O. informed us we were headed for Hawaii. That brought cheers over the phones but we still wondered why he was so stingy with liberty.

One advantage to a Victory ship was its relatively fast speed (50% faster than a Liberty). Hauling ammunition was safer as submarines couldn't keep pace with us while submerged. Still the danger of riding on top of a load of munitions was always there. As one shipmate put it, "Maybe they should issue us parachutes!"

I sat in on a poker game the third night out with five other guys in the gun crew. Joe Dylina, Signalman third-class, won all the money. We were all so broke, some of the guys borrowed money just to play. As for me, I lost a couple of bucks and chalked it up to experience. The merchant crew had their own game going next door only it lasted until breakfast. It was called pot limit — meaning you could bet up to the total amount in the pot — much bigger stakes than our little penny-ante, nickel limit game. But then they made a lot more money, too.

The crew on the *Yugoslavia Victory* was fifteen men larger than that of the *Nathaniel Currier* — three more in the deck department, six more in both Engineering and the Steward's departments. We carried a Junior 3rd Mate and a Second and Third Radio Operator in the Deck Department and had three licensed Junior Engineers in Engineering.

On May 25 we conducted structural test firings of the 5"/38 and 3"/50. After examining the foundation and bolts holding down the guns, conditions were rated satisfactory.

We soon experienced bad weather so the bow lookouts were moved to the bridge. The foul weather persisted all the way to Honolulu. But, the weather didn't dampen the spirits of those on watch. All hands were looking forward to Hawaii — especially the new men who fantasized about hula girls in little grass shacks.

On May 27 the 20-mm crews fired a few test rounds. The C.O. was satisfied. The Skipper, Clyde Bryant, held a fire and boat drill at 1630. On Sunday, 28 May, the C.O. conducted church services on the fantail for gun crew members not on watch.

We conducted a General Quarters drill with the merchant crew on May 29 and they were given instructions at their battle stations.

On May 30 we took a pilot aboard and slowly moved into Honolulu's harbor to Pier 19.

Later that night some of the crew were found drinking part of the cargo (beer). According to the *Yugoslavia Victory*'s Official Logbook:

> While vessel was alongside Pier #19 discharging Army cargo consisting in part of cased beer, Chief Officer and Captain were called and notified by 1st Lt. Everett Weston, Army Officer of the

day in charge of Army MP guards stationed on board, that one of his MPs, Private Max Reiser, had caught members of the ship's crew in the Bo'sun's locker drinking beer stolen from the cargo; seven empty cases and two full ones involved.

Upon investigation, Captain and Chief Officer found members of the crew in an Army truck on the dock, being taken to Honolulu Police Station . . .

Captain posted fifty dollars bail for each man and the men were returned to the ship and their duties.

On May 31 at 0845 Ensign White from the Port Director's Office came aboard to inspect the ship. We were pleased with grades he gave us: Guns - 4.0; Material - 4.0; Quarters - 3.9; and Discipline - 3.9. Late in the afternoon we received long-awaited mail. We also got paid, this was sometimes referred to as: "the eagle shit!"

We had four more days in Honolulu with liberty on alternate afternoons between 1200 and 1800. Pier 19 was a far better location than Pearl Harbor because everything was within walking distance. There was no long bus ride to eat up precious time.

I ate my first charcoal-broiled steak in a little tin-roofed restaurant not far from the famous Royal Hawaiian Hotel on Waikiki Beach. On the "B" section's first liberty, five of us went to the restaurant and had an unforgettable early dinner. I can still see and smell it: a big twelve-ounce sirloin steak, medium-rare, charred outside, pink inside, topped with a generous pat of butter and a sprinkling of parsley. A huge Idaho baked potato sits beside it on the plate and on the side a garden-fresh salad. I've had a lot of steak dinners, but none ever topped that. I'm not sure why, maybe, because it was the first.

Before heading back to the ship we had just enough time to wander through the Royal Hawaiian, also known as "the Pink Palace." We were told it was taken over by the Navy's submarine service for the duration of the war.

The Honolulu stevedores were fast. They had the ship unloaded in four days. Of course, they worked around the clock. The last two days in port, June 4-5, we took on a load of bulk raw sugar, tons of it. It looked like brown sugar and carried a sickly-sweet smell that permeated the ship. Every hold was filled with it.

On June 5 the Skipper and our C.O. attended a Port Directors conference, picked up our sailing orders and routing instructions, and at 1800 we sailed for the San Francisco Bay Area.

Honolulu radio stations reported the invasion of Europe shortly after we left Oahu. It was great news and boosted morale throughout the ship. Otherwise the return trip was uneventful.

Waikiki Beach, Honolulu, Oahu Island, T.H. Two soldiers on leave watch swimmers from the grounds of the Royal Hawaiian Hotel. Diamond Head Crater is in the distance, c. 1944. U.S. Army.

The C.O. set Condition 1 at 2000 for our approach to San Francisco. As we passed under the beautiful Golden Gate at 2230 we saw the lights all around the Bay. Proceeding up the North Bay to the Carquinez Straits and the Port of Crockett, California, we docked at the C&H (California and Hawaiian) Sugar pier. At exactly 2400 we secured Condition 3 and set the port security watch. It marked the end of another successful maiden voyage — and our first on a Victory ship.

It took four days to discharge the sugar. Each section had two liberties while we were there but, since there wasn't much going on in Crockett, most of us stayed aboard and saved our money for the next liberty port — hopefully San Francisco.

On June 15, 1944 the ship shifted from Crockett to Pier B of the Naval Supply Depot in the East Bay.

June 16 marked exactly one year after my first enemy action at Guadalcanal.

The following day I did something I'd been wanting to do for more than a year: hike to the top of Twin Peaks in San Francisco. I was sure that on a clear day the view was spectacular. Taking a ferry across the bay to the foot of Market Street, I asked at the Ferry Building for directions.

"Take a street car up Market Street to the end of the line; transfer to a Market Street bus and continue until you come to Twin Peaks Boulevard. From there it's an uphill hike of about one mile: elevation gain about 900 feet."

Twin Peaks Boulevard was a narrow residential street with several hairpin curves. The view improved at each turn, especially in the direction of the East Bay. Morning fog partially obstructed my view of the Pacific, but quickly burned off.

I spent a couple of hours on a grassy slope admiring the view and the beautiful day. It was so peaceful and quiet it was hard to believe there was a war on. I decided then and there to make San Francisco home should I ever decide to live in a big city.

Later I caught up on the major developments in the war:

May/June

An ammunition explosion involving several LSTs occurs in the West Loch of Pearl Harbor on 21 May.

Allied troops land on Biak Island, New Guinea.

San Francisco from Twin Peaks looking down Market Street. Man-made Treasure Island is to the left of the Bay Bridge. The Oakland hills are in the distance. U.S. Navy.

U.S. Army troops enter Rome on 4 June.

The largest Amphibious Landing in history, code named Operation Overlord, lands U.S., British and Canadian troops on the Normandy coast of France on 6 June, 1944, the beginning of the Allied Campaign in Europe. It comprises 4,000 invasion ships, 600 warships, 10,000 planes and more than 175,000 Allied troops. It takes four days of fierce fighting and heavy casualties on both sides before the two main beachhead armies are joined. (Despite the heavy casualties, the Allies send the Germans backwards toward Germany and a million Allied troops are soon on the Continent.) It was a little easier to understand why Admirals Halsey and Nimitz, as well as General MacArthur, had to go slower than they wished. We had a shortage of ships due to Operation Overlord.

On June 28 at 2000 all liberty stopped and at 0820 the following day the *Yugoslavia Victory* set sail on her second voyage with general military cargo, ammunition, military vehicles and drummed gasoline.

By lunch time we were shipping water over the bow so the C.O. moved the bow lookouts to the bridge. That extra five knots was partly responsible. Our 5"/38 gun crew changed the two storage batteries that provided the power to the firing circuit as well as to train and elevate the gun. To maintain proper voltage, we agreed to change them monthly with the second set on a slow charge supervised by the ship's electrician.

June 30 was drill day with alarm bells ringing all day long. We had a fire drill at 1310, boat drill at 1320 and a General Quarters drill in combination with the merchant crew. The C.O.'s comment in the Armed Guard Smooth Log simply stated: "Splendid cooperation!"

The next day we had target practice using helium balloons at an altitude of 1,200 yards, off the port side of the ship. The 3" and 5" guns each shot four rounds. The 20-mm guns fired a total of 480 rounds or sixty each. We were "close but no cigars" according to the C.O.

WEST LOCH TRAGEDY

Forty-seven LSTs assigned to the Northern Attack Force for the Forager Operation (Saipan), were nested in West Loch near the Naval Ammunition Depot before sailing on the campaign. Since there were only six ammunition ships in the entire Pacific Ocean area, sixteen LSTs were designated to carry anti-aircraft shells and powder. An additional ten LSTs were each designated to carry rockets, 40-mm and 20-mm machine gun ammunition. Gasoline in drums covered most of the vessel's topsides and ammunition was stowed outside of their magazines. A last minute decision was made to unload mortar ammunition out of an "LCT gunboat" mounted on the deck of *LST-353*. According to VAdm. Dyer:

> One or more 4.2-inch high explosive mortar shells being offloaded by Army personnel into an Army truck on the elevator on the forecastle of the *LST-353* exploded about 1508 on 21 May 1944. Those who saw the explosion from close aboard died. The immediate follow-up explosion was severe enough to cause a rain of fragments on all eight LSTs in the LST nest, and to start serious gasoline fires on three of these LSTs. A second large explosion at 1511 in the forward part of one of these three LSTs rained burning fragments on nearly all LSTs berthed not only in the nest but in the West Loch area. This led to a further large explosion at 1522 and the rapid burning, wrecking and loss of six LSTs and three LCTs carried aboard three of the LSTs.

Harbor tugs pulled ammunition barges and other ships clear, preventing even more disastrous explosions. LSTs *39, 43, 69, 179, 353*, and *480* plus 3 LCTs were destroyed; 163 men were killed and 396 injured.

Pearl Harbor LST explosion, 21 May 1944. Aerial photograph of the West Loch, showing the burning LSTs in Berths T-8 and T-9. Other landing ships, in the foreground, are maneuvering to escape. Credit: National Archives.

James Baird was a plankowner on *LST-353* and was aboard when she "exploded."

I was in the main Engine Room when a terrific explosion shook the ship. I climbed up to the second deck, and found the ship on fire and exploding on the bow end. I ran aft and top side to the very stern of the ship. The only crew member that I could see was a MoMM 2/c [Motor Machinist Mate] named Murphy. He started to drag a fire hose around, but it was apparent the fire main had been blown out. I could look down the sterns of the other LSTs and see men abandoning their ships from the stern, jumping into boats or into the water.

I was reluctant to leave the ship without orders. I then decided to put on a life jacket and loosen my shoes. Having heard about injuries caused by the life cables, when a ship explodes, I decided to climb to the outside of the cable. I believe this is what saved my life.

Then there was a terrific explosion that caused the main mast to fall. This was followed by another explosion, and I was blown off the stern of the ship. When I came to the surface, I spotted the stern of the ship and decided to use it to protect me as I swam away. There was another LST anchored behind the exploding ships so I swam to it as large pieces of hot metal dropped all around me. The LST had its ramp down. As I reached it, members of the crew pulled me out of the water.

I went aft to the crew's quarters. A large explosion caused one man to jump off the stern of this ship. His death was caused by one of the props as the ship was in reverse trying to distance itself from the explosions.

I was so badly shook up, I can't recall which LST picked me up. We lost everything.

James W. Baird, MoMM1/c LST-353. James Baird.

At 0330 on Independence Day the lookouts sighted the Hawaiian Islands. Lt. Rottman set Condition 1 and at 0845 we took on a pilot, entered Pearl Harbor and dropped the anchor.

The next morning the ship moved to Pier K-5. We spent the following seven days discharging. During this time the C.O. went on a lecture kick, giving talks on everything from the dangers of Dengue fever to the care of battle phones and binoculars.

On July 12 we moved from Pearl Harbor to Pier 29 in Honolulu, near the well-known Clock Tower. There we took on

5"/38 maintenance, San Francisco - Oakland Bay Bridge and Yerba Buena in background. U.S. Navy.

a partial load of used military vehicles — most of them badly in need of repair.

We spent most of our off-duty hours in Pearl playing poker or some other card game when we didn't have liberty. I was hooked on card games. I got into my first serious game of dice this trip. Lt. Rottman frowned on gambling so we used match sticks for money.

Orloski, a Chicago Polack and proud of it, liked to talk to the dice: "Shoot Luke, you're faded and fucked and so are the dice. Come once! Come twice! Come for a God damn dollar!"

On July 15 we took on a pilot and set sail "pursuant to instructions." It was with mixed feelings we said aloha as we watched those beautiful islands fade into the sunset. After church services the next morning the C.O. told us that our destination was Los Angeles.

Six days later we arrived at San Pedro, California and started discharging our cargo.

On July 22,1944 C. Mooney, J. Rasnic, and myself were detached from the "Yugo" and ordered to report to the Naval

Receiving Station on Terminal Island, San Pedro. As we headed down the gangway with our sea bags shouldered, the last thing we heard was Lt. Rottman saying, "Let's all fall in on the aft gundeck. I want to review your new gun assignments with you."

The *Yugoslavia Victory* went on to other campaigns and ports of call including the Palau Islands, Manus Island, Caroline Islands, Okinawa and New Guinea. She was scrapped in Kaohsiung in 1971.[2]

When we checked in at the Naval Receiving Station we were assigned bunks and lockers, then given a forty-eight-hour liberty. So we caught a bus and headed for downtown Los Angeles.

The greater Los Angeles area is spread out and confusing to a newcomer. According to the map, it was more than twenty miles from San Pedro to the Civic Center in downtown LA. One's sense of direction is thrown off because north and south is really east and west in the San Pedro-Long Beach harbor because of the way the California coastline dips in.

Good public transportation and helpful operators were key to visitors like us without a car. In less than an hour, the bus to the Civic Center dropped us off near Pershing Square. After wandering around the downtown section for a couple of hours, we got directions to our ultimate destination, Hollywood — home of the stars. Mooney was sure we would connect with three beautiful starlets. Rasnic and I weren't so sure, but were more than willing to follow his lead. Three bluejackets found themselves at the world-famous intersection of Hollywood and Vine looking for "action," much like the thousands of other servicemen and women who preceded them.

Later, over cheeseburgers and cokes at the Roosevelt Hotel Grill, we came up with a game plan for the next two days. We would visit the Stage-Door Canteen, NBC and CBS radio network studios to see their shows, take in a movie at Grauman's

---

[2]   Mitchell, S.A. and W. Sawyer, *Victory Ships and Tankers.* David & Charles: Newton Abbot, Devon: 1974, p. 61.

Chinese Theater, and go for a swim on Santa Monica beach — all with dates, of course. Our plan didn't include a place to stay because we weren't sure where we would be come nightfall. Hopefully, we'd get lucky and not need to rent a room. Bluejackets are known for their optimism.

Radio was still king with a console in nearly every American living room. After lunch we checked both NBC and CBS on Sunset Boulevard. In spite of the very long lines, we saw two popular network shows: "The Jack Benny Show" and "Hollywood Playhouse."

Next we went to the Hollywood Stage-Door Canteen "where movie actors and actresses entertain the troops." The place was already jumping when we arrived at 1700. As we worked our way through the crowd, attractive women passed out coffee and doughnuts. We never did find the bar. I'm not sure there was one. The few celebrities there — I didn't recognize any of them — basked in the publicity and patriotism on display. Most of the work was done by non-celebrity volunteers. Junior hostesses, as they were called, were the dance partners and the senior hostesses — chaperones really — enforced the rules which forbade hostesses dating servicemen.

The entertainment was first rate: Kay Kyser and his "College of Musical Knowledge" with a singing group. We danced several times in spite of the crowded floor but Mooney upstaged everyone when he took over the floor to jitterbug with an actress. He was some dancer.

By 1900 we were all happy to escape the crowd and get some fresh air. We decided to get something to eat, then check out the Hollywood Palladium — a big band ballroom highly recommended by the junior hostesses as well as Mooney's jitter-bugging actress.

The Palladium was everything we had heard it was and more — A nightclub with a dance floor the size of two basket-ball courts and a big band. The price of admission was steep but the entertainment alone made it worthwhile. We danced and sang along to fighting songs such as "Remember Pearl Harbor,"

"Praise the Lord and Pass the Ammunition," and "Comin' In On a Wing and a Prayer." After about an hour we wound up with four UCLA college girls who shared a two-bedroom apartment in West Los Angeles. At first it seemed like a sailor's dream made in heaven, but it wasn't to be.

After escorting them home on the bus, they invited us to spend the night, but on the condition that we sleep in the living room; no hanky panky. We were all a little high on beer, but agreed. As I recall, we ended the evening trying to harmonize to "The Last Time I Saw Paris," quietly, so as not to wake the neighbors.

After coffee and pastry the next morning, our hostesses offered us the use of the bathroom just long enough to shower and shave. They had to get ready for class, so after saying our good-byes and getting directions to the beach, "Santa Monica Boulevard runs right into it," we headed for our bus stop.

By the time we arrived at the beach, the fog was burning off. It looked like a nice day, but why were there hardly any people around? Then we remembered it was a work or school day for most people. We had breakfast at a little diner just off the beach, took off our shoes and socks and headed north across the sand. By 1100 there were still no people to speak of, so we reversed course. We probably walked ten miles, but drew a blank as far as dating prospects went. When we reached Venice Beach southeast of Santa Monica we gave up.

After hot dogs and beer, we asked our waitress for directions back to San Pedro. She said all we had to do was walk inland about a mile to the Pacific Coast Highway (State Highway 1) and head south. There we got lucky. Within minutes we got a ride with a Texas transplant heading for work at the Long Beach Shipyard on Terminal Island next door to the naval station. We were back in time for chow that night and a movie.

June/July 1944

The U.S. Marines land on Saipan on 15 June in the first assault of the Mariana Islands.

B-29 Superfortress bombers, based in Bengal, India and re-fueled in China, begin raids on Japan.

U.S. carrier forces shatter the remaining Japanese carrier forces in the Battle of the Philippine Sea, a one-sided air battle, a.k.a. the "Marianas Turkey Shoot." The enemy loses some 220 planes in air combat to only 20 American plane losses. Most military experts believe this battle broke the back of Japanese naval air power.

President Roosevelt signs the GI Bill of Rights to provide broad benefits for veterans of the war.

After the British take Caen and U.S. troops capture Saint-Lô, France, ending the "battle of the hedgerows," Patton's tank troops of the Third Army break through a German line, isolating German troops in Brittany.

Saipan Invasion. LCI(G)-725 and LCI(G)-726 fire on the beach while landing craft form up in the background, during the initial assault, 15 June 1944. National Archives.

Saipan Invasion. Marines take cover on the beach while awaiting the arrival of following troops during the initial assault. National Archives.

U.S. forces make an Amphibious Landing on Guam in the Marianas on 19 July.

President Franklin Roosevelt, is nominated for an unprecedented fourth term at the Democratic convention; Senator Harry S. Truman is nominated as his running mate, ousting VP Henry Wallace.

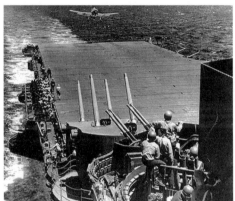

Battle of Philippine Sea, June 1944. An F6F lands on USS Lexington *(CV-16) during the "Marianas Turkey Shoot," June 19, 1944. Credit: Naval Historical Center.*

A Japanese twin-engine bomber missed this U.S. Pacific Fleet Carrier in this dramatic crash dive. The battle occurred in June 1944 west of the Mariana Islands. Credit: Naval Historical Center.

Adm. Ernest King, USN center, visits the Marianas Islands on board USS Indianapolis *(CA-35) with, left, Adm. Chester W. Nimitz, USN and Adm. Raymond A. Spruance, USN, right, 18 July 1944. Naval Historical Center.*

PORT CHICAGO EXPLOSION

An ammunition explosion rocked the San Francisco Bay area the night of July 17,1944, as the Liberty ship *E.A. Bryan* and the *Quinault Victory* loaded ammunition at the Port Chicago Annex of the Mare Island Navy Yard. There was an estimated 10,000 tons of ammunition in the ships and/or on the docks when a blinding flash filled the sky and two blasts shook buildings from Sacramento to San Jose.

Port Chicago, California, July 1944. View looking north showing wreckage of joiner building. AO7 ship pier in background. Seabees.

A plane flying 7,000 feet above Port Chicago was peppered by flying debris and made an emergency landing at Fairfield. Windows were knocked out fifty miles away. The town of Port Chicago, a mile away, was almost leveled. In ten seconds, the two ships, the dock, an ammunition train, a locomotive, and two Coast Guard boats vanished, and with them 327 men. Only twenty-five bodies were recovered.

12

IN THE MARSHALLS
AND THE MARIANAS

On July 26 Carl Mooney and I were named the Gunners'
Mates for a new crew being assembled at Terminal Island in Long Beach Harbor for the SS *David Belasco*
which had just arrived from Brisbane, Australia and Buna, New
Guinea.

The SS *David Belasco* was built by Permanente Metals
Corp., Yard No. 1, at Richmond, California and launched in
September 1943. Her engine was made by Williamette Iron &
Steel Corp. of Portland, Oregon. An EC2-Liberty freighter, she
measured 7,176 gross tons and had a deadweight tonnage of
10,550. Like all wartime merchant vessels she was owned by
the War Shipping Administration. She was chartered to Smith
& Johnson, of New York, as general agents. For armament she
carried one 3"/50 aft, one 3"/50 forward and eight 20-mm guns
(four on the bridge, two aft and two forward). Commanded by
A. Simonson, she carried a merchant marine crew of forty-three:

sixteen in the deck department; thirteen in the engineering department; and thirteen in the stewards' department. Her U.S. Navy Armed Guard Unit was twenty-eight strong with Charles K. Hackler, Lt. (jg)USNR, serving as commanding officer of a crew of twenty-four gunners and three communications men.

On July 28, the entire crew turned to, stowing gear and generally squaring things away. At 1200 liberty was granted for two-thirds of the crew, a first for all of us. This had been an option for Armed Guard crews for some time but depended on the discretion of the C.O. and, to some extent, the local Port Director's Office. Eighteen bluejackets went ashore in their dress whites that day and liberty lasted until 0900 the next morning. The duty section was kept busy checking aboard equipment and supplies . . . and looking forward to their next liberty.

On July 29 at 1200, liberty began once again for two-thirds of the crew and at 1300 our new C.O., Charles K. Hackler, Lt. (jg), came aboard to relieve Lieutenant Koller.

"Flags" Flynn had the duty that Sunday so Mooney and I decided to check out Long Beach about five miles east of us, even though we were both almost broke. An old salt on TI once said: "Any liberty is better than none. Better store up as much as possible for the future." Besides, in wartime, any liberty could be the last one.

Because the *Belasco* was berthed in Wilmington when we boarded her, we had a number of liberty options: Hollywood, Santa Monica and Malibu for long liberties or Long Beach for shorter ones.

Mooney and I met up with three of our gunners while waiting for the bus to take us into Long Beach. There were sailors everywhere, like locusts, from the bars to the beaches. Petty officers wore rating badges on the left arm for the trades, on the right for those who worked on the deck, like gunners, boatswains, and quartermasters. A white stripe around the right shoulder meant seamen deckhands, red around the left for below-deck firemen — a reflection of hierarchy and skill. You could easily spot the bluejackets with experience by their tight-fitting tailor-mades and campaign ribbons. The enlisted men owned the streets while the officers, unenvied by those below them, stayed in the better hotels.

By around 1800 we gave up on meeting women and went to a movie, returning to the ship by 2200.

For the next few days, the duty section was kept busy stowing supplies, equipment and ammunition. On August 2, twenty-four enlisted men reported aboard as passengers from the U.S. Naval Receiving Station (USNRS), Terminal Island. That evening, the C.O. secured the Port Security watch, set Condition 1 and we sailed. Early the next morning we arrived at Port Hueneme, California. Seabees immediately began loading us with military cargo of all kinds.

On August 4 an inspection of the passenger quarters, a.k.a. "doghouses", on the boat deck, revealed ticks, roaches, lice and bedbugs in the mattresses. The C.O. and Capt. Simonsen quickly went to the Port Director's Office to arrange for fumigation of the ship.

The fumigation was set for August 6. Consequently, noon and evening meals would not be served aboard. All passengers not already on liberty were granted special liberty as was the gun crew. Just about everyone went to Ventura. The weather was great for "patrolling" the beach but most of us had a serious cash flow problem that could only be solved by going back to sea.

By August 7 the Seabees were stacking pontoons all over the deck. We took on another six passengers the following morning

Military vehicles being loaded on a Liberty ship. U.S. Army.

and soon all passengers were turned to lashing their sea bags to sheltered space on the boat deck and cleaning their quarters. The pilot came aboard and we slowly moved away from the dock and sailed for parts unknown.

One hundred and one men were aboard — forty-three merchant mariners, twenty-eight Armed Guard, and thirty passengers — from all parts of the country and all walks of life. Some were trained in the ways of the sea, others fresh off the farm — all wondering where we were going, what adventures lay in store, and whether we would make it back.

Laundry was my number one priority our first day out as I was fresh out of skivvies and dungarees. Our washing machine consisted of a galvanized pail. You simply put your clothes in the bucket, added soap and water, then held the pail under the nearest steam line faucet to heat the water. After letting the clothes soak for an hour or so, you scrubbed the hell out of them with a stiff brush on a clean surface, then rinsed and dried them in the sun.

Over the next few weeks, we went through most of the sea routines I was familiar with — only with less frequency. For example, many of the weekly instructions and drills now occurred on alternate weeks. Cleaning, chipping, scraping and painting were done when there was a need — not just to keep the gun crew occupied. We still cleaned and oiled our guns like they were Swiss watches and we had plenty of aircraft identification and sight-setter drills.

On August 10, Mooney and I mustered the passengers and assigned them to stations for emergency drills. The C.O. checked life jackets, then all hands (merchant mariners, passengers and gun crew) were called to fire and emergency stations. That was followed by an abandon ship drill.

Armed Guard sea routines varied little from ship to ship. Standard watches were four hours on and eight off with life jackets and helmets nearby. An exception to this was when all hands were at battle stations (GQ) at sunrise and sunset — considered the most dangerous times of day for submarine attacks and air raids.

Fleet combatants like "battlewagons" and "flat tops" provided their crews with many services such as movies, ships' stores, a barber shop, a laundry and a "gedunk locker" (ice cream counter). Of course, on a freighter there was no place to put such luxuries. The closest we had was a "slop chest" where the purser sold cigarettes and candy. "Coffin nails" were an occupational hazard, and at five cents a pack, we smoked a lot. Unlike the Fleet, the smoking lamp was almost always lit unless we were on watch or on deck after dark.

We did other things besides stand watch and sleep. We fought a constant battle against rust with the dreaded chipping hammer, wire brush, and paint when we weren't cleaning and oiling our guns. Fortunately, as a new Petty Officer third-class, I now avoided most of the general duties and so-called "shit" details.

The food on the *Belasco* was good. The thirteen-man Stewards' Department prepared chow for 101 men three times a day on a two-oven, center-fired coal range in the galley amidships. There were three separate messrooms with table service, yet no long chow lines. The gunners and mariners mess rooms were divided by a pantry on the port side of the deckhouse. The officer's mess and lounge was on the forward end of the main deck. Meals were scheduled to catch those going on or coming off watch for breakfast (0730-0830) and lunch (1130-1230). At dinner (1700-1800), the men on watch were relieved so they could eat.

The quality of the food was generally good the first two or three weeks out until we got low on fresh supplies. Breakfast, for example, might be a choice of bacon or sausage with eggs fixed to order plus hot cakes and orange juice. Lunch and dinner might include a choice of meats and vegetables and a desert of some kind. The baker made fresh bread almost daily and you could count on a selection of cold cuts and cheeses in the pantry fridge day or night for sandwich makings before or after standing watch. Coffee was almost always available, too. Some said it was loaded with salt peter to curb the men's sex drive. I was never sure.

Of course, we ran out of fresh meat, produce and dairy products long before the end of a trip. The cooks then got creative with dried and canned fruits and vegetables, spam, beans and pasta. During longer trips in the Pacific, you might get some Australian or New Zealand mutton, but it was pretty rank.

The weather in the Pacific ranged from warm to hot — sometimes steamy hot, especially inside the ship. In such cases everyone slept on deck on Army cots. Topside the nights were usually clear and cool with a light breeze. When at anchor, the weather could be stifling and the humidity overwhelming. Then heat rash became a problem, especially for members of the engine department or "black gang."

On August 12, we practiced firing our .30-caliber rifles and .45-caliber side arms — eighty rounds of each were expended.

I got hooked on auction pinochle on the *Belasco* thanks to Mooney, Cain and Carr who apparently wanted my money badly enough to teach me the game. I lost consistently while learning the game, but got even before the trip ended. Regular pinochle is played for so much a point and scores are recorded on a pad. It is played by two to four people with a double deck. Auction pinochle, however, is played by three or four people and has many features, such as bidding, that resemble contract bridge. We played every time we had the chance at sea or in port. Watches were scheduled so we could all be available at the same time. It got so the C.O. knew exactly where to find us when off watch. During the day we played on the fantail under the guntub; nights found us in the gunner's mess.

On August 14, the cleaning section turned to painting the after 3"/50 gun tub for the upcoming Port Director's inspection in Pearl Harbor.

We berthed at dock A-13 in Pearl Harbor, said our good-byes to the passengers and the starboard section had its first liberty on August 19. That set the pattern for the next two weeks.

Because this was the first Hawaii visit for most of the *Belasco* gun crew, they peppered Carl Mooney and me with questions and the starboard liberty section soon conned me into showing them the town.

Nine of us headed straight for Canal Street, home of honky-tonks and whorehouses. In short order we were downing our first Primo Beer and discussing the pros and cons of the New Congress Hotel's "old-fashioned line" versus the "French line."

Since I had "been there, done that," I ordered another beer at a nearby saloon while I waited for "my boys." Out of curiosity I asked the bartender why all the hookers were Caucasians, at least the ones at the Congress. According to him, the U.S. Government "supervised" the whorehouses in the islands, controlling them to hold VD down. According to him the Government provided free transportation to the islands for working women. In return, they had to agree to be tested for VD every two weeks. The prostitution business itself was licensed to local operators on a contractual basis.

We were all back aboard ship in time for evening chow. Then each guy related his impressions of Honolulu for the benefit of those on watch. Naturally the stories centered around the Congress Hotel. Everyone compared notes. It was agreed the average age of the hookers was about thirty, older than God to an eighteen-year old bluejacket but not quite old enough to be his mother. The charges were five, six and seven bucks for an old fashioned, half and half, and French respectively. Everyone had his private parts washed in a pan of warm water

SS David Belasco *starboard liberty section ashore in Honolulu. August 1944. Standing left to right: Bonnalie, Carr, McGee, Cain, Burton. Front, left to right: Blum, Cassidy, Casey, Bushey. Author*

then milked down and carefully examined for VD by the hooker. And finally — and this created the most laughs — the average duration of these encounters was somewhere around fifteen minutes.

The liberty section got to take a sightseeing tour of Oahu on a bus furnished by the Fleet Recreation Office. We really enjoyed it. We circled Oahu and stopped in several places along the way, including a lunch break at the Moana Hotel — the only hotel on Waikiki Beach older than the Royal Hawaiian — and a swim stop on the northeast side of the island at Kaneohe Bay.

On September 4 the Skipper and C.O. attended a sailing conference at the Port Director's Office, a dozen Navy passengers reported aboard and in the afternoon we sailed in a convoy of thirteen Liberty cargo ships with an escort of two PCs (submarine chasers) and one DD (destroyer). Our speed was 10.5 knots.

That evening the C.O. told us we were heading to Eniwetok in the Marshall Islands. Since none of us had ever been there, little was known except what we read or heard in the news.

On September 6 during evening General Quarters, the merchant marine volunteers were drilled on loading the 20-mm guns. Two days later the General (text continues on p. 257)

Moana Hotel, Waikiki, Honolulu, T.H. seen from its pier with Banyan Tree in the center, c. 1925. Naval Historical Center.

MARSHALL ISLANDS

The Marshalls Archipelago, named after a British sea captain, comprises thirty some coral atolls between latitudes 5° and 12° N, and longitudes 160° and 172° E. Claimed by Spain, the Marshalls were annexed by Germany in 1884. In World War I both this group and the Carolines were captured by Japan and awarded to her in 1920 under a mandate from the League of Nations. Although the establishment of fortifications or military bases was forbidden, Japan closed off Micronesia in the 1930s and began fortifying strategic islands and atolls in anticipation of its military invasion of the Pacific.[1]

INVASION OF THE MARSHALLS

In May 1943, the Combined Chiefs of Staff ordered the seizure of the Marshall Islands. This assignment fell to Admiral Chester W. Nimitz, Commander in Chief, Pacific, and Commander in Chief, Pacific Ocean Areas (CinCPAC/CinCPOA), based at Pearl Harbor in Hawaii. He called on Admirals Turner, Spruance, and Hill who were experts in amphibious landings, fast carrier strikes, and shore bombardment, and MGen. Holland M Smith, USMC, Commanding General of the Marines' V Amphibious Corps.

Original plans for attacks in the eastern Marshalls were modified, and the decision was made to strike directly at Kwajalein Atoll. Kwajalein is sixty miles long and twenty miles wide, a semi-enclosed series of eighty reefs and islets around a huge lagoon of some 800 square miles. Located 620 miles northwest of Tarawa and 2,415 miles southwest of Pearl Harbor, its capture would have far-reaching strategic significance by breaking the outer ring of Japanese Pacific defense lines.

After these islands were taken, there was one more objective in the Marshalls: Eniwetok Atoll. This was targeted for attack some three months later by a task force comprised of the 22d Marine Regiment (called in the Corps the "22d Marines") and most of the Army's 106th Infantry Regiment. Brigadier General Thomas E. Watson, USMC, would be in command.

The task organization established for the Marshalls comprising 278 ships was divided into Southern ("Flintlock") and Northern ("Catchpole") Attack Forces.

With the plans in place and a very tight schedule to meet the D-Day deadline, the complex task of assembling and transporting the assault troops to the target area was put in motion.

---

[1] Morison, Samuel E. *Aleutians, Gilberts and Marshalls.*

The 23d, 24th, and 25th Marines were assigned to the Roi-Namur operation, and the 23d, 17th, and 184th Infantry Regiments of the Army's 7th Division were to take the Kwajalein Island objectives.

Forward at the main theater, an awesome pre-landing saturation bombardment was in full swing. U.S. Navy ships moved in on Roi-Namur and poured in their point-blank massed fire. Waves of planes swept in low for bombing and strafing runs. The combined total of shells and bombs reached a staggering 6,000 tons.

By nightfall, the beachheads on the neighboring islets had been secured, and for the first time, U.S. Marines had landed on a Japanese mandate.

On February 1, D plus 1, the LSTs moved inside the lagoon. Up before dawn, infantrymen filed into the cavernous holds of the LSTs and clambered on-board their amphibious tractors (amtracs). When the signal finally came to the assault waves, "Go on in!", the two lead battalions of the 23d Marines headed for Roi, with the two lead battalions of the 24th Marines churning towards Namur.

Early on the afternoon of the next day, February 2, D plus 2, the 24th Marines finished its conquest of Namur, and the island was declared "secured."

Across the sand spit, on Roi, it was a different story. When the 23d Marines hit the beaches on D plus 1, the fierceness of the pre-landing bombardment prevented the Japanese defenders from mounting a coordinated defense. Small groups of Marine riflemen joined their regiment's attached tanks in a race across to the far side of the island. By 1800 that day, D plus 1, Roi was secured.

The victory came at a cost of 313 Marines and corpsmen killed and 502 wounded. By contrast, the defeated Japanese garrison numbered an estimated 3,563 — with all but a handful of them dead.

In accordance with the overall campaign plan for the seizure of the Marshall Islands, the Army's attack on Kwajalein Island at the south end of the atoll began in exact synchronization with the Marine assault in the north. The same softening-up process was used on D-day, January 31, with a large force of warships and planes pouring on a blanket of high explosive. Then, on D plus 1, the riflemen of the 32d and 184th Infantry Regiments landed on Kwajalein Island itself.

Once ashore, the assault units found widespread devastation from the preinvasion bombing and shelling. Smashed seawalls, uprooted trees, demolished buildings, scarred pillboxes were everywhere. Dug in amidst all this debris, the Japanese fought resolutely.

It was necessary to employ heavy demolition charges to breach emplacements sufficiently for the employment of flame throwers and grenades. It was four long days until the far tip of Kwajalein had been reached and the island was declared secured. Japanese deaths reached a total of 8,122, some 27 times the number of Americans killed.

RAdm. Richmond Kelly Turner, USN, left, photographed during the invasion of Kwajalein, February 18, 1944. He was then commanding the Fifth Amphibious Force. National Archives.

Marines firing at Japanese snipers from a Communications Center in a bomb crater, on Roi Island, Kwajalein Atoll, February 1, 1944. Note wrecked Japanese G4M ("Betty") bombers in the distance. Naval Historical Center.

Marines approach a Japanese dugout entrance while clearing out snipers on Roi Island, Kwajalein Atoll, 1 February 1944. Note Japanese signpost by the entrance. Naval Historical Center.

Eniwetok Operation — Marines and Coast Guardsmen proudly display a Japanese flag, picked up by one of them during the capture of Engebi Island, Eniwetok Atoll, 19 February 1944. National Archives.

LST delivered pontoon causeway used for the Marshall Islands invasion. With four sections of the causeway joined together to form a complete bridge, heavy gear brought in by the LSTs moves ashore. Seabees.

Majuro Island, Marshall Islands — USS LST-461 beached on Majuro Island unloading supplies, c. March 1944. National Archives.

ENIWETOK

With Kwajalein Atoll in American hands, a review of the next operation immediately took place. Admiral Nimitz decided to use the 22d Marines (under the command of Colonel John T. Walker) and two battalions of the Army's 106th Infantry Regiment, since they had not been needed in the quick conquest of Roi-Namur and Kwajalein. The date for the attack was jumped forward to mid-February. The softening-up process had begun at the end of January, and the carrier air strikes increased the following month. On D-Day, 17 February, the Navy's heavy guns joined in with a thunderous shelling. Then, using secret Japanese navigation charts captured at Kwajalein, the task force moved into the huge lagoon, seventeen by twenty-one miles in size. As at Kwajalein Atoll, the artillery was sent ashore on D-Day on two tiny islets adjacent to the first key target, Engebi Island. There they set up to provide supporting fire for the forthcoming infantry assault.

The landing on Engebi came the next morning, D plus 1, February 18, as the 22d Marines headed for the beach in their amtracs. With these advances and direct fire from self-propelled 105-mm guns against concrete pillboxes, the whole of Engebi was overrun by the Marines by the afternoon of D plus 1. On the following morning the American flag was raised to the sound of a Marine playing "To the Colors" on a captured Japanese bugle. More than 1,200 Japanese, Koreans, and Okinawans were on Engebi, and only nineteen surrendered.

The main action now shifted quickly to the attack on Eniwetok Island. This mission was assigned to the 1st and 3d Battalions of the Army's 106th Infantry Regiment. When they landed their advance was slow. "Spider hole" defenses held up their advance.[2] A steep bluff blocked the planned inland advance of their LVTAs, resulting in a traffic jam on the beaches.

The attack inched forward with the repeated use of flame-throwers and satchel charges, halting for the night a few hundred yards from the tip of the island. The following morning the American attack began again, and by midafternoon the Marines and the Army battalion had secured the southern part of the island.

---

[2] "Spider holes" had many entrances. They were constructed by knocking out the heads of empty gasoline drums and making an impromptu pipeline of them, sunk into the ground and covered with earth and palm fronds. The tunnels thus constructed branched off in several directions from a central pit and the whole emplacement was usually concealed with great skill and ingenuity. If the main position was spotted and attacked the riflemen within could crawl off fifty feet or so down one of the corridors and emerge at an entirely different and unexpected spot from which they could get off a shot and dive down to concealment before it was possible to determine whence the fire proceeded.

Progress was still very slow in the northern sector, but in the afternoon of D plus 4, February 21, the northern area was also declared secure.

With the elapse of all this time (ninety-six hours instead of the twenty-four hours expected) BGen. Watson, USMC, was forced to alter his plans for the final phase of the operation: the assault on Parry. General Watson decided to hold off the landing on Parry until D plus 5 (22 February). The Navy moved its big guns in as close as 850 yards offshore and pounded the defenders with 944 tons of shells. This was supplemented by artillery fire from the neighboring islands and rocket fire from the gunboats as the Marines went in. This rain of shells crept ahead of the tanks and infantrymen as they tenaciously slogged their way across the island. For the assault troops, it was a continuing story of "spider holes," tunnels, underground strong points, and enemy resistance to the death. By evening it was nearly all over.

Early the next morning Parry was completely in American hands, and the conquest of Eniwetok was complete. Some 3,400 Japanese were eliminated there at a cost of 348 American dead and 866 wounded.

Tactically, there were a variety of innovations in the Marshalls that would prove valuable in future campaigns. There was the first use of Navy underwater demolition teams; the first use of DUKWs in combat; the first use of command ships with special communications equipment to control the battle; the first use of Marine airplanes to control naval gunfire; and the first use of armored amphibian tractors (LVTAs).

The 4th Marine Division was the first American division to use rockets mounted on jeeps, pick-up trucks, and Navy gunboats in combat. Another Marine resource was unique: the use of Navajo Indian "code talkers" in battle. They proved a perfect foil for the Japanese ability in previous battles to understand Marine voice-to-voice communications and Morse Code.

Finally, the Marshalls proved incontestably the effectiveness of prolonged and massive preinvasion naval gunfire and aerial bombing. The U.S. planes and warships had so thoroughly scoured not only the target islands, but also the other Japanese air bases in the Marshalls, that not a single Japanese plane was able to attack the American surface forces in the campaign.

To support air offensives against, and maintain surveillance over, the by-passed Japanese bases in the Marshalls and the Carolines, an advance air base, with minor fleet facilities would soon be established on Kwajalein Atoll. Complete facilities would be provided for the operation of landplanes and seaplanes.[3]

---

[3] Sources: a) *Marines In World War II - Breaking the Outer Ring* b) Dyer, *Amphibians Came to Conquer*; c) Morison, *Aleutians, Gilberts and Marshalls.*

(continued from p. 250) Alarm system was tested. Firing practice was held on the 3"/50 guns and the starboard 20s only, as we were in convoy. Five rounds of AA were expended by each 3"/50 gun and 240 rounds were expended by the 20-mms. All guns were inspected and found in good condition.

The sea routines of the merchant crew weren't that different from the Armed Guard. We both stood watches. We maintained our guns and the mariners maintained the engine and cargo gear. Our off-duty time was identical. Cards and other games of skill or chance, writing letters home, and swapping sea stories or war stories — some true, some too tall to measure.

Then there were the always popular intellectual discussions or "bull sessions" on everything from sex and politics to race and religion. Sex was by far the most popular subject. Here, everyone was an expert.

The setting for these sessions varied depending on the time of day, weather conditions and whether we had a deck load or not. The most popular time and venue was the No. 4 hatch just aft of the deckhouse in the evening after chow. Other locations included the messrooms, fantail, and the boat deck.

Race was seldom discussed but when it was, the talk could get heavy — especially if we had any southerners on board. As a country boy, I had only seen one black man in my life before leaving Montana. The "discussions" were shocking and informative, but never dull. At the time blacks, or "colored," as they were referred to, were still legally segregated by the Armed Forces. (The Navy admitted their first black messmen in 1942 before they were allowed in the Army Air Corps or Marine Corps. The Army was first. They had twelve black officers and 5,000 black soldiers in 1940.)

The war news was encouraging.

July-August 1944

Operation Globetrotter, the final New Guinea landings in Gen. MacArthur's long journey back to the Philippines are launched July 30, 1944 at Cape Sansapor on the Vogelkop Peninsula.

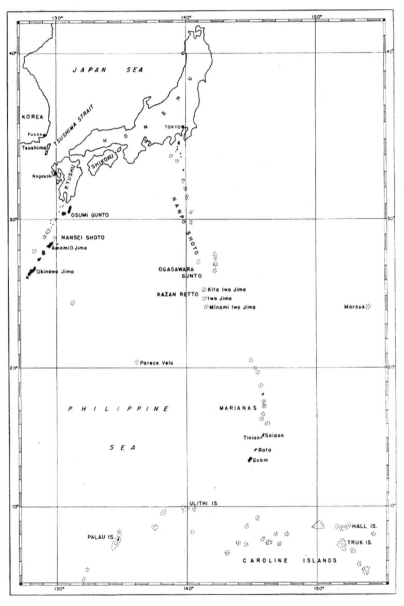

THE MARIANAS, IWO JIMA, OKINAWA, AND THE JAPANESE HOME ISLANDS

Pacific Fleet Warships and Auxiliaries anchored in a Marshall Islands atoll. In the foreground, a "Seabee" crew is building an Advanced Base for the fleet. Battleships Iowa *(BB-61) and* New Jersey *(BB-62) are among the ships in the distance. Naval Historical Center.*

American-British-French forces open a second invasion front with a major amphibious landing on the southern coast of France.

President Roosevelt and Prime Minister Churchill appeal to Stalin to aid the Warsaw insurgents; however, the Soviet Army remain halted within sight of the city while German troops savagely put down the uprising.

French and American troops liberate Paris on August 25 with General Eisenhower ordering the French 2d Armored Division to lead the Allied entry into the French capital. Frenchwomen suspected of having slept with Germans are led into the streets to have their heads shaved.

We lost a day as we crossed the International Dateline on September 10 so advanced the calendar *(text continues on p. 265)*

MARIANA ISLANDS

The fifteen Mariana Islands stretch 425 miles in a north-south arc south of Iwo Jima and the Bonins. Saipan, Tinian, Rota, and Guam, all at the southernmost end of the arc, are the only ones with any military or economic significance. Japan captured the German Marianas in World War I and was given a mandate over them by the League of Nations in 1920. By the time the war broke, the Japanese in the Marianas outnumbered the natives more than two to one.[4]

INVASION OF THE MARIANAS

The unexpectedly rapid success in the Marshalls allowed planners to advance the assault on the Marianas from October to June. Admiral Nimitz, CinCPOA, assigned overall campaign responsibility to Vice Adm. Raymond A. Spruance's Fifth Fleet. Vice Adm. Richmond Kelly Turner commanded the Joint Expeditionary Force charged with the amphibious assault. Vice Adm. Marc A. Mitscher's Fast Carrier Task Force and Vice Adm. Charles A. Lockwood's Submarine Force, Pacific Fleet, covered all landings. Lt. Gen. Holland M. Smith, USMC, Commanding General V Amphibious Corps, controlled the Marianas amphibious forces as each left U.S. Navy control at the water's edge. Three Marine Corps general officers commanded the landing forces on the targeted islands: Holland Smith on Saipan, Harry Schmidt on Tinian, and Roy S. Geiger on Guam.

No operation on so vast a scale with a final thousand-mile "hop," had ever before been planned. Inherent difficulties peculiar to amphibious warfare were enhanced by the distance of the Marianas from any Allied continental base, and by the operation's size.

No fewer than 535 combatant ships and auxiliaries carried four and a half reinforced divisions — 127,571 troops — of which over two thirds were Marines.

The destination lay 1,017 miles' steaming from Eniwetok, the nearest advanced base, which was little more than an anchorage. And Saipan lay about 3,500 miles from Pearl Harbor.

SAIPAN

The small size of Saipan dictated a straightforward plan of assault. Admiral Spruance set the invasion date at June 15. Just before dawn on D-Day, surface ships alternated with bombers and fighters in saturating the landing beaches. At 0700 on June 15 the order "Land the landing force!" boomed through the compartments of thirty-four LSTs anchored three miles off Saipan. Bow doors swung open, ramps lowered and hundreds of amphibian tractors began crawling into the water. The

---

[4] Morison, *The Rising Sun in the Pacific*, pp. 184-86.

amphibians were preceded by carefully orchestrated barrages of large-caliber naval gunfire, boat-mounted rockets, and carrier air strikes, first on the beaches and then, as the troops came across the sand, in the hills beyond. Eight thousand marines landed on the west side of Saipan north and south of Charan Kanoa in the face of moderate opposition. By nightfall they had established a beachhead 10,000 yards wide and 1,000 yards deep. That night the Japanese counterattacked at six points but were repulsed everywhere.

The next day the first Army combat units came ashore. Enemy opposition stiffened. That night the enemy counterattacked with 1,000 troops and thirty-eight tanks but was again repulsed.

On the 17th, the 165th Infantry reached the edge of Aslito Field and the next day walked across it unopposed.

On June 19, Holland Smith reoriented his corps to attack in two directions. His two Marine divisions and one regiment of the 27th Division formed a front across the island in preparation for the advance north. The other two regiments of the 27th Division, the 105th and the 165th, began the mop-up of Nafutan Peninsula.

On June 22, Gen. Holland Smith launched his attack north at 0600. The performance of Army regiments in central Saipan greatly troubled Marine Gen. Smith and on June 24 the corps commander took the drastic step of relieving Army Gen. Ralph Smith, the division commander. Army Maj. Gen. Sanderford Jarman took over the division on an interim basis. This "Smith versus Smith controversy," as it became known, threatened Army-Navy cooperation.

Resuming the two-front advance on June 25, Generals Holland Smith and Jarman tried new tactics to end the stalemate. On the Nafutan front the 2d Battalion, 105th Infantry, was assisted by 40-mm and 90-mm antiaircraft guns placing direct trajectory fire on Japanese positions, enabling flame-thrower crews to reach into caves. On the central front Army battalions no longer tried to advance in a linear fashion keeping contact with Marine units on their flanks, but instead moved diagonally across Death Valley to attack Hell's Pocket and Purple Heart Ridge from several directions.

On the 27th the 2d Battalion, 105th Infantry, overcame the last enemy strongpoint on Nafutan Peninsula. In Death Valley the 1st Battalion, 106th Infantry, cleared most of Hell's Pocket, while the other two battalions of the 106th and the 2d Battalion, 165th Infantry, secured all but the last rise on Purple Heart Ridge, "Hill Able." The next day Maj. Gen. George W. Griner took command of the 27th Division and soon could report a victory to Holland Smith when the 1st Battalion, 106th Infantry, killed the last enemy soldier in Hell's Pocket.

Now only a six-mile sweep to Marpi Point remained. Americans moved ahead rapidly. In another day-long battle the Americans regained lost terrain and in the process nearly annihilated the enemy. Two days of little more than cave demolition brought the 165th Infantry and Marine Corps units to Marpi Point, ending the battle of Saipan.

Marianas Operation, June 1944. USAAF P-47 fighters of the 73rd Fighter Sq., 7th AF, being launched from USS Manila Bay (CVE-61) for delivery to airfields on Saipan. National Archives.

Saipan Invasion, June 1944. Underwater demolition team blows up obstacles off Saipan near several LSTs. LST-390 is at right. National Archives.

Saipan Invasion, June 1944. USS Lexington (CV-16) SBD dive bombers fly over the invasion fleet off Saipan, on "D-Day." 15 June 1944. National Archives.

A U.S. sailor pays his respects to American servicemen on Saipan who gave their lives in winning the island. Naval Historical Center.

Tinian Invasion. Seabees of 302d NCB repair pontoon causeway on "White Two" beach that had broached during storm 1 August 1944. National Archives.

TINIAN

Anxious to continue the momentum of their victory on Saipan, Admiral Turner and Lt. Gen. Holland Smith quickly turned their attention to Tinian. Only five days after the invasion of Saipan, Battery B. 531st Field Artillery Battalion fired its 155-mm guns at Tinian. On July 8 three more Army artillery battalions reoriented southward, and by the time fighting on Saipan ended, XXIV Corps Artillery fired over 7,500 rounds at Tinian from Saipan.

The plan for Tinian called for a two-division amphibious assault. On the morning of July 24, the 2nd and 4th Marine divisions landed under the command of Lt. Gen. Harry F. Schmidt, USMC. Overcoming light opposition, they established a beachhead two miles wide and a mile deep by nightfall. As on Saipan, the Japanese tried to push the Americans back into the sea their first night ashore, but once again the enemy failed, losing 1,241 men in the attempt. Thereafter the rolling terrain allowed a rapid infantry-armor advance, leaving the Japanese defenders little time to reorganize. On the 26th, the marines captured their first airfield and cleared Mount Lasso, but were slowed by the weather. On July 29, the tail of a typhoon lashed across the island, destroying two pontoon causeways used to receive shipborne units and supplies from Saipan, preventing two batteries of the Army's 106th Field Artillery Battalion from reaching Tinian.

During the night of July 31 enemy survivors gathered for a last-gasp counterattack. Led by a regimental commander, the Japanese rushed the Marine line three times in the darkness but failed to break through. Daylight revealed over one hundred enemy dead, and on the evening of August 1 General Schmidt declared the island secure.

The nine-day battle for Tinian cost the attackers 328 killed and 1,571 wounded. But Marine Corps infantry and Army artillery gained one of the best island air bases in all the Pacific. From Tinian, long-range American bombers would soon bring the war to the enemy homeland.

GUAM

Guam is the largest island in the Marianas. It has a hilly surface with shoreline cliffs, many caves, and abrupt rises and draws. Unlike the rest of the Marianas, Guam was under American jurisdiction from 1898 until the Japanese invasion of December 10, 1941, a history that lent to the island's liberation the same moral imperative as that attached to the Philippines.

Admiral Spruance set the invasion date for July 21, 1944. Japanese defenders on Guam received the heaviest 'softening-up" gunfire and bombing the U.S. Navy had yet produced. On the morning of July 21, Marine units came ashore on both sides of Orote Peninsula. Opposition was surprisingly heavy but by nightfall the marines pushed about a mile inland at both points.

Over the next two days, the 306th and 307th Infantry regiments and General Bruce's headquarters waded in from the reef line, while troops ashore expanded the beachhead. On July 24 the 77th Division took over the southern perimeter; two days later the 1st Provisional Brigade began clearing Orote Peninsula. Before the attack on Orote could begin in earnest, General Takashima launched a major counterattack against Marine lines the night of July 25-26. His troops attacked one point on the line seven times but were repeatedly repulsed. Elsewhere they penetrated deeply enough that cooks and hospital patients had to take up rifles and bayonets. When it was over, the American beachhead remained intact, nearly 3,500 enemy lay dead, and the Japanese situation on Guam was hopeless.

Meanwhile, on July 27-28, the Japanese again tried to puncture the American beachhead perimeter, a failed endeavor in which they lost General Takashima to a machine gun burst. General Obata took over and frantically pulled his depleted force north to build a new defensive line. His troops were short of ammunition and rations and had only about a dozen tanks left.

By nightfall on the August 6th, Obata's last defensive line collapsed. The fight for Guam ended.

Victory in the Marianas Campaign made the continued American advance across the Pacific certain. Japan's southern flank now lay wide open, and after the Battle of the Philippine Sea the Japanese no longer had the naval air strength to counter American aircraft carrier task forces. Navy task forces and the U.S. Army Air Forces won the bases that allowed them to sever Japan's link to the East Indies oil fields, interdict its supply lines to China, and attack the Japanese home islands themselves. Furthermore, no enemy-held territory remained between American forces and the Philippines.[5]

---

[5] Sources: a) *The U.S. Army Campaigns of World War II - Western Pacific*; b) *Marines in World War II - Breaching The Marianas, A Close Encounter, and Liberation*; c) Dyer, *Amphibians Came to Conquer*; d) Morison, *New Guinea and the Marianas*.

(continued from p. 259) by one day. Fire, Emergency and Abandon Ship drills were held and the General Alarm System tested. You could feel the tension beginning to mount.

Magazine temperatures reached ninety-nine degrees for two days running. We had similar problems on the *Nathaniel Currier* at Guadalcanal. Mooney and I put some wet matting near the door of the forward magazine so that evaporation would cool the compartment.

On September 15, 1944 we arrived at Eniwetok and anchored. Our convoy of freighters was dwarfed by the awesome firepower of the Pacific Fleet moored across the lagoon. The sight of them made us all mighty proud — and more than a little envious — of our fleet brethren. Ours was a defensive role whereas the combatant crews could go looking for enemy action.

On September 16 we sailed in a smaller convoy consisting of six merchant cargo ships and one LST, plus an escort of three PCs and one YMS. Four days later two of the Liberty ships and the YMS detached from the convoy for an unknown destination. Our convoy now consisted of four Libertys and one LST plus the three PC escorts.

On September 21 we arrived and anchored at Saipan in the Mariana Islands.

On September 22 at 0830 we received our first radio alert on the *Belasco* from the shore station, warning of an air attack. The nervous phone chatter of the new men reminded me of my first encounter with the enemy at Guadalcanal fifteen months earlier. As the "old salt" now, soon to turn nineteen, I tried to calm their nerves. I also reminded them of the Fleet's huge victory in the Philippine Sea in June and that a raid of any size was a long shot at best. No enemy planes showed up so we secured from GQ after half an hour.

On September 23 we moved from our anchorage, after discharging the Navy pontoons, to Berth 3, Tanapag Harbor, Saipan. By supper time the Army stevedores were discharging our military cargo. At 1830 we received a second air raid alert from the shore station and made another mad dash for our battle stations. We didn't even have time to weigh anchor before the all clear signal was announced and we secured from GQ.

Sunday, September 24, was a surprising day. At 0900 muster the C.O. set a holiday schedule as if we were tied up in San Francisco, then announced there would be liberty for one-half of the crew between 1100 and 1800. All this in spite of air raid alerts. Obviously the "brass" knew something we didn't.

Our C.O. Charles Hackler and I escorted our first liberty party ashore that day. Starting from Tanapag Harbor where Seabees and Army stevedores were unloading our cargo, we walked into Garapan, the largest city on the island. It was hard to believe 8,000 Marines stormed ashore only three months earlier. Signs of the pre-invasion bombardments and bombings were everywhere but cleanup was well underway. The Army Engineers and Seabees were building airfields and other advance base facilities but, we were told, they also supervised Japanese civilian labor gangs assigned to various cleanup projects. Japanese civilians represented about seventy-five percent of Saipan's total population of 25,000.

For safety reasons, we were restricted as to where we could go. There were still Jap snipers in the hills who refused to surrender. We visited the Military Cemetery — a very somber experience for all of us and a picture I still see clearly in my mind's eye some fifty years later.

The Chamorro natives as well as Marine and Army entrepreneurs offered us souvenirs along the way: Japanese rifles, bayonets, and flags. Most were willing to barter for cigarettes, candy, beer, and liquor. Some of the guys got a few items, others decided to wait until they could negotiate without the C.O. present.

Lt. Hackler said that while he was at the Port Director's office the day before, he learned why it was considered safe to grant liberty. The Battle of the Philippine Sea some 600 miles west of Saipan broke the back of Japanese naval air power. In a running, two-day battle of strikes and counterstrikes with the U.S. Fifth Fleet, the Japs lost nearly all their aircraft including

100 land-based aircraft, and three carriers. We knew there had been an important battle — that much was in the news — but we had no idea it was such a decisive victory.

News coverage in the States was censored and, of course, Tokyo Rose — the traitorous American citizen who broadcast propaganda aimed at U.S. forces — called the June 20-21 battle a major Japanese victory. As we later learned, it was a major setback for Japanese air power, but did not deliver the final crushing blow we sought. The Japanese fleet was still a dangerous surface opponent.

We had two more air alerts that evening. "Washing Machine Charlie" was considerate enough to wait until the liberty party was back on board to man the battle stations.

The next day the other half of the crew had liberty and we had another call from "Charlie" at 1815 and another practice run to our battle stations.

The following days were routine. Liberty was available daily to half the crew but few took advantage of it. Most simply stayed aboard and read or played cards.

On September 28 we moved out from the dock a short distance and anchored. The discharging of cargo continued. On Sunday, October 1, we weighed anchor and moved farther from the dock and dropped the hook again to await routing instructions.

Our position was off the southern end of Saipan near Agingan Point about a half-mile west of the Ansilito Airfield. Ushi Point, the northernmost tip of Tinian was so close — or so it seemed — that seven of us decided to swim over to its beaches and look around. That was a mistake. As we learned later, it was a good two miles to Ushi Point. We also discovered the cross current was very strong.

Fortunately the Chief Mate, Charles Bennett, had the watch. He followed our swim with his binoculars and told me later, "I knew you were in trouble ten minutes after you started out. You were drifting east even though your heading was southwest." It wasn't long before we realized our dilemma and turned back. But it was like swimming upstream. The end result was five bluejackets and two merchant mariners were "rescued" by Bosun Jacobson and AB Jordan in one of the *Belasco*'s lifeboats. At first, the C.O. and the skipper were irritated at our poor judgment but they eventually cooled down. The penalty: we owed Bennett, Jacobson, and Jordan a round of beers when we got back to the States.

At 1830 the *Belasco* set sail for destinations unknown with one YMS escort: speed ten knots. On October 2 we experienced a first. The Polls opened aboard ship at 0800 for voting under the Servicemen's Voting Law. They closed an hour later. No one voted. Everyone assumed FDR's reelection was a *fait accompli*.

Just before lunch the next day we arrived at Guam and dropped the hook. Sea watches were secured and port watches set. The C.O. opened the Polls again at 1600 for an hour. Still no one voted.

Most of us were fascinated by the ongoing waterfront construction of the Seabees. We watched them sink the last several big concrete barges for temporary breakwater extensions, build more pontoon piers, and finish a causeway out to the piers.

On October 3, cargo discharging began at 0915 but went very slowly due to intermittent heavy rain squalls. By 1300 the next day discharging was stopped. A storm warning was received. The Skipper got underway and steamed at full throttle while all hands turned to securing guns and ammunition. On October 5 we were able to move back to our assigned anchorage but gale force winds and heavy rain prevented any cargo discharge. The storm hung around for another twenty-four hours before things became routine again. On October 9 at 1700, we weighed anchor and tied up to buoys in Guam's inner harbor at Apra. At 2000 discharging of cargo resumed.

On October 11, cargo discharging was completed in the early morning and a cargo of mail sacks and Japanese ammunition was loaded aboard. At 0430 we shifted to Buoy No. 1 in the outer harbor. Late that afternoon twenty-two passengers reported aboard. The following afternoon we departed in a convoy of two merchant ships and one PC escort at a speed of ten knots. Port security watches were secured and General Quarters (Condition 1) was set. As we secured GQ, our C.O. informed us we were heading back to the Marshall Islands.

During the morning of October 13, the convoy was forced to reduce speed to five knots for about an hour while the crew of one of the other merchant vessels fixed a troublesome boiler.

Between 0930 and 1415 Mooney and I established a head cleaning detail among the passengers; Lt. Hackler inspected all the guns, ready boxes and gun tubs and the magazine sprinkling systems were tested; the Skipper conducted a fire and boat drill — mainly for the passengers' benefit; and finally, we held small arms firing practice. A busy sea routine.

The rest of the trip back to the Marshalls, then on into "Pearl," was routine with a few exceptions:

We picked up 1,500 tons of aircraft engines at Engebi Atoll for Pearl Harbor.

We were able to attend movies ashore on several nights. That was a boost to our morale.

The day we left Eniwetok, October 26, was a milestone — two years in the Navy and another two to go on my "kid's cruise."

Between Eniwetok and Pearl:

The 3"/50 gun crews got to scrape and paint both guns.

We crossed the dateline (Meridian day) on October 31 so we had two 31sts.

We had firing practice of all guns with one "gun casualty." (One of the 3"/50 projectiles was not fired out by the powder charge. The bore was cleared with a short powder charge.)

On November 6 we arrived at Pearl Harbor. From the *Honolulu Advertiser*, I caught up on the major news happenings.

September-October 1944

Troops of the U.S. First Army enter Belgium and on September 10 overrun Luxembourg.

The first V-2 rocket is launched across the Channel on September 12.

Soviet troops cross the Danube River in force on September 20 and push toward Belgrade.

U.S. First Army begins siege of Aachen, Germany on October 1.

Leyte Landings 20 October 1944. TBM "Avenger" flying over the landing beaches near Tacloban during the initial landings. Naval Historical Center.

Leyte Landings. Lt. Gen. George C. Kenney (left), Lt. Gen. Richard K. Sutherland (center), and Gen. Douglas MacArthur (right) head for shore to inspect the beachhead on Leyte Island, P.I., 20 October 1944. U.S. Army.

Soviet troops enter East Prussia on October 16 and on October 18 enter Czechoslovakia.

Fourteen B-29 Superfortress bombers, flying their first combat mission from the Mariana Islands, attack the bypassed Japanese base at Truk on October 18.

U.S. Sixth Army troops land on Leyte October 20, the beginning of General MacArthur's return to the Philippines. Three days later, the Battle of Leyte Gulf results in a major Japanese naval defeat. The Japanese begin to resort to the infamous Kamikaze suicide attacks, in which Japanese pilots attempt to crash their explosive-laden planes into American ships.

Most of the gun crew went ashore while we were in Pearl, but I got into a poker game that kept going with the same players — a mix of gunners and mariners — until the end of the trip. I was becoming a pretty fair card player and gained confidence with every hand.

On November 12 we sailed for San Francisco.

The rest of the trip was uneventful until November 21 when, the ship was re-routed from San Francisco to Astoria, Oregon, by radio message. This resulted in us spending a couple of extra days at sea — one of them being Thanksgiving Day. We all had a lot to be thankful for — like arriving back in the States in one piece.

Arriving in Portland, we berthed at the McCormick Steamship Company docks. "Sea Watch secured. Port Security Watch set. Log completed for submission to Navy Department."

C.O. Hackler's Voyage Report included the following items of interest:

There were no contacts or action with the enemy.

The vessel was not unduly delayed in port.

The commercial and Navy radio operators carried out Wartime Radio Instructions for Merchant Vessels satisfactorily.

Defects in equipment: stops on the forward 3"/50 gun should be raised about one foot to prevent firing into superstructure.

Training at sea: PTS drills at general quarters; fire, emergency and abandon ship drills and lectures; use and care of sound-powered telephones; instruction in watch standing and proper method of reporting objects sighted; recognition of Japanese planes taught; antiaircraft and antisubmarine local fire control taught; gunner's mates instructed and drilled in spotting surface fire and determining sight angle in antiaircraft fire; Coxswain, GM3/c and SM2/c training course manuals issued to interested personnel; SM2/c P&E test given to SM3/c; GM3/c and COX P&E tests given to 3 non-rated men.

I had a run of luck between the Islands and Portland and won almost $200 in our ongoing poker game. Most of my winnings came from just one hand. I was holding four Jacks in a five card draw game and two other players had good hands but not quite good enough to beat my Jacks.

I hung around until everyone got paid so I could collect my winnings, then said good-bye and headed to Seattle for a visit with my family.

It was a good trip with a great bunch of guys. The *Belasco* served her country well. Like the *Currier*, she made it through the war in one piece and was finally scrapped in Portland, Oregon in April 1966.[6]

---

5 L. A. Sawyer and W. H. Mitchell, *The Liberty Ships*.

13

THE

SS *COEUR D'ALENE*
VICTORY
MISADVENTURE

On November 26, 1944, I caught a Greyhound bus for Seattle. My plan was to spend the first a few days of my leave with my family then "explore" the Cascade and Sierra ranges on my way back to the Armed Guard Center at Treasure Island. Mother and my sister, Doris, were full of questions as usual and made me more of my favorite home-cooked meals. They both worked so I was free to do as I pleased during the day.

The first thing I did was check in with the Armed Guard officer in the 13th Naval District offices in Seattle. While there I picked up the Gunner's Mate Second-Class study materials and got a couple of tailor recommendations. I was outgrowing my tailor-made dress blues. When I enlisted on my seventeenth birthday, I was a shade over six feet tall and weighed 170 pounds. I grew two inches and put on twenty-five pounds in a little over two years. "Still a growing boy," according to the tailor as he measured me for my new uniform, "guaranteed to be ready within forty-eight hours." It was a good investment of some of my poker winnings on the *Belasco*.

As with my previous leave, Mother and Doris organized a get-together with some of our friends from Malta, Montana, now living and working in the Seattle-Tacoma area.

I hoped to see my brother Bob, but he left Puget Sound a week earlier on his seagoing tug for Skagway, Alaska. I also hoped to visit Montana, but with train travel being slow and unpredictable, there just wasn't enough time.

After four days with family and friends, I picked up my new uniform and caught a bus to Portland. I planned to hitch-hike across the Cascades to Bend, then southeast to Lake Tahoe in the Sierra. But the weather was terrible: heavy rain in Portland, and wet snow at the higher elevations in the Cascades. In the end I rode the "Hound" all the way to Truckee, California then caught a local bus to Tahoe. Fortunately, my poker winnings financed the trip.

I fell in love with Tahoe and the Sierra, wandered around town, made new friends, and hated to leave when it was time to catch my train to Oakland. But I decided one day I'd be back.

I was dumbfounded to find a letter waiting for me from my father when I checked in at TI. As you may recall, my parents were divorced when I was seven, and the last time I saw my dad was in 1937, and then only for a few moments. Three years later he moved to Alaska. So we weren't exactly close. But you would never know it from the tone of his letter. Some excerpts:

> Billy:
>
> Just received your address from Betty [my sister in DC]. Hope you like your choice of service though you know my favorite has always been the Infantry.
>
> Well son, as you can see, I'm still out in the great unknown, where most everything is just as nature intended it to be. I've flown

over most of Alaska in the last two years and really like it, all kinds of game and fish. Wish you could join me after the war.

There are lots of things I would like to tell you, but I can't write about what we are doing up here, but you can bet its plenty. I know you have it in you to be a good sailor and I want you to know, I'm really proud of you. I know you will do your duty when the time comes. You know I'll be pulling for you with all I've got.

We [the OSS] are about finished with this job so when you write, mail it care of the Pastime Cigar Store, Fairbanks, Alaska. They will know where to find me.

Lots of love,
Your Dad

Amazing! He never sent us one dime all through the depression years in spite of divorce papers calling for $75 a month in child support and alimony. And he was making good money, too.

On December 15, I was assigned to temporary Shore Patrol (SP) duty until the first of the year. Most of the individual commands on Treasure Island furnished shore patrolmen to maintain order in nearby cities. The concept was not to represent law and order but to take care of the men on liberty and to see that they got back to TI without making trouble. A secondary responsibility was to protect civilians from unruly sailors. It was a thankless job but necessary.

I was issued a .45 automatic sidearm in a holster attached to a web belt that buckled around the waist, a pair of handcuffs, an SP brassard, a nightstick, and a pair of white canvas leggings reminiscent of boot camp. I joined a detail of some fifty men and boarded a blue bus for lower Mission Street in San Francisco, one of several SP "reporting stations" in the City.

Upon arrival, we were paired up and assigned beats. My partner and I drew an easy one the first night, Union Square. There were no "hot spots" here, with notorious reputations that had been placed off-limits by military officials to "protect" servicemen from unsavory activities.

We stopped a number of bluejackets and ordered them to "square that hat and roll down those cuffs." If they responded favorably that was the end of that. If they argued with us, we checked their ID and recorded their name, base or ship, and service number in our note pad.

We only had one altercation that first night and an embarrassment, at that. Two sailors got into a fist fight with some civilians after calling them names for not being in uniform. As it turned out, the civilians worked in a nearby defense plant and were exempt from the draft. We had to cuff the sailors and call the paddy wagon. Later, we had to write a report on what happened.

I had SP duty every other night in San Francisco for the next two weeks. Saturday nights were busier than others. New Year's Eve was the worst of all. There were sailors everywhere and most, it seemed, had too much to drink. Suffice it to say we had our hands full. We had long waits for the paddy wagon and it was the first time I had to bang sailors on the head to "get their attention."

On my days off, I stayed on the island and went to the movies and caught up on the news.

November/December 1944

On the home front, President Roosevelt wins an unprecedented fourth term by defeating New York Governor Thomas Dewey.

Twenty-four B-29 Superfortress bombers strike the Nakajima aircraft plant northwest of Tokyo on 24 November in the first strategic bombing raid flown from the new bases in the Marianas.

The U.S. Third Army troops cross the Saar River on December 4.

German forces stage a surprise counterattack in the Ardennes Forest of Belgium on December 16 beginning the Battle of the Bulge. On the 27th the U.S. Third Army raises the siege of Bastogne.

One day shortly before heading back to sea, or so I thought at the time, I was privileged to be one of several gunners to receive an award from the C.O. of the Armed Guard Center, Commander E.D. Flaherty. My award was a Commendation from the Chief of Naval Personnel for ". . . action against Japanese aircraft off Guadalcanal on 16 June 1943."

Sailors everywhere and from all generations know that no matter how hard sea duty can be, there comes a time when going back to sea, and leaving land behind, is a welcome relief. So it was following my Shore Patrol duty over New Year's.

C.O. Flaherty conducts Armed Guard Ceremony. U.S. Navy.

A draft of twelve men mustered outside the Center on January 2, 1945 then boarded a gray Navy bus for the short ride to the train depot in Oakland, California. Leading Petty Officer, Thomas O'Hare, GM 2/c, couldn't answer the question on everyone's mind, "Why the skeleton crew of only ten gunners and two communications people?" His trite, overworked reply, "Ours not to reason why, ours is but to do or die."

The train ride up to Portland was the worst I experienced. A grueling two-day trip on a "milk train" in an old coach car so packed you couldn't even move. When we finally arrived at about 0600 on January 4, there was no one to meet us. O'Hare made a couple of phone calls and learned our ship wasn't ready yet, so we would be staying at the nearby Naval Receiving Barracks.

The Officer in Charge of the barracks looked over our orders and said, "Ensign Binner, your Armed Guard officer, hasn't arrived as yet. So pick out an empty bunk and locker and get yourself squared away, then come by my office to pick up a liberty card if you're so inclined." Everyone was broke but seemed ready to explore Portland anyway.

For the next few days we had more liberty than anyone could afford. All we had to do was check in with the Officer in Charge each morning at 0745 and pick up a new liberty card.

On January 10, our C.O. Robert B. Binner, Ensign, USNR, greeted us with a wake up call at 0600. He had reported aboard the night before. There were a few gripes when he added morning calisthenics to our daily routine, but we figured, what the hell, we'd had it pretty easy.

The next day, the C.O. checked in with the Port Director's office and was told our ship should be ready to board sometime on Friday, January 12 at the McCormack Dock in Portland. That afternoon Binner granted me a special seventy-two-hour liberty over the coming weekend so I could visit my family in Seattle, not unusual under the circumstances.

Now here is where this story gets very confusing. Before I knew what hit me, I was accused of being Absent Over Leave

(AOL) exactly forty-eight hours on January 15 and transferred under guard to the Bremerton brig.

I don't remember the what, why, when and where of my "surrender" on January 16 but, my ship had sailed at 1235 on the 14th without me. (She steamed down to San Francisco, empty.) I do remember the train ride back to Seattle and the embarrassment of being guarded by two SPs as if I were a hardened criminal. I also remember the gray and foggy Puget Sound Naval Yard opposite Seattle and the Bremerton Brig.

The Marine Guards at the brig lived up to their reputation as mean sons-of-bitches and then some. I must have spent at least four hours a day for two days on my hands and knees repolishing hardwood floors. If you stopped to rest or talk to the man next to you, a billy club came down on your ass or across the shoulder. The guards obviously enjoyed all forms of sadism. Many a sailor vowed to get even if they ever caught them ashore unarmed. Was I ever glad to leave.

I was transferred to AGC(PAC) on January 18 under my own recognizance ("technical arrest"). The train ride was definitely more pleasant without an escort.

After checking in at the Center on January 20, I was driven to the TI Brig — a luxurious resort compared to Bremerton. At the Captain's Mast — a court of sorts at which the commanding officer metes out punishment — I was "awarded" a Deck Court for being AOL (Absent Over Leave) exactly 48 hours.

I wanted to fight the charge but a lawyer-type naval officer talked me out of it. He sympathized with me but felt I would have trouble proving my case.

Furthermore, to fight it could mean another week or more in the brig, whereas a guilty plea would be handled the next day. I pleaded guilty at the Deck Court on the 23rd and lost a half-month's pay.

Treasure Island was a welcome sight when I checked back into the "Center." In fact it was downright beautiful — the island setting, the bridges, the 1939 World's Fair buildings —

and a special place to come home to after being detached from a ship.

Even the crowded berthing and messing facilities didn't bother me any longer.

I caught up on recent developments in the war at the Recreation Center library by reading back issues of the San Francisco papers.

January 1945

On 3 January, the U.S. Unified Commands-Southwest Pacific Area (General MacArthur) and Pacific Ocean Area (Admiral Nimitz)

Across the lagoon at Treasure Island. U.S. Navy.

Fair Food and Beverage Palace, Treasure Island. U.S. Navy.

are abolished. MacArthur is placed in command of all U.S. ground forces in the Pacific and Nimitz all naval forces, in preparation for the final assaults against the Japanese.

On 9 January, the U.S. Sixth Army lands on Luzon in the Philippines.

On 12 January, Soviet forces open a massive winter offensive across the Vistula River in southern Poland.

On 15 January, the Joint Chiefs order the XX Bomber Command (B-29 Superfortresses) to transfer to the Mariana Islands from the China-India area.

I had a memorable liberty in Richmond, California — the home of Kaiser's Permanente Metals shipyards — before catching my next ship. While shooting the bull with several other bluejackets in the Recreation Center lounge one day they mentioned a country music dance hall in Richmond. They were all country boys like myself raised on Hank Williams, Roy Acuff, and Bob Wills. We decided to go see what it was like.

One of the guys had an uncle working at the yards, that's how he learned of the place. We caught a navy bus to Oakland, then took public transportation to Richmond — a very busy city that exploded with defense work during the war. Kaiser recruited workers from all over the country so we had a broad mix of patrons at the club that night, good hard-working, hard-drinking people having a ball. Of course, I had a lot in common with many of them because of my former job with Kaiser in Vancouver. After two or three drinks, I danced up a storm, especially when the band leader called a square dance.

We stayed until closing time and met a lot of good people — including some very attractive single gals — men and women building ships, home front warriors doing their part to win the war. I was especially proud to be an American that night.

It must have been 0500 by the time we made it back to TI. The fog had rolled in and I was cold, even in my peacoat, waiting for the last bus connection, while listening to the warning chorus of foghorns from around the Bay.

14

Destination: Philippine Islands

B y January 31, 1945 I was ready for more sea duty. I was pleased when my name was called along with two other gunners mates, Thomas, C. E., GM2/c, and Bagrowski, O. J., GM3/c, to take a skeleton crew of six seamen aboard the SS *Thomas Nelson* berthed at Pier 27 in San Francisco

We checked in with the C.O., Ben H. Poynor, Ensign, USNR, and got a brief tour of the ship's battle damage sustained in Leyte Gulf in November. The galley was closed for repairs so we ate chow in a small pier restaurant.

On February 2 our crew was kept busy getting ammo off the ship. The repair schedule included the use of cutting torches — not exactly compatible with high explosives. Liberty commenced at 1600 that evening but we were all too tired or too broke to take advantage of it.

The departing CO, Poynor and his replacement, Espy, spent a lot of time together the next two days. We all went to

SS Thomas Nelson *original skeleton crew, 31 January 1945. Front row L to R: Thomas, McGee, Tritt, Bagrowski. Back row L to R: Forti, Dissinger, Follmer, Dukes, Dishner. Charles Espy.*

have a farewell dinner for Poynor, except the two gunners standing port security watch.

The Liberty ship SS *Thomas Nelson* was built by Bethlehem-Fairfield Shipyard at Baltimore, Maryland and launched in May of 1942. Her engine was manufactured by the General Machinery Corp. of Hamilton, Ohio. Her gross tonnage was 7,176 and deadweight tonnage 10,550. She was owned by the War Shipping Administration and chartered to Calmar Steamship Corp. as operator. Her armament consisted of one 4"/50 aft; one 3"/50 forward and eight 20-mm antiaircraft guns (four on the bridge, two aft and two forward). With a full complement she carried a merchant marine crew of forty, headed by Capt. William F. Gayle. Within those forty were eighteen in the deck department, thirteen in the engineering department, and eight in the steward's department. *(text continues on p. 290)*

THE THOMAS NELSON

The ship received a battering from the enemy on the previous voyage. From the Enemy Action Reports for the *Thomas Nelson:*

The SS *Thomas Nelson* was damaged by enemy aircraft at approximately 1127 [0327 GCT], 12 NOV. 44, while at anchor in Dulag Harbor, Leyte, P.I., having sailed from Hollandia 23 Oct. in convoy with 23 other ships and 6 escorts for Leyte arriving 29 October, loaded with 1823 tons of cargo consisting of high explosives, gasoline, and military equipment and between 577-633 U.S. Army troops as passengers.

Between 50 to 60 Army troops and about six of their vehicles had been discharged before the attack. Vessel did not sink but returned to San Francisco (without prior repairs) under her own power.

On Sunday 12 November 1944, the SS *Thomas Nelson* was anchored in Dulag Harbor, Leyte, P.I. with more than 20 other ships — mostly of her own Liberty Freighter class. The weather was cloudy with a light wind from the northwest. Ships heading NNW (or WNW). Surface visibility good. The gun crew was in Condition 2; no Merchant Marine officer was on watch on the bridge.

At about 1127 three Japanese suicide planes came out of the clouds from the WNW relative bearing 35 degrees, and circled the ships in the immediate area. The planes then straightened out with each plane selecting a ship. One of the planes swung in a curve over the SS *Leonidas Merritt*, which was anchored off the port bow, and came in for a crash dive on the aft end of the *Nelson* where the aft magazine is located. The plane came in from about N by E relative angle 35 degrees and commenced strafing the ship with all its guns from an estimated distance of 500 feet.

The kamikaze struck the *Nelson*'s heavy lift boom at the No. 4 hatch and part of the plane sheared off the ship through the bulwark on the port side aft where pieces of the plane's engine were later found.

The Armed Guard officer stated that at the time of the attack, he was standing on the aft end of the boat deck, starboard side, when he first sighted the three planes at an altitude of about 500 feet just seconds before the crash on the *Nelson* occurred. It was impossible to sound the alarm or get any guns trained on the plane before the crash.

Two explosions occurred. The first explosion was no doubt caused by the plane crashing into the ship. The second and loudest explosion, one to three seconds later, was believed to be that of the bomb carried by the plane.

Fires caused by explosions broke out immediately on the after deck, in the 'tween deck of No. 5 hold, the gun crew's aft quarters and in the steering engine room adjoining the magazine. The gun deck above the crew's quarters for guns 8, 9 and 10 was smashed and badly burned putting all three guns out of commission.

The most dangerous fire occurred in the No. 5 hold which was nearly fully loaded with bombs and 82 octane gasoline. It took more than two hours to get the fires under control and, according to the Master, it is doubtful whether the crew could have done it without the help of a few expert firemen from a Navy LCT fireboat who came aboard.

The SS Thomas Nelson *showing damage to her after section from kamikaze attack November 12, 1944 at Dulag, Leyte, Philippines. Naval Historical Center.*

The damage was extensive with twisted steel everywhere. Naval Historical Center.

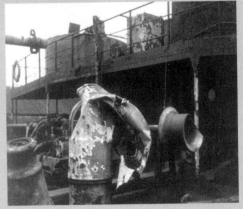

Firefighting was greatly hampered because of the deck cargo and the dead and wounded spread over the decks and in the holds of the ship. The dead and wounded Army personnel were brought up from the 'tween decks and carried to the forward part of the ship by other unwounded comrades. The Master stated that doctors and medical stores were immediately sent from shore and there was no panic and very little confusion.

Small Naval craft came alongside and took off the wounded. Total complement on board was 638, including 38 merchant crew, 27 Armed Guard and approximately 573 troops.

The entire merchant crew, who were amidships preparing for dinner, survived. Three Armed Guard were killed, four wounded — three hospitalized in forward area — and 21 survived. The U.S. troops — 107 killed, 57 missing, 84 wounded and approximately 325 survived.

Several Armed Guard personnel were commended by their C.O. Ben H. Poynor, Lt. (jg), USNR: "All stepped forward immediately during the fire when I asked for four volunteers to go aft with me to turn on the flooding system to the 4"/50 magazine and to throw the ammunition from the ready boxes overboard," said Poynor. "The whole gun deck was in flames as well as the ready boxes causing the shells to be very hot."

Three of the ship's Merchant Marine crew who volunteered to help throw ammunition overboard were also singled out.

The plane that struck the *Nelson* was described as a 'Hamp' Mitsubishi Zero-2. The Armed Guard officer and his crew were commended very highly by the Master of the ship.

Later, that same day, the ship was attacked again — this time by seven planes.

12 November 1944, 1735 hours. We were attacked by 7 planes coming in from every direction without being in any kind of formation. We shot down one plane off our port beam. One plane that we had set afire crashed into SS *Morrison Waite*.. Another plane crash dived into SS *Leonidas Merritt*. Another plane crash dived into SS *Alexander Majors*. The other three planes were shot down by the 20-odd other ships anchored in San Pedro Bay. We fired thirty-three (33) rounds of 3-inch ammunition, and eighteen hundred (1800) rounds of 20-mm.

Ira O. Schaub, staff sergeant with the 498th Bomb Squadron, 345th Bomb Group, Fifth Air Force, was a passenger on the *Nelson* when she was hit: "Our squadron was being transferred from Biak Island to the air base near Tacloban. I was a top turret gunner on a B-25J.

"I was a volunteer loader on the *Nelson*'s 20-mm cannon on the aft port side of the bridge. I bunked up under the forward gun tub on an Army cot. The deckload consisted of several trucks.

"The number 5 hold from the top down was personnel, then a layer of jeeps and trailers, then a layer of eighty-seven octane gasoline drums, then it was bombs and paraflags [bombs with parachutes] to the bottom of the hold. I still remember the Captain agonizing over turnin' the steam on to put out the fire because there was personnel down there. Our men were scattered all over the deck from midships aft."

When the attack occurred, I was "up on the bridge playin' cards with somebody. There was no alert . . . no GQ, nothin'. First time I knew anything was goin' on, one of the planes was strafin', the one comin' in on the starboard side. I looked up over the forward rail and here he comes. That's when I started runnin' for my gun. I kept goin' until he finally hit. But by the time I had the gun cocked, it was all over.

"Some of the guys on the aft guns went over the side just in time.

"One little story still sticks in my mind. We had a guy who was a practical joker, so to speak, and he got a bunch of shrapnel in his back. He was in the crew's mess lyin' face down on the table and Doctor was workin' on him, and he says, 'You know, these folks don't play fair, they're usin' live ammunition.' I can't remember his name, but I think he died from those wounds.

"I stayed aboard the *Nelson* for almost 30 days as part of the gun crew after they off-loaded our personnel. They had asked for volunteers to stay on until the ship's cargo was discharged."

C.J. (Mickey) Potter, gun director operator on the *Burlington*, remembers the Dulag Harbor action on November 12: "We knew something was going to happen because we had one snooper after another the night before. That morning we were at GQ between about 0400-0700, then we broke for breakfast. Nothing much happened until shortly before noon. Then all hell broke loose with Jap planes coming from all directions.

"We were about 1½ miles from the *Nelson* when she was kamikazied. Our chief gunner said he thought the plane that crashed the *Nelson* came in low over land. As we closed on her, we got out a couple of fire hoses — it was hard for us because we couldn't stop, you know. Anyway, the plates on the *Nelson* were red hot, you could see it. When we first played water on her, it turned to steam."

Lieutenant Poyner's Action Report described several other attacks on the *Thomas Nelson* which occurred before heading back to the States:

18 November 1944, 0745 hours. About 15 planes came in from SE about 500 feet altitude. They were quickly disposed of by our fleet and fighter planes. We fired one (1) round of three 3-inch ammunition at 7500 yards but plane was out of range.

24 November 1944, 1415 hours. One torpedo bomber came in from SE. We fired six (6) rounds of 3-inch ammunition and two hundred forty (240) rounds of 20-mm. Plane was shot down approximately 3500 yards from us by P-38 fighter plane.

6 December 1944, 1815 hours. Three torpedo planes came out of NW about 25 feet above water level. We fired three (3) rounds of 3-inch and one hundred forty (140) of 20-mm. Two of the planes were shot down by P-38 fighter planes, the other was knocked down by a Destroyer.

Of the 241 raids and alerts in Leyte during the 40 days and nights there, the above is the number of times we fired at the enemy.

The entire Navy Gun Crew is to be commended for being at their battle stations on an average of 18 hours a day, missing their meals and sleep. The crew averaged a weight loss of 20 pounds per man during this period.

The *Nelson* returned to the U.S. via Finchhafen, New Guinea and Funafuti, Ellice Islands, where she stopped to refuel and take on stores, arriving back in San Francisco on January 28, 1945.

(continued from p. 284) The U.S. Navy Armed Guard Unit contained twenty-seven men headed by Charles C. Espy, Lt. (jg), USNR. Among them were twenty-four gunners and two communications men.

On February 5 our new C.O. relieved Poynor and had his "orders endorsed by the Master of the vessel."

We spent another three weeks at Pier 27 in San Francisco doing the many things that had to be done to get the *Nelson* re-gunned. These included:

1) Remove Nos. 8 and 9 20-mm and the 4"/50.
2) Dismantle the other six 20-mm guns so the mounts could be removed from the ship.
3) When the 4"/50 replacement arrived, we found a new foundation was necessary.
4) Replace old ready boxes with new larger models.
5) Clean and paint floors of ammo magazines fore and aft.
6) Mount the replacement 20-mm guns and checked cocking lanyards.
7) Begin the systematic arrangement of the three gear lockers.
8) Replace the old Mark 4 20-mm gun sights in poor condition with new Mark 4 sights.
9) Stow the winter gear in the starboard doghouse.

The ship repair and outfitting crews made excellent progress with the battle damage repairs once all the ammunition was removed from the ship. The jumbo boom and rigging at No. 4 hatch and the No. 5 port boom were replaced almost immediately so that they could be used in other repair work and later to load cargo.

We were granted plenty of liberty during our time at Pier 27, but most of us could barely afford cigarettes and a beer now and then. We had been "on the beach" too long.

The 20-mm mounts were returned to the ship after servicing, although the No. 8 gun was replaced entirely. The next day we bundled the winter and foul weather gear together and sent it off to be cleaned. The ready boxes and magazines remained empty as welding and burning torches were still in use.

On Sunday February 16 we had to clear the ship until 0800 Monday so it could be fumigated. On February 23 we sailed from Pier 27 to the Moore Drydock facility in Oakland.

The drydock crew checked the hull, rudder, and propeller for damage and found no serious repairs were needed. We were able to start cleaning the 20-mm gun mounts to allow for proper mounting of the guns.

On February 27 the ship began feeding for the first time since docking in San Francisco — a welcome relief. The following day seventeen new men reported aboard for duty from AGC(PAC) completing our Armed Guard complement

Ollie Bagrowski, GM3/c, and I assigned the new men to quarters, then showed them the ship and their gun positions. Columbus Edward Thomas, GM2/c — nicknamed "Lum" by the crew the first day — assigned some of the experienced new men to install the new 20-mm sights and to build flooring in the ammo magazines.

We received new ammunition consisting of: 252 rounds 3"/50, 124 rounds 4"/50, and 40,000 rounds of 20-mm, plus miscellaneous ammo for small arms, fuses, primers, smoke floats, and fuse setting wrenches. The ammunition stowage in the three magazines was completed by 2130. The next day we started loading the 20-mm magazines for stowage in the ready boxes. Then everyone was sent to the Armed Guard Center for booster shots, dog tags and final paychecks before sailing.

On March 3 F. R. Booth, K.P. Brooks, and E. Prozak, all S1/c, were Absent Over Leave (AOL). They turned up voluntarily two days later after being gone fifty-nine and a-half hours. At Captain's Mast the next day the C.O. accepted guilty pleas from each of the three men who quickly became known as the "three musketeers." They lost ten days liberty.

Moore Dry-dock, Oakland, California. Naval Historical Center.

On March 9 at 0850, we finished loading the last of the 20-mm magazines and filled out all the gun ready boxes. The ship left Pier B in Oakland and moved into the Bay to the degaussing range and to check compasses. By afternoon we were back at the Naval Supply Center in Oakland to take on a deckload of railroad rolling stock.

On March 10 the C.O. and Skipper headed for the Port Director's Office for routing instructions. The C.O. returned to the ship at 1840 and mustered the duty section to be sure everyone was on board. They were. At 2145 he mustered the duty section again and found the "musketeers" AWOL (Absent Without Leave, a much more serious offense than Absent Over Leave).

On Sunday, 11 March, the three men were once again aboard ship for morning muster. The C.O. called the senior duty officer of the day on TI and requested permission to detach all three men. They were replaced the next day.

On March 12, 1945, we sailed "pursuant to routing instructions." It was forty-plus days since we boarded the *Nelson* at Pier 27 in San Francisco.

January-February 1945

Warsaw falls to Soviet troops.

Additional SS Thomas Nelson *Armed Guard personnel report aboard, February 28, 1945, prior to departure for Philippines. Front Row, Left to Right: Booth, LeMoine, Kraft, Coburn, Segars; Second Row: Cotter, Morrell, Williams, White, Moran, Brooks; Third Row: Wyman, Wohleb, Patereau, Finnigsmier, Prazak. (Fiske, Smith, Vacek not pictured.) U.S. Navy.*

Burma Road is reopened.

U.S. Third Army launches attack on the German West Wall; the U.S. First Army joins the attack the following day.

The U.S. Sixth Army attacks Japanese troops in Manila.

Allied leaders met in the Yalta Conference, the second meeting of the Big Three.

Soviet Army completed the capture of Budapest.

U.S. troops breached the main Siegfried Line on Valentine's Day.

U.S. forces recapture Bataan.

U.S. Marines land on Iwo Jima 19 February.

1,200 U.S. bombers strike Berlin.

U.S. Airborne troops recapture Corregidor in Manila harbor.

It was a guess, but most of the "old salts" in our gun crew figured we were headed for the Philippines or Iwo Jima. There's always some speculation on destinations but the field of choice was narrowing with each passing month.

We drilled at just about everything we do during our departing Condition 1 general quarters: drills on the 3"/50 and 4"/50 from the bridge phones; drills for the sight setters on the 3" and 4" guns; practiced cocking and loading the 20s; the 20-mm gunners tracked target planes . . . well, you get the picture.

An LST loaded with men and equipment for the battle of Iwo Jima. Two pontoon barges are mounted on the sides of the LST. The barges were assembled by the 70th NCB. Seabees.

Iwo Jima Operation, February 1945. An LVT(A)-4 Amphibious Vehicle is lowered over the side of the USS Hansford (APA-106), circa 19 Feb. 1945. National Archives.

We spent the next thirty-eight days steaming toward our primary destination: Manila Bay in the Philippine Islands.

As the crew got to know one another, friendships formed. Two frequently used terms in those days are still with us today: "Scuttlebutt," named after the water cask on old ships where sailors gathered for a drink of water and to exchange gossip; and "snafu," an acronym for "situation normal, all fucked up." Both words became part of every sailor's lexicon.

Shipmates who didn't join in on conversations or debates usually opted to pass the time reading, writing letters or simply staring out to sea.

Card games continued to be my favorite pastime. But now I played with the merchant crew much of the time. I had to play it close to the vest to keep from getting in over my head.

According to Lt. Espy's Outbound Voyage Report, we conducted the following training drills en route to Manila:

Training	Total Hours
1. Sight setting, pointing and training	8
2. Gun drills, fuse setting and aim-off	12
3. Message, blinker and semaphore	8
4. First aid and casualty drills	6
5. Seamanship, A to N, Progress tests	24

C.O. Espy, editor of the *Nelson*'s souvenir newspaper[1], scheduled church services every Sunday. According to him:

> The first Sunday morning at sea found a group of ten gunners attending church services on the fantail. Church hymn recordings were played including The Lord's Prayer with music. Lt. Charles Espy used as his scripture the Sermon on the Mount, and offered prayer and benediction at the end.

---

[1] The *SS Thomas Nelson Scuttlebutt*, a Navy Armed Guard newspaper, was published by the gun crew of the ship at the end of its eight month Pacific voyage. Lt. (jg) C.C. Espy, Editor; D.D. Williams, Sports Editor; Jack Fiske, Features Editor; O.J. Bagrowski, Photographer.

The second Sunday found an excellent change. Substituting for the recordings was a vocal trio consisting of A.L. Smith and K.T. Sargars, first tenors and H.B. Coleman, second tenor. They sang, "By the Deep Sea Tread." Lt. Espy gave the sermon and prayer. The group of 20, partly Merchant Marine, sang the final hymn. Benediction was pronounced by Quentin Coburn.

From the third Sunday on, there were songs by the choir, sermon and prayer by Lt. Howard Hiland, Army Cargo Security Officer aboard, and benediction by Lt. Espy. These services on the fantail, in the Officers' wardroom and in Number ten gun tub always drew about twenty men.

David Williams and Jack Fiske, two of the gun crew's "jocks" created the *Nelson*'s Gym. Feature Editor Jack Fiske:

We put our heads together and came out with some barbells made out of two cans filled with cement, nuts and bolts and a pipe as a bar. David and Jack together mitigated many exercises such as curls and presses. They worked out every evening; and although Jack slacked up, David kept on with great fortitude . . .

When leaving the States the Nelson also had a medicine ball. Every day David, Pete Morrell and Johnny Moran would work out with it for an hour or so. One day David forgot his great strength and threw it so hard it bounced off one of the fella's heads and into the sea . . .

Joe Bagrowski and Wally Folmer could often be found somewhere on the deck playing catch. When there is no deck cargo, one usually finds boxing bouts on the hatch . . .

Jule "Pop" LeMoine, S1/c, reported on a surprise birthday party in *Scuttlebutt*:

A surprise birthday party was given aboard ship on March 28 to the following men: Joe Bagrowski, who reached the ripe old age of 28, Albert Lee Smith, a polite gentleman of 23, Lloyd Finnigsmier who is now eligible to vote, 21, and Jule LeMoine who is getting younger, but still must count to 35 years. George Bissonett, chief cook of the ship, baked a very nice chocolate cake for each man. Those cakes were really good and greatly appreciated . . .

Lt. Espy reeled off some very "nice" jokes. Music and vocals were furnished by Wohleb, Segars and Smith, good old hillbilly numbers, and then some church songs. A good time was had by all 26 men of the gun crew and C.O. We four should like to thank all who made us feel at home.

Albert Forti reported on LeMoine and other Nelson "Pops" in the same issue of *Scuttlebutt*:

Jule LeMoine is better known as Pop for his accomplishments in married life. Pop is the proud father of five girls. Second to Pop is William Dishner who is the father of three children. There are two girls and one boy in his family. His youngest daughter was presented to him by his wife during the present voyage.

There are several others of the crew who are fathers of two children. They are Lt. Espy, two boys; Roy Wohleb, one boy and one girl; Raymond Kraft, one boy and one girl. Noble Morrell is the father of one boy and Johnny Moran is also the father of one boy . . .

We are hoping all of these men will be home soon to continue the life they sacrificed to become part of the Armed Forces.

We had a slightly older gun crew (22.8 years) than usual, with seven married men, four of whom had children. We single men didn't know how lucky we were. It had to be tough to leave a wife and children behind. To me it was one great adventure, but if I were married, I'm sure I would have looked at it differently.

The trip was uneventful, highlighted by:

1. The C.O. did a speed test on March 16. He rang the general alarm unexpectedly. All guns checked in by phone manned and ready in one minute, life jackets at hand!

2. On March 20 the engines were stopped at 1500 for repairs in sight of Diamond Head, Oahu, T.H. Engine repairs were completed at 2035 and ship resumed speed.

3. Bow lookout sighted Johnson Island at 1925 on March 24.

4. On March 25 at 1400 the Chief Engineer, Lloyd Ellis, again stopped the ship's engine for repairs. Repairs completed at 2300 and continued voyage.

5. We were delayed in Eniwetok two days for engine repairs.

6. On April 2 we attended a movie by invitation from the Captain of a nearby destroyer at Eniwetok.

7. On April 10 at 1115 we arrived at Kossol Passage-- sometimes called Kossol Roads--in the Palau Islands.

C.O. Espy profiled chief engineer Ellis in *Scuttlebutt.* Some highlights:

The navy men liked and respected Lt. Cmdr. Ellis, merchant marine chief engineer, from the start. Since he is as young as some of the gunners, one might believe by his calm demeanor and easy manner that he had seen little of the war. The opposite is true . . .

Ellis is possessor of the Distinguished Service Medal of the Merchant Marine which has been awarded to less than forty men. His was the 19th awarded. It was accompanied by a personal letter from Admiral Land of the M.M. A personal letter from British Admiral Ramsey commended him for 1) preparation for and participation in the Normandy invasion, and 2) voluntary work on the beachhead for four days with the Medical Corps after losing his ship.

Both officials commended him for "heroic service above and beyond the call of duty" during the Normandy invasion . . .

Mr. Ellis has been wounded seriously three different times, for which he is authorized to wear the Mariner's Medal Ribbon Bar, given only for wounds in action. It is comparable to the Purple Heart. Another ribbon sometimes seen on men of the Maritime Service is the Combat Bar, worn only after combat. When a man has lost a ship, a silver star may decorate that ribbon. Chief Engineer Ellis wears three silver stars for three ships sunk . . .

Cmdr. Ellis joined the Merchant Marine the day after Pearl Harbor withstanding since then many of the dangerous Atlantic runs. The Ellis story points to bravery; it exhibits fortitude. Yet scarcely a person on the *Nelson* knows these things besides the writer, who had difficulty in learning them.

On April 12 while in Kossol Passage, Chief Radioman Jesse Hurlbert received the information that President Roosevelt died at his retreat in Warm Springs, Georgia, after suffering a massive cerebral hemorrhage. Vice-President Harry S. Truman, former Democratic Senator from Missouri and Chairman of the Special Committee to Investigate the National Defense Program, was immediately sworn in as President. What a shock! It didn't seem right that FDR wouldn't get to see the war end.

We had a talented crew on the *Nelson* ranging from musicians to prize fighters. K.F. Segars, *Scuttlebutt* reporter:

On an average of once a week, some of the boys who were musically talented banded together to present some original and much appreciated music. Those mainly responsible for helping to while away the evening hours before G.Q. were Al Smith, first tenor; K.F. Segars, first tenor; H.B. Coleman, second tenor; Roy Wohleb, baritone; and George Wyman, bass. They were 'The Hillbilly Serenaders,' singing both hillbilly and popular songs to the crew's enjoyment. They were often accompanied by Wohleb on the Guitar.

The master of ceremonies and imitator of Cousin Minnie Pearl of WSM's Grand Ole Opery was K.F. Segars who did a lot of vocalizing too. Unusual remarks were that his songs were good but his gags corny.

Willie Williams, sports Editor:

Probably the best boxer on the *Nelson* was Wally Folmer, a hard, fast puncher at 175 lbs. Frog Forti, Pete Morrell, Jack Fiske, and Al Smith also proved their worth with the gloves. Others who

Armed Guard signalmen practice hoisting recognition flags on board a merchant ship. National Archives.

competed were Coleman, Patereau, and Williams; Coleman and Patereau being matched several times and always turning out an even match. (Williams was the wrong man to ask to write this story. As in basketball, he was easily our best man, a tricky pugilist, to say the least. — Editor) Two excellent boxers displayed their wares often. They were 'Boats' and 'Captain' Kidd, the messman . . .

One evening [later in the trip] the gun crew, merchant seamen, and Filipinos had a smoker. Numerous matches entertained us. One smooth bout engaged the Purser and Folmer. It was close, too. But the Flips, fighting for cigarettes were the audience pleasers with their wild slugging. The main event matched Boats and Lt. Weeks, an Army Security Officer.

Bielanin has boxed professionally in Pennsylvania and Lt. Weeks had punched as an amateur at an eastern university. The former weighed about 175, the latter 200. You may judge how good the bout was when you learn that each man kissed the canvas once within 30 seconds time. Yes, that inter-racial Manila mixer on No. 4 hatch was a killer-diller.

On 14 April we left Kossol Passage in convoy with fifty-four ships and three escort vessels at an average speed of 7.46 knots. Signalman strikers George Cotter and Hollis Coleman began their convoy vessel watch around the clock.

While en route to Manila, I got to know all three of the Merchant Crew radio operators. Between them they tracked the major news stories whenever they could. Since we left San Francisco:

March-April 1945

U.S. Ninth Army completes drive to the Rhine.

A massive firebombing of Tokyo kills some 100,000 Japanese as U.S. planes step up bombardment of Japan from the Mariana Islands.

U.S. Eighth Army units land on Zamboanga Peninsula on Mindanao in the Philippines on 10 March.

The month-long struggle for Iwo Jima — a rocky, eight-square mile piece of volcanic island — came to an end on 16 March. Losses on both sides are horrifying, with the U.S. Marines suffering some 25,000 casualties. (Possessing Japan's last line of radar defense to warn against American attacks, Iwo Jima was a strategically significant prelude to the invasion of Okinawa.)

U.S. Third Army begins crossing the Rhine.

U.S. Tenth Army lands on Okinawa on Easter Sunday, 1 April. (The Japanese allow the American troops to land, and then systematically attempt to destroy their naval support, beginning a fight that lasts almost three months — the bloodiest battle of the Pacific, which will eventually cost 80,000 American casualties.)

First fighter-escorted mission is flown by B-29 bombers against Japan on 7 April. (The P-51 Mustang fighter escorts were based on Iwo Jima.)

U.S. Ninth Army's 2d Armored Division reaches the Elbe River 50 miles from Berlin. (They halt to await the advancing Russian troops.)

While the convoy was en route to Manila Harbor, the gun crew conducted gunnery practice daily. However, fellow gunners mate Bagrowski still found time to work on his tan.

Left, Nelson *gunnery practice, right "Guns" Bagrowski. Charles Espy.*

On April 20, 1945 we arrived and anchored in Manila Bay at 2000. The C.O. set the port security watch as well as a port visual signal watch.

On April 22, the C.O. mustered the first liberty party, sections B and C. He then gave the first of at least two dozen lectures on the dangers of venereal disease and bad alcohol in Manila. At 1030 he took the entire liberty party ashore for a supervised tour of the Manila Hotel, piers, Santo Tomas University and the downtown area.

The next day sections C and A (my section) got the same speech and liberty tour. Radio Operator Jesse Hurlbert also went along so that the C.O. could hear the Port Director's office confirm that no radio watch was required while in port.

I'll never forget the friendliness of the Philippine people and their almost embarrassing appreciation for the long-awaited liberation. The destruction of the city was appalling. We were shocked when we saw the evidence of vengeful sacking by the Japanese occupation force. Most of the habitable dwellings were destroyed; schools gutted; bridges over the principal rivers blown up; telephone lines disrupted; and most government buildings in ruins.

All forms of transportation were destroyed or taken away, from street cars and buses to inter-island vessels. The railroads

Anchored in Manila Harbor: Liberty ship SS Jerry S. Foley *with barges alongside. The Smokestack of a sunken Japanese cargo ship is in the foreground. Naval Historical Center.*

were bombed into uselessness and most rolling stock was destroyed or taken away by the Japanese. Our deckload of rail cars would be put to good use almost immediately. But reconstruction of the devastated country had to wait because the Philippines now became the staging area for the planned invasion of Japan.

The Filipino people, most of whom spoke fairly good English, seemed to take it all in stride. They were so happy to be rid of the occupation forces that the challenge of starting life all over again didn't seem to faze them. There were other problems, too. The Communist insurgents who fought the Japanese, began trying to take power. Adding to the chaos were purges of collaborationists who held government posts under the enemy.

Remains of Great Eastern Hotel, Manila, P.I., 1945. Charles Espy.

Liberty in Manila, 1945. Charles Espy.

On 24 April, the C.O. ordered all Armed Guard to ignore the native craft called "bumboats." At 1930 an undated and unsigned notice appeared on the bulletin boards in both the crew's and officer's mess. It included the following: "Native craft will not be permitted alongside the ship."

On April 27, Capt. Gayle requested a meeting with the C.O. and Chief Mate Albert Barthez. Captain Gayle complained that K. F. Segers, S1/c, had twice called Mr. Barthez obscene names. He added that W. L. McGee, GM3/c, made insolent remarks about the Captain's policy on liberty boats. (As of April 28 we had been in Manila seven days and had only had liberty three times.) The C.O. promised to investigate.

Later that day, Lt. Espy held an Armed Guard meeting on the fantail to explain liberty boat policy. The boats were within the province of the captain, and unless he saw fit to send one ashore, no one left the ship. On the other hand, mail was the responsibility of the Armed Guard Commander since the Navy carried it for merchant ships as well as its own, and it was delivered only to authorized Navy mail messengers. Arriving in port after a long time at sea, mail became the most important item on earth. It was up to the Armed Guard to supply the mail messenger, but it was up

Vintas a.k.a. bumboats, dugouts or outriggers came alongside to trade. The native tradesmen are called Boncas. 1945. Charles Espy.

to the captain to supply the boat — and to authorize payment of the necessary overtime for the crew that ran it. From that day forward, all gunners tried to show the captain a little more respect, even if we disliked him.

That afternoon the *Nelson* was moved to anchorage 175 so that off-loading could begin. On April 29, liberty sections A and C were finally granted shore leave again, the first liberty in four days because the Captain refused to send a boat ashore.

I went ashore with David "Frog" Forti and Ray "Boats" Bielanin. Boats was an old salt who had made more than one trip to the Philippines before the war. He promised to show us the "real" Manila. For starters, we loaded up on candy, cigarettes, and a set of bed sheets from Purser Huizenga's slop chest before going ashore — items very much in demand, as we soon found out.

We hadn't gone far from the boat landing before we were propositioned by little street urchins, probably nine to twelve years old. "Hello Joe, Victoree Joe, one cigarette?" or "Hello Joe, Victory Joe. You wanna fuck my seester? Only five dolla, Joe." It was both sad and humorous. They ran alongside us until convinced we weren't prospects for what they offered.

Nelson 20-mm gun crew practice in Manila. Dissinger (right) is gunner, Williams is loader. Charles Espy

Even though the city was in ruins, "Boats" managed to find one prewar friend who still owned a little neighborhood bar and restaurant. It wasn't much to look at but the owner, Betsy Fernandez, made us feel at home. In fact, it became our "headquarters" for the rest of our stay in Manila.

We bartered with Betsy for drinks, and other "services" with our contraband goods. I'm not sure what she did with the bartered goods but she could never get too many sheets or cigarettes. Of course, we weren't the only sailors to learn the value of these items ashore. Consequently, Huizenga was forced to ration them while the supply lasted.

On my third or fourth liberty in Manila, I fell in love, or so I thought, anyway, with a beautiful little Filipina hostess working at the Fernandez club. To make a long story short, my new-found love turned out to be a part-time hooker. That ended all thoughts of a long-term relationship.

On April 30 the C.O. held a Captain's Mast in the case of Segars, K. T., S1/c, for allegedly calling Chief Mate Barthez obscene names, and for drunkenness. Although he pleaded not guilty he was sentenced to seven days solitary confinement. Segars immediately asked for consideration from higher authority ashore. The C.O. granted permission when/if a review became available. Later Segars was advised to rest his case until he reached AGC(PAC).

I later learned that Capt. Gayle demoted Barthez to an able-bodied seaman. According to entries in the *Nelson*'s official log Barthez caused trouble the rest of the trip.

The *Scuttlebutt* newspaper described some of the more traditional sporting events we took part in at Manila.

> The softball season kicked off in Manila with a 6-4 win over the SS *Island Mail* . . . The *Nelson* lineup was as follows: Bagrowski, pitcher; Morrell, catcher; Wohleb, 1st base; Coleman, 2nd base; Lt. Espy, short stop; Dukes, 3rd base; Patereau, short field; Folmer, left field; Finnigsmier, center field; Vacek, right field.
>
> The most runs batted in were by Bagrowski, the most hits by Vacek, the greatest number of assists, and without error, by Dukes. Joe pitched superb ball with no previous practice.
>
> After many disputes, the horseshoe kings appeared to be Dukes and Finnigsmier, who, pitching as a team, beat all comers. Other horseshoe pitchers who gave Dukes and Finnigsmier a bad time were "Squirrel" Thomas, "Ringer" Moran, Roy Wohleb, Pete Morrell, "Frog" Forti and "Red" Dishner . . .
>
> Outstanding beer drinkers were Johnny Moran, Red Dishner, Lloyd Finnigsmier and Pete Morrell. Almost every one else stood out in the activity also . . .

The C.O. enjoyed playing tour guide to the gun crew in Manila. He liked history and knew his subject. Here are some highlights from the *Scuttlebutt*:

> We usually came from the *Nelson* through a maze of sunken ships in a small whale boat, up the Pasig River with its floating islands of green plants. Near the Pasig's mouth is durable Fort Santiago with its 30 foot thick walls built by the Spaniards . . .
>
> Facing Pier 7 is the Manila Hotel where before the war Gen. MacArthur occupied the penthouse. Today one is warned to bring his canteen of water from his ship. The slogan is "Boil Manila water 24 hours then throw it away and drink beer."

Nelson *Armed Guard crew poses in undress blues for picture while in Manila. Lt. (jg) Charles Espy is on right. Charles Espy.*

We hitchhiked out to Las Piñas to see that unique bamboo organ built there by a priest in 1818 in which bamboos serve as pipes.

Catching rides on down to Cavite, one sees barefooted Tagolog boys riding their water buffalo through muddy patties of green rice. In Cavite, one sees a town centuries old where the galleons that plied the waves to Acapulco, Mexico were built hundreds of years ago. For many years Cavite has been a great American Naval Base. Now it is smashed to near uselessness. On the northern neck of land off Cavite City stands the old Spanish city and Fort San Filipe, as old as the Spanish conquest and half as old as Filipino civilization. The fort walls are as thick as Manila's Fort Santiago . . .

But civilization did not begin with the Spanish. Many Filipinos could read and write centuries before Magellan with characters similar to those employed in India, during King Asoka's time, long before Christ . . .

On drives to Cavite, one could see mango groves, nipa shacks, and, on Sundays, natives and soldiers gathered around cockpits betting on cockfights.

Down tree-shaded Dewey Boulevard runs an Oriental riverside drive along Manila's ocean front. Downtown, in Intramuros, "outside the walls," across the Pasig, one marvels at the former marble-white, air-cooled modern structures, now smoke-covered.   In Intramuros, or Walled City, one sees nothing but crumbled rock where the Nipponese made their last stand. Running along the top of the wall is a roadway. Near here is the statue of Legaspi, the first conquering Spaniard. Intramuros is the most graceful and extensive example of medieval architecture in the far East.

We visited Santo Tomas, a university older than Harvard, where a Jap internment camp imprisoned thousands of Americans and Filipinos. It is now used as a hospital ... .

An occasional water buffalo cart, many horse-drawn Caretellas, U.S.-made autos, G.I. jeeps and trucks crowd the streets. The interesting sights include 2 or 3 inebriated sailors with a Caretella hired as a taxi, out looking for "something or other"...

The San Sebastian Catholic Cathedral is of iron, brought in large slabs entirely from Belgium and built by Belgian engineers, much larger than Quiapo [church] but no more impressive ...

The story would be incomplete unless it was mentioned that many of us traveled out Rizal Avenue to the Chinese Cemetery. Suffice it to say, it is a marble-walled, glittering-roofed, gemmed city of fairyland holding one spellbound for hours, like a miniature village for deceased Orientals, a truly beautiful tribute to the Chinese dead.

In all the madness of war with the yellow race, Manila still had offerings for the keen observer.

The Master became a bit more generous with the use of a whale boat for liberty parties. Also, thanks to ongoing discharging of cargo, we were able to hitchhike rides ashore with the landing craft. By May 15, most everyone was so broke there were days when only one or two men went ashore.

On May 25 we set sail independently under Condition 1, then reverted to Condition 3. On May 31 we held a King Neptune's initiation for the few Pollywogs who had not yet crossed the equator.

Photographer "Flash" Bagrowski reported on the events at King Neptune's Court for *Scuttlebutt*:

It was a very hot day in May, as the *Nelson* made its way to the equator line where it met Davy Jones right on time. Yes, indeed, it was on the morning of 31 May 1945 when our good ship rendezvoused with the Royal Family of the Ancient Deep at Latitude 00° 00', Longitude 140°. It was an amazing sight to all the landlubbers as Davy Jones came up the Jacob's ladder with two pistols on his hips and a knife between his teeth, a well-bloodied scarf about his head and a patch over one eye. Yes, Siree, all the Pollywogs shivered and shook and the chill bumps were very distinctive even though the temperature was 120° in the shade.

It was noon before the Royal Family had settled down for the initiation. All the Pollywogs were blindfolded and mustered forward.

The guys were getting the real McCoy. The Royal Police would drag 'em in and force them to kneel before "His Royal Majesty, Father Neptune." Neptune was well bearded and gave a very rugged, salty appearance. He had long white hair matching his beard and crossbones with the skull branded on his chest. His wife, The Royal Queen was indeed a beautiful mermaid, wearing a grass skirt, a sea shell necklace and ear rings. Her hair hung gracefully covering the beautiful, well curved mounds of her breasts.

Father Neptune had only four words to say to those who pleaded guilty, "Give 'Em The Works," and those who failed to acknowledge their guilt of course would get batted on their one-spot until they cried for mercy. After being found guilty, they proceeded to receive their punishment. First, they had to kiss The Royal Baby's hinder which had a thick coat of mustard on it. From there it was the Royal Doctor who examined them for any defects that might stall them from becoming a Worthy Shellback. If the Royal Doctor would

King Neptune's Court aboard the Nelson. *Davy Jones, center, (Vincent the baker), with his body guards (Vacek and Wohleb), has just emerged from the deep blue sea with his ultimatum in hand for all lowly Pollywogs crouching subserviently on No. 5 cargo hatch. This portion of King Neptune's Court strode aft on the starboard weatherdeck in one of a dozen such scenes during the full afternoon's formalities. Frivolous initiation extended over two days. On close scrutiny, one can see Sparks, Dutch, Frog, Cotter, Johnson, Baker, Arden, Smith (in helmet), Chief Ellis (aft Davy Jones) and George (in white). Charles Espy.*

class them 4.0 they were led to the Royal Prostitute with whom they put on a great show indeed.

Next, it was the Royal Barber who was raring and ready to inflict his punishment. He was a typical square-headed Pollock and would grab his victim by the ears, forcing him into the barber chair. Then he would gouge the shears into their hair and if any victim got away without being scalped it was beyond Neptune's knowledge. The Royal hair tonic consisted of Stockholm tar and crude oil. It is said that this solution will wear off in a few months but I sincerely doubt it.

crude oil. It is said that this solution will wear off in a few months but I sincerely doubt it.

The most important act of all was the Royal Baptism. All Pollywogs had to be baptized in Davy Jones' presence before they were legitimate Shellbacks. This was worth seeing. They had to walk a plank blindfolded before they splashed into the blessed water of the Ancient Deep. The pool consisted of a sail full of salt water and oil, lashed to the hatch. Before the last Pollywog had been baptized, this pool of water looked worse than the muddy Missouri.

Now all the Pollywogs were classed as worthy Shellbacks and received their certificates with much pride. It was the end of a perfect day as Father Neptune, Davy Jones, and all the Royal Family departed for the Ancient Deep. The sun was sinking now and the old *Thomas Nelson* rocked and rolled into the darkness.

For the record, here are the shellbacks of King Neptune's Court who did such a super job on the prodigious equator initiation: August Rengman, Father Neptune; Charley Vincent, Davy Jones; George Harding, Royal Queen; Bill McGee, Royal Doctor; Ollie Bagrowski, Royal Barber; Lucky Sweetland, Royal Baptizer; "Boats" Bielanin, Royal Police; Junior Vacek, Royal Pirate No. 1; Roy Wohleb, Royal Pirate No. 2.

The lowly pollywogs who suffered the initiation into the land down under to become mighty Shellbacks follow: Navymen: Cotter, Dishner, Dissinger, Dukes, Folmer, Forti, and Lt. Espy. Merchant Marines: Radiomen Hurlbert, White, and Frost; Engineers Harrison, Arden, and Sidney Johnson, Holst, Brown, and Litton; Stewards' Department: Kidd, Mochel, White, Martinez, Hill and Levi; Deck Department: Smith, DeMarlo, Score, Baker, Steward, Fergason and Purser Huizenga.

The brains behind all this maneuvering belonged to Chief Ellis and S1/c Segars.

April-May 1945

Vienna falls to Soviet troops on April 13.

Soviet troops enter Berlin 23 April amidst heavy fighting.

U.S. and Soviet patrols establish contact on the Elbe River.

Benito Mussolini, his mistress, and several other Fascist officials are executed 28 April by Italian Guerrillas near Lake Como. Their bodies are hung on display in a Milan gas station.

Hitler and his wife, Eva Braun, commit suicide on 30 April in the Fuhrerbunker. Grossadmiral Karl Donitz is named Hitler's successor.

Germany unconditionally surrenders to the Allies at General Dwight D. Eisenhower's headquarters at Rheims, France. The surrender is effective at midnight on 8-9 May ending the war in Europe!

President Truman and Prime Minister Churchill announce Allied Victory in Europe on 8 May (V-E Day). The actual surrender was on May 7, at 2:41 a.m., when German Generaloberst Alfred Jodl, chief of the operations staff of the High Command of the German Armed Forces, signed the Unconditional Surrender at Allied headquarters in Rheims. Ratification in Berlin by Soviet authorities comes just before midnight on May 8. President Truman announces the surrender on May 8.

U.S. Joint Chiefs of Staff approve the directive for Operation Olympic, the invasion of the Japanese homeland scheduled for 1 November 1945.

The Armed Forces Radio network reported on the big victory celebrations in Europe and the States, dubbed VE-day. We were both happy for and envious of the Americans serving "over there."

It took *Scuttlebutt* Editor Espy the entire trip to pry the war stories out of Chief Engineer Ellis (profiled earlier) and his 1st Assistant Joao A. "Tony" Belchoir, Jr. Here's Tony's:

You've heard of men leading charmed lives. Here's just such a story. Tony had been in the merchant marine for many years before the war. However, his story really begins with the outbreak of the war in Europe. Since then Tony has earned four ribbons including the combat bar with 3 silver stars which can be worn only when a man has seen three of his ships go to the bottom. That would seem enough, but it's hardly a beginning for a man who courts Lady Fortune satisfactorily.

Besides feeling the icy water of the cold Atlantic, Tony experienced a torpedoing by a German sub in the Indian Ocean resulting in a harrowing experience on a life raft for 26 days; the last 14 without food or water. Of the nine men on the raft, six died. On the 26th day, a plane appeared and they were spotted and dropped orange juice and food. Hours later a speed boat picked them up to transport them to a British destroyer. On the trip to Bombay, one of the three men nearly died . . .

Tony made several runs to Murmansk and was in on the invasion of Normandy. Talk about a charmed life. Tony has never been wounded!

On June 2, 1945 we arrived and anchored off Hollandia, New Guinea. It was hard to believe our troops landed just fourteen months ago and now it's a major Allied base.

I ran a fever ranging from 100.5 to 102.7 degrees for several days and asked the C.O. for permission to go ashore to see a doctor. He cussed me out for not telling him sooner, but there was no boat going ashore and no Port Director's visit scheduled for this date.

On June 3 at 1045, I went ashore with the C.O. and Captain Gayle. The C.O. took me to a Naval Dispensary where I was diagnosed with malaria. The doctor advised that I be detached for treatment as soon as possible, and so on June 4 I was officially detached to the Armed Guard Pool, Receiving Station, Hollandia, New Guinea, and Coxswain Jimmie W. Benham, took my place on the *Nelson*.

The *Thomas Nelson* outlasted the enemy. In 1956 she was back in Baltimore, and was refitted as a trial conversion type EC2-M-8b (7,259 grt) at a cost of $3,070,000 under the Liberty Ship Conversion Program. She was lengthened, given

The Thomas Nelson *at anchor in 1943. Courtesy of The Mariners Museum, Newport News, Virginia.*

finer bow lines and repowered with two geared diesel engines manufactured by the Baldwin-Lima-Hamilton Corp. and these changes assured the minimum 15-knot sea speed — but this was only attained on a draft reduced to 26 feet. Other alterations included the replacing of the standard cargo gear by five deck cranes and the use of two types of sliding hatch covers. The ship operated on the Atlantic under the United States Lines flag until 1960 when she was laid up in the James River Reserve Fleet. Twelve years later she was withdrawn for scrapping at Philadelphia. Instead she was sold and converted for dredging and pipelaying purposes and renamed *Beverly M*. From 1976 to late 1980 she laid up at Hoboken, N.J., then she moved to the shipbreaker's yard at Kearny, N.J. — the former Federal shipyard. Scrapping commenced on August 13, 1981.[2]

---

[2] L.A. Sawyer and W.H. Mitchell, *The Liberty Ships*.

15

THE IMPERIAL
SUN SETS

I checked in at the Armed Guard Pool in Hollandia on June 4, 1945, then proceeded to the Base Hospital where I described my symptoms: I'd be working on the guns or just sitting on a hatch and all of a sudden would get incredibly cold, even if it was 100 degrees in the shade. Then I'd start to shake and break out in a sweat from a high fever which might last for two or three hours.

The Doc said I had a textbook case of *plasmodium vivax*, a benign form of malaria. "Expect the cycle of chills followed by fever to repeat itself ever day or so until the atabrine medication, a substitute for quinine, kicks in." I was lucky, it could have been a much more dangerous form of the disease.

Hollandia Naval Base was established to provide logistic support to services afloat and as a supply base for the invasion of the Philippines. It included a base for convoy escorts, a

Map of Hollandia showing Navy bases in 1945. U.S. Navy.

supply depot, a repair base for destroyers and lighter craft, and an ammunition depot. In addition, it was the advance headquarters of the Seventh Fleet. It seemed amazing that it was almost entirely built by the Third Naval Construction Brigade — the 102nd, 113th, and 122nd Seabee Battalions — within the previous year.

The 500-bed hospital, consisting of seventy-some structures — mostly Quonset huts — was built in the fall of 1944. One of those hut wards was my home for six weeks.

During this period, I boned up on my Gunners Mate second-class training manuals and took the test as soon as the hospital put me on out patient status, free to move about the base provided I showed up for periodic checks and medication.

Two other outpatients and I visited a nearby Papuan village. Because of the frizzled hair of the inhabitants, the Portuguese named the island Papua from a term used by the Moluccans for such hair. The irreverent Americans adopted the nickname "fuzzy wuzzies" for these proud, woolly-haired natives.

The villagers were quite friendly. In fact, it was difficult to believe that headhunting and cannibalism were still practiced in some of the more remote regions of the country.

The news on the Armed Forced Radio Network was mostly about the Pacific Theater.

Papuan men. U.S. Army Signal Corps, courtesy MacArthur Memorial Archives.

June 1945

Japan's Premier Suzuki declares that Japan would fight to the last man rather than accept unconditional surrender terms.

The U.S. Third and Seventh Armies are designated for the occupation of Europe. Other U.S. forces are scheduled for the invasion of the Japanese home islands.

Organized Japanese resistance ends on Mindanao, P.I.

The U.S. Tenth Army completes the capture of Okinawa.

General MacArthur announces the end of Japanese resistance in the Philippines.

I went to the movies almost every night, a real treat for those of us serving on merchantmen. I also had the pleasure of seeing a performance by Jack Benny and his troupe. Carol Landis, to no one's surprise, got a standing ovation each time she appeared on stage with Benny.

My treatment was officially completed the morning of July 17, 1945 and I was transferred back to the Armed Guard Pool at the Receiving Barracks. Before I could open my seabag, I was detached to the USS *Richard S. Bull* (DE-402) for transportation to Leyte: ultimate destination, the Armed Guard Pool

Benny in New Guinea — Jack Benny, radio and movie comedian, and his troupe which arrived recently in New Guinea to entertain Allied servicemen. From left, Benny, Carole Landis, Major Gerald Graham, songstress Martha Tilton, accordionist June Brunner, and Larry Adler, "virtuoso" on the harmonica. U.S. Army Signal Corps, courtesy MacArthur Memorial Archives.

USS Richard S. Bull *(DE-402). Naval Historical Center*

at the Subic Bay Naval Base on Luzon about fifty miles north of Manila in the Philippines.

There were at least two dozen passengers from all branches of the service waiting on the dock for the *Bull*'s boat that morning. I was eager to ride in a real, honest-to-God, Navy combatant. She was a beauty, too, decked out in her camouflage coat.

We boarded the *Bull* shortly before noon and were headed for the open sea by 1400. I was totally unprepared for the violent pitching and rolling we experienced in storm-tossed seas for the next three days. I soon learned why DEs, as effective as they are, were reputed to be miserably uncomfortable vessels in difficult weather.

Late that first afternoon, I was invited up to the open bridge by the Officer of the Deck (OOD). A DE's open bridge, some forty-feet above the waterline, is a miserably wet place for top watchstanders when a heavy sea is running. Visibility is much better there than in the protected wheelhouse, but I wondered if the it was worth being so miserable?

I came as close to getting seasick on that voyage as I've ever been. It was twenty-four hours before I even felt like eating some chow. But I wasn't alone. Some of the passengers stayed in their racks for the entire 1,600 mile voyage, and more than a few crew members were seen "feeding the fishes" at the rail.

Two life rafts were carried away by seas coming over the bow. When we reached Leyte, I learned some thirty-five feet of bow plating had wrinkled with the entire bow section bending upward from pounding into head seas.

The *"Bull* ride," in spite of some discomfort, was a memorable experience and made me want to transfer into the fleet.

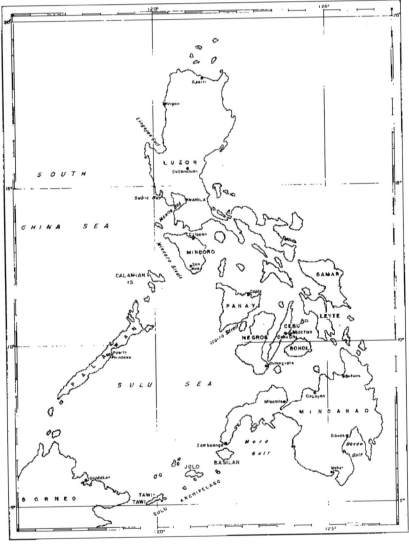

PHILIPPINE ISLANDS

Landing Craft, Infantry (Large) [LCI(L)]. Alfred J. Ormston.

Shortly before we disembarked at the Tacloban Naval Station, we were notified our destination was now Tubabao Island, a small triangular-shaped island in Leyte Gulf about fifty miles southeast of Tacloban, and separated from the island of Samar by a narrow strait.

The naval base was located on the southeastern Samar peninsula, three miles wide and eleven miles long, and on Calicoan Island, which is more than a mile wide and seven miles long, and separated from Samar by 800 feet of shallow water.

Tubabao Island, connected to Samar by a timber bridge 515 feet long and twenty-two feet wide, was the site of a Seabee-built "Quonset City" which included messhalls, recreation facilities, and utilities for 10,000 men.

I have one vivid memory of the Samar Receiving Station. There was a round-the-clock poker game at one end of our corrugated metal quonset hut. The sailors in the game and the kibitzers around them were in various stages of undress — mostly skivvies because it was hot and very humid. The staccato sound of rain beating down on the metal roof was so loud it drowned out any attempt at conversation. When one sailor checked out of the game to get some sleep or chow, another took his place. It was a sociable game: nickel ante, two-bit limit with a maximum of three raises.

It rained hard every day for hours on end. Even with a poncho on, we got soaked going to the messhall.

I was more than ready when orders came through to board an LCI bound for Subic Bay on July 30, 1945. We sailed to San Pedro Bay then up through San Juanico strait to Carigara Bay.

The LCIs provided a valuable ferry service to all branches of the Armed Forces when they weren't landing combat troops on hostile shores. Troops were assigned compartments below the weather deck. There were no bunks for the troops — it was strictly a short term voyage. (Passengers like myself were issued army cots.) The crew's quarters were also below the main deck. The three ship's officers shared a small single cabin on the main deck. Also on the main deck were the chart room and ward room where the crew and officers ate together. Above the main deck was the enclosed conning tower from which the ship was controlled. There was an open bridge above the conning tower for use in good weather or in restricted waters.

The distance between Tubabao and Subic Bay is something like 500 miles. However, our voyage which included stops at Mangarin Bay, Mindoro and Manila took seven days while covering 700 miles. I enjoyed the change of pace. With the threat of Japanese air strikes practically nonexistent, the passage was almost like a pleasure cruise.

On August 6, I disembarked the LCI in Subic Bay on a rainy, steamy day. The harbor was loaded with ships at anchor. The big question on everyone's mind was where and when do we invade the Japanese home islands?

Shouldering my seabag, I asked for directions to the Receiving Station, then caught a ride with the driver of a navy bobtail truck. He left me at the gate of my new home. I was logged in by the duty officer at the Armed Guard Pool barracks, picked out a bunk and sacked out until chow time. Later that night I went to a movie on the base with a couple of other gunners.

At muster the next morning, I learned that if you didn't draw some kind of temporary duty, you were free to do as you

Dock extension construction in Subic Bay, P.I. by 115th NCB c. 1945. Seabees.

pleased for the rest of the day. With the day off, I decided to explore the base.

Subic Bay, on the west coast of Luzon, is about thirty miles north of Corregidor and fifty miles northwest of Manila. The harbor can accommodate many deep-draft vessels. Olongapo, on the east side of the Bay was the site of prewar naval installations and a native settlement. The other large Filipino settlement, Subic City, is at the extreme northern end of the Bay. Subic Bay Naval Base was built to provide a repair base for destroyers, submarines, and small craft; major overhaul of PT engines; service and supply to fleet units, a hospital, an amphibious training center, and of course, the receiving barracks.

The Seabees' accomplishments were always impressive. Subic was my third advance base in two months since debarking the *Thomas Nelson*. The advanced naval operating bases were, of course, a must to support further operations against Japan.

"Sailor's Amusement" — Cartoon by A.H. Pool on an Olongapo dance hall, c. 1914. Naval Historical Center.

Viewing all of this new construction from the rail of a freighter was no substitute for living in and around it. It certainly opened my eyes. America's economic, political, and military commitment to winning the war was something to see. It made me both glad and proud to be an American.

That afternoon four of us decided to hit the beach in Olongapo, fast becoming the U.S. Navy's favorite R & R (Rest and Recreation) playground in the Philippines, a.k.a. "Sin City." (I learned later, the Subic Bay Naval Station (SBNS) was responsible for about ninety-eight percent of Olongapo's economy.) As the only newcomer in the group, I was glad to tag along.

We crossed the canal that separates the naval base from the town and it was as if we had entered a huge male amusement park of bars, dance halls, massage parlors, and brothels, catering to the every possible desire of America's service men.

American pop and country-western tunes blasted from the clubs; sailors and Marines with their arms slung around their Filipina companions milled about the clothing stores along the street. One store prominently displayed T-shirts in its window with bawdy slogans such as "A Woman's Place Is On My Face."

"It's twenty-four-hour partying" said "Flags" Jimmy Martinez, an Armed Guard Signalman third-class, who had been there for two months. "You can get any girl you want no matter how you look. That's what guys are told on the ships coming into port, and they get so excited, they can't wait to get out of the gates. Believe me, this is an anything-goes place — even things I never heard of."

In Olongapo, Martinez learned about "peso girl" parties when he first arrived, where women dance naked while men threw pesos [coins] on a stage. "Later," Martinez explained, "the pesos get stacked upon the floor and the women 'pick up' the coins without using their hands or feet, then drop them one by one while dancing. It was shocking. I had never seen a show like that, but I've seen weirder shows since then."

We hit five or six bars that night with "Flags" leading the way. They were jumping like it was Saturday night. Hundreds of men passed through each bar on any given night, and pretty women were everywhere, frequently outnumbering the men. "Right now," Flags said, "I could look all the way across the room and make eye contact with a girl, and that girl would be right at my side." He sucked on his beer. "If she's smart, she'll say, 'How're you doin'?' If she's not, she'll say, 'Want to buy me a beer?' That's when I turn my back on her."

Martinez was older than the rest of us by about ten years. We were impressed with his knowledge of the town and its "entertainment women" or "bar girls" — euphemisms for licensed prostitutes. If we had any doubts about his "tour guide" qualifications, he put them to rest when he introduced us to the popular game of "Smile." Servicemen sit around a table drinking beer while under the table prostitutes perform oral sex. The first guy to smile has to buy a round of drinks. But Flags was a proper host that first time. He paid the girls.

The next morning at muster, I was assigned Shore Patrol duty "effective immediately until further notice." Since I didn't have to report until 1400, I took the opportunity to put in for a transfer to the fleet: stated preference, cruisers or carriers in

Admiral Halsey's Third Fleet. With a little luck, I might get in on the invasion of Japan.

The SP Quonset was near the main gate of the base. I showed up a little early in my cleanest pair of dress whites wondering what was in store, considering what I saw in Olongapo the night before. Several other Armed Guard petty officers were also there.

Between 1400-1500, a junior lieutenant conducted an "indoctrination briefing" for all the first-timers.

> Most of the commands on the base as well as the larger capital ships in the harbor furnish shore patrol men to maintain order in Olongapo, Subic City and some of the smaller villages in the area.
>
> Everyone will be assigned a partner and walk a beat on the 1600-2400 shift in Olongapo.
>
> A 2300 curfew for all enlisted men is presently in place and must be enforced.
>
> Your primary responsibility is to take care of our men on liberty and see that they get back to the base or their ship without making trouble — not to represent law and order per se.
>
> You must also protect the Filipino people from any unruly sailors — not an easy assignment because, in many cases, it's a judgment call.
>
> If you are with us long enough, you may be assigned to the riot squad. In this case, you remain on call here at headquarters and respond, when the need arises, in one of our Jeeps.

The officer, a lawyer in civilian life, explained the Olongapo system of civic law and bar rules, dating back to pre-war days, which helped keep the flesh trade reasonably free of venereal disease and discouraged women and men from making their own agreements outside the bars. He emphasized we were not expected to enforce them but we needed to understand the system so we'd know when a sailor is out of line.

1. To legally join the ranks of Olongapo's "entertainment women" — about 10 percent of the city's population — a woman must be

eighteen years old and pay for a "mayor's permit" to work in the bars and receive regular physical exams. The fee goes directly into the town's treasury. Although the women are technically employed by the bars, they get no regular salary. Their income comes from selling cocktails on commission (about 10%) or from selling themselves.

2. A patron who desires the company of one of these women for the night pays the bar manager a "bar fine" in pesos — equal to about five to ten U.S. dollars — of which she gets one-third to half the next day if she shows up for work on time. Providing the patron pays the fine, the woman gets a "night off" pass, which she must show to local police to prove she has the manager's permission to leave the bar. Under the law, police can question any Filipina in the company of an American serviceman. Women who are caught are fined the equivalent of twenty to fifty dollars or fired. But the biggest disincentive to cutting the bar owner out of a deal is jail — reputed to be a nasty place to land.

3. In order to keep their licenses, the entertainment women must submit to tests for venereal disease twice a month at the local social hygiene clinic, jointly sponsored by the city and our Navy.

4. Well over 1,000 women are licensed prostitutes — the city won't release the actual number — and thousands more are unlicensed street walkers who ply their trade outside Olongapo's hundreds of bars, dance halls, massage parlors, and short-term hotels.

The SP officer closed his indoctrination by saying: "Some would argue that the system favors, even protects, the pimp, which, in this case, is the bar owner. But city officials insist that nightly pass checking is good business. It's like any employer-employee relationship," he said, "you have to get permission to be absent.

"The system runs smoothly as long as the woman plays by the city's and bar owners' rules, and does her best to please; but if she refuses sexual requests she can expect trouble from the manager, and, too often, rough treatment from the customer. And if that disgruntled customer happens to be a sailor or a Marine, that's when you may have to step in."

After we were dismissed, we were issued a .45 automatic sidearm, web belt and holster, brassard, nightstick, and leggings and ordered to be ready to move out at 1530. My partner, Bill Baker — a Motor Mac (Motor Machinist Mate) stationed at the Amphibious Training Center — and I were dropped off on Magsaysay Drive in Olongapo shortly before 1600 where we relieved two hot and tired looking day shift patrolmen.

The street was already mobbed with a sea of sailors in dress whites and the occasional khaki-clad Marine and, of course, many pretty young women. It was busier than New Year's Eve in San Francisco but we had a relatively uneventful shift until it was time to start enforcing the curfew. Prior to midnight, our job was to issue warnings to violators and send them on their way to the base. After that, it was the paddy wagon. In either case, the Marine guards at the base took over.

After about 2330, we did a door to door check of the bars and dance halls for stragglers. If the proprietor gave us the "all clear" signal we moved on. If not, we went in to investigate. In most cases, it would be some young sailor passed out from too much to drink. Our only real problem that night was getting two shipmates to leave their Filipina companions behind at a small hot-pillow joint (short-time hotel). We had to place them under arrest, handcuff them and call for the paddy wagon.

I had the next day off so went to the library to listen to the radio and scan back issues of stateside newspapers. The Armed Forces Radio Network (AFRN) announced a "major breakthrough in weaponry . . . with details to be announced shortly."

July 1945

General MacArthur completes the recapture of the Philippines; 12,000 Americans died in the ten month fight for the islands. With the reconquest of the Philippines and the securing of Okinawa as a base, the U.S. begins planning for the invasion of Japan.

U.S. carrier-based aircraft begin sustained strikes against targets in Japan in preparation for amphibious landings.

U.S. capital ships bombard Japan for the first time.

The world's first atomic bomb is detonated in "Trinity" test near Alomogordo, New Mexico.

The USS *Indianapolis* (CA-35) unloads components for the "Little Boy" atomic bomb at Tinian Island in the Marianas.

The *Indianapolis* is sunk by Japanese submarine *I-58* while en route to Philippines: 881 crew members are lost. Survivors are rescued two days later.

Assembly of the first atomic bomb for combat use is completed on Tinian.

August 1945

The B-29 Superfortress *Enola Gay* piloted by Col. Paul Tibbets drops an atomic bomb on Hiroshima.

The Japanese ambassador in Moscow sees Foreign Minister Molotov to seek Soviet mediation with the Allies; instead he is handed the Soviet declaration of war, effective that day.

The Soviet Union enters the war against Japan.

The B-29 Superfortress *Bockscar* piloted by Maj. Charles W. Sweeney drops an Atomic Bomb on Nagasaki. Japanese Prime Minister Kantaro Suzuki and Emperor Hirohito decide on an immediate peace with the Allies.

Japanese government accepts Unconditional Surrender.

The night of August 9, I was watching a movie in the outdoor theater with several hundred other bluejackets when the following announcement came over the P.A. system from the

August 1945 celebration in Pacific upon hearing news of Japanese offer to surrender. National Archives.

base commander: "Now hear this. The Twentieth Air Force has successfully dropped two powerful new atomic bombs on Japan which could shorten the war by a year or more. Additional details will be provided as we receive them. In the meantime, enjoy your movie."

Shouts of joy and spontaneous applause were followed by everyone trying to talk at once. What did it mean? What was an "atomic" bomb? Would the Japs surrender now? No one was sure. But it was an unforgettable moment.

I pulled two more SP shifts over the next few days without incident. Then on August 15 (14th in D.C.), the words we all had waited for were spoken over AFRN. "Japan surrenders! The Japanese Domai News Agency has announced that Emperor Hirohito and Prime Minister Suzuki have accepted the Allies' terms of unconditional surrender!"

The official announcement was made by President Harry Truman at 7:00 p.m. August 14, 1945 Washington time. Fifty years later, I still struggle to find the right words to express my feelings — and those of the millions of other Americans who experienced that climactic moment. In an instant, shouts of joy filled the morning air around the base and all across the bay.

Soon fog horns, sirens, and every other noisemaking device conceivable geared up. Work stopped everywhere as people hugged or shook hands. Sailors looked at each other and shouted, "Hey, do you know the war is over?" It was on everyone's lips: The war is over! Sailors came out of the base buildings like they were on fire. They were different men from those who had gone in. They raced to the canteen to celebrate the end of the fighting with beer and laughter.

Fire and salvage tugs began pumping hundreds of fountains of water up in the air. Other ships broke out fire pumps and portable "handy billies" to add more spray and mist to the scene. Soon, small craft, and some not so small ships, got underway and formed columns that cruised in figure eights around the Bay. The victory parade lasted several hours.

Hidden cans of beer and bottles of bourbon suddenly appeared. As I stood by the Bay and watched the parade of ships and craft, I suddenly remembered I still had over a year to go on my enlistment. What now, I wondered. I was also thankful I didn't have SP duty that day.

Later that evening, hundreds of searchlights lit up the sky in sweeping crisscross patterns as star shells and Very signals added brilliant colors to the dark canvas. Every pyrotechnic locker in the harbor was emptied that night. You could almost read by the light of the fireworks.

There were also some very somber thoughts and discussions. Everyone was relieved that they made it through the war, but there were too many memories of shipmates who weren't so lucky. Some of the reservists were already adding up their discharge points to see who would be the first to go home.

Late August 1945

Gen. of the Army Douglas MacArthur is appointed Supreme Allied Commander Allied Powers for the occupation of Japan.

Lt. Gen. Jonathan Wainwright, who was taken prisoner by the Japanese on Corregidor on May 6, 1942, is released by U.S. troops from a Prisoner of War camp in Manchuria.

Soviet troops land at Port Arthur and Dairen on the Kwantung Peninsula in China, and in the Kuril Islands.

B-29 Superfortress bombers begin dropping supplies to Allied Prisoner of War camps in China.

Chinese Communist leader Mao Tse-Tung arrives in Chungking to confer with Nationalist leader Chiang Kai-Shek in a futile effort to avert civil war.

Soviet fighters bring down a B-29 Superfortress dropping supplies to prisoners of war in Korea.

U.S. Airborne troops land in transport planes at Atsugi airfield, southwest of Tokyo to begin the occupation of Japan.

We saw scenes of pure joy in the wire services photos of victory celebrations from all over the world: a sailor kissing a nurse in New York, a jubilant crowd looking into the camera in London. San Francisco, my favorite city, had its historic pictures, too. But, unfortunately, most of them show drunken men and women, some naked or barely dressed, climbing statues or street lamps, or frolicking in fountains. Just about every downtown store suffered broken windows or looting. Liquor stores were favorite targets.

V-J Day, August 14 1945. There were casualties. It was the busiest day of Treasure Island Hospital's history. U.S. Navy.

At least thirty streetcars were wrecked. Eventually, 500 claims were filed against the city. The Associated Press:

> San Francisco, fed by two days of rumors that the fighting in the Pacific was over, was ready to explode. Many sailors in the area hadn't heard a shot fired in anger. The news meant they wouldn't have to become targets for Japanese suicide planes, a fate suffered by thousands of bluejackets at Okinawa.
>
> "The participants were mainly sailors, young women and a great number of teenagers of the bobby-sox type," *San Francisco Chronicle* reporter Stanton Delaplane wrote of the rioting on August 15, 1945, the day after the official announcement that the war was finally over.

The V-J Day surrender ceremony was set for September 2, 1945 in Tokyo Bay on the deck of the battleship *Missouri*. Allied occupation troops began arriving in Japan on August 28. On September 2, before an array of Allied representatives — including Lt. Gen. Jonathan Wainwright, a POW since the fall of Bataan — the Supreme Commander of the Allied Powers, General of the Army Douglas MacArthur, Admiral C.W. Nimitz, and Admiral W.F. Halsey, the surrender documents were signed.

Several local surrenders followed. On September 3, at Camp John Hay on Luzon in the Philippines, Wainwright accepted the surrender of Japanese forces in the Philippines. On September 9, the surrender of about 1,000,000 Japanese troops in China took place in the restored capital of Nanking; the same day, U.S. officers accepted the surrender of Japanese forces south of the 38th parallel in Korea; the Soviets accepted the surrender north of the parallel.

On October 10, the Japanese garrison at Peking formally surrendered to the Chinese Army, which had been fighting them since 1937. Other surrenders took place in the Mariana Islands, the Ryukyu Islands, on Wake, at Truk, and at Singapore.

Don Wellington, senior third assistant engineer on the *Ames Victory*, recalled the effects of the ending of the war on the supply pipeline:

While waiting for Kaiser Permanente to install a new bow, we remedied various "bugs" in the engine department and installed a new main feed pump. Sometime in July 1945, we moved the ship up river to the arsenal at Benicia, California, still without a crew.

At Benicia, we again loaded up with ammo and bombs. The crew signed on while we were at Benicia. Everyone who came through the gates of the arsenal, was frisked for booze, among other things. No booze was allowed on the premises. As we were eating dinner that night, we sailed out the Golden Gate, Captain Roy Shull remarked, "For once in my life, there is no liquor aboard my ship."

The voyage west was uneventful until one morning when we were a couple of days east of Saipan, our interim destination, the whistle started blowing. I thought it was a fire and boat drill and, having just fallen asleep after coming off watch, decided to ignore it.

A little while later, the whistle was blowing again, guns were being fired, and a god-awful racket came up from the crews' mess so I got up to see what on earth was happening.

It was V-J day! Checking out the crews' mess, I found most of the crew drunk as skunks, their mess table littered with empty liquor bottles. Since most of the celebrants were in the stewards department, we weren't fed for a couple of days. The engineers had keys to the reefers and did some cooking on hot steam pipes.

To this day, I don't know, and I don't think anyone else knows, how all that booze got aboard the ship. If any of the officers had brought it aboard before docking at Benicia, I'm sure the crew would not have had access to it.

All of a sudden, we found ourselves extremely unpopular. Nobody wanted our explosive cargo anywhere near them. We made it to Saipan and dropped anchor while somebody figured out what to do with us. Meanwhile, we learned how the war ended as a result of the Hiroshima and Nagasaki atom bomb blasts.

After spending a few weeks in Saipan harbor, we were finally given orders to proceed to Hawaii. As we approached Honolulu, a little boat came out with orders, as was the usual practice for vessels arriving in the Islands. This time we were directed to Lahaina Roads, the strait between Maui and Lanai west of the town of Lahaina. We were never cleared through quarantine so could not go ashore. Several other ships appeared and dropped anchor — all in the same fix we were — loaded with cargo which nobody wanted. We dropped the gangway and launched a lifeboat to go swimming off the ship. The captains visited each other.

After several weeks, the captains decided the crews were getting restless and should be allowed to go ashore even though we still hadn't cleared quarantine, so lifeboats were launched and ashore we went. Most of the crew headed for the Lahaina bars. I got involved in a basketball game at the Lahaina "Y." Before long, the town was inundated with drunken merchant seamen. They tore up sugar cane fields, got into fights, and one was killed trying to jump on the back of an Army truck going thirty or so miles an hour. That was the first and last day of going ashore on Maui!

Finally, we received orders to proceed to San Francisco and in late October tied up at rebuilt Port Chicago to unload the cargo that had been loaded just across the river at Benicia, California!

Meanwhile back at the Armed Guard barracks in Subic Bay, I had a discussion with the Officer in Charge. He explained that, as a regular Navy man with a little more than a year to go on my hitch, I was entitled to go back to the States for leave and reassignment to the fleet. Consequently, my request for transfer to Halsey's Third Fleet, was denied. I could expect to qualify for transportation back to the U.S. relatively soon; only married men with the necessary discharge points had higher priority. My stated destination preference was Seattle or Portland.

I was assigned to Shore Patrol duty on a full-time basis for the balance of my stay in Subic. SP Headquarters had asked for the full time service of six Armed Guard petty officers effective immediately — preferably men six-feet tall or more with experience. When I reported to the Shore Patrol office on September 4 as a "temporary full-timer," I was assigned to the riot squad day shift. There were other firsts that day in the form of perks. For example, a number of leading petty officers in Ships Service, Storekeeping, and Mess Management provided complimentary beer, ice cream, and fresh-baked goodies upon request. In exchange, they expected special treatment when on the town. One example might be a curfew violation. A confidential list of men eligible for "special consideration" was maintained by each SP duty Chief.

The SP riot squad was only called out twice my first day: in both cases to break up fights between sailors. No big deal. That night, I went into Olongapo with two other Armed Guard shipmates in the Shore Patrol force.

While we were trying to decide what to do that night, the owner of the bar came over to our table to say hello. He knew we were off duty SPs. Shortly after the owner went back to bartending, three attractive waitress joined us with an offer we couldn't refuse: "free samples." That's oral sex behind a curtain in the back of the bar. I was beginning to like this shore patrol duty! I learned later, many bars offered free samples to regular customers, especially on slow nights when the fleet was out.

For the next two weeks or so, I alternated between a regular beat with a partner and the riot squad. The duty became more challenging. At first, when the Japs surrendered, it was party time every night. Lots of happy drunks but no big problems. Later more fights developed. No one was sure why. One theory was Reservists were frustrated with the inevitable delays of going home.

On 30 September — my 20th birthday — I was on the riot squad night shift. We were sitting in the SP hut when a frantic call came in from a shore patrol team in a small native village on the eastern outskirts of Olongapo. Because it sounded serious the SP Officer on duty sent two Jeeps with four men in each vehicle. In situations like this, we always took Thompson submachine guns along. It was a good thing we did because we had a small but serious race riot on our hands.

When we arrived, there were fifty-some black Seabee construction workers in front of the main village bar wanting in and a like number of white sailors and Marines already inside denying them that privilege. The two men on SP duty who called for help were beaten up pretty badly

I was thankful the SP officer sent two units of four men with Tommy guns. It took all of us and that kind of firepower to get their attention. Even so, it was a tense half hour before we lowered our guns. Some of the men were pretty drunk and you could see them trying to figure out in their pickled minds whether we would really shoot if they charged us. Everyone was relieved to see the trucks pull in so we could separate the two sides and put some distance between them. We escorted the prisoners to the brig in our Jeeps, then spent most of the night collaborating on a report.

We decided the causes of the trouble were alcohol, women, and a territorial dispute. The white men felt they had a proprietary interest in the village since they had been there for several months. The blacks, new arrivals at Subic Bay, disagreed.

One of the pluses of riot squad duty was the chance to drive a Jeep, sometimes called a "mechanical horse." It was fun to drive but you had to be careful where you parked it or someone would steal it. Bill Mauldin drew several memorable *Stars and Stripes* cartoons of the "little truck" including one of a calvary sergeant shooting his favorite "mount" because of a broken front suspension; and another of a jeep chained to a tree and booby trapped with rifles, "Them damned LST sailors steal 'em."

I can verify that charge. The military jeep had a toggle switch instead of a key; the normal way of locking up was to remove the distributor rotor. Even then, an innovative amphibian could easily barter for a rotor from some military parts source.

My attitude toward Filipina hookers changed dramatically while I was in Subic Bay. At first, when I met a young attractive woman, I reminded myself she was just after my money. Later, when I met a girl, I understood better the challenges she faced and the poverty around her, and it made me want to help her.

Virginity was very important in the Philippine culture. But due to the war, it was a virtue many poverty-stricken women could not afford. Prostitutes were looked down on in the Philippines, perhaps even more so than in many countries. So family ties were crucial to a girl's survival and in the postwar era. The families of these girls, however, were ambivalent, accepting and even abetting the economic necessity, yet also ostracizing them for their lifestyle.

Sometimes when in town, I just wanted to talk to a woman, but while most of the bar girls were young and attractive, some even sweet, they weren't the girl next door. They made no money just sitting and talking.

Most of Olongapo's entertainment ladies were not the hardened professionals you find in Las Vegas or San Francisco. They were mainly undereducated girls from rural provinces — often areas that had been ravaged by Japanese occupation forces. Many had undergone traumatic sexual experiences at the hands of these forces. Still others, as is true the world over, were victims of incest or abandonment by a boyfriend or husband. Adding to the problem was the fact that in Olongapo, where there were no factories or other industries, staying out of prostitution was almost impossible for women.

Many young women came to Olongapo with the mistaken belief the town was saturated with American dollars, that they would find a good job as a secretary, waitress or maid on the naval base, or — if they got lucky — an American husband. Although marriage to servicemen was relatively rare, it happened just often enough to keep the myth alive. Girls who came there thinking they would be the exception to the rule, found themselves caught in a brutal game of cat and mouse with a bar owner and his customer.

The result was a young uneducated Filipina who moved to Olongapo right after the war had virtually no control over who she went with, how much she earned, or what happened to her body.

One of my favorite memories of Shore Patrol duty in Subic Bay will always be the post-curfew "tours" of the bars and restaurants along Magsaysay Drive. We had lively discussions with owners and their employees as well as their civilian customers in a relaxed friendly atmosphere. We weren't allowed to drink while on duty, but once we removed our SP gear, we became VIPs and the drinks were on the house. It was our time to relax and we enjoyed it to the hilt. Sometimes we would sing along to the juke box — tunes like "Amapola" and "Because of You" were popular then. I became very fond of the Philippine people as a result of those times together, and still am.

On October 7, 1945, I received the word that my transportation to Seattle was set for October 9 on the merchant ship, SS *Luther S. Kelly*. Later in the day, I popped in at the SP Quonset to say my good-byes, then got busy doing some laundry and various other get-ready chores.

I was up bright and early waiting for transportation to the ship on the 9th. Several other Armed Guard "nomads" were also making the trip. Altogether, about 200 passengers were collected from around the base and off various ships in the harbor for the *Kelly*.

The SS *Luther S. Kelly* was another Kaiser Permanente-built Liberty launched at Yard No. 2 in Richmond, California in July 1943. Temporary passenger quarters were created in the 'tween deck in holds 2, 3, and 4.

The Armed Guard passengers got to eat in the gunners' mess with the *Kelly*'s gun crew and shared their head. The rest of the passengers went through a chow line on the main deck next to No. 4 hold.

Everyone aboard seemed to be on a high. The sheer joy and euphoria that the ending of the war brought on was contagious. The first night out, I had the weirdest feeling to be running with lights on, after three years of sailing in absolute darkness.

The next day, I went up to the radio shack and introduced myself to the radio operators and got caught up on the latest news.

September 1945

Japanese government formally surrenders to the Allies on board the U.S. Battleship *Missouri* (BB-63) in Tokyo Bay, witnessed by an armada of U.S. warships with 1,000 carrier-based aircraft flying overhead.

President Truman proclaims V-J Day.

Gen. Tomoyuki Yamashita, the Japanese commander in the Philippines, surrenders his forces to Lt. Gen. Jonathan M. Wainwright at Baguio.

Gen. of the Army Douglas MacArthur enters Tokyo to direct the occupation of Japan.

Japanese troops in Korea surrender.

The next four weeks seemed to drag on forever. It was as if "channel fever" had set in thirty days prematurely. Shipboard activities, especially for the passengers, were much the same day after day.

The relatively few books available were passed on from man to man. Armed Forces Radio Network broadcasts when available, were piped in to the crew and gunners mess compartments as well as the ward room, a welcome addition for many of us. Some men worked on their tans while on deck, others slept the time away between meals. But the two most popular "time killers" were gambling and bull sessions.

Both pastimes attracted enthusiastic participants from the ship's company, gun crew, and the passengers — a total of about 275 men. The bull sessions could take place anytime, anywhere men gathered but, since we had no deckload, most were held on and around the No. 4 hatch after supper. Subjects ranged from reflections on events of the recent past to future plans.

Most plans were personal in nature and had to do with the immediate future like job preferences, educational choices, marriage, children, and the like. Reflections ranged from the usual war stories, both heroic and humorous, to serious intellectual subjects, usually war-related. My journal entries include the following topics: 1) The invasion of Japan — along the "what if" line of reasoning had the invasion taken place, 2) The A bomb — its use against Japan and the implications for its future use, 3) The war's impact on the U.S. — past, present and mainly in the future.

One of the favorite topics of conversation on the ship was which branch of the Armed Forces had the best deal. Since the majority of the passengers were Navy men, you can guess who won that debate. Four U.S. Navy advantages no one questioned: 1) A clean, dry place to sleep 2) Daily showers, even if they were sometimes salt water. 3) Hot meals three times a day and, 4) Burial at sea, in a worst case scenario.

Reflecting on his armed guard experiences, one of the Gunner's Mates summed up his feelings: "The men in the Armed Guard didn't get the carriers, battleships, or destroyers of their dreams, but they got something else from their time in the Armed Guard. The pride and satisfaction of knowing they fulfilled the Armed Guard motto, 'We Aim To Deliver.' The Armed Guard and their Merchant Marine shipmates delivered the troops and everything needed for their support — from food, medicine, and clothing to bombs and ammunition — to every theater of operation around the world. And in so doing, they grew up and became better men while the Navy was fulfilling its long-standing promise, 'Join the Navy and See the World.'"

The fleet sailors knew next to nothing about Armed Guard duty — not surprising since we had very little contact with them. And all servicemen considered the merchant mariners civilians which, of course, they were, but what bothered them more than anything, as far as I could tell, was the apparent lack of respect they received from the soldiers, Marines, and fleet sailors.

I spent some time with the *Kelly* gun crew and volunteered to give them a hand if they needed me. But, for the most part, I divided my time between the evening discussion groups and the poker table. You could find a game of chance on the *Kelly* any time of day or night, poker, blackjack, and craps being the most popular.

We also had some talented GI musicians aboard — I never did learn how they managed to pack their guitars, banjos, and fiddles around with them — who played some great country songs for us. And, pretty soon, we had sing-alongs almost every night on the weather deck. Not just country music either. Songs by the Andrews Sisters like "Red River Valley," "Shoo-Shoo, Baby," and "Accentuate the Positive" were very popular then. And, of course, we always had to sing a medley of songs honoring the Army ("The Caissons Go Rolling Along"), the Marines ("The Marine Hymn"), the Army Air Corps ("Off We Go Into the Wild Blue Yonder"), and the Navy ("Anchors Aweigh"). And, finally, for the old married men who had been separated for two or more years from their families, there was the pop song by that skinny guy, Frank Sinatra, "I'll Be Seeing You."

I probably averaged twelve hours a day playing poker. A few of the passengers were very good but, for the most part, they were either neophytes of the game, or were trying to beat the odds, like drawing to an inside straight. All but the better players were cleaned out two weeks into the trip.

The stakes were raised to pot limit toward the end of the trip. At this point, I was several hundred dollars ahead so started playing close to the vest. The caliber of play was much improved and it wasn't so easy to win a hand. But by sticking to my conservative philosophy — I had memorized the chances of winning with most hands by now — I walked away with more than $700.

Three recent war-related items made the news, all centered in Europe.

October 1945

All restrictions on fraternizing between Allied soldiers and German woman are relaxed by the Allied Control Council, except for certain bans on intermarriage.

Vichy French Premier Pierre Laval is executed by firing squad for his wartime collaboration with the Germans.

Wartime Norwegian collaborator Vidkun Quisling is executed by firing squad.

On November 10, 1945, a date many of the passengers will long remember, Vancouver Island was seen dead ahead through the fog. About 0920, the *Kelly* made a hard right after passing Cape Flattery and entered the Strait of Juan de Fuca. Shortly afterwards, we took on a pilot who conned the ship down the busy Puget Sound to our assigned pier on the Seattle waterfront.

We were greeted by a few families of the Army men who resided in the Northwest, but it wasn't exactly the tumultuous welcome we heard about for the big troopships. But nobody cared. Everyone was happy to set foot on Uncle Sam's soil once again.

I disembarked that afternoon and reported to the Armed Guard officer at the 13th Naval District offices in Seattle. He was holding some mail for me which included the notice that I had passed my Gunner's Mate Second-Class test with advancement effective December 1, 1945. Later the same day, I was detached to the Receiving Barracks in Seattle. After checking in and stowing my seabag, I picked up a seventy-two-hour liberty pass and headed for my mother's place, unannounced as usual.

16

DELAYED ORDERS TO NEW YORK

Mother and my sister, Doris, were just walking out the door to attend a church function when I arrived the evening of November 10. They offered to cancel their plans but I raided their fridge and listened to the radio until they returned, then we talked for hours.

The next evening almost every Phillips County transplant in the Seattle-Tacoma area came to an "impromptu welcome home party." It was an interesting mix: former hard working farmers and ranchers and small town business people who survived the drought and depression years of the 1930s, then picked up stakes and moved to the coast to fill the many defense jobs that opened up during the war.

Some of the workers were already laid off, others expected it to happen any day. But all were optimistic about the future. Mostly we talked about the good (and bad) old days in Montana and how lucky we were to have made it through the

Vivian Lyon "Fibber" McGee, author and Doris McGee, c. August 1946. Author

depression and the war in one piece. All-in-all, a most enjoyable homecoming.

The Receiving Barracks at Naval Receiving Station, Seattle, Washington, were as busy as a three-ring circus — the sudden end of the war, thanks to the atomic bomb, caught military planners by surprise. Ships arrived almost daily, overrun with servicemen on their way home.

Operation "Magic Carpet," called for the rapid return of U.S. servicemen from overseas by transport and warship after the war. This was no small task considering there were almost 15 million men and women in uniform in August 1945. (U.S. Army: 8,300,000; Army Air Force: 2,400,000; U.S. Navy: 3,400,000; U.S. Marine Corps: 486,000; U.S. Coast Guard: 170,000.)

It took me the better part of a week to arrange a meeting with the Executive Officer. He was swamped handling the needs and wants of the regular navy men passing through. I already knew that I was officially detached from the Armed Guard. The big question in my mind was what is my next billet? By the time we finally did meet, I had developed a plan to achieve my immediate objective: a tour of duty in European waters, preferably the Mediterranean.

Thanks to counseling from some old salts, here was my plan: I said that mother had recently moved to the East Coast to be near my sister, Betty. Since I had thirty days' leave coming, how about thirty days delayed orders to New York plus travel time? It would give me the opportunity to stop in my home town in Montana, then go on to New York to see my mother. (A little white lie in that mother was only *thinking* of moving east at the time. However, she and Doris did move to Washington, D.C. a few years later.)

The XO was so jammed with appointments, he seemed relieved not to have to do anything but say yes.

The next hurdle was the shortage of rail transportation. After a long wait in line, a WAVE on the transportation desk looked over my travel papers, made note of my itinerary, and said she would notify me when she had something booked. That notification finally came on November 27 — a nice Thanksgiving present. In the meantime, I had plenty of liberty.

Mother, Doris and I were invited for Thanksgiving dinner with the entire Kroon family, our best friends from the old days in Montana. And what a feast it was! Scandinavians really know how to prepare a turkey with all of the trimmings.

The next day I boarded an old Great Northern World War I-vintage coach in Seattle for the long, cold ride across the Cascade Mountains, into Spokane; past my old Farragut Boot Camp, over the Rockies into Glacier Park; along Montana's Hi-Line country into my home town of Malta. The 550 mile trip took two full days.

It seemed that we sat on one siding or another half the time waiting for higher priority trains to go by. But that wasn't the half of it. There was no heat in the car. It was "colder than a well-digger's ass" in Wyoming. Furthermore, the train was so crowded, you couldn't even move around. I'll never forget sitting up, tired and cold, trying desperately to find some way to sleep with drafts, lights, shifting from cheek to cheek trying to find some way to stretch out, and always the mildewed smell of the old maroon seats.

We finally pulled into Malta on November 30 at sunup. I heard the station master tell another passenger it was ten degrees above zero — not too bad considering the month and time of day. Buttoning my peacoat, I turned the collar up to protect my ears, shouldered my seabag and headed for the Great Northern Hotel two blocks away.

The next three weeks were a mixed bag. I guess I half-expected a hero's welcome in my little hometown of 2,500 people. But the comings and goings of servicemen were commonplace. Some — especially the older family men — had already returned. The fighting had been over for four months, people were almost blasé about the war. Nevertheless, the fact that no one seemed interested in my adventures was oddly painful.

There were still a few significant war-related items in the news.

November 1945

A Joint congressional committee in Washington opens the major postwar investigations of the Pearl Harbor attack.

Gen. of the Army Dwight D. Eisenhower is named Chief of Staff of the Army and Fleet Adm. Chester W. Nimitz is appointed Chief of Naval Operations.

Rationing of meat and butter ends in the United States.

One day I went out to the Holm ranch to visit Carl and Louella, my "country parents." It was nice to see them again and to share our experiences of the last few years, but it was somehow depressing, too. They both looked so old and tired. The hard "dirty thirties" life had taken its toll.

With each passing day, I began to realize my life and interests were no longer in Montana. That was no surprise, but I felt guilty for not feeling the same loyalty and interest most of my high school friends obviously felt. Strolling around town where nothing had really changed in five years left me depressed. Main Street was still not paved. When I mentioned this to Frank Haromas, an elder in the Community Church and one of the "city fathers," he seemed offended. "That's right, Bill, but we built a new elementary school while you were gone and I believe we have our priorities in order." And, of course, he was right.

My three week visit was more than enough. I was rest-less after only one week. Besides, I decided I would rather spend the holidays exploring New York. In the end, I was ready to leave, knowing that somehow I was leaving Montana for good and that I would never go back to stay.

My reservations for leaving Malta on December 21 called for a 0200 departure. In spite of the hour, there were several people in the waiting room when I arrived, all huddled around a stove. The forecast called for blizzard conditions with tempera-tures well below zero. What timing!

One of the people waiting for the train, an attractive gal, twenty-something, looked familiar but I couldn't place her. An older lady, probably her Mom, was seeing her off. In spite of the hour, there was the usual banter and laughter you hear in stations everywhere when people are about to separate.

Shortly before the train pulled in, the girl came over and said, "Aren't you Billy McGee?"

I said, "Yes, you look vaguely familiar, too."

"I should," she said, smiling, "we went to the same schools and church only I was two or three grades ahead of you. I'm Liz Armstrong." (Not her real name).

Trains only stop in small towns like Malta if the stationmaster signals them to stop, and then only for two or three minutes, so we boarded quickly.

Our reserved coach seats were in the same car only a few rows apart. Since the car was dark and most of the passengers were sleeping, we stowed our bags and continued our get ac-quainted conversation between our car and the car behind us for another half hour or so, in spite of the cold. Before parting at about 0300, we agreed to sit together come morning if we could get someone to move.

A few hours later, the gentleman next to Liz agreed to swap seats with me and we resumed our conversation. Liz was in her third year at Northwestern and worked part-time for a small Chicago ad agency.

We were in another drafty old coach but at least it was part of a train with a regular, through schedule, rather than a slow moving, low priority "milk train."

Liz and I were so engrossed in our conversation we hardly noticed the snow-covered plains of North Dakota flying by or the stop and go at each station. In no time we were sitting down to a very forgettable meal. But we were both ravenous and ate every bite.

On the way back to our coach we stopped and necked like a couple of teenagers on the bumpy narrow platform between cars. Liz was every bit as horny as I was by this time. Then we did the unthinkable. We ducked into the next vacant lavatory and joined the railroad's equivalent of the exclusive "Mile High Club" of airline travelers. We were two lonely people attracted to each other for the moment like many other couples, before and since.

It took the better part of the next day to make our way through Minnesota to Chicago. As we said our good-byes, we both realized we would probably never see each other again, but agreed it was nice while it lasted.

The rest of the train trip on into New York was long, boring and uneventful.

I checked in at the Receiving Station on Pier 92, West 52nd Street, the morning of December 23, 1945 in order to save money while exploring New York. However, I wasn't officially "received aboard" until 0904 on January 2, 1946. Between dates, I was free to come and go as I pleased as long as I carried my delayed orders with me.

After picking out a bunk and locker, I stowed my sea bag and headed for Times Square, "as good as any place to start" I was told by several New Yorkers at the receiving station. I had a check list of things to see or do in New York.

And see New York City I did. Once I mastered its public transportation system of subways, buses, trains, and ferries, I found it easier to get around New York than most other cities.

For starters, I visited everybody's "must sees": the Statue of Liberty and the top of the Empire State Building. Then I walked around Central Park and had drinks at the Plaza Hotel. That first night I also saw the Rockettes at Radio City Music Hall and watched people ice skating at Rockefeller Plaza.

Another day, I explored Manhattan from Greenwich Village to Harlem stopping in at interesting looking ethnic restaurants and bars along the way.

When I needed a cultural fix, I toured a museum or art gallery. My evenings were busy, too. I remember seeing the Andrews Sisters and Gabby Hayes in the "Eight-to-the-Bar Ranch" radio show at the Paramount Theater. I visited the Stage Door Canteen, went to a Broadway play and watched a radio quiz show at NBC.

I was fortunate in that I didn't have to see all of New York's sights alone. When traveling, anything can happen. There's always that element of surprise. I think that's what I like most about it. You wake up each morning and wonder: what will I see or do today? Whom will I meet? It can be pure serendipity, at times, like my meeting Liz Armstrong in Malta. But I was learning to strike up conversations with members of the opposite sex, a challenge made easier, I soon learned, if you already share a common interest.

I dreaded the thought of spending Christmas in New York alone but it turned out to be a pleasant experience. Fifth Avenue was beautifully decorated as were the many fine stores. A light snow was falling on last minute shoppers and carolers provided the sounds of Christmas everyone loves. I went to a movie on Christmas Eve and church services the next morning.

New Year's Eve on Times Square was another matter. Wall to wall people, half of them loaded, and more than a few looking for trouble. I'm convinced New Yorkers originated the saying, "New Year's Eve is for amateurs." I headed back to the station right after the crowd finished "Auld Lang Syne," mighty thankful I wasn't on SP duty, yet.

On January 3, 1946, I met with one of the officers on the staff of the Receiving Station Commander. My objective was to activate my "personal plan" to see Europe in '46 by transferring to the Atlantic Fleet. I gave him a quick run down of my previous duty in the Pacific and of my desire to see Europe before my regular Navy minority enlistment expired. He scanned my personnel file, then asked me about my long-range plans. I assured him I still planned to make the Navy my career but, before making a final decision, I needed to serve in the fleet, preferably in a cruiser or carrier in the European theater.

He looked me straight in the eye, smiled, and said, "You have it all worked out, don't you?"

I smiled back as I reminded him, "The squeaky wheel gets the grease."

He explained how difficult it was to please everyone and how their immediate priority was to process the hordes of reservists coming through the station daily based on points earned for age, length of service, and number of dependents. The men with the necessary points were then transferred to the separation center nearest their home for discharge. As our meeting was about to end, the officer assured me he and his staff would fill my request for sea duty with the Atlantic Fleet, if at all possible. Then he added, almost as an after thought, "I see you've had shore patrol duty in the Philippines. I'm going to assign you to our shore patrol unit until further notice. Hope that's okay with you."

What could I say?

If the Seattle Receiving Station was a three-ring circus, the New York station was like a beehive with bluejackets coming and going around the clock. They were so excited to be going home, they forgot some of us were trying to read or sleep. But most of us understood. After all, the war was over.

The Plan of the Day at the Receiving Station was fairly simple — at least for the regular Navy men: Muster at 0800 for assignments and keep your eye on the bulletin board for new postings. The Shore Patrol duty was straightforward compared to the Philippines. I put in five eight-hour shifts a week — some days, some nights — then two back-to-back days off. For someone wanting shore duty, it was hard to beat with a good liberty town at your doorstep.

On Tuesday morning January 22, 1946, after three weeks of SP duty, I received the news I hoped and prayed for: duty on a heavy cruiser attached to the Atlantic Fleet. I picked up my travel orders and service records later that morning, then went by the transportation desk to get my train ticket.

Now I was the one who was excited. I spent the rest of the day writing letters, making phone calls and doing laundry. That night I went to a movie on Times Square with a couple of the off-duty SPs and was back at the station by midnight. Europe was just over the horizon.

17

USS *FALL RIVER* (CA-131)

I left the U.S. Naval Receiving Station on Pier 92, West 52nd St., New York on January 23, 1946, for Penn Station. My destination was Norfolk, Virginia and the USS *Fall River* (CA-131) with a stop in Washington, D.C. to visit my sister, Betty.

The train ride between New York City and Washington was uneventful. The ugly "railroad side" of big cities like Philadelphia and Baltimore was offset by the beautiful rural scenery between them.

Betty was pretty typical of the thousands of single girls who answered the call from Washington during WWII. She left our little hometown of Malta, Montana in January 1942 and worked for nine agencies during the war, including the War Production Board (WPB) and the War Assets Administration (WAA).

Due to the acute shortage of apartments, "government girls" moved a great deal. Newcomers found it almost impossible to find a place to live. My sister lived in rooming houses with umpteen other gals, then found an opening in an upstairs apartment with five other girls. Later, these same six women rented a house for a year.

Betty and her roommate Jean, met me at Union Station and took me to lunch. They had to go back to work after lunch so I played tourist for the rest of the afternoon. The next morning, I had a bowl of cereal with Betty and Jean, then kissed them good-bye as they went off to work.

The author and sister, Betty. Washington, DC, January 1946. Author

I remembered a tip from a Chief Boatswain's Mate while stationed in New York. According to him, there were several independent limousine drivers making the Washington-Norfolk run at reasonable per-person rates operating from a "floating limo stand" near Union Station. Sure enough, a Washington-Norfolk limousine pulled into the pickup point outside the train station. The driver hustled a full load of five bluejackets and a marine corporal in less than thirty minutes. We were able to split one fare six ways — a really good deal for us — and the driver, who also owned the 1940 Cadillac limo.

Most of the other passengers were catching, or already attached to, ships in the greater Norfolk area. I was the only one assigned to the *Fall River*.

It was dark by the time the driver pulled up to the gate of the naval base, the destination for four of us. Two signalmen were already attached to the USS *Washington* (BB-64) and the third man, a coxswain, was joining the USS *Missouri* (BB-63).

USS Fall River *(CA-131), circa 1946. U.S. Navy.*

The Marine sentry at the gate checked our travel orders, then arranged for a jeep to deliver us to our respective ships.

The *Fall River* was moored to the north side of Pier 3 at Berth 35 of the naval base. I could see she was a beauty even in the semidarkness of the pier. Shouldering my seabag I headed up the gangway. The Officer of the Deck granted me "permission to come aboard" at 1830 on January 24, 1946. After reviewing my records he had an aide show me to my quarters as he wrote in the Deck Log: "Pursuant to speed letter serial 1568 of 18 January 1946 McGee, W.L., GM2c, 665 57 76, USN was received on board for duty with baggage and records."

The living quarters were confined with three tiered bunks or racks each consisting of a pipe frame into which a heavy duty canvas fabric had been laced, topped by a two- to three-inch mattress pad. The compartment — one of the largest on the ship — was home to the 6th Division. Air, warmed in cooler climates, but far from air-conditioned for warmer ones, hissed constantly through ducts. Each man was assigned a stainless steel locker approximately one foot wide by three feet high by eighteen inches deep for personal belongings — a far cry from what I had in the Armed Guard.

Before I hit the sack that night, I met several shipmates including two Sixth Division gunners mates, I.A. Bernard, GM1/c and R.C. Morgan, GM3/c. They informed me:

1) I was assigned to the Sixth Division which shares responsibility for the 40-mm antiaircraft battery with the Seventh Division.

2) A shake up of officers in the Sixth Division was underway. Our new Division Officer (DO) effective 1 February would be Lt. Edgar F. Berberet. The present three Junior Division Officers (JDOs), would soon be replaced by just one new JDO, Ensign Samuel D. Keeper. "You better write that down, McGee."

3) Few plankowners (a person who has been on board since ship was commissioned) remain aboard. The constant turnover in bluejackets due to demobilization was creating a lot of special problems. As Bernard put it, "There are times the *Fall River* seems more like a floating Receiving Station than a heavy cruiser." Drafts of men came and went almost every day. (The United States was demobilizing 1.5 million men each month. The number of servicemen would decline from a wartime high of 15 million to 1.5 million by 1947.)

4) The latest scuttlebutt had us headed for the Marshall Islands and the proposed Atomic Bomb tests. That was the last thing I wanted to hear. It seemed almost everyone aboard the *Fall River* half-expected a Mediterranean cruise. As R.C. Morgan said, "Scuttlebutt is probably only right fifty-percent of the time. So our chances of seeing Europe are still pretty good."

I knew about the proposed A-bomb tests. They made the news even before I arrived back in the states. Here's a sampling:

October 27, 1945 — Admiral King disclosed plans for A-bomb tests at a press conference in Kansas City, Missouri.

December 15, 1945 — Joint Chiefs planning staff nominate VAdm. William H.P. Blandy to head the tests.

January 8, 1946 — Navy Secretary Forrestal and Acting Secretary of War Kenneth Royall recommend tests to President Truman.

January 10, 1946 — President Truman approves tests.

January 13, 1946 — Fleet Admiral Nimitz, now Chief of Naval Operations, calls press conference in Washington to announce selection of Adm. Blandy.

January 24, 1946 — Adm. Blandy announces the tests before Senate Special Committee on Atomic Energy. Adm. Blandy also reveals Bikini test site and project code-name "Operation Crossroads."

Bernard, the Sixth Division's senior (leading) petty officer, handed me a stack of manuals later that night with the caustic comment, "Here's your reading assignment. There will be a quiz at 0900 tomorrow." But, he smiled when he said it.

The package included the ship's "Cruise Book" as well as an "Organization and Regulations Manual", the Gunnery Department's "Organization Manual", the Sixth Division's "Watch, Quarter and Station Bill" and a divisional "Organization Manual."

I finished the "Cruise Book" before lights out that night. It was a fun read covering the *Fall River*'s early history — from its August 1944 launch through the end of 1945 — ranging from the commissioning ceremonies and shakedown cruise to a Navy Victory Days Parade in Fall River, Massachusetts on October 28, 1945.

January 25 was shipboard orientation day — the U.S. Navy's system for "integrating newcomers into a ship's company in an orderly fashion."

After noon chow, I attended a group session for all newcomers covering emergency procedures, fundamental damage control, and shipboard safety, e.g., alarms (general, fire, and collision) plus abandon ship stations and drills. I soon learned that shipboard routines are different in war and peace, in port and at sea, and to some extent on weekdays versus Sundays and holidays. Of course, routines also vary by ship type and the size of the ship's company. *(text continues on p. 365)*

USS *FALL RIVER* (CA-131)[1]

The keel was laid down on April 12, 1943 and the ship was launched August 13, 1944 by New York Shipbuilding Corp. of Camden, New Jersey. The sponsor was Mrs. Alexander C. Murray, wife of the mayor of Fall River, Massachusetts. Commissioning took place on July 1, 1945 with Captain David S. Crawford, USN, in command.

Launching of USS Fall River *August 13, 1944, Camden, New Jersey. U.S. Navy.*

Statistical Data
Length: 674'11"
Beam: 70'10" Draft: 20'6"
Displacement: 13,600 tons
Speed: 33 knots.
Complement: 1,142 (peacetime), 1,500 (wartime).
Armament: Main battery - nine 8" 55-caliber guns in 3 turrets
Secondary battery - six dual 5" 38-caliber gun mounts
Antiaircraft batteries - 40-mm and 20-mm guns
Fall River Airforce: Two Seahawk airplanes.

All cruisers are named for prominent U.S. cities. The name Fall River was derived from the Indian word Quaquechan meaning

---

[1] Sources: USS Fall River "Command History;" Dictionary of American Naval Fighting Ships, Vol. II; "The Old Fall River Line" and "Straight Dope" newsletters of 8 March 1946 and 22 February 1946 respectively.

Ready to launch from catapult on Fall River. Circa. 1945. Francis V. Murphy.

falling water — the name of the stream running from Watuppa Ponds down a 200-foot drop to Mount Hope Bay. Fall River, Massachusetts was founded in 1803 on the banks of this stream.

The city of Fall River provided sports equipment, recreational facilities, and other gifts for the use of the officers and men of the USS *Fall River.* This included: two pianos, a combination radio-phonograph player, a large number of books, a substantial amount of athletic equipment, sporting goods, games and a public address system used for church services and entertainment programs such as USO shows.

SHIP'S ORGANIZATION:

The commanding officer (C.O.) and his executive officer (X.O.) were assisted by subordinate officers who controlled the major functions of the ship. These functions were divided into administrative units called departments. Each department was headed by an officer. Some departments were subdivided into divisions.

GUNNERY DEPARTMENT (887 enlisted men, 39 officers.)

Division	Responsibility
First	8" Turret No. 1
Second	8" Turret No. 2
Third	8" Turret No. 3
Fourth	5"-38, dual mount, fast firing.
Fifth	5"-38, dual mount, fast firing.
Sixth	40-mm antiaircraft guns
Seventh	40-mm antiaircraft guns

Some of the crew under one of the 8" mounts. U.S. Navy.

Eighth	20-mm guns
Ninth (Marines)	20-mm guns
"F"	Fire Control
"I"	Radar equipment
"V"	Aircraft

COMMUNICATIONS DEPARTMENT (69 enlisted men, 13 officers)

Division	Responsibility
CS	Visual communication.
CR	Radio communication.
CY	Written communication.

ENGINEERING DEPARTMENT (196 enlisted men, 12 officers)

Division	Responsibility
Auxiliary ("A")	Workshop, refrigerated spaces, air-conditioning.
Boiler ("B")	Ship's boilers.
Electrical ("E")	Electrical power.
Main Engine ("M")	Main propulsion machinery and evaporators

HULL DEPARTMENT (47 enlisted men, 9 officers)
Hull and hull systems, deck fittings and equipment. Also serving, setting up and cleaning mess gear and messing compartments.

NAVIGATION DEPARTMENT
Navigator
Training Officer
Assistant Navigator
"N" Division   Ship navigation, control, tactics, and deck watch supervision, officer and enlisted training.

SUPPLY DEPARTMENT (32 enlisted men, 5 officers)
Procurement, receipt, stowage, issue and accounting for food, clothing and pay.

MEDICAL DEPARTMENT (14 enlisted men, 3 officers)
Medical Officers
Dental Officer
"H" Division   Sick bay, isolation ward, operating room, laboratory and pharmacy.

MASTER-AT-ARMS FORCE (7 Petty Officers)
Discipline.

FALL RIVER CHAPLAIN
Religious and welfare activities.

(Continued from p. 361)
Departures from the normal routine are published in the Plan of the Day (POD). To quote from *The Bluejackets' Manual*, United States Naval Institute, Annapolis, 1990, p. 345.

This is "the word," the daily schedule of events, prepared and issued by the executive officer. It will name duty officers, assign various watches, and include any changes or additions to the normal routine and orders of the day — drills, training schedule, duty section, liberty section and hours, working parties, movies, examinations, or inspections.

The POD, distributed to the officer of the deck (OOD), all offices, officers, and division bulletin boards, is carried out by the OOD and all division officers.

The following POD for May 24 while en route to the Bikini A-bomb tests is fairly representative of a day at sea during peacetime.

Plan of the Day
Friday 24 May 1946.
Duty Section: 3rd; Standby: 1st.
Duty Commander: Lt. Cmdr. Scott.
Working Division: 1st.

0500	Call duty M.A.A. [Master at Arms]
0510	Call duty bugler, mess cooks, and petty officers.
0530	Reveille, except for mid-watch. Trice [lash] up bunks. (No coffee after 0600).
0545	M.A.A. report "Crew turned out," to O.O.D.
0600	Turn to: Commence field day. Sweep down compartments.
0630	Early breakfast for mess cooks, and M.A.A.'s. Hold late reveille.
0645	Mess gear. Clear all messing spaces.
0700	Breakfast.
0730	Muster on stations.
0800	Turn to: Continue field day. Flight quarters.
0830	Catapult two (2) planes.
0835	Torpedo defense - Conduct "AA" tracking drill.
1000	Flight quarters.
1030	Recover planes - CHARLIE METHOD.
1130	Pipe sweepers. Early dinner for M.A.A.'s, mess cooks, and men with early mess tags.
1145	Mess gear. Clear all messing spaces.

1200	Dinner.
1300	Standby for lower deck inspection. Set condition X-ray.
1315	Zone inspection.
	Zone 1 Lt. Weaver.
	Zone 4 1st Lieutenant
	Zone 2 Executive Officer
	Zone 5 Chief Engineer
	Zone 3 Gunnery Officer
	Zone 6 Lt. Cmdr. Scott.
1430	Communication drill (Exercise 23B).
1500	Secure from Zone Inspection. Set condition YOKE (less 2nd deck hatches) [See p. 388 for definitions of zone conditions].
1530	Semaphore drill.
1545	Pipe sweepers. Empty all trash cans.
1645	Early supper for mess cooks, M.A.A.'s, and men with early mess tags.
1700	Mess gear. Clear all messing spaces.
1715	Supper.
1930	Movies on top side. The movie for tonight is "Guest Wife" starring Claudette Colbert, Don Ameche, Richard Foran, and Charles Dingle.
2100	(After movies) sweep down all compartments. Empty all trash cans.
2130	Lights out in all living compartments.
2200	Blinker drill.

NOTES:

1. All Division Officers draw Master Billet sheets at Executive Officer's Office and make all corrections on separate sheet, and attach to Master Billet.
2. All hands are cautioned to use fresh water sparingly.
3. Vinegar will not be used as a cleaning agent. Use soap and water only.
4. No one is permitted aft of the movie screen during the movies. Men may sit on steel deck forward of the movie screen but

NO SMOKING. Do not throw lighted cigarettes over the side during movies - put them out on the sole of your shoe.

5. Notes from yesterday's emergency drills:

    1. Hatches near scene of the fire were not closed.

    2. Men were standing around scene of the fire waiting for men regularly detailed to break out fire hoses. Take immediate action and then turn over to fire party as they arrive.

    3. All fire, rescue, and relief parties must fall in two ranks and keep quiet to expedite muster.

    4. Move fwd. and up to stbd., aft, and down port.

    5. Seven men were still unaccounted for at secure from Abandon Ship drill.

    6. Officers and men were too slow getting to quarters.

6. There will be no SATURDAY this week. [crossing dateline].

                               M.E. Dennett, Executive Officer

The Navy standardized everything — routine, regulations, and organization — as much as possible on all ships, so you didn't have to learn a new set of regulations and a different organization every time you moved from one division, department, or ship to another. All of this and more was in the reading material Bernard gave me. (Unfortunately, there was no handy sheet comparing the "Fleet Way" with the "Armed Guard Way." So I had a lot of homework to do.)

The "Daily Routine at Sea" chart was also a big help to me when I first went aboard the *Fall River*.

Daily Routine At Sea

Wkdys Sunday Routine

0600	0630	"Up all idlers" (nonwatchstanders).
0605	0635	Announce weather.

0615	0645	"Turn to. Scrub down weather decks. Sweep down all compartments. Empty all trash cans." "Lay below to the MAA office for muster, all restricted persons." Pipe sweepers, MAA report to OOD, "Idlers turned out." Clean boats and fuel boats as necessary.
0700	0700	Pipe to breakfast. "Testing general alarm." On completion: "Test of general alarm completed." "Uniform of the day _____," or Uniform for captain's inspection is _____."
0805		Assembly.
0815	0815	Sick call.
	0815	Rig for Church. "Knock off ship's work; shift into uniform for inspections." "Uniform for inspection is _____."
	0915	Officers' call. "All hands to quarters for inspection."
	0930	"Knock off work. Shift into clean uniform of the day." Church call. "Maintain quiet about the decks during divine service." Hoist the church pennant. At the end of the service, pennant is hauled down. Commence holiday routine.
1115	1115	Pipe sweepers. "Sweepers, man your brooms. Make a clean sweep down fore and aft. Empty all trash cans." Early mess for cooks, mess cooks, and MAA.
1145		"Knock off all ship's work."
1200	1200	Pipe to dinner.
1300		"Turn to." At this time, extra duty persons muster at MAA office.
1300	1300	Pipe sweepers. "Sweepers, man your brooms. Make a clean sweep down fore and aft. Empty all trash cans."
1300		Friday, or when ordered, inspections call, "Stand by for inspection of lower decks."

1600	1600	Pipe sweepers. "Sweepers man your brooms. Make a clean sweep down fore and aft."
1600		"Knock off all ship's work."
1645		"Observe sunset." Set the prescribed material condition. Division damage control petty officers report closures to damage-control central or sign the closure log maintained by the OOD on the bridge.
1655	1655	Mess call. "Clear the decks."
Sunset	Sunset	If the ship is to be darkened: "Darken ship. The smoking lamp is out on all weather decks." If ship is not to be darkened, turn on running lights and haul down colors following motion of senior officer present afloat. (SOPA)
1700	1700	Pipe to supper. Close watertight doors, etc.: "Set material condition ____ throughout the ship."
1745	1745	Sick call.
1800	1800	Pipe sweepers. "Sweepers man your brooms. Make a clean sweep down on lower decks and ladders. Empty all trash cans." "Lay below to the MAA office for muster, all restricted persons." Rig for movies. Movie call. Time and place as designated in POD.
Dark	Dark	Dump trash and garbage. Pump bilges (Oil Pollution Act permitting). Blow tubes if wind favorable and plan requires it.
2000	2000	Hammocks. "Out lights, and silence in all berthing spaces."
2100	2100	MAA reports to the OOD "9 o'clock, lights out."
2155	2155	Tattoo.
2200	2200	MAA reports to the OOD "10 o'clock, lights out."

These excerpts do not include all routine's such as Early mess calls, Sunrise routines; Calls/Relieve the watch; and OOD, Quartermaster, Security, and Lookout routines.

It was a full day, but the shipboard organization was impressive. I guess that's the main reason I never found much fault with the Navy's Rules and Regs. They were obviously necessary, especially on ships with crews of more than 1,000 men.

The Friday January 25 log recorded the following ships present: ComBatCruLant (SOPA) [Commander Battleships and Cruisers, Atlantic Fleet (Senior officer present afloat). The senior line officer of the Navy on active service, eligible for command at sea, who is present and in command of any unit of the operating forces afloat in the locality or within an area prescribed by competent authority] was in USS *Wisconsin*. Also present were USS *Missouri*, USS *Mississippi*, and various other units of the Atlantic Fleet.

Between January 25-30, 1946, 281 officers and men were transferred off the ship for separation from the Naval service. During this same period, 138 officers and men came aboard. For every man coming aboard two were leaving. Bernard was right. The ship was a "floating receiving station."

During the above six day period, I noted the *Fall River* was assigning one, sometimes two, five-man Shore Patrol details (mostly Gunner's Mates) to temporary duty in Norfolk. Their average shift was eight hours. No doubt it was a harbinger of things to come.

On Saturday January 26 the *Fall River* moved from Pier 3, berth 35, U.S. Naval Base, Norfolk to berth No. 24, Hampton Roads, Virginia.

On Monday afternoon January 28, I watched as the two *Fall River* aircraft were hoisted out for training flights and recovered about two hours later.

On January 29 the ship received 54,642 gallons of fuel from *YOG-34*. Meanwhile we also received stores from the SS *Seminole*. Clearly, we would be heading out to sea soon. The question was where.

Wednesday morning January 30 we had back-to-back exercises: General Quarters, abandon ship stations and fire quarters.

My "plan" for a European cruise became a memory on January 31 when the *Fall River* departed Hampton Roads for the Panama Canal Zone. The skipper received orders transferring the ship to the Pacific Fleet and a significant role in Operation Crossroads with "Details to follow as they become known."

The *Fall River* crew increased by one dog while the ship was still part of the Atlantic Fleet. She joined the Eighth Division of the Gunnery Department. From *The Old Fall River Line*:[1]

Now it can be told. The "Straight Dope" on how our ship's new mascot came aboard for duty. Through a man's desire for companionship and his love of animals, the *Fall River* recently had her crew increased by one dog.

Let's call her Guns.

One night in January 1946, while visiting some friends in Newport News, Welsh, 8th Div., was completely carried away by a small bundle of fur behind two large brown eyes. Nothing would do but sole possession of the then unknown Guns. After much bickering, Welsh drove a bargain, and the dog was his.

All that remained was to get her aboard. After much conspiring between Ullrich, Pop Finley, Farrel, and Hodkinson, it was decided that Welsh should shanghai her aboard under his peacoat.

The scheme proved successful, and the dog was kept hidden until the day before sailing, when she was discovered and ordered off the ship. All hands turned to, however, and through a special chit signed by Gun Boss Little and Executive Officer Dennett, Guns was allowed to stay.

Guns has been known by several names since first coming aboard. Some of the better known ones are: "Flags," from her week's stay

---

[1] The USS *Fall River*'s newspaper, *The Old Fall River Line* a.k.a. "Straight Dope" was published bi-weekly by members of the crew beginning February 22, 1946.

on the Signal Bridge; "Hashmark," from her anticipated long naval career; and "Shanghai," for obvious reasons.

However, no one has seemed to be able to give the dog a name that will stick, and because the pooch is the ship's mascot, the "Straight Dope" has decided to help all hands name her. Ballots will be printed and distributed in chow line in the near future. Put in your vote, and we'll let you know the outcome in the next issue.

Saturday February 2: Another exercise and drill day. GQ, Fire drill and Collision Quarters. Then at 1017 we had a Man Overboard drill (first boat manned and ready at 1035). In the afternoon we had a Fire and Rescue drill.

As I became more acquainted with the shipboard routines, I got to know members of the 6th Division a little better. The 6th Division was largely made up of young, "wise guys" from New York — mainly Brooklyn and the Bronx — with the accent and attitude to prove it. Most of them were fresh out of Boot Camp. R.C. Morgan and I nicknamed them our "Dead End Kids." They looked and talked much like their namesakes in the movies. But once you earned their respect, they were good sailors.

On Sunday February 3 divine services were held for the crew. It was announced: "Now hear this: Sixth Division detail, rig for church on the fantail." Duties such as this were rotated among various divisions.

Sundays were more relaxed. Perfect for bull sessions on deck in these warm waters. At noon we were just south of Cuba and the Dominican Republic.

According to Guns Bernard, the *Fall River* developed quite a sports program in 1945 but due to the many transfers, all the teams needed replacements.

On Monday February 4 we had more drills and exercises between 0845-0955 followed by a special sea detail exercise. At 1205, the C.O. held mast and awarded the guilty party five days solitary confinement on bread and water for striking a Petty Officer.

THE BOATSWAIN'S CALL

The Boatswain's Call or whistle, was once the only method other than the human voice of passing orders to men on board ship. Today many ships still use the Boatswain's call preceding important PA announcements as well as a mark of respect to pipe the Captain or special visitors on board.

The boatswain was the petty officer in charge of rigging, sails and sailing equipment. He therefore needed to issue orders more often than other petty officers and so the whistle was named after him.

In the old days men were rigidly trained to respond immediately to the piping of the Call. At sea, in moments of danger they could hear the high-pitched tones of the Call, and react without delay whereas a shouted order may not have been heard above the howling winds and lashing waves. Instructions to hoist sails, haul or let go ropes were conveyed by different notes and pitches.

The boatswain's pipe was first used on English ships in the thirteenth century, during the crusades, and became known as "The Call." About 1670 the Lord High Admiral of the Navy wore a gold whistle of rank. This was known as the "Whistle of Honour."

Each section of the Boatswain's pipe has a nautical name. The ball is the buoy; the mouthpiece is the gun; the ring is called the shackle, and the leaf is called the keel.

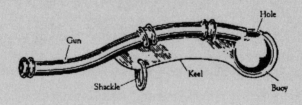

"Now hear this: Sweepers, man your brooms. Make a clean sweepdown fore and aft. Empty all trash cans." That PA announcement and many others were usually preceded by the call of the Boatswain's pipe or whistle. This was another Navy tradition I didn't experience in the Armed Guard. So I didn't know one call from another when I joined the *Fall River*, let alone why and how the tradition started.

I was surprised to learn that the "N" Division of the Navigation Department had a Chief Buglemaster and two Buglers in addition to the Quartermasters, an Aerographer's Mate and a Photographer's Mate. However, only on some occasions, such as Mail Call and Taps, would a bugle call precede a PA announcement. There are always exceptions to the rule. Richard W. Camp, QM3/c, N Division remembered one: "Every once in a while some OOD would have a bugler look through his book. On one occasion, he ordered the call for 'shine all bright work' and nobody had any idea what it meant. Everyone was running around but hell, nobody knew what it meant, let alone what to do!"

On February 5 the *Fall River* entered Limon Bay, Panama Canal Zone. After a pilot came aboard, the ship was maneuvered on various courses and speeds with the pilot at the con, and the Captain, Executive Officer and Navigator on the bridge. By 0826 the ship was moored to Pier 10 and the special sea detail was secured. At 0915 we commenced taking on fresh water and fuel from the dock.

At 0815 muster, I.A. Bernard ("Guns," from now on) informed me I had been "awarded" SP duty for the day. Just after lunch, our Shore Patrol detail of twenty-five Petty Officers plus two officers, left the ship for duty in Cristobal.

The naval shore establishment on the Atlantic side of the Canal Zone was primarily limited to an air station for seaplanes and the submarine base at Coco Solo bounded by Margarita Bay on the west and Manzanillo Bay on the south. Colon and Cristobal, across Manzanillo Bay, were the liberty towns. Our detail was divided into two units to cover both towns.

The afternoon and evening were relatively uneventful with the usual number of "drunk and disorderlies." Lots of bars and bar girls hustling "blue moon cocktails" — blue-colored soda pop. But the guys would order them just to get to talk to the girls.

"Red Light" houses were at street level and run much like retail stores. The lines to the whorehouses and prophylactic stations were long, especially at night. One of the biggest beefs my partner and I had to break up that night was between several sailors and Marines. As it turned out, two Marines joined their buddy in line ahead of the sailors and that triggered it.

At about 2000 my partner and I were ordered to escort one of the *Fall River*'s "deck apes" (his words) back to the ship. He had been held by the Canal Zone Police on a charge of "operating a motor vehicle without a driver's license." He was delivered back to the Shore Patrol headquarters in Cristobal where someone would take him to the Canal Zone Police to answer the charge.

I had my first liberty in Panama on the 6th with Guns Bernard, R.S. Morgan and two other men from the sixth division. By the looks of the only photo I have of our Panama visit (taken by the night club photographer) we were reasonably sober and well behaved.

For the most part, Panama was disappointing. The towns seemed dirty. They had plenty of bars and night clubs for the sailors of the world, but I guess I was spoiled by the young and pretty Filipina girls. The Panama hookers were old and tired by comparison. Nevertheless, some of us learned the true meaning of a "trip around the world" that night. As the crew reported back on the liberty opportunities ashore, the lyrics to that still popular WWII calypso tune took on more

Liberty in Colon, Panama Canal Zone. Left to right: author, ????, Bernard, Morgan and ????.

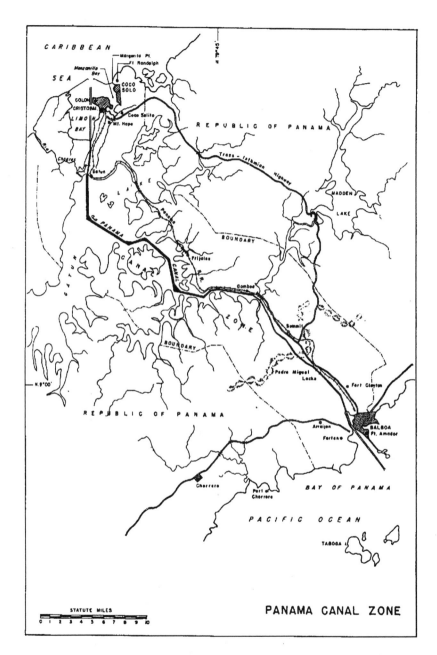

PANAMA CANAL ZONE

meaning: "Drinking rum and Coca Cola . . . Working for the Yankee dolla."

Roy L. Swalm S2/c, 7th Division: "The things we saw in Colon . . . these fast women. Coming from a little Pennsylvania town in the coal region, I didn't know what a fast woman was. The little kids, ten to twelve years old, the mannerisms and the vocabulary that they used. I was utterly shocked. I couldn't believe there was such a thing in the world. But that's the way it was."

On February 8 a special sea detail commenced preparations for getting underway. Yard tugs *Cardenas* and *Alhegueza* came alongside and a pilot reported on board. At 0611 the *Fall River* was underway from Pier 10, Cristobal, Canal Zone for San Pedro, California. At 0631 yard tugs cast off and at 0655 the ship entered the Gatun Approach to the Panama Canal Zone

The trip through the canal was beautiful and exciting to all of us first timers. I learned that the six locks operate strictly by the force of gravity. No pumps are used. Each lock holds 66 million gallons of water — enough to supply an average American city for one day. Lock gates are seven feet thick, eighty-two feet high, and weigh up to 730 tons. Ships are stabilized and towed by electric locomotives called "mules."

Monday was another day of General drills and exercises: 0846-0941 General Quarters. 1302-1318 Fire drill (1304, first stream of water at scene of fire). 1325-1358 abandon ship drill.

The C.O. held mast at 1415 and awarded punishment to two men for "illegal possession and use of camera on board ship," one a Quartermaster 3/c, the other a Seaman 2/c; punishment; two weeks restriction. That really surprised me, now that it was peacetime.

We had a new drill the next day. At 0800 Flight Quarters was sounded. At 0825 the course was changed to 060 (from 297) in preparation for catapulting one plane to port. At 0821 Pilot Lt. (jg) Aronson in plane No. 2 was launched by catapult. At 1027 they were recovered and lowered on the starboard catapult. Meanwhile the ship's crew was called to GQ and a Fire Drill.

At 1300 Flight Quarters was sounded again. This time it was Lt. R.S. Hardwick in plane No. 2. He was catapulted and recovered between 1330 and 1424. Finally, Ensign W.W. Ellis took the same plane up between 1447 and 1526. Later that evening we saw the lights of Acapulco, Mexico off to the east.

The following day we had our first antiaircraft firing practice of the voyage using balloons.

At 1100 it was the 4th and 5th Division's turn. They also conducted a 5-inch Variable Time (VT) fuse projectile test. The VT fuse, also called an influence or proximity fuse, became available to the Fleet in 1943 but the Armed Guard never received any of this new ammo so I was particularly interested in the test. The VT fuse detonated 3-inch and larger antiaircraft shells at the closest point to an enemy airplane thus increasing the probability of destroying the aircraft.

At 1125 all firing practice ceased. Ammunition expended: 538 rounds of 40-mm; 1700 rounds of 20-mm; and 74 rounds of 5'/38 cartridges and 50 rounds of 5'/38 special projectiles (VT fuses).

That afternoon, I had another first. At 1431 the ship commenced steaming at various speeds to stream paravanes (a torpedo-shaped device towed on either side of a ship's bow to deflect and cut adrift moored mines). The paravanes were streamed at 1527 and recovered fifteen minutes later while the ship was making ten knots. That night we passed by Mazatlan, Mexico.

By February 14 I noticed the weather was improving. The daytime temperatures were about 90 degrees in Panama even though it was winter. Now they were around 80 and were expected to drop to about 70 by the time we reach L.A.

It was another "drills and exercises" day. They were becoming routine for all of the new men — the objective of all training. We had GQ in the morning and exercised at emergency drills in the afternoon — away Fire and Rescue Party, Fire drill, and Collision drill. At 1900 we changed to Zone plus 8 time. We passed Cabo San Lucas on the southern tip of Baja California later that night.

February 15 was payday for the crew. Another new "line experience." There was no line when a fifteen to thirty man

Armed Guard crew got paid. Between 1300-1530 the skipper conducted an inspection of the lower decks. My only previous experience with this type of inspection was in Boot Camp and one or two times on Treasure Island. You should have heard the howls and bitching from my

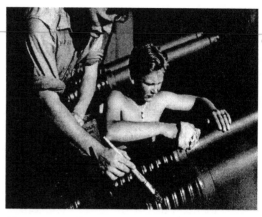

Cleaning and greasing 40-mm guns.   Naval Historical Center.

Dead End Kids! All that griping reminded me of a little item in *The Old Fall River Line*:

> Intercepted Mail
>
> Dear Ma:
>
> I joined the Navy because I admired the way the ships were kept so clean and tidy. This week I learned who keeps them so clean and tidy.
>
> With love, Junior

Looking aft from bridge while Fall River *is underway. Note Seahawk scout plane on port catapult. U.S. Navy.*

Everyone was up bright and early on February 16 for our arrival in Los Angeles. Many of the younger guys who grew up in the East had never been to California, so this was a major port for them.

At 0706 a Pilot boat came alongside and we entered San Pedro harbor through the east entrance of the breakwater.

Above, 40-mm quad guns in action. Note shell cases being ejected to the deck in front of the gun mounting, and loaders feeding fresh cartridges. Naval Historical Center.

Right, crew of a 40-mm quad A.A. gun mount loads four-round clips into the loaders of guns. (Gun captain is in "Talker" helmet.). Naval Historical Center.

At 0733 we passed the USS *Lexington* close aboard to port. At 0753 the ship anchored in Berth C-8 in seven fathoms of water. Other ships present included USS *New Jersey*, USS *Alabama*, USS *Massachusetts*, USS *Springfield*, USS *Salt Lake City*, USS *Dayton*, USS *Wilkesbarre*, USS *Astoria*, and various units of the U.S. Naval Force, and various yard and district craft.

At 0952 the Agriculture and Sanitation Inspectors came on board. They left the ship at 1026. At 1100 the Customs Officer came on board. He left at 1203. Transfers of personnel began right after noon chow: Two Marines were transferred to Camp Perry, Virginia; three men, including our Engineering

Officer, went on leave; and twelve men reported on board for temporary duty.

At 1400, seven men left the ship for temporary Shore Patrol duty at the SP Headquarters, Pico Avenue Landing, Long Beach. A large liberty party was right behind them.

Sunday was uneventful but early Monday morning (0130) three of our illustrious Dead End Kids were "arrested and returned to the ship under the custody of the XO; offense, Misconduct ashore."

The front page of "Straight Dope" headlined our arrival on the coast:

Fall River liberty party files down the gang plank to explore sunny California. Dominick Di Guiseppe.

> *Fall River* Joins Pacific Fleet
>
> San Pedro, California. On Saturday last, the USS *Fall River*, embarking on her first real tour of duty, joined the Pacific Fleet as a member of Cruiser Division One. A far cry from her weekly sorties out of Norfolk. This duty may someday take her to many of the colorful spots of the Orient: Shanghai, Hong Kong, Singapore, or Manila. There is also the possibility that she may figure in the forthcoming atomic bomb tests late this spring. However, her future is still a mystery: in the meantime, the ship is preparing to take her place in the Navy's peacetime Fleet, and many of her crew are enjoying sunny California for the first time.

February 19 started out with heavy fog and visibility of only fifty yards. Shipboard routines were much the same as they were in Norfolk. Work parties in the morning and afternoon. Liberty parties were taken ashore in an LCI (Landing Craft, Infantry) at 1600.

USS Fall River *(CA-131) anchored in San Pedro Bay, February 1946. Kenneth J. Tinker.*

David Shafer, S1/c, 3rd Division, remembered a favorite Southern California liberty: "A group of us went to Hollywood and on to San Fernando Valley to ride horses. We ended up at the Brown Derby to quench our thirst. Two older women were seated next to our table and sent over a bottle of champagne. They eventually joined us and one woman asked to sit beside me. She said I looked so much like her son who was killed in action while in the Navy. I felt she got comfort in talking about the matter. My brother was killed a year earlier during the 'Battle of the Bulge' so I understood her situation."

February 20 was a busy Mast day for the skipper:

Twenty-four men each lost one liberty for "improper wearing of uniforms while on authorized liberty."

Two men were found guilty of sleeping during working hours; punishment, twenty hours extra duty.

Six men were each restricted to the ship for one week for the following offenses: 1) Improper uniform, 2) Altered ID, 3) Possessing another man's ID card, failure to cooperate with Shore Patrol and out of uniform, 4) Improper uniform and altered ID, 5) Improper wearing of uniform, failure to salute superior officer and altered ID.

Sometimes there are ways to avoid problems. Larry Trueax, GM striker, 6th Division remembered R.C. Morgan,

Life aboard a cruiser, clockwise from left: showering, working over the side, in the chow line, morning wash-up and holy-stoning. U.S. Navy

Franklin and Casey returning from liberty in Long Beach: "I had the watch and they tried to bring a bottle of whiskey aboard in a shoe box. The Officer of the Deck asked to see the shoes so R.C. dropped the box over the side and said, 'Hell, they didn't fit anyway.'"

I went ashore several times while we were anchored in San Pedro Bay, usually with one or more guys in the 6th. One time we made the rounds of Hollywood. Some stops, like the

Left, two of the 6th Division's "Dead End Kids," P. Chini S2/c, and H.J. Callabretta, S2/c, tour Beverly Hills. Right, actor James Gleason opened his house and pool to several Fall River *6th Division guests. Author.*

Brown Derby and the Palladium, were familiar from an earlier visit. Another time, we headed south for a change of pace and had a ball on Balboa Island next to Newport Beach.

One twenty-four-hour liberty with Guns Bernard, R.C. Morgan, and one other 6th Division man stands out. We ended up with six very nice teachers who had all attended the same small midwestern college before the war. We partied until the bars closed, went skinny dipping in the ocean, then spent the night with all six gals in this little house in Culver City. Bernard was the only one to get laid that night. He cut out the best looker in the bunch and had her behind closed doors before the rest of us had our hats off. We felt like country bumpkins, but we admired Bernard's expertise.

There was a second bedroom but it soon became obvious there would be no more sex play that night. We sat around and talked until sunup. End of story. However, Morgan and I never let Bernard forget the "selfish act" he committed that night and swore to get even if we ever get the chance!

On Tuesday March 5 the "black gang" began turning over the main engines for dock trials. At 1430 a draft of 126 men, most reservists, was transferred with bags, records, and pay accounts to report to the C.O. Terminal Island, California for further assignment while awaiting discharge.

Shortly after the preceding draft left the ship, a draft of fifty men was received on board with bags, records and pay accounts for further transfer to Receiving Station NAVY 128 (Pearl Harbor) for assignment by Commander Service Pacific.

On Wednesday March 6 1946 we got underway for Pearl Harbor, Territory of Hawaii at a speed 15 knots.

The March 8 "hot off the press" issue of *The Old Fall River Line* lead with this cover story:

> *Fall River* in Crossroads
>
> Putting a sudden and dramatic end to her West Coast stay, the *Fall River* on Wednesday slid out of her anchorage at San Pedro, Calif., bound for Pearl Harbor. Her new assignment: to take a large part in the coming atomic bomb tests in the Marshall Islands this spring.
>
> Although her exact role has not been officially released as yet, the *Fall River* will undoubtedly be a part of the Naval operating forces at the scene of the tests.
>
> Opening in early May, America's atomic bomb tests will be conducted under the command of Vice Admiral W.H.P. Blandy at Bikini Atoll in the Marshall Islands. This Navy-Army-Civilian operation, which bears the code name of 'Crossroads,' will be staged by Joint Task Force One, which will consist of 97 target ships and at least 50 operating ships, of which the *Fall River* is to be one.
>
> A B-29, flying more than five miles high, will drop the test bomb, while other B-29s and B-17s outfitted as flying laboratories will make observations of the tests. The target fleet will be anchored in waters ranging from 66 to 120 feet in depth, in a lagoon on Bikini Atoll.

There are some interesting sidelights to the forthcoming tests. Admiral Blandy reassures many letter-writers that the A-bomb will NOT puncture the seabed and let the water run out.

The 167 natives which comprise the population of Bikini Atoll will be evacuated to a safer home, as will all personnel on Eniwetok, which is 235 miles to the east. Whereas the *McKinley* will be only a few miles from the explosion, it is estimated. Too damn close for us? (Or will it be) . . .

Admiral Blandy has announced that live animals, sheep, goats, etc., will be used for the tests. Although the resulting flood of letters and protests from animal-lovers is tremendous, there have been very few from men who will be there . . . Instead, the rumor has been circulating that all men connected with the experiment will be given an 80% raise in pay. Believe that one and we'll tell another.

On March 12 we sighted Makapuu light, Oahu Island, in the early morning. At 1016 we passed Diamond Head Light abeam to starboard. With the aid of the tugs *Nachinga* and *YTB-340* we moored port side to the west side of berth Baker No. 3, Pearl Harbor, T.H. We then set material condition X-Ray and secured the special sea detail.

CONDITIONS OF READINESS

For damage control purposes, Navy ships have three material conditions of readiness, each representing a different degree of tightness and protection. They are X-Ray, Yoke, and Zebra.

Condition X-ray provides the least protection. It is set when the ship is in no danger of attack, such as when she is at anchor in a well-protected harbor or secured at home base during regular working hours. During this condition, all closures marked with a black X or circled X are secured; they remain closed when setting condition Yoke and Zebra.

Condition Yoke provides somewhat more protection than condition X-Ray; Yoke is set and maintained at sea. In port, it is maintained at all times during war, and at times outside of regular working hours in peacetime. Yoke closures, marked with a black Y or a circled Y, are secured during conditions Yoke and Zebra.

Condition Zebra is set before going to sea or when entering port during war. It is set immediately, without further orders, when general quarters (GQ) stations are manned. Condition Zebra is also set to localize and control fire and flooding when GQ stations are unmanned. When condition Zebra is warranted, all closures marked with a red Z, a circled red Z, or a Z within a black D, are secured.

Once the material condition is set, no fitting marked X-ray, Circle X-ray, Yoke, Circle Yoke, Zebra, Circle Zebra, Dog Zebra may be opened without permission of the commanding officer, through the damage control assistant (DCA) or officer of the deck.

18

OPERATION
CROSSROADS

A draft of thirty-nine passengers was ready to disembark the *Fall River* when the gangway was lowered — the first of many drafts to come and go during our stay in Pearl Harbor. The first liberty party was right behind them.

On March 13, Rear Admiral Frank G. Fahrion, USN, and his staff came aboard for a brief tour of his new flagship for the Bikini Atomic Bomb Tests. Fahrion and his staff would be responsible for organizing and directing the target ships and salvage units during the "Crossroads" tests as well as commanding all of Joint Task Force One (JTF-1) when VAdm W.H.P. Blandy was elsewhere.

The second half of March was relatively uneventful except for one thing. On March 23 word was received that President Truman postponed the Bikini tests for six weeks to accommodate members of Congress. Six weeks of waiting around was exactly what the crew didn't want.

Some of the crew decided to get better acquainted with the "ladies of the night" now that they had more time in port. Vitto Rossi, electronics technician: "One time when I was coming back from liberty in Honolulu, I remember the Marines were bringing back one of our guys who had been on liberty and all he had on was a pair of Marine skivvies. He had been rolled and I remember him saying, 'I lost $365.' I said to myself, one dollar for every day of the year. When they found him, he was completely naked. The Marines loaned him the undershorts."

Honolulu liberty, Spring 1946, while awaiting orders to proceed to Bikini for A-bomb tests. Top L to R: Dave, McGee, Burnier. Bottom L to R: Chuck and Roberti. Author.

Fall River sailors continued going and coming to and from various schools. Half of the 6th Division went to the Antiaircraft Training Center in Waranae in Oahu for two weeks on March 25. In the meantime, we received almost daily drafts of new men as crew additions or as part of Fahrion's flag allowance.

On March 27 the ship moved to berth F-8 in Pearl Harbor, and at high noon the flag of RAdm. F.G. Fahrion, USN, Commander Task Group 1.2 in the *Fall River* was hoisted for the first time.

The *Fall River* was attached to First Division Cruisers, Pacific Fleet and became temporary Flagship for Commander Task Groups JTF-1 at Pearl Harbor, T.H.

The week of April 7 saw 263 men depart the *Fall River* for temporary training or transfers and ninety-one men return to the ship, so the churn continued.

The week of April 15 brought a change in the routine. From ship's log:

Monday 15 April: 1006 Underway from berth H-1, Pearl Harbor, Territory of Hawaii in accordance with Commander Training Command speed letter . . . Maneuvered on various courses and speeds conforming to the channel. Pilot Lieutenant Commander Liberg at Conn, Captain, Executive Officer, Navigator on Bridge. Standard speed is 15 knots (142 rpm). 1059 Pilot left the ship. 1113 Secured special sea detail, set regular sea detail. 1146 Commenced swinging ship on various courses to calibrate Radio Direction Finder . . . 1302 Exercised at fire quarters. 1303 First stream at scene of fire. 1320 Secured from fire quarters . . . 1332 Exercised at torpedo defense for anti-aircraft tracking drill. 1333 Changed speed to 8 knots, (074 rpm). 1340 Loading drill for all turrets . . . 1540 Secured from all loading drills . . . 1545 Set special sea detail. 1554 Captain took Conn . . . 1613 Anchored in anchorage number 5, Kewalo Basin, Oahu, T.H.

Tuesday, Wednesday and Thursday were almost identical to Monday's exercises except that each day short range runs were made on a fleet tug with two target sleds in tow. April 22-25 were filled with more training drills, tests and practice runs while underway. We did have two drills I hadn't experienced before: a message dropping drill from a plane and a steering casualty drill where steering control was shifted to aft steering.

On April 27, following Captain's inspection, the *Fall River* shifted to the east side of Berth Baker 12 in the U.S. Navy Yard in Pearl Harbor.

BIKINI TESTS — WHY, WHEN AND WHERE

When the Japanese surrendered, the United States found itself the only global power capable of producing the atomic bomb. Since the race to produce the bomb had precluded all but a cursory analysis of how it would affect military operations over the long term, many important questions remained such as what to do with the bomb and how to control it. Furthermore, there was no reliable information available on the bomb's effects on ships, airplanes, and military equipment, or defense against it.

Both Adm. Blandy, when Chief of the Bureau of Ordnance in 1943, and Senator Brian McMahan (D-CT) in a 1945 speech, called for the use of enemy ships and surplus U.S. vessels to test the effects of new weapons on Navy ships. McMahan:

> In order to test the destructive powers of the atomic bomb against naval vessels, I would like to see these Japanese naval ships taken to sea and an atomic bomb dropped on them. The resulting explosion should prove to us just how effective the atomic bomb is when used against giant naval ships.

Momentum in favor of the A-bomb tests started to build. Soon other politicians and military strategists, as well as the media, were calling for tests. Subjects debated in the media included:

Has the A-bomb made navies obsolete?

Would it affect the future size and composition of the armed forces?

Would nuclear weapons be controlled by civilian or military authorities?

The Joint Chiefs of Staff (JCS) created JTF-1 and assigned it the mission of atomic bombing a target array of naval ships. Vice Admiral W.H.P. Blandy was designated Commander. This task Force would soon comprise a total of more than 200 ships, 42,000 men, and 150 aircraft. It would include members of the Navy, Army Air and Ground Forces, and civilian scientists. Its directive ordered one test of the bomb in air above the target fleet, and a second detonation in the water, slightly below the surface.

Bikini Atoll met all but two of the Joint Staff Planner's criteria for a test site: the island had 167 inhabitants, and the fishing industry was concerned that large numbers of fish would be killed but these problems were resolved. The Bikinians were relocated, and the Fish and Wildlife Service of the Interior Department argued that the concerns raised by the fishing industry were unfounded.

The test dates were originally set for May 15 and early July 1946. Time was an important factor for several reasons — most related to postwar demobilization. The Army and Navy were rapidly downsizing, affecting the number of personnel available to man the ships, planes, and instruments required for the tests and scientists were leaving the government's employ. Furthermore, civilian scientists insisted they be back at their universities by September.

In the meantime we began to understand just how complicated the atomic bomb tests would be. The assembled task force was comparable to a major wartime battle plan.

JOINT TASK FORCE ONE ORGANIZATION
Operation Crossroads July 1946

VAdm. W.H.P. Blandy, USN, Joint Task Force Commander

Flagship-*Mount McKinley* (AGC-7) Capt. W.N. Camet, USN

Maj. Gen. W.E. Kepner, USA, Deputy Task Force Commander for Aviation

RAdm. W.S. Parsons, USN, Deputy Task Force Commander for Tech. Direction

Maj. Gen. A.C. McQuliffe, USA, Ground Forces Advisor

TECHNICAL GROUP (TG1.1)-RADM. W.S. PARSONS, USN
Laboratory Unit (TU1.1.1)

Capt. E.H. Eckelmeyer, Jr., USN

Flagship *Albemarle* (AV-5)-Capt. Eckelmeyer

LSM-60 Cmdr. H.A. Owens, USN

LCT-1359 W. Wannstedt, QM2/c, USN

INSTRUMENTATION UNIT (TU 1.1.2)-CAPT. A.C. THORINGTON, USN

Flagship *Haven* (APH-112)-Capt. A.C. Thorington, USN

Kenneth Whiting (AV-14) Capt. A.R. Truslow, Jr., USN

USS Fall River *(CA-131) at anchor, Kewalo Basin, Oahu, T.H. Kenneth J. Tinker.*

Cumberland Sound (AV-17) Capt. H.R. Horney, USN
Wharton (AP-7) Capt. V.F. Gordinier, USN
Avery Island (AG-76) Cmdr. D.E. Pugh, USN
Burleson (APA-67) Capt. C.L. Carpenter, USN

DRONE BOAT UNIT (TU 1.1.3) CMDR. R.R. BRADLEY, USN
Flagship *Begor* (APD-127) Lt. Cmdr. R.K. Margetts, USN

TARGET VESSEL GROUP (TG 1.2)-RADM. FRANK G. FAHRION, USN
Flagship *Fall River* (CA-131) Capt. D.S. Crawford, USN

BATTLESHIP AND CRUISER UNIT (TU 1.2.1)-CAPT. W. DEWEESE, USN

All together JTF-1 would have eight task group commanders:

TG-1.1 RAdm. W.S. Parsons, Technical Group,

TG-1.2 RAdm. F.G. Fahrion, Target Vessel Group,

TG-1.3 Capt. W.P. Davis (Navy), Transport Group,

TG-1.4 Col. J.D. Frederick, Army Ground Group,

TG-1.5 Brig. Gen. R.M. Ramey, Army Air Group,

TG-1.6 RAdm. C.A.F. Sprague, Navy Air Group,

TG 1.7 Capt. E.N. Parker (Navy), Surface Patrol Group,

TG 1.8 Capt. G.H. Lyttle (Navy), Service Group.

[*A complete list of Operation Crossroads target and support vessels can be found in Appendix C.*]

Admiral Blandy also maintained liaison with two boards in Washington: The JCS's Evaluation Board and the President's Evaluation Commission. The Evaluation Board was appointed by the JCS and had two broad functions: (a) to be available to the Task Force Commander for advice during the preparation for the tests and (b) to evaluate for the JCS the results of the tests as reported by Commander JTF One. The Evaluation Commission appointed by the President also had two functions: (a) to cooperate with the Secretaries of War and Navy in the conduct of the tests and, (b) to study the tests and submit to the President the Commission's observations, findings, conclusions and recommendations.

A Rear Echelon Staff was established in Washington to assist the Task Force in the field and coordinate with the War and Navy Departments and other government agencies.

A Fleet of more than ninety vessels was assembled as a target for the tests. It consisted of older U.S. capital ships, three captured German and Japanese ships, battleships, destroyers, submarines (some on the surface and some submerged), transports, cargo ships, landing ships, concrete barges, and a concrete dry-dock.

The plan was to moor the target ships in a corner of Bikini's lagoon which was approximately twenty miles long and ten miles wide. Every effort was made to ensure the target vessels were watertight. The ships were partially loaded with fuel and ammunition to better simulate real conditions.

JTF-ONE staff meeting. Seated, L to R: Major General W.E. Kepner, Deputy Task Force Commander for Aviation; Vice Admiral Blandy, Commander; Rear Admiral W.S. Parsons, Deputy Task Force Commander for Technical Direction; Major General A.C. McAuliffe, Ground Forces Advisor. Rear: Brigadier General T.S. Power, Assistant Deputy Task Force Commander for Aviation; Brigadier General K.P. McNaughton; Captain C.H. Lyman, Assistant Chief of Staff for Operations;Colonel T.J. Betts, Assistant Chief of Staff for Intelligence; Colonel D.H. Blakelock, Assistant Chief of Staff for Logistics; Dr. Ralph A. Sawyer, Technical Director; Captain Robert Brodie Jr., Assistant Chief of Staff for Personnel, and Captain G. M. Lyon, Safety Adviser. U.S. Navy.

On several occasions, the planners explained to the press that the mooring plan for the ships bore no resemblance to the steaming formation of a task group at sea or of a fleet at anchorage. They were not simulating an attack. The target ships were moored to guarantee a maximum amount of damage to the bull's-eye group of ships and graduated damage outward from that center. There would be twenty-three ships moored in an area that normally was used for two or three capital ships at anchor and one at sea.

At one press conference, Adm. Blandy said of the arrangement, "It is our intention to inflict damage deliberately, not

Operation Crossroads, 1946. Target and Support ships at Pearl Harbor, in early 1946. Ships present include: USS Crittenden *(APA-71),* USS Catron *(APA-71),* USS Bracken *(APA-64),* USS Burleson *(APA-67),* USS Gilliam *(APA-57),* USS Fallon *(APA-81),* USS Fillmore *(APA-83),* USS Kochab *(AKS-6),* USS Luna *(AKA-7),* LSM-203 *and* LSM-465. *National Archives.*

to prove that the damage may or will not be inflicted in a real attack." Simulation of an actual bombing attack was precluded by the fact that only one bomb was to be used. A step to ensure bomb accuracy was painting the battleship *Nevada*, the center target, a bright red-orange and installing a radar beacon on board.

The support fleet of some 150 ships would provide quarters, experimental stations, and workshops for most of the 42,000 men in JTF-One. Additional personnel would be billeted on nearby atolls such as Eniwetok and Kwajalein. Bikini Atoll's small islands would be used as recreation and instrumentation sites.

One ship was included for biological testing. The *Burleson* (APA-67), carried 200 pigs, 60 guinea pigs, 204 goats, 5,000 rats, and 200 mice. A refitted assault transport, she also carried grains so that the insects within the grain could be studied for genetic effects by the National Cancer Institute. One reason for exposing the animals to the bomb detonations was to study the bomb's effects on humans. The primary purpose was to show the symptoms generated by the explosions, to provide experience cataloging injuries and detecting the onset of slowly developing ones, to provide experience in treating injuries, and to reveal any new effects.

Before each test, all personnel would be evacuated from the target vessels and Bikini Atoll and temporarily placed on board ships of the support fleet which would sortie from Bikini Lagoon at least ten miles east of the atoll. (See Appendix C for makeup of support fleet.)

On May 11 the *Fall River* commenced taking on fuel and fresh water. Scuttlebutt had it we'd soon be getting underway for the Marshall Islands. The *Fall River*'s now familiar role as a "receiving station" continued with men transferring ashore and aboard almost daily.

Many of the target ships and support vessels began arriving at Pearl Harbor. They included veteran combatants like *Independence, Saratoga, Nevada, New York*, and *Arkansas* plus various other vessels of the Pacific Fleet.

On 12 May, another forty-seven men — thirty-two of them Signalmen and Radiomen — were received on board for temporary duty with ComTaskGroup 1.2.

On Tuesday May 14 at 0823, Amphibious Force Command Ship, USS *Mount McKinley* (AGC-7) stood in and the following day Vice Admiral W.P. Blandy, USN, Commander Joint Army-Navy Task Force One hoisted his flag on it for the first time.

The *Fall River* deck log for the next few days was filled with last minute transfers and additions to both crew and flag allowance prior to departure for Bikini.

On Tuesday May 21 1946 the USS *Fall River* got underway from berth K-8, Pearl Harbor en route to Bikini Atoll. We

USS Fall River *(CA-131) ComTaskGroup 1.2 Flagship just before steaming for Bikini from Pearl Harbor for Atomic Bomb tests. Circa May 1946. Kenneth T. Tinker.*

would serve as Rear Admiral Fahrion's headquarters for the entire Crossroads Operation.

The next five days were fairly routine. We steamed in company with USS *Walke* (DD-416) and USS *Laffey* (DD-724). The Officer in Technical Command (OTC) was Commanding Officer, USS *Fall River*. Formation guide was the *Fall River*.

In spite of the many Crossroads stories in the Honolulu media, RAdm. Fahrion's staff tried to play down speculation as to the potential dangers to participants. Stuart Hepburn, RM2/c, CR Division:

> I clearly recall receiving dispatches quoting scientists while we were on duty in the radio shack, including comments on the probabilities of a tidal wave to chain reactions that might obliterate the entire task force. We were told in no uncertain terms not to take this information outside of the radio room.

On May 26, the formation crossed the International Dateline and all clocks were set ahead twenty-four hours to minus 12 zone time.

On May 27 Bikini Island showed on the radar bearing 284 degrees at a distance of nineteen miles. We anchored at

1141 in nineteen fathoms of water, coral bottom, with seventy-five fathoms of chain to the port anchor. Several other ship were already present.

Two days later the *Pensacola, Arkansas,* and *Salt Lake City* stood in and anchored.

That afternoon I went ashore for the first time with about two dozen 6th Division shipmates for a look at Bikini Island. Our plan was to have a couple of cold beers and play some softball. As it turned out, the beer was warm and the temperature was about 100 degrees, without even a trace of a breeze, so the intra-division ball game was called off and we spent most our time swimming in the lagoon.

May 30 was a quiet day. Three more ships stood in: *Independence, Rhino,* and *Mustin.*

The 31st wasn't much different. Our pilots made flights and the target ships *Saratoga* and *Anderson* plus submarines *Dentuda, Parche,* and *Pilotfish* arrived.

On June 1, 1946, the C.O. inspected the crew, weather decks and living spaces. We had a close brush with a court martial. Our 40-mm quad was mounted on a square tower about

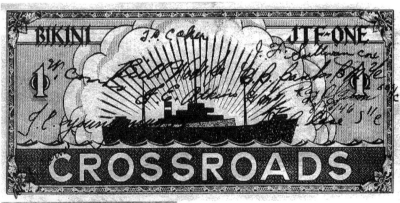

Photo of Short Snorter JTF-1 dollar bill and 5 cent chits good only at the Coral Reef Tavern during Operation Crossroads. Note shipmate signatures. Author.

five feet square and twenty feet tall. The base which was secured to the main deck (within the well-defined limits of the
quarterdeck), also served as a storage locker for ammunition and
gun maintenance tools and supplies.

The 6th Division was lined up awaiting the arrival of the
C.O. when I noticed the sweet aroma of Raisin Jack (moonshine
made from raisins). Following my nose, I discovered a small
puddle of "Jack" just outside the locker door. Opening the door,
I grabbed a cleaning rag and quickly wiped it up. (It left a dark
stain on the beautiful wood deck but I was able to stand over it
during the inspection.)

Investigating afterward, I learned the makings for the
"Jack" were provided by friendly galley slaves. The container,
a small keg, was lifted from one of the ships boats — a serious
no-no. Unfortunately, it was a fresh batch of "Jack" and popped
its cork when it was moved. Otherwise it might not have spilled.
I reminded the crew that the quarterdeck was the last place on
the ship they should be making Raisin Jack and that if it happened again, they wouldn't be so lucky.

On June 2 Admiral Blandy, arrived in his flagship, the
USS *Mount McKinley.*

In the "Forward" to *Operation Crossroads, the Official
Pictorial Record*, W.A. Shurcliff, JTF-1 historian, summed up
the preparations, instrumentation and pre-test training:

Preparations: Plans for the Operation went forward during the
Spring and early summer of 1946. Surveys of the Bikini lagoon
were made, its waters combed for truant Japanese mines, its natives
evacuated to another island. The islands were sprayed with DDT to
insure healthful conditions for Task Force personnel. Towers to
house cameras and television apparatus were built.

At Kwajalein, the available airfield installations were readied
for the arrival of the Air Group. Laboratories for chemical analysis
and photograph processing were constructed.

Little by little the ships of the target array assembled and were
brought to Bikini, most of them through Pearl Harbor, which hummed

with activity. Installations of special equipment had to be made on many vessels. Salvageable ship materiel was removed. Army equipment scheduled to be secured to the decks of the target ships and exposed to the bomb's destructive force was placed aboard.

The German cruiser *Prinz Eugen* moved from European waters to Philadelphia and on to the Pacific. From Japan steamed the captured Japanese battleship *Nagato* and the light cruiser *Sakawa*. Also to their rendezvous with destiny came the valiant old battleship *Pennsylvania*, commissioned in 1916 and once flagship of the United States Fleet, the 30-year-old veteran *Nevada*, first of the Navy's oil-burning super-dreadnaughts, the rugged carriers *Saratoga* and *Independence*.

Several plans for the arrangement of the target fleet were considered and revised. The directive creating the Operation specified a disposition of ships to give a graduation of damage from maximum to minimum. Major damage to ships at the outskirts of the target circle, would provide valuable means of analyzing the bomb's elusive fury.

The concentration of ships, from a Navy point of view, was obviously artificial. More than 20 ships were compressed within 1000 yards of the bulls-eye ship. Ordinarily such an area would be used to contain but a single capital ship in a carrier force at sea, or three capital ships in a normal anchorage. The principle of using an arrangement that would provide graduated damage, instead of one representing a tactical formation or anchorage, was followed in both tests.

Instrumentation: The instrumentation program at Bikini constituted the heart of the Operation. More than 10,000 instruments were placed about on target ships, [as well as] in shore, observer ship, and aircraft installations. Simple and complex, the instruments included many that were familiar long before Bikini, many developed specifically for these tests.

Various staff divisions under the Technical Director concentrated on apparatus. Their names hint at the breadth of scientific observation planned: bomb operation; pressure and shock; wave motion and oceanography; electromagnetic propagation and electronics; radiological safety; radiation; radiometry; technical photography.

The ships themselves were in a real sense instruments, their recorded behavior in the face of the explosions revealing much of the nature and development of the gigantic forces produced. Ingenious instruments on the ships measured roll and pitch, recorded strain experienced by plates and ribs, wrote down the temperature of ship interiors, tested surrounding air for contaminating radioactivity, radioed their findings to the observer fleet miles outside the lagoon.

Drone, or unmanned, radio-controlled boats and planes played an important part. The boats collected samples of the radioactive lagoon water when it was still too "hot" to handle. Drone planes penetrated where no man could have ventured, flew through the mushroom cloud on photographic missions, sampled its poisonous content, televised to remote onlookers their instrument panel readings for flight analysis.

Cameras at Bikini took more than 50,000 stills and 1,500,000 feet of movie film. One camera, presumably the world's largest aerial camera, used a 48-inch focal length telephoto lens capable of taking a legible photograph of the dial of a wrist watch a quarter of a mile away. One high-speed movie camera operated at the rate of 1,000 pictures per second.

Pre-test Training: The tests required special training of the 42,000 men who serviced the Operation. Procedures were set up for placing the thousands of instruments, for their care and activation, the collection of their data. Underwater photography techniques were developed as an aid in recording the data from sunken ships. The drone plane and boat programs, Army and Navy, greatly advanced the art of radio control apparatus and its manipulation.

The fact that Test Able was but the third atomic bomb ever dropped from a bomber provided the Army Air Forces with an incentive for considerable valuable and much-needed training in a practically untried field. AAF training for Bikini began in January 1946 at Roswell Field, New Mexico. It concerned drone operation and the bombing mission, the crew for which was selected after rigorous competition.

At Pearl Harbor, the Navy trained fire-fighting and damage control teams for the exacting work of first reboarding the target ships after each test. This work was important in saving instruments from destruction from secondary causes following the explosions, and in advancing the time for safe general inspection of the ships. To safeguard personnel from radioactivity, radiological monitors were schooled in the use of Geiger counters, which detect contaminated areas.

Fast minesweeper USS *Thompson*, (DMS-38), a converted flush deck destroyer, was on her way home from Japan to San Francisco when she received a change in orders at Saipan to escort a squadron of small YMS motor minesweepers to Bikini. Charles P. Minton:

> As I recall, we entered the lagoon on March 7, 1946, and witnessed the natives departing for Rongerik Atoll aboard *LST-1108*. Their outrigger canoes were on the top deck of the LST. Each had its sail hoisted, perhaps as insurance against engine failure on the part of the LST.
>
> *Thompson* and her YMS "chicks" swept the Sunburst (east) part of the lagoon for Japanese mines but found none. What we found were coral heads which wrecked our equipment.
>
> Much sonar work was required and it was hard work. Sweeping started at dawn and went on until dark. *Thompson* remained in one position and controlled the sweeps by radar. Under our XO, Lt. B.W. Moulton, the atoll was also mapped by radar, probably in conjunction with underwater work by surveying ship *Sumner* (AG-32) [a converted submarine tender].
>
> From time to time *Sumner* would detonate small explosive charges underwater, and even though she was usually several miles away, they sounded as if someone had hit *Thompson* with a sledgehammer especially if you were sitting near the side of the mess compartment.
>
> Thanks to our Loran system [LOng-RANge electronic navigation] we discovered the old charts they gave us were wrong. We passed the word on to higher authority. No doubt *Sumner* had already discovered the error — too bad we weren't informed.
>
> Our orders sending us to Bikini were sealed and stamped "Secret." The bridge gang was quite surprised to hear a commercial radio station tell all about Operation Crossroads. This happened one

LST-1108 moves outrigger canoes from Bikini to Rongerik, while the native owners watch anxiously, wondering whether Uncle Sam's sailors will handle their primitive craft as well as they do their own. These sailing canoes are used for hundred-mile trips in the open sea from atoll to atoll. U.S. Navy.

night when several quartermasters and signalmen decided to sleep in the pilothouse and on the bridge wings because of the heat below decks. We asked the radiomen to pipe us some music and they succeeded in picking up a Midwestern station (I think it was Minneapolis) which not only played music to lull us to sleep but which also gave a news item identifying in some detail what was happening at Bikini.

I went ashore only once during our week to 10 days at Bikini. The abandoned village was spotless. Most of the liberty party sat and drank beer until it was time to return to the ship.

My main impression of our stay at Bikini is how hard we worked, the radar and sonar people especially. The sweep was completed just as the first ships arrived to start the work ashore. Before we were out of sight of Bikini islet, the Seabees already had camera towers erected.

Bikini shack used to store R & R beer. Charles P. Minton.

June 3 was another "Receiving Ship" day with several men being transferred to LCIs and LSTs throughout the atoll.

It was about this time the McGee-Oyer Blackjack partnership began. I met Gerry Oyer, GM2/c, the day he came aboard in Pearl and we became good friends. At first we played doubledeck pinochle. Then we graduated to poker and blackjack when the opportunity arose. One night we both got lucky in the same blackjack game and before it was time for lights out, we controlled all the money on the table. That's when we first got the idea to form a partnership. Our game plan was that one of us would deal, the other would be banker anytime either one of us won the deal. The regular players were skeptical of our motives at first, but liked the faster pace of the game.

As I look back, one simple rule was key to our eventual success as "casino operators," and it was in effect before Oyer and I joined forces. Simply stated, any player with enough money on the table could "tap" the dealer when it came his turn to bet, meaning he could bet an amount equal to the dealer's total bankroll on the table. If the player won, the dealer was "tapped out" and had to give up the deal to the player.

In other words, the deal was up for grabs at all times if you had enough money to tap the dealer and the intestinal fortitude to risk it.

It wasn't long before we had visitors from other divisions wanting to sit in when/if a seat opened up. This increased activity forced us to create "funny money" to use in the game as a safety precaution. We knew gambling was against the "rules and regs," but assumed it was not being enforced now that the war was over.[1]

Some of the more fortunate bluejackets were able to indulge in a special form of shipboard entertainment. Connie (The Greek) Kontopirakis, EM3/c, "E" Division, was one of the lucky ones:

Verse of the People

"Bikini Blues"

This is the story of John and his men,
Who'll never sail the seas again.
They have no teeth, they have no hair,
Their eyes pop out, their ears cave in.
They now drink milk instead of gin!
But after all is said and done,
And if by chance I have a son,
No matter how much the "A" bomb
    harmed me,
I'll make the beggar join the Army!

As an electrician and gyrocompass tech, I was allowed to draw pure grain alcohol from the ship's supply to clean the electrodes that go into the salinity indicators of the fresh water condensers. They had to be cleaned with pure grain alcohol because anything else would leave a residue and affect the readings. But this was pure stuff. We would retire to the IC [Interior Communications] room which was on the fifth deck down. About an hour or two later when we would come back up, our eyeballs would look like road maps, but we never got caught.

Each test day had a "dry run" scheduled, and a code name was assigned to it. The rehearsal date for Test Able was "Queen" Day and for Test Baker, "William" Day. The hour of detonation of the bomb was "How" hour.

We began to realize how formidable a weapon the atomic bomb was when Cmdr. Dennett, the *Fall River*'s exec, issued Ships Order #2-46 on June 22, 1946:

---

[1] Imagine my surprise some fifty years later to learn it was still against the rules and regulations of the U.S. Navy even in peacetime. The proof of this was that the Commanding Officer held mast and assigned seven men (all petty officers) ten days restriction for gambling!

Subject: Atomic Bomb Test Safety Precautions.

Enclosure: (A) Potential Hazards to Personnel.

(B) Radioactivity Test Plan.

(C) Air Contamination Action Plan.

(D) Water Contamination Action Plan.

1. Certain safety precautions in regards to the Atomic Bomb Test must be very carefully observed by all hands on test and rehearsal days to insure against any form of injury. Potential hazards are enumerated and described in enclosure (A), and actions to be taken in order to guard against injury from post effects of the explosion are listed in enclosures (B), (C), and (D).

2. Enclosure (B) will be placed in effect at How -24 hours on all test and rehearsal days and executed as directed by Fall River Senior Medical Officer. Enclosures (C) or (D) will be placed in effect by the Commanding Officer instantly only if warning is received from higher authority indicating necessity therefor.

3. Safety precautions and actions on test rehearsal days will be governed by the following schedule:

TIME	ACTION
How -30 Min.	All hands to quarters.
How -5 Min.	Read special safety precautions to all hands over 1MC [footnote: The ships general announcing system.] from Conn.
How -2 Min.	All hands
	(1) Face away from Bikini as ordered over 1MC
	(2) Sit on Deck
	(3) Close eyes tightly
	(4) Cover eyes with bended arm against the face
How -?	"Carry on" when word is passed on 1MC. At this signal, all hands may safely observe the beautiful display of colors in the incandescent column of cloud and the gigantic clouds which follow the explosion.

M.E. Dennett, Cmdr., USN Executive Officer
APPROVED:D.S. Crawford, Commanding Officer

Monday 24 June, preparations were made for getting underway at 0400 for "Queen" day. The OODs logged the following entries:

0445 Set material condition "YOKE." 0517 Tested main engines. 0520 Hove short. 0522 USS *Cumberland Sound*, USS *Kenneth Whiting*, and USS *George Clymer*, underway standing out. 0531 Got underway for operating area outside BIKINI ATOLL, MARSHALL ISLANDS in accordance with COMMANDER JOINT TASK FORCE ONE, operation plan number 1-46. Maneuvered on various courses at various speeds to clear Atoll; Captain on the con, Executive Officer and Navigator on the bridge. Standard speed 15 knots (145 rpm). 0624 ENYU ISLAND abeam to port. Distance two miles . . .

Maneuvered on various courses at various speeds maintaining our position, bearing 102 degrees (t), 18 miles from target for the official rehearsal "Queen Day" of the Atomic Bomb test, Operation Crossroads. 0914 Executed official rehearsal "Queen Day" of the Atomic Bomb test, Operation Crossroads . . . Maneuvered on various courses at various speeds en route to BIKINI ATOLL harbor entrance. 1038 Set the special sea detail . . . 1107 Stopped all engines. 1113 Anchored in berth 386, BIKINI ATOLL, MARSHALL ISLANDS, in 24 fathoms of water, course sand bottom, with 60 fathoms of chain to the port anchor . . .

1620 Made preparations for getting under way. 1621 Set material condition "YOKE." 1634 Task Group One Point Eight standing in. Underway for berth 91, BIKINI ATOLL, MARSHALL ISLANDS on various courses and speeds conforming to channel. Commanding Officer at the con. Executive Officer and Navigator on the bridge. 1819 Anchored in berth 91, BIKINI ATOLL, MARSHALL ISLANDS, in 21 fathoms of water, coral bottom with 75 fathoms of chain to the port anchor . . .

On Wednesday morning, June 26, two officers and nine enlisted men of the U.S. Army left the ship to return to Prayer

Operation "Crossroads," 1946 — Officers involved with Army Air Force and Navy Participation in the Atomic Bomb tests, (l-r): BGen. Roger M. Ramey, who is directing AAF participation in the test; unidentified AAF Officer; Col. Paul W. Tibbets; Unidentified AAF Officer and RAdm. Thomas L. Sprague.

Island, having been on board for evacuation of Bikini Atoll on "Queen" Day. Two days later we received two Marine Corps sergeants on board for temporary duty in connection with Operation "Crossroads" photography.

On June 29 the Secretary of the Navy, James V. Forrestal, broke his flag in USS *Mount McKinley*. That evening Vice Admiral George F. Hussey, USN, Chief of the Bureau of Ordnance, reported on board unofficially as a visitor to observe the "Able" day Atomic Bomb test.

June 30 was filled with activity. From the ship's log:

1320 The following ships got underway and stood out: *Sumner, Moale, O'Brian, Huntington, Ingrham, Barton, Trippe, Flussen, Rolette;* 1343 *Furse;* 1345 *Reclaimer;* 1358 *Appling;* 1400

Saidor; 1401 *Begor*; 1420 *Ajax*; 1435 *Artemis*; 1437 *Coasters Harbor*; 1445 *Pollux*; 1446 *Henrico*; 1505 *Bountiful*; 1507 *Wharton*; 1524 *Benevolence*; 1540 *Bexar*; 1542 *LST-861*; 1554 *Haven*; 1600 *Blue Ridge*; 1604 *Panamint*; 1606 *Saint Croix*; 1610 *Appalachian*; 1623 *Gunston Hall*; 1625 *San Marcos*; 1626 *LST-817*; 1648 *Burleson*; 1651 *Orca*; 1654 *George Clymer*; 1658 *Avery Island*; 1715 *Fulton*.

Ensign John K. Larsen remembered the "advance" media coverage:

Prinz Eugen *(IX-300) (ex-German CA) ready for target duty in the operation "Crossroads" A-bomb tests, 14 June 1946. (Note radar van parked atop her bridge, and German radars atop the director and mainmast.)* National Archives.

We saw them being transmitted back to the States the day before the test. I saw them in the Ward Room and I remember complaining about it. I remember asking them, "How the heck can you guys write, 'It was a bright sunny day this morning when the bomb went off' you know that kind of stuff when it hasn't even happened yet?'" Well somebody explained to me. "Well look, from a practical point of view, there's only so many communication lines out of here and its easier to call and say 'correct the following paragraphs' than to try to send a four-page transcript. That gives everybody a better chance of getting their words back.'"

Continuing from the deck log on the day the bomb dropped:

United States Ship: *Fall River*
Monday 1 July 1946

4 to 8

Anchored as before.   0357   Tested safety valves on boiler
number three, by hand.   0445   Set material condition "YOKE."
Made all preparations for getting underway.   0500   Cut in boiler
three on the main steam line.   0510   Tested main engines.   0515
USS *Cumberland* underway.   0517 USS *Mount McKinley* underway.   0520   USS *George P. Clymer* underway.   0524   USS *Kenneth
Whitting* underway.   0526   Underway en route BIKINI ATOLL to
Operating area in accordance with JOINT TASK FORCE ONE
operation plan number 1-46, for Atomic Bomb test "Able."   Maneuvered on various courses at various speeds to clear anchorage
area;   Captain at the conn, Executive Officer and Navigator on the
bridge.   Standard speed, 15 knots (145 rpm).   0600 Nun buoy
number 6, abeam to port, distance 20 yards, standing out ENYU
channel.

At 0540 on July 1, Commander Joint Task Force One
ordered the drop aircraft, a specially modified B-29, to take off
from Kwajalein.   Twelve hours prior, all air operations within
500 miles were stopped.

Observers present included a Presidential Evaluation commission, the JCS Evaluation Board, U.N. representatives from
eleven countries, including the Soviet Union, and media representatives.

And, again from the deck log:

8 to 12

Steaming on various courses and speeds to keep station in
sector for Operation Crossroads.   0900   Atomic Bomb number 4
exploded . . .[2]

The bomb was released at 0859 and detonated with a
yield of twenty-three kilotons fifteen seconds before 0900, 1,500

---

[2] The first was at Almogordo, New Mexico, the second at Hiroshima and
the third at Nagasaki.

TEST ABLE: *Officers and men of the carrier* Saidor, *assembled on the flight deck, rehearse the safety procedure followed on Able Day to protect their eyes from the blinding light emitted by the explosion. The most intense portion of the flash, many times the brilliance of the sun, lasts for a few millionths of a second. To guard their eyesight, persons without goggles were ordered to stand with their backs toward the blast and to remain in this position until the all-clear signal was given several seconds after the instant of explosion. U.S. Navy.*

to 2,000 feet west of the planned detonation point above the *Nevada.* The pool news report described the blast:

> The mushroom broke out suddenly at the top, and the cloud changed colors. It was a fascinating picture. For a few minutes, it looked like a giant ice cream cone as it turned completely white. Looking at it then through binoculars, it seemed like floating layers upon layers of whipped cream. Again it changed colors, now to peaches and cream. All this time, the trade winds were driving it hard. In 30 minutes the cloud began to disintegrate into a crazy pattern of fat Zs. In an hour, the wind had so battered it that the disintegrating cloud began to look like a giant, willowy dragon in a small boy's dream.

John Reilley: "I was standing in front of the hanger deck with some newsreel people. We just shaded our eyes with our hands. I remember seeing the *Pennsylvania*'s bow being lifted out of the water."

John Skarzenski: "They stressed that personnel not required to be below decks were to be at quarters topside sitting down with their arms over their eyes and heads cradled between their legs. And even though we did that, we could still see the light from the bomb with our eyes closed.

Operation Crossroads, 1946. "Able" day A-bomb cloud seen from USS Fall River *(CA-131) off Bikini, 1 July 1946. Naval Historical Center.*

Another thing I still remember. Right after the explosion — we had these dignitaries aboard and one of them had a stateroom on the starboard side near the exec's cabin — here was this gentleman calmly painting the cloud as it was forming. Amazing."

Louis V. Brence: CRM, CR Division USS *Pensacola*: "We had our eyes covered with our forearms and leaned on our raised knees. I still saw the flash of light of the explosion even though my eyes were covered and my back was to the target. I've often wondered if my late-in-life development of cataracts may have been triggered by this experience.

The news reports described the damage to the ships and aircraft:

> A destroyer and two transports sunk 'promptly' and another destroyer capsized. It later sank and the cruiser *Sakawa* sank the following day.
>
> The light carrier *Independence* and the submarine *Skate* were damaged severely also. These ships were within one-half mile of the explosion point.

Operation Crossroads. "Able" day explosion, 1 July 1946. Note effect of shock wave on water, below. Left, As seen from Bikini, with USS Saratoga at left. Aerial view, bottom. Bottom photo National Archives, others, Naval Historical Center.

All target vessels within 500 yards of actual surface zero, the detonation point, were sunk or seriously damaged.

Ships beyond 750 yards had little induced activity or contamination.

In stations normally occupied by people were 176 goats, 146 pigs, 109 mice, 57 guinea pigs, and 3,030 white rats. During Test Able, 35% of these were killed — 10% by air blast, 15% by radioactivity, and 10% during later study. Because of the facilities provided to the press, the first picture of the blast was received in San Francisco one hour and 20 minutes after the bomb's detonation.

According to the Department of State Bulletin issued on 21 July, no significant unexpected phenomena occurred — no large water wave formed; the radioactivity dissipated as expected; and

Correspondents aboard an LCT view the badly damaged USS Independence *(CVL-22) on July 3, 1946, two days after the "Able" day burst. (This was the unengaged side of the ship.) National Archives.*

no damage occurred on Bikini Island, located about three miles from the explosion center.

Knowing what I do now, I find it surprising that we returned so quickly to Bikini. From the ship's log for July 2:

> 0 to 4
> Anchored in berth 386, BIKINI ATOLL, MARSHALL IS-
> LANDS in 23 fathoms of water, coarse sand bottom, with 75 fath-
> oms of chain to the port anchor . . .
> 8 to 12
> Anchored as before.   1020   Underway to berth 91, BIKINI
> ATOLL, MARSHALL ISLANDS. Captain at the conn. Executive
> Officer and Navigator on the bridge, steaming on various courses
> and speeds conforming to channel.   1037 *Sakawa* sank.   1040
> USS *Sumner* relieved this vessel as Harbor Entrance Control Ves-
> sel.   1147 Anchored in berth 91, BIKINI ATOLL, MARSHALL
> ISLANDS . . .

Soon after the first test, the collection of data began — the reading of apparatus, the amassing of facts which would take months to appraise. Wednesday July 3 was completely uneventful if you go by the ship's Deck Log. At 0715 the Secretary of the Navy hauled down his flag in USS *Mount McKinley*. A few men were returned to their ships having completed temporary duty on the *Fall River*.

On Independence Day, a contingent of U.S. Army personnel left the ship for Prayer Island, Bikini Lagoon after completion of temporary duty aboard the *Fall River*. Two days later Task Group 1.2 began rearranging the target array for test "Baker."

The days dragged on between tests. There wasn't much to do aboard ship except work during the long, hot summer days, so most of us went ashore in the afternoons when we had liberty. There was always softball, warm beer and a swim to break the monotony. Dick Camp, QM3/c, "N" Division: "I remember going swimming after one of the test shots. I also remember a cheap crappy beer, Acme, I think it was, always out in the sun. We would drink that crap and then go throw up, then swim in the salt water. I think there was a raft out there but we would cut our feet on the coral anyway."

On July 8, VAdm. William H.P. Blandy paid the *Fall River* an "unofficial visit" and presented RAdm. F.G. Fahrion a Gold Star in lieu of a second Legion of Merit medal.

On July 19 the *Fall River* got underway for "William" day. The rehearsal was very similar to "Queen" day.

Commander Dennett, the *Fall River*'s X.O., invited me up to his office on July 22 to find out my plans now that my kid's cruise (four year minority hitch for seventeen-year olds with parental consent) was coming to an end. I told him I'd given it a lot of thought and decided I would be better off taking my discharge and getting an education first.

Cmdr. Dennett congratulated me on what he called "an intelligent approach to your future," then surprised me by asking, "Would you consider shipping over, if we made you a gunner's mate first?"

I answered, "No, but thanks for the offer anyway."

With that, he said, "We'll arrange transportation for you back to the States as soon as possible after the Baker test."

On July 23 VAdm. G.P. Hussey, USN, Chief of the Bureau of Ordnance unofficially came aboard as a guest of RAdm

Left, view of the blast damage to the conning tower area of USS Skate *(SS-305), two days after the "Able" day aerial burst. Bottom, despite the damage, USS* Skate *(SS-305) gets underway the same day.   National Archives*

Fahrion to observe the "Baker" Atomic Bomb Test. On July 24, ships began to stand out one by one much like the day before the "Able" shot.

For the "Baker" test, the target vessels were moored in new positions centered on a bomb situated in a caisson submerged beneath the *LSM-60* at the center of the array. The LSM had been refitted extensively with special rigging facilities, a laboratory, and radio and electronic equipment. Wire cable, electrical wire, and a coaxial umbilical — which transmitted the

Submarine Rescue Vessel USS Coucal *(ASR-8) divers being lowered into Bikini Lagoon during Operation "Crossroads" resurvey activities in July 1947. National Archives.*

ultrahigh frequency signal that detonated the bomb — linked the weapon to the ship.

Based on our deck log entries, one would never know we witnessed what most news services considered the most important news event of 1946:

DECK LOG — REMARKS SHEET

United States Ship: *Fall River*

Thursday 25 July 1946

0 to 4

Anchored as before in berth 91, BIKINI ATOLL, MAR-SHALL ISLANDS. Ships present: various units of US Naval Force. SOPA is COMMANDER JOINT TASK FORCE ONE in USS *Mount McKinley.*

4 to 8

0400 Made all preparations for getting underway. 0416 Cut in boilers number two and three on the main steam line. 0440 Tested main engines. 0450 Set material condition "YOKE." 0500 Hove short. 0507 USS *Cumberland Sound* underway. 0511 USS *Kenneth Whiting* underway. 0514 USS *Albermarle* underway. 0517 USS *George Clymer* underway. 0518 USS *Rockridge* underway. 0520 USS *Mount McKinley* underway. 0522 Underway en route to operating area, in accordance with orders of COMMANDER JOINT TASK FORCE ONE, Operations plan 1-46. Maneuvered on various courses at various speeds to clear anchorage area; Captain at the con, Executive Officer and Navigator on the bridge. Standard speed 15 knots, (145 rpm). 0600 Lighted fires under boiler number one and four. 0616 Can buoy number one abeam to starboard, distance, 350 yards. 0617 Set course 137 degrees (t) and 131 degrees (psc), at standard speed. 0635 All engines ahead one-third speed. 0643 All engines stopped. 0648

TEST BAKER: In a caisson slung at a predetermined depth below LSM-60 is the atomic bomb used in Test Baker, which occurred at 0835 on July 25. The test was designed to determine the effects of an underwater atomic bomb explosion upon ships, particularly ship hulls. Use of a surface vessel from which to suspend the bomb made possible a detonation at exactly the predetermined depth and at the exact center of the target array. U.S. Navy.

On station for Atomic Bomb Test "BAKER," of Crossroads Operations, BIKINI ATOLL, MARSHALL ISLANDS. 0656 Let fires die out under boiler number one. 0700 Set condition of readiness twelve in aircraft. 0728 Let fires die under boiler number four. 0730 Mustered crew on stations: no absentees.

8 to 12

Steaming as before. 0820 Made daily inspection of magazines and smokeless powder samples: conditions normal. Lying to on station for test "BAKER." 0835 "HOW" hour. Fifth Atomic Bomb exploded in underwater test. 0837 Large white mists cover target area. Smoke clouds rising above area.

Bob Greening: "We could watch the underwater test with the naked eye. I saw this huge roll of water coming. The ship just shuddered."

Vitto Rossi: "I had a pair of binoculars and I was look-ing at the battleship, *Arkansas*, one of the biggest targets that I could see, and I remember there were two or three of us watch-ing together from the I Division. As soon as the smoke cleared all of us exclaimed at the same time, 'the *Arkansas*'s gone.' That was a strange feeling."

Chet Romano: "I was inside our 5"/38 mount for the Baker test. I trained the gun around in the direction of the target ships. I looked through the scope. Another guy was in there with me in the pointer's seat. We both saw the underwater blast. It was frightening at first. I was amazed."

The "Baker" bomb had an estimated weapon yield of twenty-three kilotons. The pool news report read:

> So violent and swift moving was the cloud and so great the scale of the explosion that to those of us, peering at the lagoon from our plane 15 miles away, it seemed almost as though the whole floor of the target anchorage had flung itself straight into the sky. We were flying at 7,000 feet and the fiery blast seemed to reach for our wings . . . It is impossible to guess what the enormous shock of the underwater bomb has done to rudders and propellers of the target ships . . . The full destructive power of the bomb of course can be determined only after close range stud-ies, but it is evident that the underwater atomic charge probably is more lethal than the air blast.

During Baker, the first subsurface atomic burst in his-tory, 200 white rats and 20 pigs were in four target ships. Only a small number were used since the direct blast and heat of Able were not expected. Radiation sickness was fatal to all the pigs because of the residual radioactivity on the ships generated from the "dirty" water.

The JCS Evaluation board described the aftermath as fol-lows:

View of the "Baker Day" A-bomb blast from USS Mt. McKinley *(AGC-7), 25 July 1946. National Archives.*

Aerial view of test "Baker." Note target ships on edge of base surge.   Naval Historical Center.

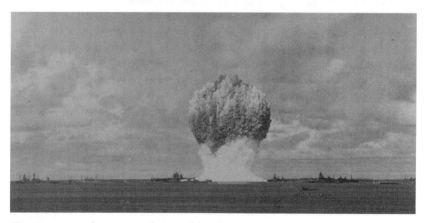

Frame seven of a series of ground level views, taken about six seconds after detonation. Identifiable ships are (l-r): USS Pennsylvania, USS New York, USS Salt Lake City, Nagato and USS Nevada. Naval Historical Center.

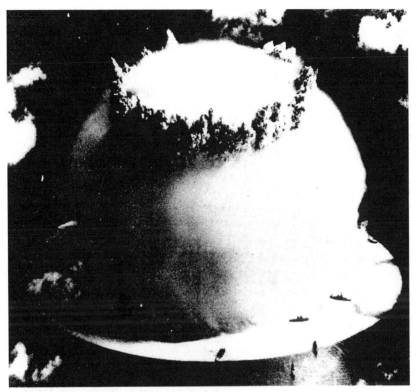

"Baker Day" atomic bomb test on July 24, 1946. A condensation cloud formed after the explosion sprays a wall of water on target vessels. Defense Nuclear Agency.

The explosion produced intense radioactivity in the waters of the lagoon. Immediately after the burst, it is estimated to have been the equivalent of many hundred tons of radium. A few minutes exposure to this intense radiation at its peak would, within a brief interval, have incapacitated human beings and have resulted in their deaths within days or weeks.

Great quantities of radioactive water descended upon the ships from the column or were thrown over them by waves. This highly lethal radioactive water constituted such a hazard that after four days it was still unsafe for inspection parties, operating within a well established safety margin, to spend any useful length of time at the center of the target area or to board ships anchored there.

As in Test ABLE, the array of target ships for Test BAKER did not represent a normal anchorage, but was designed instead to obtain the maximum data from a single explosion. Of the 84 ships and small craft in the array, 40 were anchored within one mile and 20 within about a half-mile. Two major ships were sunk: the battleship *Arkansas* immediately, and the heavy hulled aircraft carrier *Saratoga* after seven and one-half hours. A landing ship, a landing craft and a concrete oil barge also sank immediately. The destroyer *Hughes*, in sinking condition, and the transport *Fallon*, badly listing, were later beached. The submerged submarine *Apogon* was sent to the bottom, emitting air bubbles and fuel oil, and three other submerged submarines sank; but two of these were later raised. The badly damaged Japanese battleship *Nagato* sank after four and one-half days. It was found impossible immediately to assess damage to hulls, power plants and machinery of the target ships because of radioactive contamination. External observation from a safe distance would indicate that a few additional ships near the target center may have suffered some hull damage. There was no obvious damage to ships more than a half mile from the burst.

Connie "Greek" Kontopirakis: "I was up on the superstructure of the ship by fire control. I had a good view of the Baker blast. I saw the *Arkansas* go up in the air and as it rose, it broke in two and kept rising. That's what I saw. I didn't see it come down because of the cloud."

Again we returned to the site of the blast. From the deck log:

0935 Secured evaporators. 1032 Maneuvered at various courses and speeds to stand in to channel entrance. 1044 USS *Appling* standing out, passed abeam to starboard, distance, 450 yards. 1049 Salvage Unit 1.2.7, passed abeam to starboard, standing toward lagoon. 1051 USS *Artemis* standing out. Passed abeam to starboard, distance, 450 yards. 1056 USS *Henrico* standing out passed abeam to starboard, distance, 400 yards. 1058 Can buoy number one abeam to port, distance, 30 yards. 1106 Anchored in berth 386, BIKINI ATOLL, MARSHALL ISLANDS, in

20 fathoms of water, coarse sand bottom, with 75 fathoms of chain to the port anchor.

16 to 20

Anchored as before. 1608 USS *Saratoga* sank. 1658 USS *Lowry* stood in to berth assigned. 1700 USS *Mount McKinley* stood in to berth assigned. Set material condition "X-RAY." 1710 USS *Panamint*, USS *Blue Ridge*, and USS *Appalachian* stood into the anchorage and proceeded to assigned berths. 1845 USS *Sumner* and USS *Moale* stood into the anchorage. 1848 USS *Albermarle* underway standing out of anchorage.

Stanley W. Smith, Radioman 3/c, USS *Saratoga*:

After the Able test, there wasn't much damage to the *Saratoga* — a few fires on the flight deck and some dead test animals. We went back aboard for about two weeks and, after surveying the damage, decided "Sara" was unsinkable. So a couple of buddies and I elected to leave our full seabags aboard three weeks later for the Baker bomb.

Seven plus hours later, we watched "Sara" sink from an APA troopship with tears in our eyes. As she slipped under the surface, I don't know what mattered most — my ship or my gear. Shortly after that, I was transferred to the *Fall River* with a ditty bag my sole possession.

Kenneth J. Tinker, Seaman 2/c, USS *Saratoga*:

I watched the *Saratoga* go down from the deck of the *Rockwall* (APA-230). I went on the "Sara" fresh out of boot camp in about March 1946. We only had a skeleton crew of about 620 men to take her to Bikini. We worked eighteen hour days. They didn't have near enough men for that big flattop.

We were taken off the "Sara" for the Able test, then went right back aboard until the day before the Baker shot. It was one sad day for all the guys who had called her home.

After the second bomb sunk the "Sara," our crew got split up — detached to a lot of different ships. That's when I came on the *Fall River*.

Vitto Rossi remembers watching the *Saratoga* go down, too: "The *Fall River* was back on station at the mouth of the lagoon when the *Saratoga* went down. One of our buglers played taps and there wasn't a dry eye in sight. It was a sad moment for lots of us, but especially for former 'Sara' crew members."

Historian Shurcliff described the Target Fleet research ahead:

This time the work of reentry was retarded by the contamination of the water. Ships were washed down and made "Geiger sweet," that is free from harmful radioactivity. Concerning the atomic bomb, time for bombast had ceased, the time for analysis of results had begun.

The only *Fall River* test-related log entries were two days after "Baker" on July 27:

0000 Ship is on one hour notice for getting underway, boilers two and three steaming.
1403 USS *Fulton* was beached on Enyu Island.

Captain Thomas M. Daly summed up the differences between the two shots and the challenges ahead in cleaning up the contaminated target ships and support vessels:

The major difference between the effects of tests Able and Baker was the radioactivity Baker generated. More than 90% of the target vessels were contaminated. This result had not been anticipated. The fatality figures of the animals suggested that exposed humans would have also had a high mortality rate. The radioactivity was so severe, in fact, that it was not until ten days after Test Baker that all target ships could be reboarded; all animals had been removed by the five-day point, however.

As Hanson Baldwin wrote in *The New York Times*:

The tests showed that the destructive radius of the atomic blast against ships was considerably more localized than the general public had expected, but only slightly less than Operation Crossroads personnel had anticipated. The form of the waterspout in the second test, which was much shorter than forecast, and the extent of the cloud of vapor, mist, spray, and gas, which had a diameter of perhaps 3 miles were definite surprises.

The cleanup after Test Baker was an information-gathering process also — particularly regarding decontamination of the target ships. The opportunity was used to determine which decontamination methods were successful. Some of the support ships, those not directly involved in the tests, were contaminated from radioactive lagoon water ingested into their salt water lines and evaporators (which are used for distilling water on board ship).

Underwater photography was used at Bikini to record damage to hulls and superstructures of sunken vessels. This work was especially significant after Test Baker, in which a large part of the damage occurred on ships which sank. The diver shown is preparing to descend from the specially equipped LCM used in this work. He wears a simple face mask and a quick-release type of lead-weighted belt. U.S. Navy.

On 8 September, President Truman indefinitely postponed the third test, ostensibly because sufficient information was now available for scientific analysis.

Admiral Blandy gave his impressions of the tests' value and their implications for the future in a speech in Boston on September 5, 1946:

> . . . I believe that if there is atomic warfare in the future, naval war will not be exempt from it. There are those who believe that in future conflicts, great guided missiles will cross the oceans and continents and explode atomic warheads over cities, and that therefore there will be no need for navies. Such weapons may indeed become a reality, but I do not subscribe to the belief that they will eliminate all other kinds of warfare. The ships, weapons, and tactics of sea fighting may change radically, and we should always take the lead in such changes. But I can visualize traffic on the sea for a long time yet, even in war, and therefore fighting on the sea.
>
> Unless some plan which is at the same time practical, reliable, and acceptable to all nations, is devised for outlawing the atomic bomb, there will be atomic warfare, and I believe it will include naval warfare. But as a result of Operation Crossroads, the United States will at least be better prepared for such warfare than any other nation on earth.

Machinist Mate Albert Fickel and Chief Quartermaster Michael Ganitch, USS *Pennsylvania* (BB-38), were part of the skeleton crew that steamed her down to Bikini. Both were career men who were on the "Pennsy" when she was bombed in Pearl Harbor in December 1941 and torpedoed in Okinawa in August 1945. Mickey Ganitch:

> We went back aboard after both tests. I was in charge of the animals — you know, the typical duties of a Chief Quartermaster. We also placed the Geiger counters around the ship. The civilian scientists went back aboard with us. I had to show them where we had put the animals and Geiger counters. After we showed them where they were, they took them away.

After we had been back on board the Pennsy, they would tell us to take a shower and throw away our clothes as soon as we got back to the support ship.

Al Fickel:

We had to escort the civilian scientists and engineers through the ship to evaluate the damage. We also took readings off the instruments down below decks.

I'll tell you one thing, when we went back aboard after the underwater test, we tried to clean it up. I can tell you this: You couldn't actually see it, but you had an eerie feeling there was something aboard you didn't know anything about. When we returned to the *Rockbridge*, they had people waiting for us with Geiger counters to sweep us. Some days they'd say, 'You've got to stay aboard the *Rockbridge* for a few days. You've had enough rems for now.'

Some of us wore badges to measure radiation, some didn't. Hell, we were doing things we didn't understand. There was no control. The scientists and engineers didn't even know what they were doing. They knew they were messing around with something they had no control over.

I went back aboard many times after both tests but I didn't have any follow-up physicals or lab tests. I turned in lots of information when the Bureau of Personnel was hot on that stuff years ago — information like where I was and what I did, and how long I was out there, all that crap because I was one of the last to leave that damn place.

The Pentagon claims there's no cover up but if you've been reading the papers, they're hindsight experts. They had hindsight as far as the atomic tests are concerned — exposed people to radiation. They've also got hindsight about Agent Orange over in Viet Nam, and now they're developing 20-20 hindsight about chemical warfare exposure in the Gulf.

They are also experts at losing records. I've got about as much faith in the U.S. government now as I have in my damned cat.

Mickey Ganitch:

> They towed the *Pennsylvania* down to Kwajalein and for two
> years they tried to decontaminate her but she was too radioactive.
> So they took her outside the harbor and pulled the plugs but she
> still didn't sink. They ended up torpedoing her off Kwajalein in
> early 1948.

Radiation dangers and warnings were largely ignored for
the first ten days following the Baker test which ultimately led
to long term health problems for many test participants.

The *Fall River*'s hull below the waterline was checked
for radiation. Ensign John Larsen:

> Radiation readings were taken of the *Fall River*'s bottom while
> we were still in Bikini. It was only about a fifteen degree list but
> it felt like thirty when you tried to walk. They took a whaleboat
> and went along the waterline where the hull was exposed, and
> checked it with a Geiger counter. Later in the day they reversed
> the whole process and checked the other side.

Wednesday 31 July was a big day for the *Fall River*. At
1100 "pursuant to orders of the Bureau of Personnel of 23 May
1946, Captain Theodore R. Wirth, USN, relieved Captain David
S. Crawford, USN, as Commanding Officer." It was also a big
day for two 6th Division POs! Dave Morris and I were notified
at morning muster that our transportation back to the States was
all set and that we would be detached to a troopship the next
day.
At 1230 an officer and three Petty Officers left the ship
for temporary duty as Shore Patrol on Bikini Island. They were
followed by three Stewardsmates who left the ship for temporary
duty in the Bikini Officer's Mess, so I guess no one was too
worried about ionizing radiation at this point. All seven men
were back aboard ship later that evening.

Gerry Oyer and I ran our last blackjack game that night. Shortly before "lights out," we closed down the game and got together up by my Quad 40 to divide the spoils — a total of a little more than $3,700.

The USS *Fall River* remained in the Marshall Islands during post-Crossroads evaluation, then returned Rear Admiral Fahrion to Pearl Harbor, arriving September 14, 1946. During October she underwent tender repairs in San Pedro, then departed for Portland, Oregon where she arrived October 25, 1946. There she took part in that city's Navy Day celebration. For three days, "open house" was held aboard.

At the conclusion of Navy Day, the *Fall River* left Portland for San Diego where she arrived on November 1. The next two weeks were spent in and near San Diego in intensive drill and refresher training for the officers and the crew.

Considerable time was spent in the Long Beach-San Pedro, California area decontaminating the parts of the ship declared radioactive from the Bikini Operation. This included drydocking to scrape the ship's bottom.

On December 30, 1946, the *Fall River* sailed for Japan arriving January 12 after a stormy passage. In Japan, the *Fall River* relieved the USS *Chicago* (CA-136) as the Base Force flagship. On February 4, the ship set sail for training exercises with HMAS *Shropshire*, upon completion of which she took departure for Otaru, Hokkaido, arriving February 7 after a freezing, stormy trip.

On February 12, the ship left the Hokkaido area and moored in Yokosuka 13 February. During the last two weeks of February and the first two weeks of March the ship engaged in gunnery exercises.

Beginning April 20, she toured ports in Japan including: the Japanese Naval Base at Kobe, Nagasaki, Sasebo and Kure plus Pusan, Korea. Kure was the Headquarters of the British Commonwealth of the Far East.

After a brief return to Yokosuka, the ship visited Shanghai, China, then returned to Yokosuka long enough to transfer

Navy Day visitors line up to visit the Fall River *(CA-131) in Portland, Oregon, October 26, 1946. Dominick Di Guiseppe.*

RAdm. Bledsoe and his staff to the USS *Toledo* (CA-133) and on June 17 sailed for Bremerton, Washington.

The *Fall River* docked at Pier 91 in Bremerton. Overhaul at the Puget Sound Naval Shipyard, Bremerton, Washington, started June 30. Inactivation Ceremonies were held on October 31, 1947.

At the end of her career, the *Fall River* (CA-131), received the Navy Occupation Service Medal, Asia, for the periods 12 January - 17 April 1947, and 27 April - 17 June 1947. She was awarded the China Service Medal for the period 18-26 April 1947. The Fall River was finally struck from the list on February 19, 1971 and scrapped in Portland, Oregon in 1973. However a small portion of her bow rests in Fall River, Massachusetts in the company of two complete ship memorials — the USS *Massachusetts* and the USS *Kennedy*.

BIKINI 'WITCH'S BREW'
by Jonathan M. Weisgall

"Baker Day" Atomic Bomb Test, Bikini Atoll, 25 July 1946. Frame 1 of a series of ground level views, taken about a half-second after detonation. Identifiable ships are (l-r): USS Pennsylvania, USS *New York, USS* Saratoga, USS *Salt Lake City, USS* Arkansas, USS *Independence, Nagato and USS* Nevada. *Naval Historical Center.*

[Naval Institute Press Book Adaptation, Proceedings/*February 1994. Mr. Weisgall is an attorney in Washington, D.C., and adjunct professor of law at Georgetown University Law Center.]*
 Thousands of radio stations around the world broadcast the tests. More than 42,000 military and scientific personnel were assembled at Bikini Atoll, a tiny ring of islands in the Pacific some 2,500 miles southwest of Hawaii, for the world's fourth and fifth explosions of an atomic bomb. The first three at Alamogordo in the New Mexico desert, then over Hiroshima and Nagasaki — were shrouded in wartime secrecy. But these, code-named Operation Crossroads, were different. At Bikini, the world watched and listened in July 1946, as Army-Navy Joint Task Force One tested the bomb on a guinea-pig fleet of 95 ships. More than 175 reporters from around the world were there, as well as congressmen, senators, Secretary of the Navy James V. Forrestal, and United Nations observers.

The first test — Able — on 1 July, was an air drop similar to Hiroshima and Nagasaki. The bomb sank five ships, but it disappointed most observers, many of whom did not even see the blast through the dark goggles they were ordered to wear. However, the second test — Baker — on 25 July, was at once a magnificent and terrifying spectacle. In one second, an underwater bomb pushed a one-mile-wide dome of water into the sky. It looked like Niagara Falls in reverse. Then, a full 10 seconds later, the water column collapsed back into the lagoon, creating enormous, rolling waves of spray, mist, and air that crept over the target fleet and swallowed the ships from view. "Why doesn't the captain take this ship out of here?" spouted one reporter on an observation ship 12 miles away. This unexpected radioactive cloud bank, later called a base surge, was not predicted by any of the scientists, and it was about to become America's Chernobyl.

"The base surge contained enormous quantities of radioactive material," wrote Ralph Sawyer, the operation's technical director, in a secret report. Billowing outward, it spread more than three miles across and 1,800 feet high, engulfing all the target ships within minutes and leaving what Sawyer called a "kiss of death" on the ships. The base surge "heavily contaminated" all but 9 of the 95 target ships, wrote the Navy, and "its radioactive mist settled on the decks, moistened every bit of exposed metal, wood and canvas." The blast, which sank the 26,000-ton battleship *Arkansas* (BB-33) in a matter of seconds, unleashed the greatest waves ever known to humanity, one of which lifted the huge aircraft carrier *Saratoga* (CV-3) 43 feet. It also unleashed the greatest amount of radioactivity ever known up to that time.

As more information comes to light about U.S. government research that exposed human subjects to radiation in the decades after World War II, the time has come to reexamine the 1946 Baker test, which was both a great technical success for the Navy and a near-disaster for many of the 40,000 sailors who were overexposed to radioactivity from the blast.

At first, an underwater atomic explosion had seemed too reckless. Scientists from Los Alamos National Laboratory warned the Navy in December 1945 that an "underwater test against naval vessels would contain so many hazards that it should be ruled out at this time." If the muffling effect of the water were to prevent the radioactive material from rising high enough into the atmosphere, there would be trouble. "A rise of only 10,000 feet . . . would present the greatest hazard," one study concluded, "because most of the contamination would fall on the target ships or back into the lagoon," and another report predicted that the water column would rise only 5,000 to 8,000 feet. "The water near a recent surface explosion will be a witch's brew," warned Los Alamos.

"There will probably be enough plutonium near the surface to poison the combined armed forces of the United States at their highest wartime strength."

The warnings could not have been clearer, and they all came true, as nearly half the bomb's fission products fell back into the lagoon's water or onto the target ships. Scientists knew from studies of radium-dial workers that only a few millionths of a gram of radium lodged within human bones could prove fatal. Plutonium, the main component of the Baker bomb, has the same effect and is even more toxic. The Baker test, though, did not involve millionths of grams of radium, or even hundredths of grams. "The radiation was roughly equivalent to that from several thousand tons of radium," wrote Ralph Sawyer.

Colonel Stafford Warren, the operation's radiological safety (radsafe) director, warned that Baker would cause severe contamination in the lagoon and that the target ships "may remain dangerous for an indeterminable time thereafter," but these warnings were ignored. Despite drone boat readings of 730 roentgen per day near the center of the target array (more than twice the lethal dose), the first patrol boats entered the lagoon 41 minutes after the shot, followed by a salvage group, radsafe monitors, and technicians, who boarded 12 target ships to retrieve data and instruments. By the end of the day, 49 support ships returned to Bikini's lagoon with nearly 15,000 men on board.

Radiation levels on some of the target ships remained dangerously high, even a week after the shot, and boarding them was unsafe, except for brief visits. To make matters worse, radioactivity in the lagoon's contaminated waters spread quickly to the support ships. Warren's radsafe plan cautioned that no apparatus on the support ships that used salt water cooling should be operated until the sea water in the lagoon was declared safe. Nevertheless, the day after Baker, the support ships were authorized to operate their evaporators, which distilled sea water for drinking. As a result, every nontarget support vessel became contaminated, just as the planners had feared, and fission products became concentrated on underwater hulls and in condensers, evaporators, and salt water pipes.

Despite all the warnings that the highly radioactive column of water would come crashing down on the ships, no one had planned for the disaster that had been predicted with such amazing accuracy. "Since the nature and extent of contamination of the targets was completely unexpected," the Navy later admitted, "no plans had been prepared for organized decontamination measures." The Navy tried dissolving action with hydrochloric and sulfuric acid and detergent action with foamite, soap power, lye, and even naphtha and diesel oil. Using air compressors other men blasted the ships with rice, barley, ground coffee, sand,

and coconut shells. Crews even worked in two-hour shifts using the tried-and-true Navy method — scrubbing.

After the Baker test, more than 40% of the men at Bikini were assigned to work on decontamination, inspection, towing, or salvaging the target ships, with the brunt of the boarding and decontamination efforts being borne by the 8,463 crew members of those ships. All personnel on tugs were ordered to stay windward of the target ships to minimize contamination, but it was impossible not to get wet. In fact, one tug became so contaminated that it was put out of service.

Few of the 42,000 men at Bikini were even aware of the hazards and the need to take radsafe precautions, and others did not care. One of Warren's radsafe colleagues wrote about a captain "who insists on a 'hairy-chested' approach to the matter with a disdain for the unseen hazard, an attitude which is contagious to the younger officers and detrimental to the radiological safety program." Two other monitors wrote of "an attitude of indifference on the part of the ship's officer" of one target vessel, the [former German heavy cruiser] *Prinz Eugen*. Despite readings of 50 times the maximum daily tolerance dose, some crew members were ordered to spend the night there, because the ship's officer believed that there was "such a large safety factor that it can be ignored." Radioactive material "was scattered over the decks of the ships," said a Navy speaker at a 1947 conference on defensive atomic warfare. "Men walked through it, tracked it around, and got it on their clothing and hands and faces. There was some tendency on the part of the men to disregard a danger which they could not see, nor touch, nor smell."

It is impossible to recreate with any accuracy radiation levels on every part of the target ships over specific periods of time. It is equally impossible to determine who may have ingested or inhaled radioactive materials or received high doses from open cuts or wounds. One sailor sleeping close to salt water lines may have received much higher doses than another sleeping three feet away. One man may have worn protective boots and gloves during a decontamination shift, while another just a t-shirt. "The erratic location of high and low intensities on the target ships does not permit an accurate estimate of any one individual's exposure," noted Warren shortly after the tests. Virtually all the available evidence, though, points to the conclusion that radiation dangers following the Baker test were serious and that not enough steps were taken in time to prevent serious and widespread overexposures. A host of factors--the overwhelming amount of contamination from the base surge, lingering radiation on the target and nontarget ships, malfunctioning radsafe equipment, a shortage of monitors, failure to observe radsafe regulations, and the ignorance and indifference displayed toward the radiation hazard by officers and enlisted men alike--caused many men regularly to receive radiation doses in excess of the daily tolerance dose of .1 roentgen. Moreover, this tolerance dose, deemed appropriate in 1946, has now been lowered for the general population by a factor of 365, so that today the current recommended maximum dose for one year is approximately the same dose that was recommended as the maximum exposure for one day at Operation Crossroads.

The anecdotal documentary evidence of overexposure, even at the .1 roentgen level, is simply overwhelming. Warren's radsafe section detected 67 overdoses in one three-day period, with some men exposed to 20 times the daily limit, and one batch of 125 film badges showed 26 overexposures. Work on two target ships was stopped because of the crew's overexposure from working and living in the ships. Ten days after the tests, 35 target ships had average topside readings more than 10 times the daily tolerance dose, and some had readings 70 time greater.

In early August, Warren warned Vice Admiral William H.P. Blandy, the commander of Operation Crossroads, that "some of the most important ships have had many lethal doses deposited on them and retained in crevices and other places." He warned Blandy that plutonium "is the most poisonous chemical known," that "it is insidiously toxic in very minute quantities," and that his monitors lacked the equipment to measure it. Nevertheless, for weeks after the test, men routinely boarded target ships, swept them, scraped them, ate their meals in them, and even slept on board; they were constantly exposed to the danger of inhaling plutonium and fission products from Baker.

On 3 August, nine days after Baker, Warren was convinced he had a disaster on his hands. He told Blandy that decontamination efforts were largely useless and that the target ships "should be declared hopelessly contaminated." He warned that there was "increasing evidence" of overexposures, and he called for an immediate end to Operation Crossroads.

Blandy rejected this recommendation at a staff meeting on 6 August, but Warren did not let matters rest there. "Control of the safety of the target ships' crew is rapidly getting out of hand," he asserted bluntly the next day. "The target vessels are in the main extensively contaminated with dangerous amounts of radioactivity. Quick decontamination without exposing personnel seriously to radiation is not possible under the present circumstances and with present knowledge." Worried about the breakdown of much of his monitoring equipment, he also sent an urgent cable to Los Alamos, requesting 300 new Geiger counters and 50,000 film badges. "Strongly urge that . . . this [be] treated as an actual emergency involving safety to life," he teletyped.

Blandy changed his mind on 10 August. "This stops us cold," he said, faced with Warren's clear evidence, now buttressed by analyses flown in from Los Alamos. All decontamination work was halted, and most of the target vessels were towed to Kwajalein Atoll, 250 miles away. Operation Crossroads "was conducted as an emergency and a lot of compromises were made to meet this emergency," Warren wrote to a radsafe monitor later that year. "I never want to go through the experience of the last three weeks of August again." While the documentary records of Operation Crossroads do not suggest a conspiracy or deliberate intent to cover up the test results, they do show a deliberate attempt by the scientific and medical experts to cover their hindquarters by refusing even to consider the possibility that a serviceman's presence at Bikini might later result in a radiation related disease. In fact, one of the main purposes of a Medico-Legal Board established at Bikini by Stafford Warren was to provide a paper trail designed to lay the groundwork for future denial of legal claims that might be brought against the U.S. government arising from Operation Crossroads. Robert R. Newell, Chairman of the Board, readily admitted just weeks after the tests that the board "initially . . . served to reassure Col. Warren that the safety measures adopted by RadSafe were such as to attract no justifiable criticism, and to give what assurance was possible that no successful suits could be brought on account of the radiological hazards of Operation Crossroads."

Nevertheless, lawsuits were on the minds of top Crossroads officials at an October 1946 meeting to discuss decontamination issues. "Having in mind both medical and legal protection," the participants, led by Blandy, agreed that documents relating to decontamination efforts should be classified "and that the public relations angle should be considered carefully to remove confusion and the impression that the Navy is 'covering up.'" And at a meeting in late November to discuss possible litigation from the sale of target ships as scrap, one participant noted that Leslie Groves, the head of the Manhattan Project that developed the atomic bomb, "is very much afraid of claims being instituted by men who participated in the Bikini tests."

Although the instantaneous bursts from Able and Baker sank only 14 ships, radiological contamination eventually sank almost the entire target fleet. Most of the ships still showed high levels of radioactivity one year after the tests. "They're still hot enough to make it inadvisable to have men on them more than 24 hours at a stretch," Admiral Blandy said in July 1947. In the end, all but six vessels were sunk by the bombs or deliberately scuttled or sunk because of lingering radioactivity.

"We want ships which are tough, even when threatened by atomic bombs," wrote the official Navy historian of Operation Crossroads in 1947. "We want to keep the ships afloat, propellers turning, guns firing; we want to protect the crews so that, if fighting is necessary, they can fight well today and return home tomorrow." His comment captured the Navy's attitude toward the bomb after the war. No one yet recognized that the greatest danger of atomic warfare--or of weapons testing--lay not in the immediate blast and heat from the atomic bomb but from the deadly lingering radioactivity. The ghost fleet would not steam back under the Golden Gate Bridge, triumphant and invincible. The ships survived the familiar enemies of heat and blast, but the Navy had never fought an alpha particle.

OPERATION CROSSROADS
By Oscar Rosen, Ph.D.
National Commander, National Association of Atomic Veterans 1960-1996

Forty-two thousand military personnel including some women, many government officials, foreign and domestic, and numerous members of the media witnessed the first post World War II series of atomic bomb tests known as Operation Crossroads. As of this year, according to the Institute of Medicine of the National Academy of Science, 22,000 of the 42,000 military participants have died. According to our sources, many of them died of causes that can only be attributed to radiation poisoning while many of the survivors are still suffering from a variety of radiogenic diseases. We don't know the causes of death of the non-military observers but it would be very useful to have that information. Somewhere in the top secret archives of the Manhattan Project of the Atomic Energy Commission, the names of the invited non-military observers must exist. What a story that would make!

The Veterans Administration acknowledges that many of the diseases to which participants in all the atomic bomb tests 1945-1963 and the occupation of Hiroshima and Nagasaki succumbed are radiogenic but makes it fiendishly difficult for these veterans to receive compensation and adequate medical care. We believe that the Defense Special Weapons Agency (DSWA) formerly the Defense Nuclear Agency (DNA), Science Applications International Corp. (SAIC) which does dose reconstructions for the VA and DSWA, the VA, other government agencies and the National Academy of Science do all that they can to keep the Atomic Veterans and their families at bay. At the rate we are dying off, we will all be fossils by the 21st century. Gulf War veterans who may have participated in an atomic bomb test can only say deja vu.

One of the most disturbing aspects of Operation Crossroads is that when Manhattan Project Director Oppenheimer learned that the military wanted to conduct nuclear bomb tests using live military personnel as participants, he argued that the tests could be simulated in the laboratory but he was overruled. Countless lives could have been saved had his advice been taken. Instead he was eventually stripped of his clearances and nearly sent to prison because of his concerns about the testing and development of more destructive weapons such as the hydrogen bomb. This earned him the implacable enmity of Edward Teller, the "father" of the hydrogen bomb. Oppenheimer was later accused of being a communist sympathizer, stripped of his clearances and cast into limbo. At one time veterans organizations such as NAAV were designated as terrorist organizations and therefore subject to infiltration by the CIA.

Another very disturbing aspect of Operation Crossroads concerns the fear expressed by the chief radiological officer, Dr. Stafford Warren that many veterans would file lawsuits as a result of their exposure to radiation during Crossroads. He even succeeded in persuading President Truman to cancel the scheduled third test, Test Charlie, because the Bikini test area was already so badly contaminated by the first two tests. Nevertheless, thousands of military personnel were kept at Bikini for a month or more after the testing was terminated.

More than 90 target ships and over 150 support ships were assigned to Operation Crossroads. The majority of both groups had seen service in World War II including the aircraft carriers Saratoga and Independence, various submarines, destroyers, battleships and auxiliary vessels. After the testing when high death rates were being reported for the crews of some of the target ships, survivors were calling ships such as the Ingraham and Orca death ships. Some target ships such as the *Niagara* were remanned when they were declared "Geiger sweet" following a period of so-called "decontamination." Details of the health problems and causes of death of the *Niagara* crew would be very useful.

In the Foreword to the official history of Operation Crossroads published in 1946, Task Force Commander Admiral William Blandy wrote, "The Atomic Age is here. It is no myth. Nor is the atomic bomb 'just another weapon.' It is the most lethal destructive agent yet devised by man. It's energy release is staggering: it's radioactivity is slow-killing poison." [See Operation Crossroads-The Official Pictorial Record, The Office of the Historian, Joint Task Force One, Wm. H. Wise & Co., Inc., New York 1946.]

The only atomic bombs of which Admiral Blandy had any knowledge were the 21 kiloton Trinity, 15 kiloton Hiroshima and 21 kiloton Nagasaki bombs whose yields were 21, 15 and 21 kilotons respectively. As an informed well educated individual, he must have known the story of the Curies and how exposure to minute amounts of radium caused their deaths, about the fate of many of the young women know as radium dial watch painters. We already know about the enormous amounts of radioactivity the aforementioned bombs released. We also know about the effects of fallout from the Nevada tests upon the Downwinders.

Admiral Blandy also complained that the Crossroads personnel were not provided with adequate protective equipment.

When inquiries began to be made into the dangers of radioactive fallout from the Crossroads bombs, authorized government spokesmen announced that all the fallout from the first detonation, Test Able, was blown away by prevailing winds. It is curious, therefore, that personnel were not allowed to go aboard the carrier Independence until the fifth day after Able because of contamination. What is even more curious is that much of the contamination was caused by transuranic elements with half lives of thousands of years such as Plutonium 239. Was five days long enough to wait to avoid exposure to the radiation that Admiral Bandy called [a] "slow-killing poison?"

This writer served on the floating dry-dock ARD-29 during Operation Crossroads. On the morning of June 30, 1946, a seagoing tug towed us to a safe distance from Bikini Atoll where Test Able was to be detonated the next morning. The bomb was to be dropped from a B-29 and was to explode in the air over the array of target ships. The bomb detonated in the air above the target ships but at a considerable distance from their center. While standing on the deck of the ARD-29 on the morning of July 1, 1946, an announcement was made over the PA system that if anyone wanted to see the bomb go off, to look toward Bikini while listening to the countdown. The same announcement was probably made on all the support ships some of which were much closer than we. When the countdown reached zero, an enormous bright white flash appeared above the horizon. We were not told to shield our eyes or to wear special glasses. As a child, I remember being warned to avoid looking at the sun during an eclipse. Years later, I read in an official government publication that all personnel serving aboard ships during tests such as Operation Crossroads were to be issued special goggles. This directive apparently didn't apply to us. Maybe Admiral Blandy knew what he was talking about when he wrote that better protective equipment was needed for the test participants.

In the years following the tests, many of the participants reported cataracts which the government was forced to declare were radiogenic. But the VA and certain members of Congress fought us tooth and nail to prevent us being acknowledged as disabled from exposure to radiation during the tests and other "radiation risk" activities.

This year, the Institute of Medicine of the National Academy of Science issued its report on Operation Crossroads that took 13 years to complete. The report contains numerous demonstrable flaws but no member of congress is willing to challenge it.

Why? Who is telling the truth? Who knows the truth?

19

HOMEWARD BOUND

O n Thursday, August 1, 1946 at 1600 twenty men were "transferred with baggage, records, and accounts to the USS *Saint Croix* for transportation . . . to San Francisco for discharge." All were regular navy soon to be at the end of our enlistments.

The USS *Saint Croix* (APA-231), a Haskell Class attack transport, was built by Kaiser Inc. in Vancouver, Washington and commissioned by the Navy on December 1, 1944. She was a Victory ship designed to carry 1,562 troops with a crew of 536. Her armament consisted of one 5"/38 and twelve 40-mm guns.

We had at least 1,500 men on board. Dave Morris and a few other shipmates joined me in the 5"/38 gun tub on the fantail for a last look at the *Fall River* as we passed through the channel entrance and out to the open sea. There was a very deep feeling that we were losing something. We kept looking until she was out of sight.

The troop compartments were crowded, hot, and stuffy with long lines for the heads. Messing facilities weren't much better. They were temporary quarters for the movement of troops during wartime. The passengers spent as little time below decks as possible. Consequently main deck space was at a premium.

Shipboard activities were the same day after day. Reading, listening to the radio, and sunbathing, were augmented by that popular sport, "talking story." Of course, there was always cards and dice for the more adventurous.

The bull sessions knew no boundaries. Subjects ranged from the Atomic bomb tests and other events of the recent past to future plans.

The sixteen-day voyage to San Francisco was uneventful.

On the morning of August 18, 1946, we disembarked the *Saint Croix* in Oakland, California, and split up into groups according to destination. I boarded a blue-gray Navy bus with fifty-some other men. Destination: Shoemaker Separation Center about twenty miles southeast of Oakland.

Shoemaker was no stranger to me having spent a month in the Naval Hospital there in the spring of 1944.

The drab gray buildings, typical World War II two-story, frame construction, had been used as a separation center since early 1946.

According to my Service Records, it took forty-eight hours to separate me from the naval service. My records revealed:

1. The end of my enlistment was officially September 29, 1946.
2. The "Marks Assigned Upon Transfer" [from the Fall River] were good: Proficiency in Rate: 3.9; Seamanship: 3.7; Mechanical Ability: 3.9; Leadership: 3.9; Conduct: 4.0.
3. Total authorized leave taken during enlistment: 54 days.
4. Net service (for pay purposes) 3 years, 9 months, 24 days.

Receiving Barracks, Shoemaker, California, Circa 1945-46. National Archives.

5. Total payment upon discharge: $460.79 (including $37.75 travel allowance).
6. Honorable discharge button, a.k.a. "ruptured duck," received on 20 August.
7. Enlisted for four years in Class V-6, USNR, from 21 August 1946 as GM2 and was ordered to inactive duty under Commandant 13th Naval District.

As I walked out of the Shoemaker gate after midday chow on the 20th and surveyed the autumn beige-colored, parched hills around the base, my feelings were mixed. I was sad in a way to be leaving the Navy but exhilarated by the challenges ahead. I had a "free at last" feeling. Now I would call the shots, go anywhere, do anything I wanted — within the law and assuming I could afford it. I could look forward to developing my own Plan of the Day, or, Year.

Appendix A

The United States
Merchant Marine
at War

This summary of the U.S. Merchant Marine during World War II was condensed and edited from a report submitted to the president of the United States by VAdm E.S. Land on January 15, 1946, and was provided through the courtesy of the Office of External Affairs of the Maritime Administration.

During World War II the United States fighting team was made up of three major entities: our fighting forces overseas, the production army at home, and the link between them — the difference between victory and defeat — the United States Merchant Marine.

The United States Merchant Marine possessed the largest number of merchant ships in the Allies pool of shipping and was the greatest single strategic factor in the defeat of the Axis powers. American sea power kept the Allies supplied with the raw materials and products essential to victory.

Germany launched a U-boat fleet to choke off supplies from Britain and Russia. The antisubmarine warfare carried on by British and Anglo-American navies, forced Germany into a long war she could not sustain. Later the *coup de grace* was given by the combined air fleets and the Russian steamroller, both of which owed their power to the stream of supplies carried in American ships.

Against Japan the role of our Navy was reversed. It fought an offensive war and succeeded in closing Japan's sea lanes and sinking her merchant fleet while ours sailed in comparative security.

Our fighting forces were never knocked off an important beachhead, nor, thanks to the merchant fleet, did we fail to develop each landing with a steadily increased flow of supplies that enabled our armies to meet their objectives.

What It Took To Win

For the United States Army the high point was on the beaches of Normandy and Okinawa; the Air Forces in the great sky battle over Regenberg; the United States Navy in the Battle of Midway; the United States Marine Corps atop Mount Surabachi. For the Merchant Marine the stuff of legends was the Murmansk run. The ships ran innumerable gauntlets of air, surface, and submarine attack ranging around the globe, from the Red Sea and the Indian Ocean to the mid-Atlantic and the Mediterranean, and the kamikaze attacks in the Pacific. But none of these combined all elements of danger as did the Murmansk run.

The most direct route to Russia was through the Denmark Straits between Iceland and Greenland, around the North Cape of Norway and into Murmansk. Through icy, fog-bound seas, their flanks exposed to the dive bombers, surface raiders, and submarines moving out from the Nazi-held fjords of Norway, the slow gray convoys kept moving. Nor was there sanctuary at their destination, for every hour on the hour, the *Luftwaffe* blasted delays in the grim business of unloading the ships in the ice-cluttered harbor of Murmansk. Yet the cargoes were delivered. The Murmansk run exemplified the high price of victory. Through the first part of 1943, casualties among the seagoing force were greater proportionately than in all branches of the armed services combined, except the U.S. Marine Corps. Unreported thousands of our seamen and officers were injured under attack or suffered the nightmare of waiting aboard boats and rafts for rescue. Seven hundred thirty-three American merchant vessels of over 1,000 gross tons were sunk. A total of 6,700 merchant seamen and officers were dead and missing; 581 were made prisoners of war.

The cold evaluation in dollars and cents of the cost of building and operating our wartime merchant fleet reached a grand total of more than $22,500,000,000.

The Cargo Lift

The final measure of accomplishment of the Merchant Marine during the war is the amount of cargo transported. Since the war had to be planned on the amount of shipping available within certain dates, fluctuations in cargo were an index to the progress of the war from Pearl Harbor to Tokyo Bay. The total dry cargo and bulk liquid shipments[1] rose rapidly from 44,117,000 tons in 1942, to 62,113,000 in 1943, 78,553,000 in 1944, and 83,469,000 in 1945. During the last year of the war, this meant an average rate of delivery of 8,500 tons of cargo every hour of every day and night. The total cargo lift from the United States between December 7, 1941, and the capitulation of Japan was 268,252,000 long tons, of which 203,522,000 were dry cargo and 64,730,000 were petroleum products and other bulk liquids carried in tankers.[1] Approximately seventy-five percent was carried by ships of the WSA [War Shipping Administration]-controlled fleet.

---

[1] Data not available on amount of bulk liquid cargo carried by WSA tankers for Army and Navy.

Ships of America's merchant fleet also carried the great majority of the 7,129,907 Army personnel and 141,537 civilians moving overseas between December 7, 1941, and November 30, 1945, and the 4,060,883 Army personnel and 169,626 civilians returning to the United States within the same dates.

The Wartime Fleet

The unprecedented growth of the United States merchant fleet was the primary reason for the WSA's ability to meet the tonnage demands of the war. Upon America's entry, the fleet, augmented by foreign vessels acquired by negotiation, requisition, and seizure in American ports, totaled about 900 dry-cargo vessels of 6,700,000 deadweight tons and some 440 tankers of 5,150,000 deadweight tons. The curve rose rapidly. At the end of 1942, there were 1,639 ships in WSA operation; in 1943, 2,847; 1944, 3,744. By the end of the war with Japan the WSA controlled fleet numbered 4,221 with a deadweight tonnage of 44,940,000.

The race between ship construction and sinkings by the enemy was won by the Allied convoy system and naval superiority in combating the submarine menace, and an unprecedented shipbuilding technique. WSA losses, including marine casualties during 1942, were equivalent to thirty-nine percent of new construction in that year. This was reduced to eleven percent in 1943 less than eight percent in 1944, and four percent in 1945.

About seventy-five percent of the vessels under WSA control consisted of Liberty ships, a relatively slow vessel of eleven knots speed and 10,800 deadweight tons. Victory ship construction began in 1944, when turbines became more readily available for merchant fleet building. The Victory was an emergency type vessel of about the same tonnage as the Liberty, but more modern in its propulsion machinery with speeds ranging from fifteen to seventeen knots. It supplanted the Liberty building program in 1945.

The remainder of the fleet included the "C" types which varied from the small coastal vessels of 5,000 deadweight tons to the C4 freighters of 13,500 deadweight tons. In addition, there were special types built prior to 1939 made up primarily of freighters, combination passenger and cargo ships, refrigerator ships, and bulk carriers. Many were converted to Army or Navy aircraft carriers, troopships, cargo vessels, and modified tank carriers.

The tanker fleet was made up principally of the "T" or standard type tanker varying in size from 15,900 to 23,000 deadweight tons and emergency type tankers converted from Liberty ship hulls. Privately built tankers and miscellaneous types built prior to 1939 comprised the remainder of the tanker fleet.

What We Shipped

Cargo ranged in size from pins and ball bearings to locomotives and landing craft; from drugs, medicines, hospital supplies, and clothing to explosives and firefighting equipment; from foodstuffs to agricultural machinery and Army tanks — the tools of destruction and construction, the means to help sustain the war overseas, the implements and materials that are basic to the support of civilian populations. Some of the commodities were stowed compactly in the holds of ships, others required space out of all proportion to their weight, and were carried on the decks of cargo vessels and tankers. Planes, tanks, trucks, and other vehicles require enormous quantities of fuel and lubricants to keep them in operation. Exclusive of shipments for the Army and Navy, we sent overseas from January 1943 through August 1945, 18,907,089 tons of gasoline, 7,235,999 tons of fuel oil, 1,498,034 tons of Diesel Oil, 1,440,459 tons of gas oil, and more than 667,979 tons of lubricants. In all, petroleum and its products totaling some 35,109,145 tons comprised ninety-nine percent of the total bulk liquid shipments; inedible oils and chemicals made up the remaining 326,204 tons.

Where the Cargo Went

Cargoes were carried across every ocean into practically all inhabited areas of the world, along many sea lanes never before used, to old established ports and to wartime destinations which were ports in name only. The distribution in 1944 indicates the proportion of dry cargo each major area received: fifteen million tons to the United Kingdom and Continent of Europe; thirteen million tons to the Pacific areas; eight million to the Mediterranean area; six million to South America and the Caribbean; five million to the U.S.S.R., and three million to India and Ceylon.

The Big Customers

There were five major accounts: the Army, the Navy, the lend-lease program, civilian exports to Allied Nations, and shipments to Latin America and other countries. Imports included strategic materials for war industries and essentials for civilian use. Each of these programs was essential to winning the war, and the problem of meeting the cargo needs of each, without jeopardizing the other and with the amount of shipping available, was the principal task of the War Shipping Administration. To carry it out successfully meant assembling a staff of ship operations men of tested ability and the organization of this staff on a worldwide basis. It meant constant liaison with military and political leaders, and civilian agencies in charge of production, finance, and economic coordination with our Allies. There was no precedent for guidance, no time for training or experimentation.

Aid to Our Allies

The gallant stand of Great Britain and Russia in the months before Pearl Harbor and in the early days of our participation was of incalculable value to the United States in gearing up its war machine. As the war proceeded, it was necessary to increase the flow of supplies and equipment. Vessels of various nations carried these lend-lease cargoes, but the bulk was transported overseas in WSA-controlled ships: in 1942, thirty-nine percent of all shipments for lend-lease and civil requirements; in 1943, fifty-three percent; in 1944, sixty-two percent; and in the first ten months of 1945, fifty-eight percent.

During 1942 and the early part of 1943, thirty percent of the carrying capacity of the WSA fleet was used for lend-lease and civilian commodities for our Allies, principally Great Britain and Russia. This percentage dropped only one point by the end of 1943, but by that time the total tonnage of our merchant fleet had increased materially, so that the actual weight of cargo increased. In fact, the lend-lease shipments during 1943 to Russia exceeded our commitments by more than thirty-five percent.

In 1943 WSA ships made 2,876 sailings with lend-lease supplies. Of the total, 2,267 sailings were for Great Britain, her colonies and dominions, 328 for Russia, and 281 for other lend-lease countries. The improvement in antisubmarine warfare was especially helpful. In 1942 an average of twelve percent of ships carrying lend-lease for Russia was sunk, principally along the dangerous Murmansk run, but by the end of 1943, barely one percent of such vessels were lost.

Although the principal function of the WSA in the lend-lease program was the delivery of war materials, there was another and highly important phase: the servicing, supplying, and repair of ships belonging to foreign governments who had lend-lease agreements with the United States, and the allocation of ships to replace their excessive war losses. The WSA transferred 509 vessels to serve under Allied flags. These were principally Liberty-type and prewar ships. Of the total, 341 went to the United Kingdom, ninety-three to Russia, twenty-three to Norway, fourteen to Greece, thirteen to France, seven to Belgium, six to Netherlands, six to Poland, four to Chile, and two to China. In addition, WSA handled the transfer of small boats, tugs, and barges. Under the lend-lease program our shipyards repaired damages to foreign vessels and converted many of their merchant ships into troop carriers and hospital ships .

Latin America

Latin America's participation in the war further emphasized the economic and social ties between them and the United States. The export program with these Latin American nations was arranged by the State Department and Foreign Economic Administration (FEA). Shipping quotas were set, and met, for cargo space in the WSA-controlled fleet. The export part of this program was dovetailed with the WSA's import operations by utilizing homeward-bound vessels. The WSA officials made every effort to simplify the procedures in licensing and booking shipments to these countries. This process led naturally into a smoother transition from lend-lease shipments to relief shipments for war-torn countries at the war's end.

Dry cargo exports in WSA ships for both the lend-lease program and civilian commodities totaled 10,242,000 long tons in 1942, 16,221,000 in 1943, 16,485,000 in 1944, and an estimated 21,733,000 in 1945. Tanker exports in the same categories amounted to 4,246,000 in 1942, 6,370,000 in 1943, 13,874,000 in 1944, and an estimated 9,389,000 in 1945.

War Sinews from Abroad

To keep war production at peak efficiency, the Merchant Marine had to bring home essential raw materials in great amounts. Commodities were brought into the United States from every continent. Bauxite, copper, coffee, sugar, nitrates, manganese, and other essentials came from South American and Caribbean ports; burlap was brought back from India and Ceylon; wool from Australia; hides and skins, cocoa beans, sisal and henequen from Africa, chrome came from Turkey via the Red Sea and from North and Transpacific Russia.

During the first two years of the war, our armies demanded a swiftly rising flow of supplies. Submarines took a heavy toll. The resulting pinch on imports fell most heavily on civilian commodities. With tankers burning in sight of our own Atlantic shores, many homes were cold from lack of fuel. American families experienced lack of coffee, spices, sugar, and other commodities.

The Big Lift

During the war years, the War Shipping Administration allocated as much as three-quarters of its tonnage to Army and Navy cargoes. The armed services were always the Number One customers of the Merchant Marine. The first two years of the war saw the buildup of the military powerhouses of Africa, the United Kingdom, and the South and Southwest Pacific. This process called for a steady stream of cargo ships. During 1942 and the early part of 1943, the WSA merchant fleet devoted forty-one percent of its capacity to Army cargo and thirteen to the Navy. This ratio changed slightly toward the end of 1943, when WSA ships were devoting forty-nine percent of their capacity to the Army and ten percent to the Navy.

Invasion of the Mediterranean area was the first large-scale action engaged in by ships of the WSA fleet. Hundreds of merchant vessels were in the initial attacks on North Africa and the landings on Sicily. Seizure of these areas created another problem for the WSA operations staff. The campaigns of our armies in that area called for the diversion of a large fleet of merchant ships for initial attacks and required a sufficient number of vessels to maintain the stream of men and supplies moving in as the invasion developed. This withdrew from other world services a sizeable proportion of our cargo fleet. Fortunately, success in North Africa came ahead of schedule and large numbers of ships again were available for multiple tasks in other oceans.

Toward the end of 1943, we built up in the British Isles the greatest invasion force ever assembled. The great convoys, some with as many as 167 ships, shuttled across the Atlantic bearing essential cargoes.

In the southwest Pacific area, the situation was different. The circuitous route necessary during the early days of the war to send supplies to General MacArthur in Australia greatly cut down the tonnage an individual vessel could deliver in a given period of time. Ships diverted to that area for shuttle runs between Australian ports and New Guinea and interisland services were sometimes detained for months.

In 1944, seventy-four percent of WSA tonnage was allocated for the Army and Navy, compared with fifty-nine percent so employed toward the end of 1943. Ships allocated to the Army alone comprised about sixty percent of the WSA fleet, while the dry-cargo tonnage allocated to the Navy amounted to fourteen percent.

In 1944 the Allies took Sicily, went into the Italian boot, and hammered at the Cassino gateway to Rome. The beaches at Anzio were occupied with substantial losses. General Eisenhower returned to England and opened wide the valve on the great flood of American troops and gear needed to build up overwhelming power for the assault on the Normandy coast. The vast war raging along the Russo-German front from the Baltic to the Black Sea called for more and more shipments of American war materials for Russian armies.

And in the Far East the tempo increased. At the start of the year, the incredibly difficult Burma campaign was in its opening phases, and General MacArthur established a firm hold on eastern New Guinea. On the eastern sea approaches to Japan, Admiral Nimitz began investment of the Marshall Islands. The long stretches of the Pacific were now American highroads to numerous powerful bases where supplies were assembled to attack the Philippines and the home islands of Japan. Our forces were successfully installed on the northern flank, the Aleutians.

All of these movements needed steady maintenance of supplies by the merchant fleet.

By mid-1944, the war reached maximum fury. The greatest sea-borne invasion in history crossed the English Channel on June 6. In the van were thirty-two American merchant ships to be sunk off the beachhead to form a breakwater. They were manned by more than 1,000 merchant seamen and officers who volunteered for the hazardous duty. They sailed from England through mined waters, filed into position off the Normandy beach under severe shelling from German shore batteries, and were sunk by the crews to form the artificial harbor. Behind this breakwater, prefabricated units were towed in to handle the subsequent debarkation of men and equipment. Ten oceangoing tugs operated by the WSA and manned by merchant crews assisted in the famous MULBERRY operation by towing the harbor units into position. From D-day until the last tug departed the Channel area, they towed 182 units. This project stands as one of the most remarkable water-born engineering accomplishments of all time. Later, the English Channel was nicknamed by the merchant crews "Liberty Lane" because of the number of these cargo ships shuttling between England and France. In all, 150 American merchant vessels were operated by the WSA in this cross-Channel service.

By June 1944, in the Central Pacific, the Marianas were attacked and Saipan fell; Tinian and Guam in July; in the southwest Pacific, General MacArthur bypassed strong Japanese forces by the capture of Hollandia on New Guinea and was looking northward toward the Philippines. The second invasion of France from the south was mounted, and our forces raced up the Rhone Valley to join with those from the Normandy break-out.

The weight of shipping needed in the assault of western Europe was tremendous: on January 1, 1944, 1,970,000 deadweight tons were employed by the Army in the United Kingdom-Continent area. By September this had increased to 6,508,000 deadweight tons, largely in shuttle service. In the western Mediterranean Army tonnages increased from 3,118,000 on July 1, to 5,658,000 on November 1, most of which had been built by the Maritime Commission since the war began.

In the latter part of the year, the full flood of shipping poured into the rapidly moving forward drives in the Central Pacific, into the Philippines, and to sustain the great battle of France and the Low Countries. By November, the port of Antwerp, vital to the supply of the northern armies, was in our possession. In the south, Toulon and Marseilles were used while facilities in Antwerp were improved, even in the face of a constant rain of V-bombs. By the end of the year, interior lines of supply connecting the Allied armies with the ports were functioning, and merchant vessels were discharging matériel for use in the final assault across the Rhine into Germany itself.

Bombers now mounted the assault on the Japanese homeland from bases on the Marianas, and the signal was given by the combined Chiefs of Staff to General MacArthur to hit the Philippines at Leyte. The buildup of his supplies and the seaborne invasion of that island was made possible by the thousands of tons of war matériel carried by hundreds of WSA cargo ships, and by the end of 1944 American invasion fleets steamed for Manila.

As this great expansion of power was taking place in the Pacific during the year, more and more WSA tonnage was allocated for the Army and Navy. On January 1, 1944, 2,301,000 tons; on December 31, this had increased to 4,526,000 tons. Tonnage placed at the disposal of naval needs was primarily for use in the central Pacific, where from January 1 to December 31, allocations were increased from 570,000 deadweight tons to 2,629,000 tons.

The year 1945 saw our maritime power at its peak. The nation's gigantic wartime shipbuilding program and the development of convoy operations, the perfection of antisubmarine warfare devices and techniques, and the training of Navy personnel to man them, and to serve aboard the merchant vessels as gun crews, all combined to put overwhelming strength into the overseas operations of the United States Merchant Marine. By

June, the WSA-controlled fleet numbered 4,125 Vessels, with a deadweight tonnage of 44,435,000. Ship sinkings, which during the years 1943 and 1944 showed a steady decline, were consistently lower during that period. The terrific power shown by our Navy in the Pacific cleared the sea approaches to our forward-moving forces.

With the sustained airborne blows at Japan from the hard-won fields on Okinawa and Iwo Jima, and the hammering the enemy received from the great naval fleets ranging the shores of her home islands, followed by the atomic bombing of Hiroshima and Nagasaki, the WSA made ships ready for the occupation forces and matériel taken by General MacArthur into the beaten enemy territory.

The men in command of the armed services had high praise for the merchant marine.   Fleet Admiral Ernest J. King, Commander in Chief of the United States Navy and Chief of Naval Operations:

> During the past 3½ years, the Navy has been dependent upon the Merchant Marine to supply our far-flung fleet and bases. Without this support, the Navy could not have accomplished its mission. Consequently, it is fitting that the Merchant Marine share in our success as it shared in our trials,
>
> The Merchant Marine is a strong bulwark of national defense in peace and war, and a buttress to a sound national economy. A large Merchant Marine is not only an important national resource; it is, in being, an integral part of the country's armed might during time of crisis. During World War II, this precept has been proven.
>
> As the Merchant Marine returns to its peacetime pursuits, I take pleasure in expressing the Navy's heartfelt thanks to you and through you to the officers and men of the Merchant Marine for their magnificent support during World War II. All hands can feel a pride of accomplishment in a job well done.
>
> We wish the Merchant Marine every success during the years ahead and sincerely hope that it remains strong and continues as a vital and integral part of our national economy and defense.

General Dwight D. Eisenhower:

Every man in this Allied command is quick to express his admiration for the loyalty, courage, and fortitude of the officers and men of the Merchant Marine. We count upon their efficiency and their utter devotion to duty as we do our own; they have never failed us yet and in all the struggles yet to come we know that they will never be deterred by any danger, hardship, or privation.

When final victory is ours there is no organization that will share its credit more deservedly than the Merchant Marine.

General Douglas MacArthur:

I wish to commend to you the valor of the merchant seamen participating with us in the liberation of the Philippines. With us they have shared the heaviest enemy fire. On this island I have ordered them off their ships and into fox holes when their ships became untenable targets of attack. At our side they have suffered in bloodshed and in death. The high caliber of efficiency and the courage they displayed in their part of the invasion of the Philippines marked their conduct, throughout the entire campaign in the southwest Pacific area. They have contributed tremendously to our success. I hold no branch in higher esteem than the Merchant Marine services.

How the Fleet Was Obtained and Operated

The global aspects of World War II presented demands out of all proportion to the tonnage available. Virtually all European and Mediterranean ports were closed to us. From the Aleutians to Australia, we had to fight our ships through to the few ports remaining out of Japanese hands. The key lay in the length of the shipping lanes and the condition of the ports. If a ship must go farther, and spend more time when it gets there, more ships must be added to the run if a given amount of cargo is to be handled. Furthermore, the composition of our pre-Pearl

Harbor fleet must be considered. Many were built between wars, or even before World War I. Many were small. Less than one-third of our tonnage was in the foreign trade fleet. The net result was that December 7, 1941 found us with an alarming shortage of ships.

But we had one great advantage we did not have at the start of our war in 1917: the governmental machinery, the industrial know-how, standard ship designs, and the results of previous experience in terms of statistics and analyses. To some extent the job ahead was foreseen between the start of the war in Europe in September 1939 and Pearl Harbor. The ever-growing danger of war during those days was evident to the United States Maritime Commission.

Created under the Merchant Marine Act Of 1936, this agency was already established to direct the national phases of merchant shipping and shipbuilding, and prepared the national defense aspects of the United States Merchant Marine, particularly in shipbuilding. Emergency-type cargo ships were not mere makeshifts invented under the pressure of war; development began before Pearl Harbor. Bigger and faster ships designed under the Maritime Commission's long-range policy were built by shipyards encouraged by the Nation's new maritime program. Building schedules were stepped up. Cooperation with naval authorities resulted in fast production to meet the auxiliary needs of the United States Navy. The Japanese attack at Pearl Harbor pressed the button for full-speed construction.

It was early seen that the immense shipbuilding function would absorb the complete attention of the United States Maritime Commission, and that there was urgent need for a special agency to handle the wartime merchant fleet. This was created on February 7, 1942, by Executive Order. The Chairman of the United States Maritime Commission was named two days later as War Shipping Administrator, directly responsible to the President of the United States.

The WSA was empowered to control the operation, purchase, charter, requisition, and use of all ocean vessels under the control of the United States, except for those of the armed services and those limited domestic water-borne services under the Office of Defense Transportation.

Before establishment of the WSA cooperation by American ship operators in transporting military, lend-lease, and other cargoes was on a voluntary basis. The responsibility of the WSA included the purchase or requisition of vessels for its own use or for use of the Army, Navy, or other Government agencies; the repairing, arming, and installation of defense equipment on WSA-controlled vessels and Allied vessels under Lend-Lease provision; the conversion of vessels to troop transports, hospital ships, and for other special purposes; the training and providing of ship personnel; the operation, loading, discharging, and general control of the movement of the ships; administering of marine and war risk insurance laws and funds, and the control of port and terminal facilities, forwarding and related matters.

Efficiency Means More Lift

WSA officials operated under the maxim "there are never enough ships." The utmost use was squeezed out of each vessel. Throughout the war new ways were devised to carry more cargo per ship. Previously unused deck and under-deck space was pressed into service. Aircraft, tanks and landing craft were loaded on the decks of tankers. During the early days of the war this saved time and dry-cargo shipping space. During 1944 from Pacific ports alone 2,727 airplanes, 993 boats, 296 amphibious craft, and 1,223 vehicles were shipped as deck cargo. Deep tanks of dry-cargo vessels served to carry excess bunker oil to the United Kingdom at a time when shortage of oil threatened the success of Britain's war effort. This was equivalent to the capacity of 475 dry-cargo vessels carrying an average cargo of 400,000 cubic feet. The amount of surplus fuel loaded in deep tanks of dry-cargo vessels was equivalent to the cargo capacity of fifty-seven tankers carrying an average cargo of 12,000 tons. Unusual cargoes were carried for special military uses overseas.

A number of vessels were specially outfitted so that un-boxed vehicles could be rolled out in rapid fashion to save turnaround time in their shuttle across the Channel. Ingenious wooden false decks were prefabricated in this country, stowed knocked-down ready for installation. Plans and instructions were carried for the Army to erect them when the ships arrived. Bulk ore carriers were fitted out and loaded the largest cargoes of grain ever carried.

Every effort was made to prevent the port congestion so common in World War I. Port authorities smoothed out a number of defects in the interval between wars, and the WSA coordinated operations with port officials, the Office of Defense Transportation, Army authorities, rail, barge, and truck lines and private port and terminal operators. A master stevedoring contract was agreed upon. Contracts were made giving the WSA control of deep-sea terminal facilities during the war period and permitting equitable allocation of ships among terminal operators. WSA operations officials in New York met daily with those from the British Ministry of War Transport. Ships on berth loading or discharging at Atlantic coast ports were reviewed and checked by daily tele-type. Immediate steps were taken to ensure the meeting of convoy deadline dates.

To meet the various needs of the different theaters of war traffic was allocated to points along our coastlines best suited as outports. Atlantic ports served the European theater while the Pacific slope was set up as a separate administrative region. Columbia River and North Pacific ports, for instance, served much of the Russian lend-lease trade with two-and-a-half million tons moving from them during 1944. Gulf ports served in the import of strategic materials and essential commodities from South and Central America, and excess traffic to the Southwest Pacific moved from them through the Panama Canal.

Efficiency in handling the WSA fleet was complicated by problems peculiar to wartime. About one-third of all dry-cargo vessels during any one period during 1944, for example, were in foreign areas discharging cargo or engaged in local military operation. Inadequate port, storage, and transportation facilities in Europe and in the Pacific also tended toward delays in returning ships quickly to the United States. Nevertheless, figures for 1944 show that despite an increase in the average number of ships handled daily, ranging from 416 at Atlantic and Gulf ports in January to 581 in December, the average time spent by these vessels in port declined from twenty-five days in January to less than seventeen days in October. The improvement was a result of reducing time spent discharging, loading, repairing, awaiting sailing orders, and other miscellaneous operations in port. This speedup added the equivalent of 125 ships to the East Coast fleet during each of the critical three months of the final buildup for the invasion of France.

Keeping the Fleet in Shape

Worldwide facilities for quick repair were essential to keep the ships sailing. War service is hard on ships. They are pushed in convoy to meet exacting time schedules regardless of weather, and loaded to maximum capacity. This called for discharging cargo under every conceivable handicap ranging from refueling of fighting ships from tankers at sea to manual unloading under enemy air attacks at wrecked piers, emergency docks, and from ships to barges and lighters. All this added up to abnormal wear on gear, equipment, and personnel.

Military demands called for numerous devices, equipment, and conversions below and above decks of standard type ships; and sudden calls were common. Shortages of certain type combat ships meant conversion of merchant vessels to fit wartime specifications. Maintenance, repair, and conversion of the ships of our wartime merchant fleet was another responsibility of the WSA. This called for an immense amount of legal and financial activity and dealings with hundreds of repair concerns, agents, and organizations.

Because the task was primarily concerned with the operation, rather than with the construction of ships, the Division of

Maintenance and Repair of the United States Maritime Commission was transferred to the WSA. It was greatly enlarged. In addition a Division of Foreign Repairs and Salvage Operations was created maintaining personnel in numerous ports overseas. To coordinate the function with similar operations of the Navy, an Office of Coordinator for Ship Repairs and Conversion was set up in New York. This office maintained an orderly flow of work to some 100 repair yards throughout the country.

During the first eighteen months after the establishment of the WSA's Maintenance and Repair Organization on May 7, 1942, primary stress was put upon expanding ship repair facilities in the United States. Many new yards were established. A system of inspection was devised. Standard plans and specifications were set up to insure uniform changes and modifications. This unit of the WSA directed the arming of merchant ships, installations of defense gear such as degaussing equipment and special cargo handling devices. Some vessels were "winterized" — heating coils installed and other adaptations for Arctic and North Russian runs. Auxiliary tanks were set aboard ships going into war theaters where there were inadequate water supplies. In addition to repairing damage, specific accomplishments included conversion of ships to transport mules; fitting Liberty ships for carrying prisoners of war and their subsequent refitting as troop carriers to return military personnel from overseas. The troop-carrier program called for the conversion of about 400 vessels, including the liner *George Washington,* and ninety-seven Victory ships at a total cost of about $290,000,000. Similar conversions of foreign-flag vessels were accomplished. Of great military importance was the fitting out of several Liberty ships to transport and lay special hollow cable used as a pipeline spanning the English Channel — a source of supply for our fast moving motorized equipment in the Battles of France and Germany. Four Soviet vessels were converted to floating fish and crab canneries. Numerous tankers were fitted out with oiling-at-sea gear and special decks to deliver aircraft and other cargo.

The WSA's Repair and Maintenance Organization handled more than 42,000 jobs at an approximate total cost of $1,480,087,-000. Of these, 36,476 were for the WSA, costing about $1,168,740 000, while 5,600 jobs were carried out on foreign vessels under lend-lease arrangements, costing some $311,347,000.

Ship-repair contracts were negotiated with Australia, Belgium, Egypt, England, and South Africa to assure WSA vessels rates and conditions equivalent to those of the nationals of each country. Thousands of routine repairs were handled under the supervision of sixty-two engineering representatives stationed all over the world. Stock piles of parts and equipment were maintained at strategic and advance foreign ports for making quick battle-damage repairs.

Husbanding the Fleet

The WSA-controlled fleet consumed over 300 million barrels of all types of bunker fuel. To insure adequate supplies WSA maintained close cooperation with the Petroleum Administration for War, the United States Navy, and major oil suppliers as well as with the British Ministry of War Transport.

To assure an adequate supply of the best food available, the WSA saw to it that suppliers had large quantities of essential foods. More than 450 food suppliers were approved to sell these set-aside and restricted foods to WSA ships. Through such means the WSA made available during the period February 1943 to January 1946, more than 1,812,000 tons of such foods. This included 350,000 tons of meat and poultry, 286,511 tons of fresh fruits and vegetables, and correspondingly large amounts of butter, canned foods, eggs, cheese, milk, coffee, and other scarce items. Additional training was given stewards, cooks, and bakers.

So that merchant seamen would be able to purchase personal supplies of good quality aboard ship, a standard slop chest was adopted comprising fifty-two items in addition to tobacco and cigarettes. Handling and delivery of mail to and from merchant ships was improved steadily. Husbanding the fleet also called for provision for other supplies, such as deck and engine gear, turnbuckles, lashings, lumber, instruments, and safety devices. WSA storage yards were set up, with new and reconditioned supplies available. Special stock piles of equipment were ready in England prior to D-day, particularly for the "block ship" phase of the invasion operations.

The Men Who Sailed the Ships

The early months of the war brought public attention to merchant seamen. Initially there were not enough men. About 55,000 merchant seamen and officers were sailing in December 1941. Many more were ashore, often in permanent, well-paying jobs. The need for a program to procure and train merchant seamen and officers crystallized shortly after the creation of the War Shipping Administration when, in the spring of 1942, ship delays from lack of crews reached a critical point with an average of about forty-five a month. The WSA administered three organizations under the direction of a Deputy War Shipping Administrator: the Recruitment and Manning Organization, the Training Organization, and the Maritime Labor Relations Organization. The personnel system thus evolved resulted in a peak seagoing force of 250,000 kept within the framework of the civilian maritime industry, despite the fact that the seamen and officers carried on their work under combat conditions.

Records of the Recruitment and Manning Organization (RMO) show a steadily growing and unbroken flow of seagoing manpower. Delays in sailings for temporary want of crews shrank steadily from twelve to fifteen a fortnight in mid-1942 to two or three a fortnight at the end of 1943. During the war, the turnover rate of men in the industry was less than one fourth of what it had been before the war.

The immediate task of the RMO was the recruitment of ex-merchant seamen back into the industry. The first large-scale step was a nationwide registration of seamen in September 1942.

Direct recruitment began early the following year, augmented principally by a recruitment campaign carried out with the cooperation of the Office of War Information and the National War Advertising Council. Nearly 100,000 men with previous sea experience working ashore were recruited by WSA into the wartime Merchant Marine.

It was not easy to recruit experienced seamen, many of whom were reluctant to leave well-paying, protected shore jobs, particularly when there was no guarantee of reemployment. So Public Law 87 was passed by Congress during the summer of 1943, guaranteeing seniority and reemployment rights to men who went back to sea.

The RMO made 346,100 assignments of men to ships. A large percentage of these were from training stations. On numerous occasions, such assignments meant the difference between the sailing or delay of a great convoy. Yet RMO actually hired only twenty-five percent of all seamen, the ship operators and unions hiring the remaining seventy-five percent. Its responsibility was to fill in where regular means of hiring could not meet the sudden demands caused by deliveries of new ships, last-minute sailing dates and other wartime exigencies.

There was little object in recruiting and training seamen if they were not retained in the industry. Therefore the Selective Service System delegated to RMO the authority to certify active seamen to their draft boards for occupational deferment.

A New Generation of Seamen

As part of the Merchant Marine Act of 1936, there was in effect since 1938 a training program for officers and seamen. Shortly after the war began, it was transferred to the WSA and expanded to meet the demand for new men. The program was carried on by three units under the Training Organization: The United States Merchant Marine Cadet Corps, the United States Maritime Service and State Maritime Academies under Federal supervision.

The Cadet Corps provided merchant-officer training in deck and engine departments for young unmarried men with high school or college education. Entry into the Corps was conditional upon meeting qualifications as midshipmen in the Merchant Marine Naval Reserve. The principal institution of the Corps was the United States Merchant Marine Academy at Kings Point, N.Y., established in January 1941. This is a federal academy bearing the same relationship to the Merchant Marine as West Point does to the Army and Annapolis to the Navy. Two basic schools, at Pass Christian, Mississippi, and San Mateo, California, provided preliminary training. All cadet midshipmen served an intermediate period at sea aboard merchant vessels. During the war, 123 were reported dead and missing, and many displayed conspicuous bravery under combat conditions.

The United States Maritime Service operated large training stations for unlicensed seamen in deck, engine, and steward departments at Sheepshead Bay, New York; Avalon, California and St. Petersburg, Florida. Further training was provided as carpenters' mates, radio operators and purser-hospital corpsmen. Special radio schools were maintained at Gallups Island, Boston Harbor, Massachusetts and at Hoffman Island, New York Harbor. Officers' schools were maintained at Fort Trumbull, New London, Connecticut and Alameda, California, where deck and engine men with at least fourteen months' sea service were given a four-months' course to qualify them to sit for their licenses and which provided refresher courses for officers renewing expired licenses.

The United States Maritime Service also conducted special courses of instruction in diesel engineering, turboelectric and high-pressure turbine propulsion, signalling, use of barrage balloons aboard ship, and chief steward training.

The Maritime Service's upgrading program was particularly effective in helping officers, seamen, cooks, and bakers raise their grades. This was an essential process to fill continuous vacancies in the higher ranks and ratings. Upgrade schools were located in Baltimore, Boston, New York, New Orleans,

Seattle, San Francisco, Los Angeles, and Wilmington, California.

There were five State Maritime Academies which came under Federal supervision. They were located in California, Maine, Massachusetts, New York, and Pennsylvania.[2]

From 1938 to December 1, 1945, the training program graduated 31,986 officers (7,291 from the Cadet Corps, 21,988 from the Maritime Service, and 2,707 from the State Maritime Academies), 7,727 radio operators, 150,734 unlicensed seamen in all ratings, 5,034 junior assistant purser-hospital corpsmen, 2,588 junior marine officers for the Transportation Corps, United States Army Service Forces, 36,620 from deck, engine, and steward upgrade schools, 996 from license refresher schools, 3,653 from turboelectric and 642 from high-pressure and geared turbine schools, 1,066 Diesel engineers, 2,024 6-weeks' engineers, and 127 river-pilot trainees. The following special schools graduated: Barrage balloon, 7,980; visual signalling, 10,001; safety at sea, 1,316. There was a grand total of 262,474 graduates turned out under the WSA training program.

Employee-Employer Relations

When the American Merchant Marine was taken over by the WSA in April 1942 most seagoing personnel were members of maritime labor unions and were covered by collective bargaining agreements. Maritime unions agreed that the right to strike would not be exercised for the duration of the war, that the authority of the master of a ship in wartime operations would be strengthened, and that no changes would be made in collective bargaining agreements without WSA approval.

---

[2] As of 1997 the Pennsylvania school has long been closed. State academies now also exist in Texas and the Great Lakes.

Homes at Home and Abroad

Almost entirely lacking at the start of the war were facilities on a large enough scale to provide a health, welfare, and convalescence program in the United States, or housing, recreational, and medical aid for American seamen abroad. In 1942 the United Seamen's Service was set up as a nonprofit organization sponsored by WSA. It became a participating agency of the National War Fund November 1,1943. The USS was to the merchant seamen what the USO and Red Cross were to members of the Armed Forces. At its peak, USS operated 126 facilities — rest homes, clubs, hotels, recreation centers — on six continents with a total personnel of 2,000. In 1944, about 170,000 American merchant seamen paid more than 2,600,000 visits to these establishments and, from 1942 to May 1, 1945, approximately 1,503,595 overnight accommodations were provided for seamen.

Medical Service for Seamen

Under public laws, dating back to 1798, the United States Public Health Service was charged with providing medical care for merchant seamen.[3] Wartime situations, however, made the provision of additional medical services imperative.

The WSA, in cooperation with USPHS and other Government departments (Coast Guard, Navy, Army) and the United Seamen's Service, worked out a comprehensive health service. Administration of the program was put in the hands of the Medical Director, WSA. The program provided health protection for the individual seamen, other crew members, and military personnel and passengers traveling aboard merchant ships, through the control of communicable, neuropsychiatric, and other diseases. Services of specialists in the field of communicable disease,

---

[3] During the Reagan administration legislation was enacted abolishing the several Public Health Hospitals and denying American merchant seamen their medical care.

dentistry, nutrition, psychology and psychiatry, and sanitary engineering were obtained.

The urgent wartime need for merchant seamen made it imperative that every man be medically able to do his job at sea, that he be immunized and free from communicable diseases. Because of the necessity for quick action and the shortage of medical personnel available to the industry to perform examinations, WSA established a sign-on medical examination program to supplement existing medical programs of general agents. The WSA prescribed the minimum standards and the examinations were carried on in WSA Port Medical Representatives' offices or through offices of agents.

Realizing that there were not enough doctors for one to be assigned to each merchant ship, the WSA in December 1942 established a hospital corps school at the United States Maritime Service Training Station at Sheepshead Bay, N.Y. This school graduated nearly 5,000 men with the rating of junior assistant purser-pharmacist's mate. Utilization of these men made it possible for nearly eighty-two percent of all merchant ships to carry a medically trained staff officer.

WSA medical authorities and the United States Public Health Service established a sanitary engineering division to develop standards and procedures to insure proper sanitary facilities and conditions on vessels operated by the WSA. In addition the WSA medical office prepared two books, *Ship's Medicine Chest and First Aid at Sea* and *Syllabus for Hospital Corpsmen* and a periodical, "Purser-Pharmacist's Mate Journal."

Rewards for a Job Well Done

Congress and the President with the War Shipping Administration and United States Maritime Commission awarded medals for outstanding conduct and service insignia for public identification of the contribution made to victory by the men of the Merchant Marine.

The Merchant Marine Distinguished Service Medal (DSM) is the highest award for the men of the Merchant Marine. It was authorized by Congress in April 1942, to be awarded in the name of the President of the United States for outstanding conduct or service in the line of duty. During the war 141 such medals were awarded. Next in scale is the Merchant Marine Meritorious Service Medal for outstanding conduct or service which does not justify the award of the DSM, a category into which fell many cases of heroism and devotion to duty. A total of 362 were awarded.

The Merchant Marine unit award is called the "Gallant Ship" citation. It is awarded to a ship which has served in outstanding action against the enemy, in marine disasters or other emergencies at sea, during which time each member of the crew performed in an exceptional manner. A plaque upon which appears the citation is presented to the ship; and to the master and each member of the crew, including the Naval Armed Guard, a Gallant Ship Bar is presented. Throughout the war, two merchant ships were so rewarded.

Similar to the Armed Service's Purple Heart is the Mariner's Medal, authorized by Congress to be awarded to any person serving on a vessel of the United States Merchant Marine during the war period who loses his life, is wounded, or suffers physical injury or dangerous exposure as a result of enemy action. A total of 5,099 Mariner's Medals were awarded, a large proportion of them posthumously to the next of kin.

The Merchant Marine Decorations and Medals Board issued War Zone Bars, Combat Bars, and Merchant Marine Service Emblems. These were authorized by Congress in May 1943. The Combat Bar signifies service aboard a vessel attacked or damaged by the enemy, with a star attached if the wearer has been forced to abandon ship. War Zone Bars denote service in the Atlantic, the Mediterranean, Middle East, and Pacific zones. Officers and seamen who served in the Merchant Marine between September 8, 1939, and Pearl Harbor, are eligible for the Merchant Marine Defense Bar, and the President approved the wearing of the Philippine Defense and Philippine Liberation Ribbons by Merchant Marine personnel.

The Cost of the War Years

Total net obligations and disbursements by WSA chargeable to its various appropriations, including its revolving fund, the maritime training fund, State maritime schools fund, lend-lease allocated funds, and the marine and war-risk insurance fund, from February 7, 1942, to June 30, 1945, were $7,581,917,854. Of this amount, purchase, charter, and operations of vessels, reconditioning, outfitting, defense installations, operation of warehouses and terminals and other obligations and expenditures from the revolving fund amounted to $3,900,489,753. From February 7 to June 30, 1942, expenses were $183,527,851; in 1943, $1,242,554,696; in 1944, $1,150,017,004; and in 1945, $1,324,390,202.

Obligations, and expenditures from the maritime training fund covering the training of officers and seamen, recruitment and manning of seamen, seamen's medical program, and maritime labor relations for the entire period were $235,476,144, of which $39,285,226 was expended in 1942; $60,273,015 in 1943; $65,828,116 in 1944, and $70,089,787 in 1945.

Total obligations in support of State maritime schools amounted to $943,434, of which $180,814 was expended in 1942; $344,258 in 1943; $224,598 in 1944, and $193,764 in 1945.

The marine and war-risk insurance fund for the entire period shows an excess of $82,892,248 in receipts over disbursements and recorded obligations.

Funds expended or obligated for lend-lease purposes by WSA from inception to June 30, 1945, totaled $3,527,900,771.

The War's End

The end of hostilities did not mean the cessation of WSA activities. The final month of 1945 found the merchant fleet operating at a rate never before reached in wartime. During that month there were 1,200 sailings as against 800 in the busiest months of the war. The reasons were the final liquidation of our wartime military operations and the increase of our responsibilities to provide relief for liberated nations.

Even before V-E day, work began on converting cargo ships and preparing passenger vessels to bring home the men of the Armed Services. A total of 546 such vessels comprised the WSA troop return fleet. Ninety-seven Victory ships were converted to troop carriers with a capacity of 1,500 men each. More than 300 converted Liberty ships were in the fleet, in addition to numerous large converted dry-cargo vessels. This fleet, operated in a common pool of WSA, Army, and Navy vessels, by the first of December brought back about three-and-a-half million men from overseas. From V-E day to V-J day, practically the whole troop-return responsibility was on the WSA, which accomplished better than eighty-five percent of the troop return up to September 1, 1945. The remainder was for the most part carried on British vessels, including the liners *Queen Mary* and *Queen Elizabeth.*

From V-E day on, the number of ships sailing with relief cargoes of food, clothing, medical supplies and other supplies increased. A great number of these carried goods under the United Nations Relief and Rehabilitation Administration program. Others were destined for Allied military authorities in charge of relief for civilian populations in certain areas. To a large extent, the relief program filled shipping space previously used for lend-lease cargoes.

APPENDIX B
NAVY ARMED GUARD
— UNSUNG HEROES

by Justin F. Gleichauf[1]

This article first appeared in the April 1986 issue of American Legion Magazine *and is reprinted with permission.*

Out-manned and out-gunned, the gallant seamen of the Navy's Armed Guard were tasked with a near-impossible mission: to protect U.S. shipping from the U-boat menace.

Whitson Lloyd's luck ran out May 5, 1945. He had survived the sinking of his ship off Newfoundland in 1943, returned safely from the deadly Murmansk Run in 1944, but went down with the SS *Black Point*, in sight of land, off Rhode Island. The young Lloyd was the last member of the Navy Armed Guard to die, on the last American ship sunk by a German torpedo in World War II. The war in Europe ended two days later.

---

[1] Justin F. Gleichauf is also the author of *The Naval Armed Guard in World War II, Unsung Sailors* (Annapolis: Naval Institute Press, 1990).

One of the most dramatic, but least-known stories of the war, is that of the U.S. Navy Armed Guard service. A comparative handful of men, it suffered losses far out of proportion to its size and to the Navy as a whole.

At a time when German U-boats, planes and armed raiders were sinking allied supply ships faster than they could be built, the Armed Guard, dormant since the end of World War I, was reactivated and rushed to sea to man guns aboard U.S. merchantmen and tankers. Their armament was puny compared with torpedoes and dive bombers, but they performed valiantly, and on one occasion fought a German sea raider to the death, with both ships going down.

The need for protection of supply lines was desperate. Winston Churchill wrote, "The only thing that ever really frightened me during the war was the U-boat peril . . . the Admiralty shared these fears." Britain's situation was indeed precarious; it needed one million tons of food and raw materials per week just to survive, let alone the massive flow of materiel needed to carry on the war. The USSR was in equally desperate straits for war supplies. The key was to provide protection for available shipping, while building more than was being sunk — much easier said than done.

In World War I, German U-boats had taken a fearful toll of Allied shipping: More than 5,000 ships, totaling more than eleven million tons, were sunk. One German captain alone sank 194 Allied ships. In the early days of World War II, there were not enough escort vessels, and many ships had to sail unprotected. In one six-month period in 1943, German U-boats sank 603 vessels.

The U.S. Neutrality Act, passed after the outbreak of war in 1939, barred U.S. vessels from the war zone, but in 1940, by a bit of Roosevelt sleight-of-hand, the United States made fifty old coal-burning destroyers available to the British Navy and shifted some 150 U.S. ships to other flags to keep the vital supply line open.

A vast program of ship building was inaugurated, and by 1943 there were eighty U.S. yards building ships, mostly slow, ugly 'Liberty' ships. The Liberty ships were based on a modified 1879 British design for tramp steamers; they were about 10,000 tons and had a top speed of eleven knots. Construction time was four to six weeks, but the Kaiser yards built one Liberty in the incredible time of four days, fifteen hours. By the end of the war, 2,710 Liberty ships had been built, of which 943 were sunk by enemy action. It was during this period that "Rosie the Riveter" made history.

However, before the "Bridge of Ships" became a fact, the German High Command revised strategy and began operating in "wolf packs," spread over a vast area of ocean. When a convoy was spotted, the sub would trail it until joined by others. In one joint attack in 1942, forty-two U-boats sank twenty-two merchant ships, destroying 161,000 tons of cargo and killing 360 persons, including fifty-one armed guards.

Herb Norch, a former armed guard now living in El Paso, Texas, described a typical wolf pack attack:

> Convoys could consist of up to 100 or more ships, spread out from horizon to horizon. Tankers and ammo ships were assigned locations in the center to provide some additional protection, but sub commanders countered by moving inside. Tankers were easily recognized by their silhouettes, and when set ablaze they lighted up a whole area, giving a better choice of targets. Tankers were hard to sink, and could burn for hours, or days.

Convoy speed could be as slow as five knots, and it was easy for a ship to get lost or outdistance its convoy. Stragglers or damaged ships were sitting ducks for U-boats. There was a large area in the mid-Atlantic where no air power could be delivered until late in the war and it was a happy hunting ground for submarines, as was the U.S. East Coast, where ships were silhouetted against lights on shore. Fires of burning ships were a common sight along the East Coast.

The Navy Armed Guard had only one job aboard ship, to man the guns. Gun crews generally were from eight to twenty-four men, headed by one officer. Lonnie Lloyd of Raleigh,

N.C., reported that at first men received as little as one to two weeks training before going to sea, and some ships had creosote poles as "guns." Later, more effective armament, 20mm and 40mm, three-inch 50s and five-inch 38s were installed, and training was expanded to six weeks at centers in Brooklyn, New Orleans and Treasure Island, Calif.

Armed Guard pay started at a princely $20 per month, later raised to about $65, but far below rates of merchant seamen on the same ships, who faced the same hazards. Hazards there were, aplenty. Don Geib, Colonia, N.J., was torpedoed twice in five months. Three of a total of ten survivors from the SS *Jonathan Sturges* were reunited recently, forty years after their ship sank in the North Atlantic. They spent sixteen days and nights in a lifeboat before they were rescued.

The SS *James Iredell* made it back from Palermo, Sicily, after sustaining a torpedo attack, three direct bomb hits, concussion damage from an ammunition ship blown up just ahead of it, and after fighting a three-day fire in the hold. Norch survived several runs in the North Atlantic, and unloading ammunition under heavy air attack at Anzio beachhead, before being seriously injured in a Japanese kamikaze attack in the South Pacific.

All runs were dangerous, but by far the deadliest was the notorious Murmansk Run to the USSR. Edward Stettinius Jr., former head of Lend-Lease, reported twenty-five percent of all ships to Murmansk were lost, including seventy-seven U.S. merchantmen.

The British Navy tried to provide protection for such convoys, but in 1942 it lost two cruisers, ten destroyers and other ships damaged on this run. One convoy, the ill-fated PQ-17, was an absolute disaster, losing twenty-three of thirty ships. Others were almost equally hard-hit.

Ed Wilmer, of Baltimore, who served on the SS *Louisa M. Alcott*, reported,

We left Norfolk in 1944 as part of a 108-ship convoy. Part of us split off to Murmansk. Past Iceland we were hit by U-boats and later by planes and shore batteries. A ship directly ahead of us was hit by a torpedo and the men took to the lifeboats, but by the time we reached them, about five minutes, we found them frozen stiff at the oars.

Death was the constant companion of the seamen on the Murmansk Run, with Nature assisting the enemy. Ice often locked convoys into paths from which there was no escape. The SS *Henry Brown* was lost but shot down five German planes before going down. Crewmen had no illusions about their life expectancy when their ship joined a convoy to Murmansk.

Possibly the most dramatic direct encounter of the Armed Guard occurred when the SS *Stephen Hopkins*, on its first (and last) voyage, fought a duel to the death with the German sea raider *Steir*. Their ship mortally wounded by the bigger and heavier armament of the *Steir*, the Armed Guard inflicted such damage on the *Steir* that it had to be scuttled. A young cadet engineer, Edwin O'Hara, stepping in to replace members of the gun crew who were killed or wounded, scored several direct hits on the raider before he, also, was killed.

One of the most horrifying acts of the war occurred in the South Pacific, when the SS *Jean Nicolet* was sunk by a Japanese submarine. Several crewmen and armed guards were picked up by the sub, tied up on deck and killed in cold blood when the submarine submerged.

Of total Navy enrollment of 3,380,817 in World War II, Navy losses were 36,950, including armed guards. Maximum strength of the Armed Guard was 144,000 men, of whom 1,710 were killed, or one out of every 185 men, plus scores of POWs, only a handful of whom were ever found.

In 1941 the U.S. Merchant Marine had 900 dry cargo ships and 440 tankers. By V-J Day, in spite of losses, it had 4,421 vessels, with a carrying capacity of more than 45 million tons. More than 1,700 U.S. ships had been lost in action, but the Merchant Marine (defended by Naval Armed Guards) had moved 268 million tons of cargo, a figure neither the German High Command nor the Japanese believed remotely possible. Losses of ships, based on new construction, fell from thirty-nine percent in 1942 to four percent in 1945.

World War II Naval Armed Guard — by the numbers.[2]

A grand total of 144,970 Armed Guard officers and enlisted men served in 6,236 merchant ships from December 7, 1941 to September 30, 1945. Seven hundred ten ships were sunk and many others damaged (216 Libertys, fifty on their first voyage).

Armed Guard officers totaled 9,390, of which 8,587 were gunnery officers and 803 were communication officers.

Armed Guard enlisted personnel totaled 135,580, of which 119,811 were petty officers and seamen, and 15,769 were signalmen and radiomen.

Armed Guard personnel peaked on November 1, 1944 with 106,661 enlisted personnel and 5,447 officers for a total of 112,108.

Armed Guard personnel transferred into the fleet or to other duty assignments after the victory in Europe and in preparation for the anticipated invasion of Japan totaled 86,198, of which 5,896 were officers and 80,302 enlisted personnel.

Personnel still on Armed Guard duty as of September 30, 1945 totaled 58,772 of which 3,494 were officers and 55,278 were enlisted personnel.

Armed Guard personnel classified as dead, missing in action or prisoners of war from December 7, 1941 to September 30, 1945:

Deaths:	105 officers, 1,578 enlisted men.
Missing:	7 officers, 120 enlisted men.
POWs:	1 officer, 13 enlisted men.
Totals:	113 officers, 1,711 enlisted men.

---

[2] *Arming of Merchant Ships and Armed Guard Service*, Appendices I and III, U.S. Naval Administration in WWII, Officer of the Chief of Naval Operations, covering 7 December 1941 - 30 September 1945.

Appendix C

Operation Crossroads

Vessels

OPERATION CROSSROADS TARGET VESSELS[1]

Battleships and Cruisers (Task Unit 1.2.1)

Arkansas, BB-33   *Nagato*, Japanese BB
Nevada, BB-36   *New York*, BB-34
Pennsylvania, BB-38   *Pensacola*, CA-24
Prinz Eugen, IX-300   *Sakawa*, Japanese CL
Salt Lake City, CA-25

Aircraft Carriers (Task Unit 1.2.2)

Independence, CVL-22   *Saratoga*, CV-3

Destroyers (Task Unit 1.2.3)

Anderson, DD-411   *Conyngham*, DD-371
Hughes, DD-410   *Lamson*, DD-367
Mayrant, DD-402   *Mustin*, DD-413

---

[1] Sources: Shurcliff, *Bombs At Bikini*, pp. 190-91; Weisgall, *Operation Crossroads*, pp. 317-22. Note: Weisgall includes the disposition for each target vessel.

Mugford, DD-389	*Rhind*, DD-404
Stack, DD-406	*Talbot*, DD-390
Wainwright, DD-419	*Wilson*, DD-408

Submarines (Task Unite 1.2.4)

Apogon, SS-308	*Dentuda*, SS-335
Parche, SS-384	*Pilotfish*, SS-386
Searaven, SS-196	*Skate*, SS-305
Skipjack, SS-184	*Tuna*, SS-203

Landing Ships and Craft

LSTs 52, 125, 133, 220, 545, and 661
LSM-60; LCIs 327, 329, 332, 549, 615, and 620
LCMs 1, 2, 3, 4, 5, and 6
LCTs 412, 414, 705, 745, 746, 812, 816, 818, 874, 1013, 1078, 1112, 1113, 1114, 1175, 1187, and 1237
LCVPs 7, 8, 9, 10, 11, and 12

Attack Transports

Banner, APA-60	*Barrow*, APA-61
Bladen, APA-63	*Bracken*, APA-64
Briscoe, APA-65	*Brule*, APA-66
Butte, APA-68	*Carlisle*, APA-69
Carteret, APA-70	*Catron*, APA-71
Cortland, APA-75	*Crittenden*, APA-77
Dawson, APA-79	*Fallon*, APA-81
Fillmore, APA-63	*Gasconade*, APA-85
Geneva, APA-86	*Gilliam*, APA-87
Niagara, AP-87	

OPERATION CROSSROADS SUPPORT VESSELS[2]
Mount McKinley (AGC-7)
Force Flagship, JTF-ONE
Fall River (CA-131)
Target Vessel Control Group, Task Group 1.2

---

[2]   Shurcliff, *Bombs At Bikini*, pp. 186-189.

Technical Group (Task Group 1.1)

Albermarle, AV-5	*Avery Island*, AG-76
Begor, APD-127	*Burleson*, APA-67
Cumberland Sound, AV-17	*Haven*, APH-112
Kenneth Whiting, AV-14	*Wharton*, AP-7
LCM-60	*LCT-1359*

Transport Group (Task Group 1.3)

Appalachian, AGC-1	*Appling*, APA-58
Artemis, AKA-21	*Bayfield*, APA-33
Bexar, APA-237	*Blue Ridge*, AGC-2
Bottineau, APA-235 *LST-817*	*George Clymer*, APA-27
Henrico, APA-45	*Ottawa*, AKA-101
Panamint, AGC-13	*Rockbridge*, APA-228
Rockingham, APA-229	*Rockwall*, APA-230
Rolette, AKA-99	*Saint Croix*, APA-231
LST-881	

Navy Air Group (Task Group 1.6)

C P Cecil, DD-835	*Furse*, DD-882
N K Perry, DD-883	*Orca*, AVP-49
Saidor, CVE-117	*Shangri-La*, CV-38
Turner, DD-834	

Surface Patrol Group (Task Group 1.7)

A.M. Sumner, DD-692	*Barton*, DD-722
Flusser, DD-368	*Ingraham*, DD-694
Laffey, DD-724	*Lowry*, DD-770
Moale, DD-693	*O'Brien*, DD-725
R.K. Huntington, DD-781	*Walke*, DD-723

Service Group (Task Group 1.8)

Ajax, AR-6	*Cebu*, ARG-6
Chickaskia, AO-54	*Chowanoc*, ATF-100
Coasters Harbor, AG-74	*Creon*, ARL-11

Dixie, AD-14

Fulton, AS-11

Limestone, IX-158

Phaon, ARB-3

Quartz, IX-150

Sioux, ATF-75

Telamon, ARB-3

Wenatchee, ATF-118

ARD-29

388, 861

YFs 385, 733, 735, 752, 753, 754, 990, 991, 992

YOs 132, 199

YW-92

Enoree, AO-69

Hesperia, AKS-13

Munsee, ATF-107

Pollux, AKS-4

Severn, AO-(W)-61

Sphinx, ARL-24

Tombigee, AOG-(W)-11

Wildcat, AW-2

ATAs 124, 187   LSTs

YC-1009

YO-Gs 63, 70

Salvage Unit (Task Unit 1.2.7)

Achomawi, ATF-148

ATRs 40, 87

Clamp, ARS-33

Coucal, ASR-8

Deliver, ARS-23

Gypsy, ARSD-1

Oneota, AN-85

Preserver, ARS-8

Skakamaxon, AN-86

Widgeon, ASR-1

LST-1184

ATAs 180, 185, 192

Chickasaw, ATF-83

Conserver, ARS-39

Current, ARS-22

Etlah, AN-79

Mender, ARSD-2

Palmyra, ARST-3

Reclaimer, ARS-42

Suncock, An-80

LCT-1420

Dispatch Boat and Boat Pool Unit (Task Unit 1.8.3)

Gunston Hall, LSD-5

San Marcos, LSD-25

LCTs 1116, 1130, 1132, 1155, 1268, 1341, 1361, 1377, 1415, 1461

PGMs 23, 24, 25, 29, 31, 32

Presque Isle, APB-44

LCIs 977, 1062, 1067, 1091

Medical Unit (Task Unit 1.8.4)

Benevolence, AH-13

Bountiful, AH-9

Survey Unit (Task Unit 1.8.5)

Bowditch, AGS-4   *James M. Gilliss*, AGS-13
John Blish, AGS-10   YMSs 354, 358, 413, 463
YP-636

Evacuation Unit (Task Unit 1.8.7)

LSTs 871, 989

APPENDIX D
ADDITIONAL SOURCES OF
INFORMATION

I have drawn on numerous sources for this factual memoir. If a reader wishes to research his career and any ships he might have served on, a complete story can be obtained by visiting or writing the places listed below. If by chance the data desired are not at these places, the capable personnel there will be able to direct you where to look.

A. U.S. Government

1. Archives and Records Sources.

a) *National Personnel Records Center (Military Personnel Records) 9700 Page Blvd., St.Louis,MO 63132-5100*; TELEPHONE: 314-538-4141 (Navy/MarineCorps/CoastGuard)

When telephoning the above number you will receive a tape recorded statement. You will be able to leave your name and address and the center will send you the proper form to fill out. You can fax your request in. The number is 314-538-4175. Response will be made by U.S. mail.

This Center maintains individual Personnel Records ("service records") and Medical Records (only to 16 October 1992) of Navy Commissioned officers and enlisted personnel, Marine Corps officers and enlisted personnel, U.S. Air Force Commissioned Officers and enlisted personnel and Army Commissioned Officers and enlisted personnel. The Center will honor requests for information at no charge for veterans and members of their immediate families. Write and request Standard Form 180 to submit inquiry.

(Author's note: If you plan to research your own story or that of an immediate relative, <u>start</u> here. It will give you important leads; specific dates when/where you served on ships or shore duty.)

b) *National Archives, Textual Reference Branch, 700 Pennsylvania Avenue, NW, Washington D.C. 20408*; TELEPHONE: 202-501-5305

This branch holds all records prior to 1 January 1941 and has no World War II material on file.

c) *National Archives II, Textual Reference Branch, 8601 Adelphi Road, College Park, MD. 20740*; TELEPHONE: 301-713-7230 (textual material) or 301-713-6795 (photographic material)

This branch holds all records from 1 January 1941 to present.

"Armed Guard Logbooks" prepared by the Armed Guard Commander aboard each ship during WW II comprising a brief daily account of events of the Armed Guard crew (Record Group 24)

"Armed Guard Officer Reports" include Armed Guard crew lists, voyage reports, data relating to armaments and supplies provided by the Navy as well as correspondence relating to recommendations for medals, miscellaneous orders, and correspondence.

The Textual Reference Branch in National Archives II also maintains the deck logs of Navy ships dating from 1 January 1941 through 31 December 1961.

A very large majority of all World War II War Diaries, Operational Plans, Action Reports, Damage Reports, etc. formally kept at the Operational Archives Branch, Naval Historical Center, was transferred to "NATIONAL ARCHIVES II" in June 1996. This includes Action Reports from Commander-in-Chief, Pacific Fleet (Ser 001100 of 6 September 1943) and Commander, Service Squadron, South Pacific Force (Ser 0486 of 25 July 1943) which include the actions of 16 June and 9-24 June 1943.

d) Regional Offices of the National Archives

The National Archives has 14 Regional Offices located as follows:

National Archives-New England Region
380 Trapelo Road
Waltham, Massachusetts 02154
TELEPHONE: 617-647-8100
(NOTE: covers Connecticut, Maine, Massachusetts, New Hampshire, Rhode Island, Vermont)

National Archives-Southwest Region
501 West Felix Street, P.O. Box 6216
Ft. Worth, Texas 76115
TELEPHONE: 817-334-5525
(NOTE: Arkansas, Louisiana, New Mexico (Most records from Federal agencies in New Mexico are at the Rocky Mountain Region.) , Oklahoma, Texas.

National Archives-Pittsfield Region
100 Dan Fox Drive
Pittsfield, Massachusetts 01201
TELEPHONE: **413-445-6885**

National Archives-Rocky Mountain Region
Building 48-Denver Federal
Denver, Colorado 80225-0307 (Microfilm only) TELE-
PHONE: 303-236-0817
(NOTE: covers Colorado, Montana, North Dakota, South
Dakota, Utah, Wyoming, New Mexico)

National Archives-Northeast Region
201 Varick Street
New York, New York 10014
TELEPHONF-: 212-337-1300
(NOTE: covers New Jersey, New York,
Puerto Rico and the Virgin Islands)

National Archives-Pacific Southwest Region
24000 Avila Road
Laguna Niguel, California 92656
TELEPHONE: 714-360-2641
(NOTE: covers Arizona, Southern California, and Clark
County, Nevada)

National Archives-Mid Atlantic Region
9th and Market Streets, Room 1350
Philadelphia, Pennsylvania 19107
TELEPHONE: 215-597-3000
(NOTE: covers Delaware, Maryland, Pennsylvania, Vir-
ginia and West Virginia)

National Archives-Pacific Sierra Region
1000 Commodore Drive
San Bruno California 94066
TELEPHONE: 415-876-9009
(NOTE: covers Northern California, Hawaii, Nevada (except Clark County), the Pacific Trust Territories and American Samoa)

National Archives-Southeast Region
1557 St. Joseph Avenue
East Point, Georgia 30344
TELEPHONE: 404-763-7477
(NOTE: covers Alabama, Florida, Georgia, Kentucky, Mississippi, North Carolina, South Carolina and Tennessee)

National Archives-Pacific Northwest Region
6125 Sand Point Way NE
Seattle, Washington 98115
TELEPHONE: 206-526-6507
(NOTE: covers Idaho, Oregon and Washington)

National Archives-Great Lakes Region
7358 South Pulaski Road
Chicago, Illinois 60629
TELEPIIONE,: 312-581-7816
(NOTE: covers Illinois, Indiana, Michigan, Minnesota, Ohio and Wisconsin)

National Archives-Alaska Region
654 West Third Avenue
Anchorage, Alaska 99501
TELEPHONE: 907-271-2441
(NOTE: covers Alaska only)

National Archives-Central Plains Region
2312 East Bannister Road
Kansas City, Missouri 64131
TELEPHONE: 816-926-6272
(NOTE: covers Iowa, Kansas, Missouri and Nebraska)

"Deck Logs" of merchant ships are usually available in the regional archives nearest the port city where each voyage terminated. Microfilm of crew lists may also be available. Call or write your nearest branch for more information.

Records preserved at regional archives (except Pittsfield) are documents from Government agencies at the local and regional levels.

e) Department of the Navy, Naval Historical Center, Washington Navy Yard, 901 M Street SE, Washington, DC 20374-5060; TELEPHONE: 202-433-4132 (Navy Library), 202-433-6773 or 76 (Ships Histories Branch), 202-433-2765 (Photo Archives Section); 202-433-3224 (Operational Archives Branch)

The Deck Log Division of the Ships Histories Branch of the Naval Historical Center has control of all Navy ships deck logs dating from 1 January 1962 to present. For that period, inquiries have to be made through that office to gain access to the logs. They are stored in the Suitland Federal Records Center.

The Ships Histories Branch also contains data on individual ships filed alphabetically by the name. These files contain a wealth of source material other than deck logs not found in any other Archives. Copies of Citations, Action Reports,, War Diaries, etc. may also be found in these files, especially for those ships that served in World War II. Files are also kept on unnamed ships, such as LSMs/LSTs, but these files are not complete.

The Navy Library has extensive collections of World War II publications such as the "Combat Narrative" monograph series (32 booklets), put out by the Office of Naval Intelligence shortly after the battles had been fought; the "Battle Experience" series (26 booklets) put out by Headquarters, Commander-in-Chief, Pacific Fleet; and "United States Strategic Bombing Survey" reports. While the publications are antiquated by research from World War II to the present, they are extremerly useful in showing the thinking, policies, impressions, etc. of the time. In addition they have marvelous illustrations.

Just at right angles to the building, on the right side of Leutze Oark is the Marine Corps Historical Center. Its library, while not as extensive as the Navy Library, is very good for its size and holds Marine Corps World War II publications. Should the research include Marine Corps actions in the War, one should visit the library while there and stop in at the Research Branch across the floor from the library. The Research Branch also holds valuable data on Marine Corps actions.

A very large majority of all World War II War Diaries, Operational Plans, Action Reports, Damage Reports, etc. formerly kept at the Operational Archives Branch was transferred to "NATIONAL ARCHIVES II." Call them to see what remains.

2. Other Sources of Information (Textual and Photographic).

a) *History Division, Photographic Section, United States Naval Institute, United States Naval Academy, 118 Maryland Avenue, Annapolis, MD 21402-5035*; TELEPHONE: 410-295-1022 or 1020

This organization has a wealth of photography of U.S. Naval Ships from 1775 to present. It is easily accessible and less costly to purchase photographs from them then it is from "National Archives II." It is recommended that you try here first.

A quantity of reference material is also available.

b) *Special Collections and Archives Division, Nimitz Library, United States Naval Academy, 589 McNair Road, Annapolis, MD. 21402-5029*; TELEPHONE: 410-293-6903

The Nimitz Library has a wealth of textual material covering all periods. Photographic reference material in the library is very limited. *Entrance to the library is limited to Naval Academy associated personnel.* Anyone else desiring to use the library to conduct research should first write or call to get permission. This is just a formality, but required. Permission is usually given.

c) Government Photographic Sources

Defense Nuclear Agency, 6801 Telegraph Road, Alexandria, VA 22310-3398.

Department of the Navy, Nimitz Library Special Collections and Archives Division, United States Naval Academy, 589 McNair Road, Annapolis, MD 21402-5029 (301) 267-2220.

National Air and Space Museum, Archives Division, Smithsonian Institution, Washington, D.C. 20560 (202) 357-3133A3.

Naval Historical Center, Photographic Section, Washington Navy Yard, Building 108, Washington, D.C. 20374-5060 (202) 433-2765.

National Archives at College Park, Nontextual Division, Still Pictures Branch (NNSP), 8601 Adelphi Road, College Park, MD 20740-6001 (301) 713-6660

d)   Newsletters

Additional information is available through the following association newsletters:

Armed Guard Newsletter. *The Pointer.* Bi-monthly. Annual dues: whatever you can afford. Phone: (919) 876-5537. USN Armed Guard WWII Veterans (USNAGWWIIV). 5712 Partridge Lane, Raleigh, NC 27609-4126.

Atomic Veterans Newsletter. Quarterly. Annual dues: $15. Phone: (609) 822-9714. National Association of Atomic Veterans (NAAV). P.O. Box 2558, Ventnor, NJ 08406-0558.

Brownies' Bights. Monthly. Annual dues: $25. Phone:(410) 661-1550. SS *John W. Brown*, a.k.a. Project Liberty

Ship. P.O. Box 25846, Highlandtown Station, Baltimore, MD 21224-0846.

Farragut News (Farragut N.T.S. Reunions). Phone: (503) 325-9620. Bud and Ruby Darren, 1420 Madison, Astoria, OR 97103.

Guns. Quarterly. Annual dues: $25. Phone: (219) 845-3747. The Association of Gunner's Mates. 7217 Belmont Ave., Hammond, IN 46325.

SS Jeremiah O'Brien. Quarterly. Annual dues: $25. Phone: (415) 441-3101. Fort Mason Center - Bldg. A., San Francisco, CA 94123-1382.

National Association of Radiation Survivors Newsletter. Bi-monthly. Annual dues: $15. Phone: (800) 798-5102. P.O. Box 2815, Weaverville, CA 96093-2815.

Treasure Island Museum Newsletter. Quarterly. Annual dues: $25. Phone: (415) 362-4473. The TI Museum Assn., 410 Palm Avenue, Treasure Island, San Francisco, CA 94130-0413.

USS *Fall River* Newsletter. Bi-Monthly. Annual dues: $25 or whatever you can afford. Phone fax: (954) 484-3898. *Fall River* Shipmates Association, 3740 Inverrary Dr. Apt. E1L, Lauderhill, FL 33319.

U.S. Navy Cruiser Sailors Association. Quarterly. Annual dues: $15. Phone: (508) 252-3524. USN Cruiser Sailors Assn. (USNCSA), 21 Colonial Way, Rehoboth, MA 02769.

U.S. Merchant Marine Veterans of World War II. *The Anchor Light.* Monthy. Annual dues: $36. SS *Lane Victory*, PO Box 629, San Pedro, CA 90733. Phone: (310) 519-9545.

Bibliography

Government Publications

Arming of Merchant Ships and Naval Armed Guard Service, Guide No. 172, micro-fiche, U.S. Naval Administration in WWII, Office of CNO covering period 7 December 1941 — 30 September 1945.

Building the Navy's Bases in World War II. Washington: US Government Printing Office, 1947.

Dictionary of American Naval Fighting Ships. Naval Historical Center, Washington, D.C.

Dyer, VAdm George C. *The Amphibians Came to Conquer: The Story of Admiral Richmond Kelly Turner.* 2 vols. Washington, D.C.:GPO, 1971.

"Exchange of Destroyers for Air and Naval Bases." U.S. Department of State Bulletin, 7 September 1940.

History of Armed Guard Center (Pacific), Treasure Island, San Francisco. Appendix H (12th Naval District, 13 November 1945), micro-film, Office of Naval History.

History of Naval Armed Guard Afloat, World War II Guide No. 173, (OP 414), Director of Naval History, Fleet Maintenance Division (micro-fiche). Operational Archives Branch, Naval Historical Center, Washington, D.C.

Land, VAdm Emory S. *U.S. Merchant Marine at War.* Final report of the Administrator, War Shipping Administration, to President Truman, January 1946.

McDevitt, E.A. (Ed). *The Naval History of Treasure Island.* San Francisco: U.S. Naval Training and Distribution Center, 1946.

Merchant Marine Official Logs, NARA Regional Archives filed in branch nearest port city where ship's voyage ended.

Report Of The President's Advisory Committee On The Merchant Marine. Washington: GPO, 1947.

Mersky, Cmdr Peter B. USNR. *Time Of The Aces: Marine Pilots In The Solomons, 1942-1944,* a pamphlet in World War II Commemorative Series, (Washington, D.C.: Marine Corps Historical Center, 1993).

Melson, Charles D. Major, USMC (Ret.). *Up The Slot: Marines In The Central Solomons,* a pamphlet in World War II Commemorative Series, (Washington, D.C.: Marine Corps Historical Center, 1993).

B. Interviews and Correspondence

Marvin Acree (1)
Walter P. Ballow (3)
Bernard Barker (3)
Tom Borden (8)
Lawrence Brence (8)
Harry Brownell (8)
Dick Camp (8)
Rollie Cannon (8)
John D. Case (4)
John Clancy (8)
Duane Curtis (9)
Charles Espy (10)
Dominick Di Guiseppe (8)
Ray Donnelly (8)
Bill Eissler (8)
Jim Fawcett (8)
Albert Fickel (11)
Mickey Ganitch (11)
Anthony Gray (2)
Bob Greening (8)
Stuart Hepburn (8)
Bill Hartman (1)

David Haugh (3)
Edval Helle, Sr. (3)
Erwin Holan (3)
Leonard D. Honeycutt (7)
Eugene M. Hopper (1)
Mike Hosier (3)
Kenneth F. Keller (3)
Connie Kontopirakis (8)
John Larsen (8)
Roy Lucy (1)
Merle Luther (1)
Charles Maiers (3)
Cal McGowan (6)
Dave Morris (8)
J. B. Morrison (3)
Ross Osborn (1)
Pat Paones (3)
Bob Parker (3)
John Parry (8)
Robert B. Phillips (3)
John Reilly (8)
Jay S. Rider, Jr. (3)

Richard T. Rogers (3)
Chet Romano (8)
Vitto Rossi (8)
Primo Saraiba (1)
George Schieltz (8)
David Shafer (8)
John J. Skarzenski (8)
Clinton Slater (1)
Stanley W. Smith (8)
Joe Sony (8)
Don Sterling (5)
Roger Stormes (8)
Roy Swalm (8)
Tony Tesori (5)
Ken Tinker (8)
Lawrence G. Trueax (8)
Stan Voorheis (3)
Robert E. Vorhies (3)
Donald R. Waterhouse (3)
Ray Weathers (3)
Steve Young (8)
John Zett (8)

(1) USS *Aludra* survivor (AK-72)
(2) USS *Celeno* (AK-76)

(3) USS *Deimos* survivor (AK-78)
(4) Guadalcanal Beachmaster
(5) USS *LST-340*
(6) USS *LST-353*.
(7) USS *Skylark* (AM-63)
(8) USS *Fall River* (CA-131)
(9) SS *Nathaniel Currier*
(10) SS *Thomas Nelson*
(11) USS *Pennsylvania* (BB-38)

C. World War II Books

Allard, Dean C; Crawley, Martha L.; and Edmison, Mary W.:
US Naval History Sources in the United States. US Naval
History Division, Washington, D.C., 1979.

Barbey, Daniel E. *MacArthur's Amphibious Navy.* Annapolis:
Naval Institute Press, 1969.

Bearden, Bill (Ed). *The Bluejackets' Manual.* Annapolis: Naval
Institute Press, 1990.

Berry, Lieutenant Robert B. *Gunners Get Glory.* New York:
Bobbs-Merrill Co., 1943.

Brinkley, David. *Washington Goes to War.* Ballantine: New
York, 1988.

Buell, Thomas B. *Master of Sea Power: A Biography of Fleet
Admiral Ernest J. King.* Boston: Little, Brown, 1980.

———. *The Quiet Warrior: A Biography of Admiral Raymond
A. Spruance.* Boston: Little, Brown, 1974.

Bunker, John G. *Liberty Ships.* New York: Arno Press, 1980.

Calhoun, Capt. C. Raymond. *Typhoon: The Other Enemy.*
Annapolis: Naval Institute Press, 1981.

Carpenter, D., and N. Polmar. *Submarines of the Imperial Japanese Navy.* Annapolis: Naval Institute Press, 1986.

Chelemedos, Capt. Peter. *Peter, the Odyssey of a Merchant
Mariner.* Seattle: Peanut Butter Publishing, 1992.

Churchill, Winston S. *The Hinge of Fate.* Boston: Houghton
Mifflin Co., 1950.

_____, *Memoirs of the Second World War*. Boston: Houghton Mifflin, 1959.

Cook, Capt. Charles. *The Battle of Cape Esperance*. Annapolis: Naval Institute Press, 1968.

Costello, John. *The Pacific War (1941-44)*. New York: Rawson Wade, 1981.

Cravan, W.F. and J.L. Cate. The Army Air Forces in World War II. Volume 4. *The Pacific: Guadalcanal to Saipan (August 1942-July 1944)*. Chicago: University of Chicago Press, 1950.

Dyer, VAdm George C. *The Amphibians Came to Conquer: The Story of Admiral Richmond Kelly Turner*. 2 vols. Washington, D.C.:GPO, 1971.

Galati, Bob. *Gunner's Mate*. Irving: Innovatia Press, 1993.

Gibson, Charles D. *Merchantman? Or Ship of War*. Camden: Ensign Press, 1986.

Glans, Roger E. *United States Naval Training Station, Farragut, Idaho*. Minneapolis: 1992.

Gleichauf, Justin F. *Unsung Sailors: The Naval Armed Guard in World War II*. Annapolis: Naval Institute Press, 1990.

Halsey, FAdm William F. and LCmdr. J. Bryan, III. *Admiral Halsey's Story*. New York and London: McGraw-Hill Book Company, Inc., 1976.

Hayes, Grace Person. *The History of the Joint Chiefs of Staff in World War II: The War Against Japan*. Annapolis: Naval Institute Press, 1982.

Hoehling, A.A. *The Fighting Liberty Ships*. Kent: Kent State University Press, 1990.

Hoyt, Edward P. *How They Won the War in the Pacific: Nimitz and His Admirals*. New York: Weybright and Tally, 1970.

Hughes, T. & J. Costello. *Battle of the Atlantic*. New York: Dial Press, 1977.

Irving, David. *Destruction of PQ-17*. New York: Simon & Schuster, 1968.

Ito, Masanori. *The End of the Imperial Japanese Navy.* New York: Berkeley Press, 1984.

Jaffee, Walter W. *The Last Victory.* San Pedro: U.S. Merchant Marine Veterans WWII, 1991.

————. *The Last Liberty.* Palo Alto: Glencannon Press, 1993.

————. *Appointment In Normandy.* Palo Alto: Glencannon Press, 1995.

Kahn, David. *The Code Breakers.* New York: Macmillan, 1967.

Kernan, Alvin. *Crossing The Line.* Annapolis: Naval Institute Press, 1994.

King, Adm. Ernest J. & Cmdr Walter Whitehill. *Fleet Admiral King.* New York: W.W. Norton, 1952.

Lewin, Ronald. *The American Magic: Codes, Ciphers and the Defeat of Japan.* New York: Farrar Straus Giroux, 1982.

Lundstrom, John B. *The First Team and the Guadalcanal Campaign.* Annapolis: Naval Institute Press, 1994.

Mason, John T., Jr. *The Pacific War Remembered.* Annapolis: Naval Institute Press, 1986.

McCormick, Harold, J. *Two Years Behind The Mast.* Manhattan: Sunflower University Press, 1991.

Middlebrook, Martin. *Convoy.* London: Penguin Books, 1976.

Miller, Thomas G., Jr. *The Cactus Air Force.* New York: Harper & Row, 1969.

Mitchell, C.B. *Every Kind of Shipwork.* New York: Todd Shipyards Corp., 1981.

Moore, Captain Arthur R. *A Careless Word...A Needless Sinking.* Kings Point, NewYork: American Merchant Marine Museum, 1983/1985.

Morison, RAdm Samuel Eliot. *History of United States Naval Operations in World War II*, Boston: Little, Brown, 1947-1990.

————. Vol. I. *The Battle of the Atlantic, September 1939-May 1943.*

————. Vol. III. *The Rising Sun in the Pacific, 1931-April 1942.*

_____. Vol. IV. *Coral Sea, Midway and Submarine Actions, May 1942-August 1942.*

_____. Vol. V. *The Struggle for Guadalcanal, August 1942-February 1943.*

_____. Vol. VI. *Breaking the Bismarcks Barrier, 22 July 1942-1 May 1944.*

_____. Vol. VII. *Aleutians, Gilberts and Marshalls, June 1942-April 1944.*

_____. Vol. VIII. *New Guinea and the Marianas, March 1944-August 1944.*

_____. Vol. XII. *Leyte, June 1944-January 1945.*

_____. Vol. XIII. *The Liberation of the Philippines, Luzon, Mindanao, The Visayas, 1944-August 1945.*

_____. Vol. XIV. *Victory in the Pacific, 1945.*

_____. Vol. XV. *Supplement and General Index.*

Newcomb, Richard F. *U.S. Cruisers--A Century of Service.* Paducah: Turner Publishing, 1994.

Noel, Capt. John V. Jr. and Capt. Edward L. Beach. *Naval Terms Dictionary.* Annapolis: Naval Institute Press, 1988.

Polmar, Norman and Thomas B. Allen. *World War II: America At War, 1941-1945.* New York: Random House, 1991.

Potter, E.B. *Bull Halsey.* Annapolis: Naval Institute Press, 1985.

_____. *Nimitz.* Annapolis: Naval Institute Press, 1976.

Sawyer, L.A. and W.H. Mitchell. *The Liberty Ships.* Second Edition. London: Lloyd's of London Press Ltd., 1985.

_____. *Victory Ships and Tankers.* Devon, England: David & Charles: Newton Abbot, 1974.

Schofield, William G. *Eastward the Convoys.* Chicago: Rand McNally, 1965.

Smith, VAdm William Ward. *Midway: Turning Point of the Pacific.* New York: Crowell, 1966.

Snouck-Hurgronje, Jan. (Ed.) *Ship Organization and Personnel.* Annapolis: Naval Institute Press, 1972.

_____. *The Rising Sun: The Decline and Fall of the Japanese Empire.* New York: Random House, 1970.

van der Vat, Dan. *The Pacific Campaign.* New York: Simon & Schuster, 1991.

Warner, Denis and Peggy Warner. *Disaster in the Pacific: New Light on the Battle of Savo Island.* Annapolis: Naval Institute Press, 1992.

Wells, Arthur W. *The Quack Corps.* Chico: DelArt Publishing, 1992.

Wheal, Elizabeth-Anne; Pope, Stephen; and Taylor, James. *A Dictionary of the Second World War.* Grafton: London, 1989.

D. Nuclear Weapons Testing and Its Aftermath

Armbruster II, Cecil. "50th Anniversary-Operation Crossroads." *Sea Classics*, August 1996.

Bradley, David. *No Place to Hide.* Boston: Little Brown, 1948.

Cook, C. Sharp. "The Legacy of Crossroads." *Naval History*, Fall 1988.

Daly, Capt. Thomas M. "Crossroads of Bikini." *Proceedings*, July 1986.

Delgado, James P. "Bombshell at Bikini." *Naval History*, July/August 1996.

Gallagher, Carole. *American Ground Zero.* Cambridge: MIT Press, 1993.

Gould, Jay M. and Benjamin A. Goldman. *Deadly Deceit.* New York: Four Walls Eight Windows, 1990.

Graeub, Ralph. *The Petkau Effect: Nuclear Radiation, People and Trees.* New York: Four Walls Eight Windows, 1992.

Grahlfs, F. Lincoln. *Voices From Ground Zero.* Lanham: University Press of America, 1996.

Ito, Timothy M. "Birth of the Bomb." *U.S. News and World Report*, July 31, 1995.

Office of the Historian, Joint Task Force One. *Operation Crossroads: The Official Pictorial Record.* New York: Wm H. Wise, 1946.

Rhodes, Richard. *The Making of the Atomic Bomb.* New York: Simon & Schuster, 1986.

Saffer, Thomas H. and Orville E. Kelly. *Countdown Zero.* New York: Putnam and Sons, 1982.

Shurcliff, W.A., Historian of Joint Task Force One. *Bombs At Bikini: The Official Report of Operation Crossroads.* New York: Wm H. Wise, 1947.

Strope, Walmer Elton. "The Navy and the Atomic Bomb." *Proceedings,* October 1947.

Weisgall, Jonathan M. *Operation Crossroads.* Annapolis: Naval Institute Press, 1994.

E. Periodicals

American Society of Mechanical Engineers. "Liberty Ship." September 18, 1984.

Barger, Mervin D. "Getting the Goods to the Beach." *Surface Warfare.* January/February 1980.

Bennett, James. "Forgotten Heroes." *Sea Classics,* August 1987.

Britton, LCdr. Beverly. "Stepchildren of the Navy." *Proceedings,* December 1947.

Dorn, David R. "Ships for Victory." *Proceedings,* February 1985.

Gleichauf, Justin F. "Navy Armed Guard: Unsung Heroes." *American Legion Magazine,* April 1986.

Guillen, Michael. "The S.S. *John Brown.*" *Sea History,* Autumn 1986.

Kortum, Karl and Adm. Thomas J. Patterson. "How We Saved the Jeremiah O'Brien." *Sea History,* Winter 1988-89.

Miller, Ian. "The Sea Raider Michel." *Sea Classics,* June 1985.

Ruark, Lieutenant Robert. "They Called 'Em Fish Food." *Saturday Evening Post,* 6 May 1944.

Rubin, Hal. "The Last of the 'Libertys'." *Oceans,* March 1979.

Sudhalter, D.L. "How Hurry-Up Henry [Kaiser] Helped to Win the War." *The Retired Officer,* August 1986.

Weisgall, Jonathan M. "Bikini: Witch's Brew." *Proceedings,* February 1994.

Various Authors. "50th Anniversary WWII" articles. *VFW Magazine,* 1991-1995 issues.

F. Newspapers and Wire Services

Some of the national and international information for this book, including the periodic "War Milestones" data, came from United Press International, Associated Press, and/or local news coverage in one or more of the following daily newspapers: *Honolulu Advertiser, Honolulu Star Bulletin, Long Beach Press-Telegram, Los Angeles Examiner, Los Angeles Times, Oakland Tribune, Portland Oregonian, San Diego Union-Tribune, San Francisco Chronicle, San Pedro News Pilot, Seattle Post Intelligencer, Seattle Times* and the *Vancouver Colombian.*

G. Miscellaneous

"Kaiser's World War II Shipyards." Text of an address by James F. McCloud, retired president, Kaiser Engineers, given at the dedication of the site of Kaiser's Shipyard No. 2 as a Richmond, Calif., Historic Landmark. May 8, 1992.

"The Lessons of the Liberties" Text of an address by Robert T. Young, chairman and president, American Bureau of Shipping, given before the Propeller Club of the U.S., New York, NY. 8 May 1974.

USS *Fall River* (CA-131) "Cruise Book." Shipboard publication, 1945.

INDEX